# DIMENSIONS OF ANTHROPOLOGY

# DIMENSIONS OF ANTHROPOLOGY

## A Prismatic Panorama

Amitabha Sarkar
Samira Dasgupta

KALPAZ

ISBN: 978-93-5128-194-8

Price: ₹ 1450/-

First Published 2016

*Published by*

**Kalpaz Publications**

C-30, Satyawati Nagar,

Delhi -110052

E-mail: kalpaz@hotmail. com Ph.: 9212142040

*Printed at:* G. Print Process, Delhi

**Cataloging in Publication Data--DK**

Courtesy: D.K. Agencies (P) Ltd. <docinfo@dkagencies.com>

**Sarkar, Amitabha, author.**

Dimensions of anthropology : a prismatic panorama / Amitabha Sarkar, Samira Dasgupta.

pages cm

Includes bibliographical references and index.

ISBN 9789351281948

1. Ethnology--India. 2. Tribes--India. I. Dasgupta, Samira, 1953- author. II. Title.

GN635.I4S27 2016 DDC 305.800954 23

# Contents

# Preface

In the course of long association with Anthropological Survey of India for more than 35 years we, the authors, were involved in number of national and regional level research projects under the able guidance of renowned Social Scientists of international fame. Professionally, we are in anthropological research work since 1977. In College and University we were taught anthropology predominantly at theoretical aspect. However, when such knowledge is put into practice in the professional field, it translates itself into an altogether new, different and distinct dimension of experience.

The present treatise is a collection of number of articles which were either published or read in national Seminars etc. During the long period of research experiences authors undertook field work in Rajasthan, Gujarat, West Bengal, Jharkhand and Chhattisgarh area, especially in the tribal pockets. After the superannuation from Anthropological Survey of India, the authors were engaged for a considerable period to carry out a research project at Kandhamal, Odisha on the theme of 'Social Identity'. In this treatise valuable published materials of several eminent anthropologists are also incorporated to get support in our present work; we really are grateful to them.

There was a great feeling of nostalgia for those research projects in which we carried out intensive field-work for a prolonged period (maximum six months at a stretch, in one occasion only) for generating empirical data. In anthropology field-work is very much essential which is considered as laboratory. But it is sad to see that present generation is not eager to carry out intensive field-work; without such field-work one cannot get detailed insight of the problem. In this connection we clearly remember one incident with one of our colleague with whom there was a hot exchange for about forty five minutes on ethnographic study. We were infavour of ethnographic field work and thereafter by churning the ethnographic data, problem oriented focused study can be made. According to Gopala Sarana (The Methodology of Anthropological Comparisons, Arizona: The University of Arizona Press, 1975) – "ethnography is vital to anthropology, but comparison is equally basic. The ultimate aim of anthropology is to understand the similarities and differences among human cultures and to throw light on what is glibly called 'human nature'. This cannot be attained through the contextual explanations"..."observation and the recording of the data together constitute one phase of the anthropological method, called here the ethnographic procedure. The other phase consists of comparison done in the library". Now the authors feel that time has come to select some of their favorite topics for this volume for the posterity to get an impression how intensive field work is essential in anthropology. In some selected Chapters there is a small write-up as 'Prologue', which is primarily theoretical framework for the field work on the respective topics.

We also sincerely express our thanks to various Directors during the last 35 years of Anthropological Survey of India for their approval in involving us in various research projects and helping us in making foot prints of those arena of anthropology, which are of immense help for the present generation of practicing anthropologists of the country. We are also thankful to Shri Debashis Biswas, EDP Section of Anthropological Survey of India for his painstaking help in preparing the charts. Authors express their sincere gratitude to Shri Pradip Josh of Chandannagar for language editing and suggestions.

We also express our deep sense of gratitude to our seniors and well-wishers like Professor A. K. Danda, Dr Biman K. Dasgupta, Dr B. B. Goswami, Dr M. K. Raha, Dr R. K. Bhattacharya, Dr J. K. Sarkar, Shri Sadhan Sengupta, Mr William Ekka, Mr Hasan Ali and Professor R. M. Sarkar for their active support in preparing this manuscript.

**Amitabha Sarkar**
**Samira Dasgupta**

# 1

# Introduction: The Basics of Anthropology

## How was the discipline formed

Anthropology never attained its present status all on a sudden. It has been enriched by the ideas which are the products of experience of life-long trial and error method. The knowledge of different communities given by voyagers and travellers on the customs of peoples attracted the attention of educated men in Europe. The travelling was facilitated due to the invention of steam engine and steam ship which happened at the period of Industrial revolution in Western Europe and the impetusfor such revolution came from the renaissance.

In the seventeenth-eighteenth century anthropology first came into existence. Darwin's theory of evolution played a great role for the formation of anthropology. The impact of Darwin's theory of evolution brought a revolutionary thought process at that time. With the idea of evolution some social reformers of that time thought that there were some simple societies (which were described in travellers account) from where the complex society developed through many successive stages; the society developed from simple (which were found among primitive, savage people etc. ) to complex (man is not the creation of God). Man came into being through evolution. It is also sure that before entering these developed complex society there were some simple society and certainly those were the primitives. In this way anthropology came into existence.

Now, it is a question before us that, how the idea of Darwinian theory of evolution emerges?

In the thirteenth-fifteenth century there occurred the 'Renaissance'. The cause of renaissance was that after the destruction of important sites of learning by foreign invaders, many scholars, learned social reformers and scientists took shelter in neighbouring country like Italy. They sowed the seed of renaissance which ultimately turned the society into new prosperous life. And Darwin got impetus from this revolution.

So far as the cause of renaissance is concerned contradiction is inevitable. But a major cause was definitely the "Crusade". It happened to be proved that it was a "fake war between the Christians and the Islam". Assumption substantiated by facts is that it may have assisted the existing feudal system. Due to the inequal distribution of wealth in agrarian economy, –a vast wealth was accumulated to a restricted band of men enjoying every facility backed by the Kings. The poor peasant class many times showed sign of dissent over the existing system and then and there the potential young power and majority of peasants were requested to save the Christianity from the Islamic invasion. On this ground they were sent to Palestine and M. E. Asia. On the way due to extreme desert climate majority among them either faced extinction or perished and the rest were killed at the war and thus the revolt was suppressed by the tactful destruction of man power. Simultaneously one very illuminating thing has happened. The soldiers, who returned home, exchanged their experiences about the prosperous sites of learning and of the cities which they passed on their way. In this way, the light of renaissance and its tenets of development were spread.

## I

We can begin our discourse with the question—what is anthropology? Each discipline of knowledge develops around certain basic questions which determine its aim, object, and scope. What are such questions in anthropology? In anthropology such basic questions are around man himself and it is the study of man in totality.

Anthropology has developed around three basic questions about Man. The first is: how man came in the earth and got such physical features of erect posture with the ability of speech? The answer is, by evolution. Evolution is the process of change through which the man got the present appearance which took a long way. It is known that the animal kingdom started with amoeba-a unicellular creature and after several prolong phases of evolution and several changes mammals came in the earth. Again, from the mammals through evolution the anthropoid apes have appeared in the earth and finally the human beings emerged on the earth. Study of this arena of anthropology is known as Biological or Physical Anthropology.

It was one million years ago when man appeared in this earth; the evidence of agricultural economy is found only ten thousand years ago. So from the appearance of the man on the earth up to 10,000 years ago, he lived a hunting-gathering life and we have no direct evidences how he lived and led the socio-cultural life. The definite account of his cultural life is however available from history, that is, from the rise of scriptures, five or six thousand years ago. From the first appearance of man on the earth up to the beginning of the historical period, he definitely had a social/cultural life, record of which we do not possess. These vast period before history is known as 'Pre-history' or 'Palaeo-anthropology'. It is definite that our present culture for their basic part owes to the deem dawn of civilisation during the vast pre-historic period. This deals with the second arena of anthropology—how he lived in that period, what were the cultures and what their environment was like. During these pre-historic periods the four pillars of inventions were there upon which the kaleidoscopic range of present culture stands. The first invention was the '**cutting tools**', along with this the human culture immediately became different from the animals. The second invention was '**fire**', that is, the technique of fire-making. The third invention was the '**wheel**', and the fourth one is the producing of '**cereals**' in the period of cultivation. This period is otherwise known as '**revolution**'—which also brings drastic social change in the human society. The time of pre=history is divided into lithic ages of which Palaeolithic, Mesolithic represent the hunting-gathering stages and Neolithic initiates the period of cultivation; perhaps the first evidences of such is obtained from Badari, Egypt some 10,000 years ago. Since Neolithic through Metal ages man's culture advanced very rapidly. The main aspect of study of pre-history is to observe scientifically the cultural development of man through the development of tool technology and other artefacts of archaeological evidences. When the cultural development of the pre-historic period is studied in the background of and in the development of physical evolution of fossils, ape and men along with the changes of geo-morphology it is called palaeo-anthropology.

The third question of anthropology deals with the question around the study of present day socio-cultural aspect of man both earlier and indigenous people or the son of the soil and contemporary. In the initial period the study was confined to the tribal or the native people but later on the horizon of such study is expanded to contemporary modern societies and their culture, such as, problem oriented, focused study on current day issues. Among these problems is Study on indigenous knowledge and sustenance, Old age problem, Women empowerment, Problem of weaker section, Identity being the tool of stigma of development, Social impact assessment in relation to development, Regionalism and Social unrest, Inter cultural communication especially in border area, Social identity, Anthropology of culture and space, Anthropology of culture and communication, Ethno-ecology, Ethno-medicine etc. are the major arena of Social-cultural anthropology in our country.

## II

According to Penniman (1935), there are four phases of development of the world anthropology.

(i) **Formulatory period (before 1835):** Travellers account. Herodotus (484–425 B. C.) - was father of Greek ethnography, considered as the father of anthropology. Herodotus was the first to report about the prevalence of *couvade*—a custom in which the husband observes labour pain and other taboos which are to be imposed on his wife;

(ii) **Convergent period (1835-1859):** During this period divergent views about the origin of biological and social aspects of human beings by scholars of different countries were expressed which ultimately shaped the theories of culture;

(iii) **Constructive period (1859-1900):** This phase started after the publication of Darwin's *Origin of Species*. Tylor, Frazer, Maine and Morgan's contribution belong to this period. During this period anthropology started as an independent discipline of teaching and research in many universities like Oxford, Cambridge; and

(iv) **Critical period (1900 onwards):** Many anthropologists have pointed out that during this period various anthropological concepts were propounded which led to the foundation of different schools of thought in anthropology viz, functional school, structural school, diffusion school, culture and personality school etc.

In India teaching of anthropology as discipline was first started in Calcutta University in 1920.

### III

Histoprically, anthropological studies in India started with tribal studies. These studies were given priority by the British administrators and scholars as well as by foreign missionaries and travelers for the purposes of: (a) colonial administration, (b) cultural-historical study of religious conversions and (c) adventurous memoirs.

As such, we found books on Khasi by Gurdon, Garos by T. C. Sinha, Ao-Nagas by J. P. Mills and beside these there are many ethnographic accounts by the missionaries and travelers. In India review of tribal research activity made from time to time by scholars like S. C. Roy (1921), D. N. Majumdar (1950-56), G. S. Ghurye (1956), S. C. Dube, N. K. Bose, K. P. Chattopadhyay, L. P. Vidyarthi, S. C. Sinha and others.

The development of tribal research in India historically may be reviewed in three phases: Formulative (1774—1919), Constructive (1920—1949) and Analytical period (1950 onwards).

**Formulative period:** Since the foundation of the Asiatic Society of Bengal in 1774, the British administrators, missionaries, travelers and a few other anthropologically oriented individuals collected data on tribal and rural groups and wrote about their life and culture in journal of the Asiatic Society of Bengal (1788), Indian Antiquary (1872) and later in the journal of Bihar and Orissa Research Society (1915) and Man in India (1921). They also collected ethnographic data and published a series of District Gazetteers and Handbooks on tribes and castes and also a number of monographs especially on the tribes of Assam. During the census, especially in 1931 and 1941 some British and Indian anthropologists were associated with the collection of anthropological data on the tribes and castes of the different parts of India.

Some scholarly British administrators posted in different parts of India, such as, H. H. Risley, E. T. Dalton and L. S. O. Malley in eastern India, Russell in middle India, E. Thurston in south India and W. Crooks in northern India, wrote Encyclopaedia inventories of the tribes and castes of India which even to-day provide basic information about the life and culture of the people of the respective regions. In addition to the Handbooks on the tribes and castes of different regions, general books on Indian ethnology were also published by administrators like J. M. Campbell (1856), R. S. Latham (1859) and Risley (1891), with a view to acquainting government officials and provide persons with classified descriptions of tribes and castes of India.

Detailed accounts of specific tribes and some castes were written by J. Shakespeare (1912), Gurdon (1914), Mills (1922), Parry (1932), Grigson (1938) and a few others who wrote competent monographs on specific tribes and castes. For example, W. G. Briggs (1922) wrote on the 'Chamar', P. O. Bodding (1925) on 'Santal Medicine' and several others in different parts in India were also influenced by British anthropologists like Rivers (1906) 'The Todas', ' the Veddas of Ceylon by Seligman (1911), 'the Andaman Islânders by Radcliffe Brown (1922).

Under these influence the first Indian to write exhaustive monographs on the tribes of India was S. C. Roy who published 'the Munda' in 1912, 'the Oraon' in 1915, 'Oraon Religion and Customs' in 1928, 'Hill-Bhuiyas' in 1935 and 'the Kharia' in 1937. Hutton described 'Roy' as the "father of Indian anthropology". In 1916 R. P. Chanda published his book on the Indo-Aryan race which created great interest in the study of early cultural history of racial admixture in India.

**Constructive Period**—Social anthropologist in India witnessed a phenomenal change when it was included in the curriculum of the two important universities in Bombay (Sociology in 1919) and Calcutta (Anthropology in 1921). These two universities attracted academicians and scholars to undertake significant researches. Very soon, specialised subjects like kinship studies, social organisation etc. were undertaken by scholars like Ghurye, K. P. Chattopadhyay, M. N. Srinivas, D. N. Majumdar, I. Karve and a few others. In 1938 under the joint session of the Indian Science Congress Association and the British Association on the occasion of the Silver Jubilee of the former, reviewed the progress of anthropology in India and discussed plans for future studies. During this period, after completing doctoral assignments, a few anthropologists provided some theological leads in social anthropological researches. For instance, Srinivas' work on 'Marriage and Family in Mysore' (1942) and N. K. Bose's publication on 'Hindu Method of Tribal Absorption' (1941) were a turning point in Indian Anthropology.

The entry of Verrier Elwin and his studies on the tribes of Madhya Pradesh (undivided) and Odisha like the Baiga, the Agaria etc. gave further recognition to Indian anthropology. Furer Haimendorf's publication on the tribes of Hyderabad and other successive works provided refined models for prospective research workers in India.

Thus, Indian anthropology, born and brought up under the influence of British anthropology, matured during the constructive period also on the lines of British anthropology. Except for a few studies of Indian caste by Briggs, Iyer and Hutton and the tradition of making tribal studies continued till the end of the 1940s. On the lines of anthropology taught at that time at Cambridge, Oxford and London, Indian anthropology was characterised by ethnological and monographic studies with a special emphasis on researches in kinship and social organisation.

**Analytical period**—After independence there was a positive increase in contacts with the American social anthropologists. Some anthropologists like Opler (Cornell University), David Mandelbhaum (California University), Oscar Lewis (Illinois University) and several students from Cornell University came and stayed in Indian villages with a view to testing certain hypothesis and refining some of the methodological framework developed elsewhere and to assist the community development programs in the Indian villages.

In addition to the village, caste and urban studies as well as the problem oriented researches of power structure and leadership of religion, culture and personality were carried out in this period. The tribal studies were also given an analytical and action–oriented approach. Now the tribal communities are studied in terms of inter-relations as well as in terms of differences among the tribal and non-tribal communities. Mention may be made of Majumdar's and Barreman's study of Polyandrous Khasa, S. C. Sinha's village and mixed tribal village of Dhalbhum area etc. Majumdar focused the characteristics of the Tribe-Hindu continuum through the polyandrous Khasas. Barreman studies these people as Hindus. Sinha brings up clearly the prevalence of the Bhumij-Rajput continuum. Vidyarthi shows that the 'Manjhi' tribe has attained the status of a caste in the Munda village of Ranchi (1965). These researches opened up a new era of understanding regarding changes among tribes in the setting of mainstream of Hindu social organisation.

Robin Burling (1963-an American) in his study of 'Rensanggri'-a Garo village provides a first rate of model with reference to family and Kinship. Vidyarthi points out in his study of Maler culture of Santal Pargana in the nature-man-spirit complex.

All these studies provide a model for understanding tribal complex in terms of inter-relatedness of ecology, economy, society and spiritual belief and practices. Anthropological Survey of India-one of the premier institute of the country, conducted several empirical research works under the aegis of several renowned social scientists, like Material culture of India, Culture trait and culture area survey, Weaker Section studies, Agrarian Situation in India, Land use Pattern especially Shifting Hill Cultivation, Ethnography study on tribal groups, Tribal Stratification, Tribes in Contemporary India, Weaving in India, Tribal Education in India, People of India—a mega project, extensive survey, Impact of Industrialisation in selected tribal pockets, Urban Anthropology in selected pockets of the country, Regionalism and Development, Study of women, Management of environment and Natural resources with traditional Wisdom, Study on Cultural Syncretism, Cultural Dimension of Tourism, Study on Traditional Knowledge System, to understand man-nature interaction focused study has been made on Biosphere Study and so on.

It is sad but true that due to prolonged absence of regular Director (from 2000 onwards to till date, that is, December, 2015) at Anthropological Survey of India, the structure of the premier institute is like a ship in the deep ocean without Captain. Therefore, the research output from this premier institute now becomes markedly insignificant.

## IV

## Aim, Objective and Method of study in Social-cultural Anthropology

### A. Social–Cultural Anthropology

I. Object of Study: Human behaviour

(Human= Physical part)

(Behaviour = Cultural part)

II. What is behaviour: Sum total of relations belong to three levels according to mode of interaction—

a. Material

b. Social

c. Religion/Ideology

III. Each behaviour has two components:

a. Explicit/Norm

b. Implicit/Value

### B. Relations

I. **Relation by nature:** For existence requires a container that is, society or a Village etc./Community–a Physical Proximity.

II. Relation between behaviour and society that is, Culture and Society is like a Container and Content.

III. Therefore, Society = Container of relations.

IV. Relations = It is all through some certain roles and status, that is, Actors —Individual.

V. Society = Container

Relation = Content.

Role = Individual.

**C. The Method of Science = Comparison and Classification.**

I. **The Method of Science:** This explains nexus between cause and effect. This study starts from present to the future, if necessary, study of the past is also included on ostensible historical ground.

II. **Method:**

(a) Concrete to Abstract,

(b) Classification,

(c) Comparison.

III. **Experiment → Observation → Inference**

Data————————————→ Inference.

**D. Method of study of Relations**

For understanding and observation of relations they can be approached chiefly from four dimensions–

a. Ethnographic–Descriptive

b. Social–Analytic i. e, Inter-relation and Inter-action Analysis. Inter-relations = Structure + Inter-action = Function. i. e, Inter-relationship and Inter-action analysis = Structural-functional analysis.

c. Cultural—Each relation has a social norm and value = Value analysis.

d. Change Perspective.

e. Thus, the main method of Social-Cultural Anthropology = Relational analysis.

**References**

1. *A Survey of Researches in Sociology and Social Anthropology*, Vol. III, ICSSR.
2. Bose, N. K. *Fifty Years of science in India (Anthropology).*
3. Banerjee, Biswanath and Amitabha Sarkar, 1996, *Fundamentals of Social and Cultural Anthropology*, Calcutta: Firma KLM Pvt. Ltd.

# 2

# Field Methods and Techniques

Relationship between social-cultural anthropology and the research oriented field work may be compared with fish and water. The proposition of this discipline mostly comes out of field observations. In the formative phase subject matter of this discipline was based on the accounts provided by the missionaries and the travellers. But soon the drawbacks of such speculations were felt and the scholars themselves tried to collect information from the people and they were primitive people in the early period. L. H. Morgan visited the Iroquois to collect information. But actual field expeditions began in America with the work of F. Boas in 1880s in Baffin land and British Columbia and were initiated in England by A. C. Haddon of Cambridge who led a group of scholars to the Torres straits of the Pacific in 1898 and 1899. The field work trend was soon added with the teaching of qualification that is, staying in the field for a long period to understand the society and culture of the people under study for practical reasons. As the field work upto 1930 were done among the primitive societies to understand their culture through native languages, prolong staying among them was necessary. Thus, since 1850s, the scholars in social cultural anthropology tend to use the information collected by themselves, and field work qualification and study of small society (small universe) began to gain ground. After 1930s, contemporary societies–rural, urban, industrial also were studied by social-cultural anthropologists. Meantime W. H. R. Rivers in the course of his own field work showed the importance of genealogical technique to collect fruitful information. The direct observation interviews, and recording of cases by the techniques of genealogy etc. became common. In the early twentieth centuries between 1905 to 1910 Radcliffe Brown, a pupil of Rivers and Haddon, for the first time attempted to investigate sociological theories in a primitive society and to describe the social life of the people in such a way as to bring out clearly what was significant in it for those theories. At the sametime B. Malinowski's field work among the Trobi and Islanders opened a new horizon for all time field workers in socio-cultural anthropology.

Information collected by the social-cultural anthropologists are data to them but all information are not data. For example, if one is interested to find out the way of selecting mates of the youths at the present moment, one begins to collect information from all marriageable youths by taking their opinions in the matter. Such opinions will be information only but not data. For the same purpose if a person begins to note the cases of married youths of the same time along with following what method they used to select mate for the marriage, the information will be taken as 'data' as they are true cases.

Thus, the field for the social-cultural anthropologist's observation is broadening with inclusion of many new methods and techniques for collecting data for the wider fields. From a pluralist approach, they study societies not society, cultures not culture and realise in some way or other that all societies and cultures are interlinked and interdependent, may be at different degrees.

At the present moment, it is necessary to distinguish certian terms for the field work for very practical reasons. The terms like "technique", 'method" and "methodology" are to be understood.

A technique is an actual device, a means or a procedure for collecting and processing data in the particular contexts of a scientific inquiry. A method is the broad category which includes many techniques by which a goal or an end is to be achieved for a particular field of inquiry.

A methodology is the analytical studies of methods. Specific studies are examined here as to the procedure adopted, the assumptions made, and the results obtained. At present social-cultural anthropology depends on classification and comparison in some places. Its generalisations are based on controlled comparison. For ethnographic approach the method is deductive. For social anthropology the trend is analytic and in most cases deductive. In cultural anthropology generally inductive principles are adopted. An inductive trend that is 'inside out' is traced, among a number of social-cultrual anthropologists in the recent time. After 1960s, study of social-cultural anthropology of one's own society and culture has been encouraged. Pioneers of such studies are David Schneider (1968), Clifford Greetz (1973) *et al.*

In the above lines the general nature of development and aim of field work has been stated very briefly. Now, the very important features regarding the methods and techniques of field work in social-cultural anthropology are stated. Observations and understanding of society and culture (relations and values behind) start with the facts or data. The method of collecting data in the field is an important factor; the value of reports depends on the methods of enquiry.

The entire field work procedure has two elements:

1. The observation and collection of data (facts).
2. A systematic analysis of the collected data and writing a report on it.

The data collection is done by either of the two sources for both

1. Textual i.e. from written documents

Contextual, data collected from the field.

The method: Direct observation can be divided into two parts:

a. The Direct extensive observation.
b. The Direct intensive observation.

Each method has several techniques. Direct extensive observation method is suitable for a wider or big area under study. The most popular form of this observation is by Polls, that is; a small sample of a large community is examined and the conclusion drawn from it are generalised. This is valid only if the sample is really representative. This technique has three essential phases: the drawing up of a list of people to be questioned (the sample), the questioning of this sample (the inquiry) and the utilisation of the results of the inquiry.

Direct extensive observation is done by sampling and questionnaire techniques. Sampling may further be done following two procedures: one is the quota and the other is the random sampling.

In questionnaire the poll procedure is done in interviews of questions. The questionnaires are classified according to the degree of freedom in reply. These can be of : (a) open and closed question, (b) questions with a series of alternative replies and (c) evaluating questions.

**Direct intensive observation:** It is carried out on small groups and even on individuals. It is not therefore, as wide but it is more detailed and has greater depth. This is the main method used in social-cultural anthropology. Direct observation is the technique per-excellence used by the anthropologists and the other technique is the interview. But actually observation and interview both are done for the purpose of collecting field data.

The four main techniques of this method are —

a. Observation

b. Interview

c. Case studies and genealogical technique

d. Questionnaires, schedules

(a) Direct observation is based on individual contacts between the observer and the people observed. There is an attempt to define the behaviour or the attitudes or obtain information on the life of the groups by examining some of the members of the group. Participant observation consists of examining the group itself as a whole. It is called *participant observation* because the observer always involves himself to some extent in the life and activities of the group. The participation is often more active and can be divided into two types. Either the observer is external to the group to start with and involves himself in the group to be able to observe or he is originally a member of the group who endeavours to acquire the quality of an observer. It is important to distinguish participant observers and observer participants.

### Participant Observers

They are observers first and participants second. In order to observe collective behaviour, ceitain groups become involved in the life of the group and participants in its activities. The participation can vary in intimacy and duration; sometimes the observer involves himself only briefly and superficially in the life of the group but sometimes the symbiosis is long and profound.

### Observer Participants

(a) 'Participants'–observe the social realities of their own group. Two main techniques are the observer either practices introspection and studies social reality through the medium of his own consciousness or he observes his colleagues in the group, the institutions in which he operates etc.

**(b) Interview:** Interview technique is an informal effective non-verbal and verbal conversation used for specific purposes and is focused on certain planned content areas. It involves collecting of information pertaining to provide range of data.

## The interviews can be classified in two categories

i. *Unstructured interview:* In this type, the interviewers do not follow a list of predetermined questions, and the interviews are encouraged to relate their concrete experiences with no or little direction from the interviewer, and reveal their attitudes and opinions as they see it.

ii. *Structured interview*: This is a highly standardised technique and a set of pre-determined questions. Hence, this requires a pilot study before hand. The directive interview often takes the form of a schedule. It is often criticised as it imposes selection of topics controlling the content of response; as it prescribes length of responses and thus in-hibits full revealing of informatin; as it indicates form of response thereby hampering informants in their attempts to relate situations as they see them.

Following types of interviews are often used to collect and check up data on required situations.

*Repeated (Panel) interviews:* This technique was per-fected by Lazarsfeld. A group of people were subject to repeated interviews at various intervals.

(a) Technique of the Panel.

Essentially the panel is based on two ideas.

1. Repetition of the same questions at regular intervals.
2. The same people are interviewed throughout the in-quiry.

*Repetition of the interviews*: Panels are designed mainly to study the evolution of attitudes and opinions over a short period of time. The group is questioned at regular intervals to obtain a series of 'snapshots' of its opinions and a com-parison of these gives an accurate idea of evolution of opinion. The interviews can be about attitudes and opinions, about those things which are likely to influence opinion and about attitudes and opinions which are thought to be linked with the inquiry.

The frequency and the total period of interviewing vary considerably depending on the nature of the inquiry and composition of the groups interviewed.

*Interviews in depth*: Under this general heading various interview techniques are grouped which attempt a deeper understanding of opinions, attitudes and even the whole personality of the subject. The terminology is not well established in this field and classification is not easy. Some techniques differ very little from one another but two categories can be clearly distinguished.

*Memoir interviews*: This type of interview has been little used until now but it seems to have great possibilities. The procedure is for an investigator to obtain permission from a person to see him regularly over a period of time to question him on events in which he has been involved. The inter-viewer must of course have a profound knowledge of the period studied and can be sympathetic and tactful. The type of person who could be interviewed are retired politicians of the second rank, directors and secretaries of committees, parties and groups, local elites and notables, higher civil servants, etc.

*Focused interviews*: This technique was invented by the American Sociologist R. K. Merton. It consists not so much of an interrogation as assisting people to illuminate some factor or stimulus acting on them and the impacts/effects of this on their attitudes. The interview takes place following a particular situation common to all the people being interviewed–a film by the reading of a newspaper, listening to the radio etc. The aim is to study in depth the influence of this situation. The procedure was invented to analyse the effects of communications.

### (c) *Case studies and genealogical techniques*

*Case Studies:* Case study is the technique of exploring and analysing the life of a social unit, be it a person, a family, an institution, culture group, or even an entire community. Its aim is to determine the factors that account for the complex behaviour patterns of the unit and the relationship of the unit to its surrounding milieu. Case-data may be gathered exhaustively on the entire life-cycle or on a definite section of the cycle of a unit, but always with a view of ascertaining the natural history of the social unit, and its relationships to the social factors and forces involved in its environment. In other words, through the case method, the social researcher attempts to see the variety of factors within a social unit as an integrated whole.

*Genealogical Technique*: Sometimes for particular topics case studies are collected with the help of genealogy which is otherwise known as genealogical technique. Particularly 'data' on kinship, inheritance and succession etc. are collected by this technique. First of all, a short genealogy of informant is taken. In applying this method, the simplest kinship terms as father, mother, son, daughter, brother, sister, husband and wife are generally used. The informant is asked the name of those who stand in this relation with him. He is given to understand that only biological kins are to be included. He is also asked as to how he addresses others and how others address him and thus the kinship terminology is built up. In the study of concrete cases, roles of kins are often required.

After the collection of genealogy of the informant, he is asked to narrate an event in which he himself is or was directly or partially involved. He is asked to describe the happenings or roles, he himself played. Thereby, he furnishes a concrete case experience by himself. As in this technique the case is studied centering the genealogy, which form the basis of investigation, this technique is generally known as 'Genealogical Technique'.

Through this technique, concrete cases are studied and the investigator takes upon him the duty of analysing, instead of putting it on the shoulders of the informants.

### (b) *Questionnaires, Schedules*

*Questionnaires:* They may be structured questionnaire with concrete and prearranged questions prepared in advance. Then they may be 'closed' or 'open ended'. In an 'open' ended question, it is possible to obtain a wide variety of reactions. It allows the respondent to give any type of answer he wishes, long or short. 'Closed' or 'fixed alternative' type of questions require the respondent to choose from a set of categories. The first requires consider-able work in the form of coding and content analysis before quantified analysis is possible. Further, comparability is not possible because vague and indefinite answers may be obtained. This is why any effective interview schedule often contains a mixture of both types of questions.

*Schedules*: This may be of different kind -Observation Schedules or Forms, Document Schedules, Institutional Survey Forms of Evaluation Schedules, Interview Schedules. Use of schedules requires fairly thorough knowledge of local cultural patterns and social groupings.

The field-worker must identify potentially significant questions by means of participant observation and key informant interviewing. They can be useful in cross-checking the data. So preliminary field work is necessary as it makes possible the construction of an interview schedule suited to local data and conditions. It has to be pre-tested in a com-munity similar to the main research site chosen, in order to ascertain people's responses to the style and content of questions.

Questionnaires can be distinguished from interview schedules in that the respondent himself fills out the answers to the questions on the form provided by the investigator. Questionnaires are generally sent through mail, while the schedule is filled out by the research worker. Both questionnaires and schedules are beneficial as supplementary and extending devices in observation, interview, and in evaluating personal behaviour and social situations. They also aid in standardising and objectifying observations and interviews. Further, they are useful as devices for isolating the element at a time and thus intensifying observation of it.

*Selection of Informants*: In the entire procedure of collection of data in the field, selection of informant plays vital role. The right person for particular information should be chosen and the informants with the knowledge of current affair experiences can provide with dependable data. Thus the role of informant is very important in the entire course of the field work.

## References

Banerjee, Biswanath and Amitabha Sarkar, 1996, *Fundamentals of Social and Cultural Anthropology*, Calcutta: Firma KLM Pvt. Ltd.

Basham, A.L. (ed), 1984, *A Cultural History of India* (2nd impression) Delhi: Ox-ford University Press.

Baneijee, S. 1981, *Impact of Industrialisation on the tribal population of Jharia -Ranigunge Coal Field area*, Calcutta: Anthropological Survey of India.

Beals, R. L. and H. Hoiser 1959 (2nd edition), *An Introduciton to Anthropology*, New York: The Mac-milan and Co.

Becker, H. and A. Boskoff, 1957, *Modern Sociological Theory: In Continuity and Change*, U.S.A: Rinehart and Winston Hott.

Bose, N. K., 1948, *Hindu Samajer Gadan* (in Bengali), Calcutta: Viswa Bharati Granthalay.

Bose, N. K., 1951, "Caste System in India", *Man in India*, Vol. XXXI.

Bose, N. K., 1953, *Cultural Anthropology and other Essay*, Calcutta: Indian Associated Publishing Co. Ltd.

Bose, N. K., 1961, *Cultural Anthropology*, Calcutta: Asia Publishing House.

Bottomore, T. B., 1971, *Sociology*, Bombay: George Allen and Unwin (India) Pvt. Ltd.

Duverger, Maurice, 1961, Introduction to the Social Sciences: With special reference to their Methods, London: George Allen and Unwin Ltd.

Geertz, Clifford, 1973, The Interpretation of Cultures, New York: Basic Books.

Sarana, Gopala, 1975, The Methodology of Anthropological Comparisons, Arizona: The University of Arizona Press.

Schneider, David, M. 1968 American Kinship: A Cultural Account, New Jersey: Prentice Hall, Inc.

# 3

# Development of Social Thought

Ideas about society existed in ancient times. But it was not until the nineteenth century that science of society developed as a specific field of knowledge. Before the nineteenth century there was no rigid differentiation between the various theories about society, philosophy, religion, economics and political science. During the eighteenth century, the term anthropology was often used to designate a consideration of the whole mental activities of man. In the early part of the eighteenth century the concept of the subject took a shape when L. H. Morgan, Edward Tylor and others attempted to classify primitive and contemporary peoples basing on cultural facts. They attempted to define and point out the scope of the discipline still in a formative phase.

At that period some intellectuals of comparative law contributed some valuable ideas to this subject. Swiss Jurist Bachoffen (1815-1887) expressed the idea of the matrilineal descent of the first time. J. F. Mclennan (1827-1881) also thought about the importance of matrilineal descent. Henry Maine (1822-1888), Professor of Law at Cambridge, advocated for the priority of patriarchy in the source of origin of the civilisation and tried to classify the society on the basis of status and contract.

The above mentioned anthropologists along with the jurists and other intellectuals of that period like Kant, Hume and others were influenced by the achievements of the Industrial Revolution as well as by the Theory' of Evolution. Such influences are often traceable in their thinking and ideas on societies and cultures.

In this formative stage of sociology and anthropology appeared Sir Herbert Spencer, (1820-1903) who could very sucessfully frames the scope of both the subjects. He classified worldly objects into three orders: inorganic (non-living), organic (living) and super-organic (socio-cultural). Anthropology in general, according to him, was related to both organic and super-organic orders. In the organic level it studied man as a biological organism and in the super-organic, the cultural traits. He further distinguished three principal types of institutions in the society: sustaining institutions, economic institutions, and regulating institutions i.e. religious and political systems. Social structure was therefore, conceived of as a kind of equilibrium maintained by interrelated functioning of the component institutions.

Thus, anthropology in general, by virtue of its scope, deals both with the organic and the super-organic orders and as such it seems to occupy a position between natural science and humanities. The two main divisions of anthropology i.e. physical and social-cultural are still independent to a great extent and are based on their own respective theories. It is often stated that one of the ultimate objectives of anthropologists lies in finding out corelation between these two levels. Social-cultural anthropology has been dependent on sociology since the period of its inception, for its theories at least, though later the former deviated considerably both in the fields of interest and methods from the latter. Since its inception, social-cultural anthropology has been related to philosophy, history, etc. on the one hand and with the biological theory of evolution on the other. It is true that initially social-cultural anthropology was evolutionary.

In any scientific approach the systematic classification of the phenomena is essential. In the case of sociology and in socio-cultural anthropology also, endeavours towards classification have been made mostly on the basis of: (i) social relations, (ii) social groups and (iii) structures of the society. In this field along with Morgan, Tylor, Frazer, social-cultural anthropology owes to the eminent sociologists like Comte, Spencer, Durkheim, Hobhouse, Simmel, Tonnies, Max Weber and Karl Marx.

Evolutionist L. Morgan (1818-1881) classified seven statutes of society as based on marriage and family. To him the history of human race was one in source, one in experience and one in progress. Contemporary European civilisation was placed at the top of his scheme of seven statutes from primitive savagery to civilisation. He used the Australian aboriginals to the Roman empires as examples in support of his theory. In search of suitable example for his purpose this genius did not depend only on traveller's or missionary reports like others, but also conducted field tours among the Iroquois of New York State as early as in 1850s, establishing thereby, a record of field work for the first time in the history of this subject. He was also the founder of systematic study of kinship system for tracing cultural evolution.

Tylor (1832-1917) was neither a field worker nor he was one of those armchair anthropologists. One of his major contributions was the definition of culture. He was interested in studying religious institutions and through religious practices tried to focus the evolution of societies.

James Frazer (1854-1941) postulated three stages of development through which he believed all societies passed i.e. Magic. Religion and Science.

These victorian anthropologists tried to trace evolution with utmost sincerity and spent all their energies in arranging types and forms neglecting the perspectives of time and space. None of them except Morgan, attempted to apply their hypotheses to the whole of the culture, they rather dealt with selected aspects. For tracing evolution these scholars laid much importance upon the basic technological inventions particularly those related to food quest. There is an underlying assumption in the writings of some of them that technological changes stimulated major changes in all other spheres of culture. The evidence for such a deterministic view is not yet very convincing. Some areas of culture such as language, arts, and systems of religious beliefs apparently seem to be independent of technology.

But social-cultural anthropology of ages will remain grateful to these great thinkers for the foundation of the discipline and some positive contribution towards the concept of society and culture. They differentiated very carefully the cultural traits from the biological traits and they perceived quite clearly the systematic nature of the cultural phenomena.

The contribution of some pioneers in sociology to the field of social-cultural concepts is briefly described below:

August Comte (1798-1857) was the founder of systematic thinking in sociology. He surveyed fully the history of science. To him the study of sociology was to be used as a tool for attaining certain social goals. He believed that each branch of knowledge passed through three stages: the theological or fictitious, the metaphysical or abstract and the scientific or positive. To him the society and state formed the organic whole. He advocated that man should be viewed sociologically, that is, holistically.

The French genius Emile Durkheim (1858-1917) was closer to Hegel in thinking and held that social facts could not be explained in terms of individual psychology only because they exist outside and apart from individual minds. The collective consciousness or group habits were much more important objects of sociological studies. Society provided a large number of predefined conventions and norms which governed the behaviour of an individual. He emphasised the autonomy of sociology and tried to specify the range of phenomena with which it should deal. He showed how sociology differed from psychology, philosophy and economics. To him social solidarity was of two types: mechanical and organic.

To L. T. Hobhouse (1864-1929) sociology was a science which had the whole social life of man as its sphere of study. His theory of social development described the growth of knowledge. His three broad types of social unions were based on kinship, authority and citizenship. He classified primitive societies in terms of economic condition.

Mention can be made here on certain original contribution towards the conception of social process. Sociological thoughts in Germany were mostly influenced by the ideas of Simmel. G. Simmel (1858-1918) who was in favour of dissociating sociology from psychology. He attempted to classify all social relationships in terms of their tendency towards association or dissociation, towards increasing or decreasing of social distance between individuals.

Ferdinand Tonnies (1855-1936)'s 'Master Concept' of gemeinschaft (community) and gesellschaft (society) was a turning point in German sociology and it established a new era in the world sociology.

Von Weise's relational sociology aimed at an analysis and classification of social process. It showed how social structures arose through the activities of simple social process and association and dissociation. Vier Kant again stated sociology as concerned with the analysis of fundamental social relationship as leadership, respect, submission, strength and power.

Many basic ideas regarding sociology reflected in the writings of Max Weber (1864-1920) were stimulated by materials from history, law, economics, politics and comparative religion. He was a historian-cum-sociologist. In his attempts towards classification of societies and in his ideas of 'ideal type' he was not free from Marx's influence. He classified the society in terms of social action. He also classified social relationship between traditional, affective, rational in terms of means and rational in terms of ends. In the process of his interpretation of social relations he classified authority of three types: traditional, charismatic and bureaucratic.

Karl Marx (1818-1883) was an economic historian. His economic interpretation of history was a classic work. Though he was not a sociologist, his interpretations were mostly based on sociological ground. He defined society as an organised multitude of productive forces. He analysed the economic structures as social institutions characterised by productive technique of social division of labour expressed in patterns of ownership of the instruments of production and in a corresponding class structure. To him social changes could be defined by the changes in productive techniques. He concluded that social systems contained contradictions between the economic and other spheres and insisted that these provoked class struggles and thus social changes were related to social evolution. His theory of social change contained two important features: 1. that the change could be investigated by analysing the reactions of implicated groups, and 2. that the change was often accompanied by maladjustments and group conflicts on physical and ideological levels.

The influence of Hegel on Marx was fundamental. The basic concept that the world is not to be comprehended as a complex of readymade things, but as a complex of process, in which things apparently look stable, but they constantly go through an uninterrupted change of coming into being and again passing away. Marx's achievement lies in bringing together two schools of thought, viz, Hegelianism and Utilitarianism. Hegelianism emphasised collectivism and its method was historical, while, utilitarianism emphasised individualism and its method was analytical. Marx claimed that he had corrected the anomalies in Hegel and had discovered the 'rational kernel within the mystical shell' (Behura, 1988). Marx believed that social history would culminate in the rise of the proletariat and he looked forword to their dominance in society. For Hegel, the mechanism of progress was welfare between nations; for Marx, it was antagonism between social classes.

Marx's materialism was dialectical and not mechanical. He had the idea that man could become the master of his own destiny. He maintained that economic causes could be found for all political and legal institutions. Engels said that the economic situation was 'in the last instance the determining factor of history, which was finally deceisive'. (Behura, 1988). Marx sought to explain the historical and economic phenomena not through natural sciences, but through dialectics. Marx was obliged to reject religion. Marx did not believe in Hegel's idea that a spiritual state was to emerge in the ultimate analysis. His ultimate goal was the classless society. **Dialectical materialism** of Marx was a panoramic interpretation of the worldly phenomena. Dialectical materialism studies the dynamism in the universe, in the external world and in the world of thought. In dialectical materialism, evolution is the development of matter from within unlike mechanical materialism, where evolution occurs under external pressure.

The historical materialism is an economic interpretation of history, and a means for the application of dialectical materialism to the development of society. According to Marx production is the most important of all human activities. Men in association produce more food than the men in isolation, and society is thus the result of an attempt to secure the necessities of life. There have been four main stages in economic life of mankind:

(i) The primitive, communistic or Asiatic stage in which the forces of production are slight and communally owned.

(ii) The Ancient Stage,

(iii) The Feudal Stage, and

(iv) The Capitalist stage.

According to Marx, economic factor is the most important factor in history. Marx maintains that 'all the social, political and intellectual relations, all religious and legal systems, all the theoretical outlooks which emerge in the course of history, are derived from the material conditions of life'. All other motives of men are subordinate to the economic motive.

In the primitive stage, there is a crude sort of communism; in the ancient stage, private property arises, and with it arises the system of slavery; in the feudal stage, there are feudal lords and serfs in the society; the relationship between lord and serf is personal; the serf is better than the slave, for he cannot be killed; while, in the capitalist stage, land is no longer important. It is the industrial stage, with capitalists and workers, between whom exists an impersonal relationship. Marx is of the opinion that until the stage of perfect production is attained, all societies will be transitory and thus each step is a step nearer to ultimate classless society.

It appears that major contributions in methods the theory in social-cultural anthropology came from Durkheim and Max Weber. In the field of social classification different criteria have been used by Spencer,

Comte, Marx, Hobhouse, Tonnies and others, to distinguish the forms of society. Durkheim and Spencer based on size and associated phenomena. Comte and Hobhouse classified in terms of intellectual development and Marx did it on the basis of economy. All the mentioned attempts of classification were based on evolutionary scheme. In the studies of social stratification, Marx's contribution was fundamental.

Regarding classification of social groups, some distinguished primary and secondary group or groups, quasi-groups etc. while discussing Simmel and Max Weber, their attempts to classify social relation and social action have already been mentioned. At present the industrial societies, problem of underdeveloped countries in the process of industrialisation offer new lines of thinking to the sociologists and the anthropologists.

### Social-Cultural Anthropology rests on three principal approaches

1. The theory of evolution, 2. Theory of diffusion and 3. Structural-functional approach. The theme of theory of evolution has been briefly discussed previously. Still many anthropologists of the present time believe in the process of cultural evolution. One of the vehement critics of evolution in culture, R. H. Lowie states that "evolution is far from dead, and our duty is merely to define it with greater precision" (Lowie, 1937). The idea of evolution at present, has been followed up by anthropologists like V. G. Childe (1892-1957), J. Steward and L. A. White. They treat culture as a whole than particular cultures. V. G. Childe states that "the multiplicity of cultures revealed by ethnographic and archaeological research is a handicap if the objective is to establish general stages in the evolution of cultures.......discover general laws descriptive of the evolution of all societies" (Childe, 1951).

J. Steward's evolutionary studies are in the same line as other evolutionists with the implication that cultural evolution is always progressive. According to Steward similar necessities may give birth to similar effects in many areas and it is called as Multilineal evolution. L. A. White is the most outspoken evolutionary among the three anthropologists mentioned here. He had added much in the process of classification and precision to Morgan's contribution. The idea of Morgan, was re-established by him in terms of technology and energy. He is of opinion that specialisation comes after substantiating local condition which is one in progress and one in source. He also states that social evolution is a consequence of technological evolution. According to him culture is the product of energy and technology.

The theory of diffusion states that culture traits are often borrowed, and the total culture does not emerge in similar forms in different societies by spontaneous growth due to certain common social potentialities and common human nature. In the process of borrowing and incorporation of traits of culture from the other groups, the diffused traits may undergo all sorts of change.

The theory of evolution was criticised both by the diffusionists and the functionalists. Diffusionist Friedrich Ratzel (1844-1904) in Germany was perhaps the forerunner in this aspect. "Ratzel did not invent the principle of diffusion which Tylor and Pitt-Rivers applied quite as radically. But . . . did give special emphasis to uninventiveness of mankind. . . . Ratzel added the notion that the globe so far as inhabitable, is actually everywhere occupied by man where he referred far reaching migrations dating back to a very early period" (Lowie, 1937). Since then three distinct trends in social-cultural anthropology in England, Germany and America can be traced.

In England, Elliot Smith (1871-1937) and W. H. R. Rivers (1864-1922) were pioneers. Rivers made valuable contributions to kinship systems. In Germany, diffusion studies were initiated by Ratzel and Graebner and followed up by Schmidt. Later on important research works were done by Gusinde.

In America, the former anthropologists as L. H. A. Morgan, O. T. Masion and others were under the spell of evolution. F. Boas (1858-1942) emphasised the importance of field work, linguistics and psychology studies in anthropology. "He also introduced the concept of 'pattern' in the description of tribal or area cultures; he rejected evolution and environmentalism in their crude classical forms and accepted diffusion, independent development, parallelism and convergence, not as dogmatic postulates but as tools to aid research" (Haddon. 1934).

"Age and Area", theory of naturalist was applied in anthropology by N. C. Nelson in 1919 and later on elaborated by Clark Wissler, a contemporary of F. Boas. A. L. Kroeber, student of F. Boas, stated that culture and age area concepts existed in biological sciences and used in anthropology before Wissler without methodological formulation. Regarding the point of origin of characteristic traits in culture area Kroeber stated the centre "as a locus of superior productivity" (Kroeber, 1931). In his book 'Anthropology' published in 1923, he gave a diagrammatic representation of accumulation and diffusion of culture traits. Students of F. Boas worked in different fields of anthropology.

Ruth Benedict worked on Patterns of Culture, R. Linton worked out culture area for Madagascar and he also devoted himself to the culture and personality studies. Herskovits sets up culture areas for Africa, Clyde Kluckhohn studied themes and value configuration among the Navahos. Later on Herskovits and Linton initiated acculturation studies.

Everywhere in England, Germany and America these diffusionists commonly laid much importance to: (i) the study of history and (ii) the field work. On the whole it may be said that diffusion is not a mechanical process, it is exceedingly complex one and subjected to many conditions, cultural, sociological, geographical etc. The concept of age area and culture area as formulated by Clark Wissler is an important contribution to social-cultural anthropology.

Functionalism originated in Durkheim's writings and B. Malinowski proposed to explain social phenomena by referring them to individual biological needs and derived cultural needs. In practice Malinowski oscillated between ethnographic description and psychological explanations. A. R. R. Brown's theory of structure seeks to act in the following ends: 1. Precise description of functioning social structures as these exist in various parts of the world. The usages and institutions found in human societies are to be described with special reference to their roles in maintaining the social structure, 2. a systematic classification of social phenomena together with a suitably exact terminology, 3. formulation of the general laws that underlie social phenomena by scientific methods paralleling those of the natural sciences (Beals and Hoijer, 1959). A. R. R. Brown laid much stress on the study of society than on culture. Works of B. Malinowski and A. R. R. Brown inspired their disciples as M. Fortes, E. Pritchard, R. Firth in British Island and also influenced many American anthropologists. As a result, some of the American anthropologists attempted to redefine their methods and approaches for their earlier concentration on historical studies. For example Linton's analysis of the culture traits may be mentioned. In the studies of R. Redfield. Fred Eggan and Sol Tax the influence of A. R. R. Brown can be traced. Thus, A. R. R. Brown cleared the path by generalising science of social anthropology.

Social-cultural anthropology still shares the theories of sociology in common and is benefited by the theories of social conflict and group integration, Marx's theory of class.

Now earnest endeavors should made by empirical researches so that the validity of these concepts may be tested. At the present moment the problems of social-cultural anthropology are in no way different from the problems of sociology. Here classification of problem drawn by M. Ginsberg may be mentioned. He sorted out the problems in the following order: (a) Social morphology: which includes the investigations of the quantity and quality of the population in so far as they affect social relations and character of social groups and the study of social groups and the study of social structure: the description and classification of the principal types of social groups and institutions, (b) Social control: the study of law, morals, religion and other regulating agencies, (c) Social process: the study of various modes of interaction between individuals or groups, including cooperation and conflict, social differentiation and integration, development and decay, (d) Social pathology: the study of social maladjustment and disturbances and of the methods used for dealing with them (Ginsberg, 1939). Each of the above mentioned items is conceptually rich undoubtedly but to be proved valid they should be placed on empirical base.

Before proceeding to methods it should be mentioned that organic and social-cultural fields are different in two respects: the organic objects are observable and so explanation from surface is possible, while social-cultural world in most part has to be comprehended in terms of the inner working of the mind. The organic world rests on mechanical relations but social-cultural world rests on the relation of value and purpose. Again, in social-cultural behaviour there are some activities, i.e., material pursuits which may be directly observed and handled. Social activities i.e. kinship behaviour, marriage ceremony etc. can also be observed. Religious concepts or supernatural ideas, however, can only be recorded through utterances and have often to be understood through empathy. So each field deserves different treatment in the empirical procedure.

It has already been stated that social science or general anthropology occupies a place between natural science and humanities. Therefore, neither the methods of natural science nor that of the humanities are adequate for the pursuit of this discipline. Again to cope with the varied field, on one method can possibly be effective. Broadly, comparative method as set out by Durkheim is still followed up. But it is to be ascertained whether the institutions compared are of similar or of different backgrounds. Comparative method is based on the general rule of inductive logic. The method provides scope of using data derived from different regions and different times. This method aims at formulation of sociological laws as natural laws, which however, is still a very controversial issue. B. Malinowski pragmatically tried to find out functional connections between man and culture or interrelation of institutions and moved from description to psychological ends. Later on, of course, he condemned his own attempts. On the other hand, A. R. R. Brown believed that the utility of the comparative method will depend upon proper definition of the units of comparison. It is still a very difficult problem. With many modifications of the earlier ideas of H. Spencer he advocates the study of social structure. He regards it "as . . . a part of the social structure all social relations of person to person" etc. (Radcliffe Brown, 1952). To R. Firth the above seems to be too broad a definition as it makes no distinction between the ephemeral and the more enduring elements in social activities and make it almost impossible to distinguish the idea of the structure of a society from that of the totality of the society itself. A. R. Radcliffe Brown, of course, was in hope that by studying the social structure intensively, formulation of social laws would be possible. S. F. Nadel later on criticised structural studies for its narrow compass. He tried to make this sort of approach more effective by analysis of social structures in terms of status and roles (Nadel, 1955). But R Firths later on commented that . . there is . . . . no such isolable entity as the social structure .... no such isolable entity as the social structure......the social structure, viewed as something within grasp of the ethnographer's account, is a myth. . R. Firth's (1952) veryown specific opinion on the study of social structure is "It is an analytical tool, designed to serve us in understanding how men behave in their social life. " The essence of this concept is those social relations which seem to be of critical importance for the behaviour of members of the society, so that if such relations were not in operation, the society could not be said to exist in that form.

The idea of the structure of society if it is to be in conformity with the general concept of structure must fulfill certain conditions. It must be concerned with the ordered relations of parts to a whole, with the arrangement in which the elements of the social life are linked together. These relations must be regarded as built up one upon another—they are series of varying orders of complexity. They must be of more than purely momentary significance—some factor of constancy or continuity must be involved in them.

The structural study itself is a formal one of the basic relations only. It is necessary to study social adaptation as well as social continuity. A structural analysis alone cannot interpret social continuity. So, analysis of the organisational aspect of social action is the necessary complement to analysis of the structural aspect. It helps to give a more dynamic treatment.

Therefore, the study of social organisation always states the concrete activity. It includes the recognition of time factor in the ordering of social relations. The concept of social organisation is important also for the understanding of social change.

Still structural method stands as a fruitful analytic tool in studying the social morphologies. (Since Redfield's attempt towards synchronic comparison of village or total communities in space in relation to model types, folk and urban is mentionable as a new technique in comparative method). E. E. Evans Pritchard's approach in this respect is perhaps, more towards reality. To him in social-cultural anthropology methods of historical interpretation are more suitable. In sociology or in social-cultural anthropology ideas of causal connection or attempts to formulate laws as in natural science are absurd. This discipline provides knowledge of human societies and thus facilitates better understanding of human problems. His own studies of Azande religion, Nuer tribe are more devoted to contextual understanding rather than to formulation of laws like natural science (Evans-Pritchard, 1951).

So far anthropologists engaged themselves in studying primitive societies only but responding to the demands of situation they have turned towards the study of their own societies. Naturally, present anthropologists should also be aware of sociological methods to some extent.

Among the pioneers of sociology, some considered it as a natural science and some as history of philosophy. Earlier Durkheim, Karl Marx and others regarded sociology as a natural science and attempted to the formulation of universal sociological laws. They tried to study society as a chemist studied the salt or a zoologist studies the nervous system of a toad.

Dilthey and Rickert successfully differentiated natural or organic spheres from socio-cultural spheres of study. They stated that: (i) in natural level objects could be observed and studied from outside but in social-cultural level it could be observed from inside. And relation between man and a machine or salt or a toad and relation between one man and another man was never of similar kind and (ii) in the natural world the relations were obviously mechanical so it might be related by causality whereas in social-cultural domain the relations were always value oriented and purposive (Bottomore, 1962).

Dilthey further specified that in natural science investigators' attempts were directed to "knowing about" the object but in social-cultural level there was enough scope of 'knowing' the subject directly that is, through insights about the working of the human mind. So human studies should be made with the construction of types of culture and personality which might serve as an . outline or frame work for understanding the human situations in time and space. To Dilthey sociology thus differed from natural science in the object of study. And considering the object of study the social scientists should always be realistic or conscious about their working limit. Here E. E. Evans Pritchard is closer to Dilthey in his views.

Basing on understanding Max Weber tried to balance the two concepts—Marx at one pole and Dilthey at the other. In his study of relation between the protestant ethics and capitalism he attempted to show how protestant ethics and growth of capitalism could be historically studied and basing on the fact thus obtained, causal explanation of development of western capitalism could be inferred. Regarding methods followed by him in his studies of capitalism, economic influence of world religion etc., he carefully examined the historical changes in structures and forms of society and attempted both historical interpretation and causal explanation (Max Weber, 1930). A strong influence of Max Weber is seen among the today's social-cultural anthropologists.

However, Social-cultural Anthropology is a science as its generalisations are based on controlled comparison which includes co-ordination between induction as well as deduction. Subject matter of social-cultural anthropology (institutions, groupings, ethic, norms, values etc. ) in most part functionally depend on or are related to each other. The aim of science is to find out and explain their meaning and nexus. In case of ethnographic approach the method is deductive or 'outside in' or '**centripetal**'. If the analysis starts from individual or family of domestic units and extends to find out its relation with all other institutions economic, political, religious etc., the method is inductive or 'inside out' or '**centrifugal**'.

In India "the nucleus for the study of anthropology dates from the foundation of the Asiatic Society of Bengal by W. Jones towards the later part of eighteenth century. Pioneers were Dalton, Ibbetson, Nesfield, Senart, Hiralal, Russel, Thurston, Crooke, Risley and others. Ethnographic accounts of tribes and castes were written by these administrative officials. Among them Herbert Risley's works are the most valuable and fundamental. Rai Bahadur S. C. Roy, L. K. A. Iyer, some missionaries and the civilians as Hutton, Shakespeare, Johnstone, Parry, Smith, Gurdon, Playfair, Hodson, Mill's monographic studies and K. P. Chattopadhaya's analysis of marriage regulations as affected by culture contact, T. C. Das's analysis of the culture complex centering round the use of fish; the problem of fish, fishing and fishermen of Bengal by M. N. Basu are mentionable. D. N. Majumdar, W. G. Grigson, G. S. Ghurye's contributions towards the domain of social-cultural anthropology are also notable.

Analytic trend in Indian social-cultural anthropology was noticed for the first time in the writings of N. K. Bose. His most original thinking regarding the concept of culture was published as early as in the year 1929, and the study of caste system was published later on (Bose. 1951). His unique methods of studying Indian societies are best represented in the book 'Hindoo Samajer Gadan', written in Bengali. Next to him, most valuable contribution to the Indian social-cultural anthropology comes from M. N. Srinivas (Srinivas, 1952). S. C. Dube's studies on social process are notable for its methodology (Dube, 1958) and Karve (1968). Except the works of these few anthropologists general condition of social-cultural anthropology in India is quite precarious. Students often read this subject, take post graduate degrees, but even then in most cases it is seen that a proper understanding of the subject eludes them since they lack training in analytic lines. Things become worse when such students do research work. They take research degrees which only fetch some monetary gains in the service line, academic position and prestige in the society. In most cases these studies are not based on adequate statement of hypothesis tested and so these unrelated research findings produce only a miscellany of curiosa, nothing in lineament of this science while its vast field is waiting for systematic treatment.

Post-Independent India has been changing in somewhat faster pace. Improved communication, raised standard of living, industrial planning and political atmosphere prevailing at present in India have imposed certain definite changes in the system which is quite a long way from what it had been earlier. It has affected the rural as well as tribal areas of course, in different degrees and ways. In rural areas even, it has lessened the impact of caste system, given birth to a kind of sentiment of 'ethnic' and new classes, mostly on the basis of wealth and completely new power groups mainly based on politics.

Different social problems were reflected in the writings of Sarat Chandra Chatterjee and Rabindranath Tagore. Besides these literatures such problems and related themes have occasionally been imparted by the historians, economists, political scientists and philosophers of the country. Recently the effects of Community Development Projects on minds of the Indian people have neatly been portrayed by a Journalist (Nair, 1961). Social-cultural anthropologists should be aware of these facts. Ideas from these varied sources certainly help a social-cultural anthropologist at work.

For research works in social-cultural anthropology at the present moment, piecemeal studies of communities will never produce any result of practical value. Research taken on regional basis on modes of interaction between communities is sure to fetch fruitful results, valuable both for academic and administrative purposes. To understand such regional problem, emic view is necessary and to understand the emic situation one has to take methodological knowledge of Cognitive Anthropology.

## Functionalism

The scholar of evolution did not give satisfactory answer to the integrative elements of culture; some scholars came forward with a scheme of penetrating ethnographic description and the analysis of integration and of inter relations between institution—which give birth to *functionalism.*

Emile Durkheim (1858-1917) studied group relation to understand function. He never provided a specific theory of functionalism, but he used functional method in explaining the function of social phenomena of primitive societies.

On the other hand, Malinowski has a clear cut methodological perception to understand function. He studied individual relations which ultimately affects culture. To him study of inter relationship between custom and institution is functionalism. The basic meaning of function is activity. Malinowski was of opinion that all the cultural components have function to perform while interpreting the 'concept of culture and need'

Malinowski and his associates were of the opinion that a cultural trait which is functionless could not survive and hence has no cultural survival. One trait of culture is integrated with another and when one is disturbed the other gets paralysed. Malinowski understands and interprets culture in terms of function. Thus he became champion of the functional school.

- The first aim of every society is its survival,
- Every society has some personnel, who have some norms with a set of values,

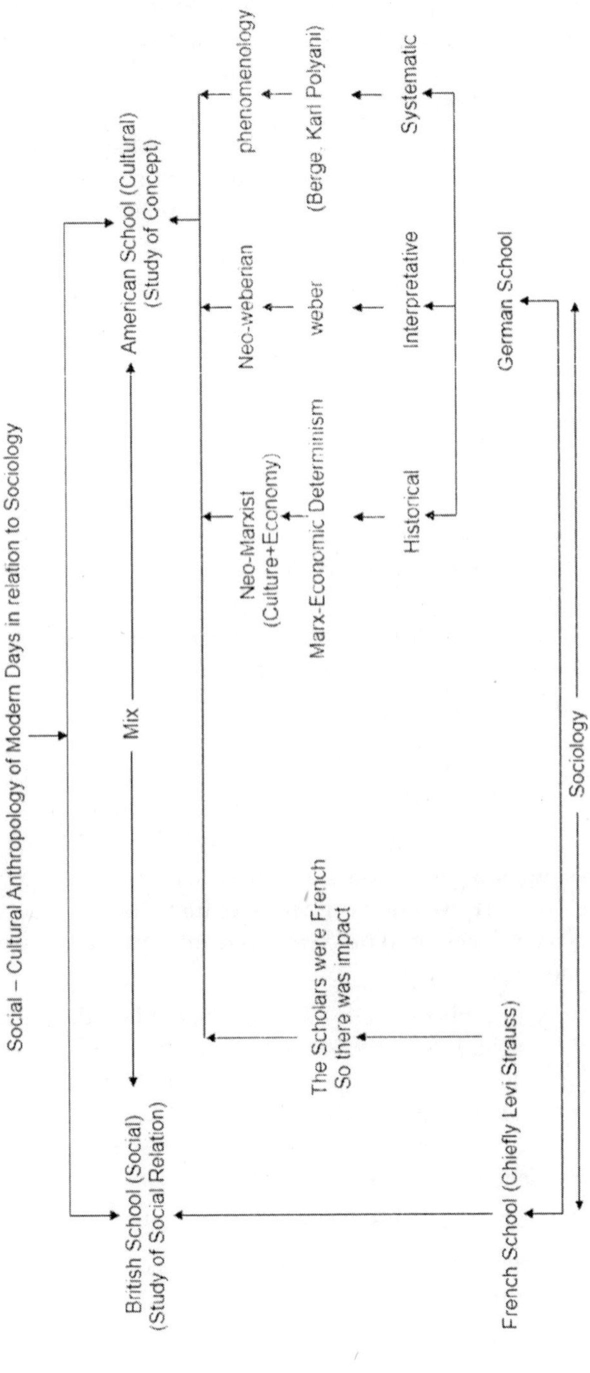
Social – Cultural Anthropology of Modern Days in relation to Sociology
American School (Cultural)
(Study of Concept)
British School (Social)
(Study of Social Relation)
Mix
phenomenology
(Berge. Karl Polyani)
Systematic
Neo-weberian
weber
Interpretative
Neo-Marxist
(Culture+Economy)
Marx-Economic Determinism
Historical
German School
The Scholars were French
So there was impact
French School (Chiefly Levi Strauss)
Sociology

- Malinowski said these norms and values inspired the personnel for material apparatus,
- Which ultimately creates activities,
- For performing such activities there is need of function.

In functionalism society is conceived as a system of inter related parts in which none can be understood in isolation from the other.

## Structuralism

Social structure is the actually existing network of relations and the essential component are the family, marriage, clan etc. The essential relations are not individual relation but group relation. Radcliffe Brown (1881-1955) studied the social structure on the basis of two fundamental needs: (a) to analyse social phenomena, (b) to classify society on the basis of certain distinctive characteristics of their own as simple or complex.

## Differences of functionalism between Malinowski and R. Brown

1. Malinowski never said anything could function without an ordered arrangement, while, Radcliffe Brown said in 1935 the concept of function as have been defined involves the notion of a structureconsisting of a set of relation amongst unit entities.
2. Malinowski said the essential concept is organisation. In order to achieve any purpose to reach any end, human beings have to organise.

## Difference to the Idea of Structure

1. According to Malinowski 'organisation implies a very definite scheme or structure the main features of which are 'universal'. He called this 'universal' unit of human organisation an institution, while, Brown did not have any pre-determined ordered arrangement as social structure.
2. Malinowski structure was applicable to all organised groups, while, Brown's structure did not have any fixed parameters. It had to be deciphered in each specific case from the complexity of empirical data.

## Difference of Structuralism between Radcliffe Brown and Lévi-Strauss

1. According to Brown and Lévi-Strauss structure is an ordered arrangement of parts or components.

2. Radcliffe Brown adopted inter personal relation, while, Levi-Strauss was interested in structure not from the aspects of inter personal relationships but he wanted first and foremost to discover the 'structure of human thought process' and he was not concerned with such functions and considers them 'self-understood'.

**DEVELOPMENT OF SOCIAL THOUGHT**

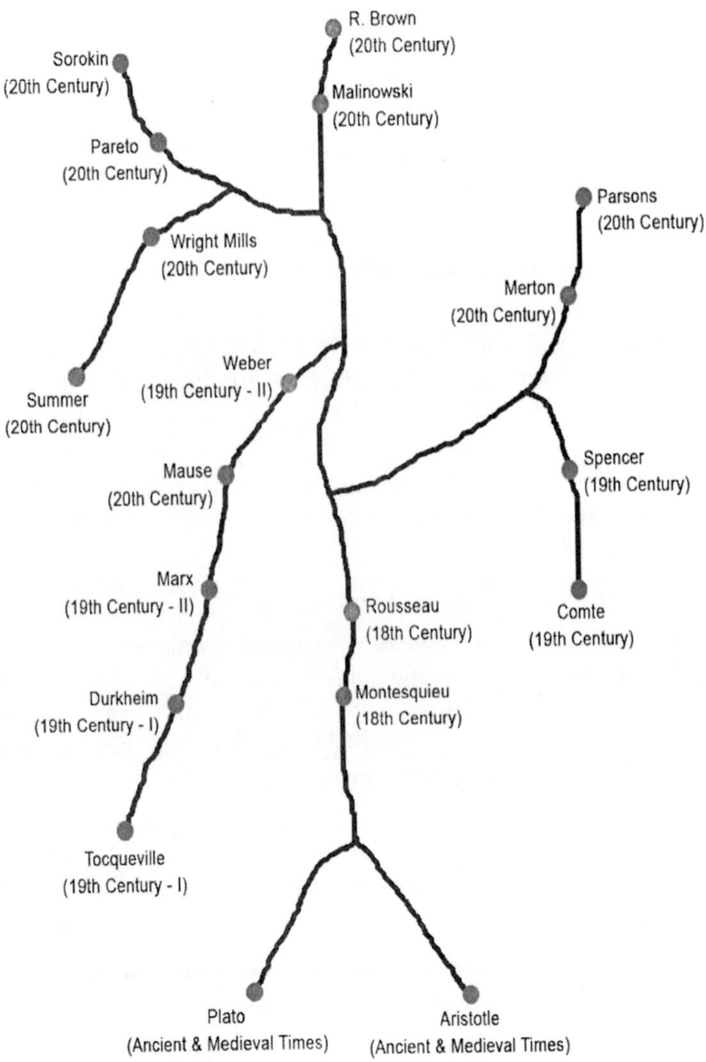

**References**

Abraham, J. H., 1973, *Origins and Growth of Sociology*, England: Penguin Books.

Banerjee, Biswanath and Amitabha Sarkar, 1996, *Fundamentals of Social and Cultural Anthropology,* Calcutta: Firma KLM Pvt. Ltd.

Beals, R. L. and H. Hoiser, 1959 (2nd Edition), *An Introduction to Anthropology*, New York: The Macmilan & Co.

Behura, N. K., 1988, *Anthropological Thought and Theories*, Calcutta: Institute of Social research and Applied Anthropology.

Bose, N. K., 1948, *Hindu Samajer Gadan* (in Bengali), Calcutta: Viswa Bharati Granthalay.

Bottomore, T. B., 1971, *Sociology*, Bombay: George Allen and Unwin (India) pvt. Ltd.

Childe, V. G., 1951, *Social Evolution*, London and New York: Copyright by H. Schuman.

Dube, S. C., 1958, *Indias Changing Village*, Ithaca, New York: Cornell University Press.

Evans Pritchard, E. E., 1951, *Social Anthropology*, New York: Free Press.

Firth, Raymond, 1952, *Elements of Social Anthropology*, London: Watts and Co.

Firth, Raymond, 1954, "Presidential Address", in Journal of Royal Anthropological Institute, Vol. 84.

Ginsberg, M., 1934, *Sociology*, London: Oxford University Press.

Ginsberg, M., 1957, *Essays in sociology and Social Philosophy*, London.

Haddon, A. C., 1934, *History of Anthropology*. London: Watts and Co.

Hobhouse, L. T., 1924, *Social Development–its Nature and Conditions*, London: George Allen and Unwin Ltd.

Lowie, R. H., 1937, *The History of Ethnological Theory*. New York: Farrar and Rinehart.

Nair, Kusum, 1961, *Blossoms in the Dust*, London: Gerald Duck Worth and Co. Ltd.

Radcliffe Brown, A. R., 1952, *Structure and Function in Primitive Society*, London: Cohen and West Ltd.

Spencer, H., 1872, *Study of Sociology*, Kanpur: Kitab Ghar (Indian Edition).

Weber, Max, 1930, *Protestant ethics and the Spirit of Capitalism*, London: George Allen and Unwin (Translated by Talcott Parson).

Wissler, Clark, 1929, *An Introduction to Social Anthropology*, New York: Henry Holt and Co.

# 4

# Kinship Pattern and Systems

In human society people are found together in groups by various kinds of bonds. The most universal and basic of these bonds is that which is based on reproduction, an inherent human drive called kinship. Firstly, there is the bond between spouses and their relations on either side; and secondly, there is bond between parents and their children, and that between siblings, i.e. children of the same parents. The first kind of bond is called affinal kinship and the relatives so related are called affinal kin. The second kind of bond i.e. the relationship based on blood ties is called consanguineous kinship and the relatives are called consanguineal kin.

To understand the social structure of a society through kinship behaviours of the people within the family and its outer world is important one. Social structure means an arrangement of persons in institutionally controlled or defined relations. Social structure provides a framework on which the social actions occur. Therefore, social structure consists of the major component of the society which form a systematic (i.e. the inter-relationship of basic groupings and institution) arrangement and serve to regulate further social action along with the same line.

Brown has pointed out that specially the range of application of the kinship terms and the specific behaviours of the persons give the full account of the dynamic relations within a society. Eggan has shown among the Hopi Indians the classification of relatives into categories is not only simply a matter of terminology or language, but is the basis of much of the regulation of social life. Among the Hopi Indians system all the members of the lineage of a grandparent are included in one category with the grandparents and the attitude that is appropriate towards a grandparent is extended to them.

Social aspects of kinship system deal mainly with relations, terms and functions: regular and occasional i.e. structure and functional ends. The cultural aspect of kinship study is a recent development, after D. M. Schneider's (1968) efforts which deal with the norms and values behind the relations expressed by different terms in different kinship systems in different language.

Now, coming towards structure types of relationship may be real or artificial. The real relationships are those by blood affinal are those by marriage. Artificial relations are those like ceremonial friends, which is otherwise known as *putative kinship,* for example, *Soi patano* (in rural Bengal), *Karam daiyer* or *Phool daiyer* (in Jharkhand), *Sahu domanga* (in Odisha) etc.

The term 'cognate' is used for the relations of both mother's and father's side. While, 'agnate' marks for relations through male line only and 'uterine' relations through female line only.

For understanding the function of kinship system or associated behaviour, Mayer (1960) is quoted. He primarily classified the function of kin in the following levels–in the Household, outside the household among consanguine, outside the household among affined behaviour of kin at wedding, at mortuary rites and at secular matters.

Numerous field studies have shown that societies differ markedly in how they group or distinguish relatives under the same or different terms. The kinship terminology may reflect the kind of family prevailing in a society, its rule of residence and its rule of descent and also other aspects of social organisation. The kin term may also give clues to prior features of the social system, if, as many anthropologists believe, the kin term of a society are very resistant to change. The major systems of kinship terminology are the Omaha, the Crow, the Iroquois, the Hawaiian, the Eskimo and the Sudanese system (Ember and Ember,1977).

## A. Omaha Kinship Terminology

Fa Si Da and Mo Br Da called by different terms and terminologically differentiated from sisters and parallel cousins, but Fa Si Da is terminologically classed with Si Da and or Mo Br Da with Mo Si. A type of kinship terminology usually found in conjunction with patrilineal descent.

(Patrilineal descent: affiliates the child exclusively with the consanguineal kin group of the father).

**Table 4.1**

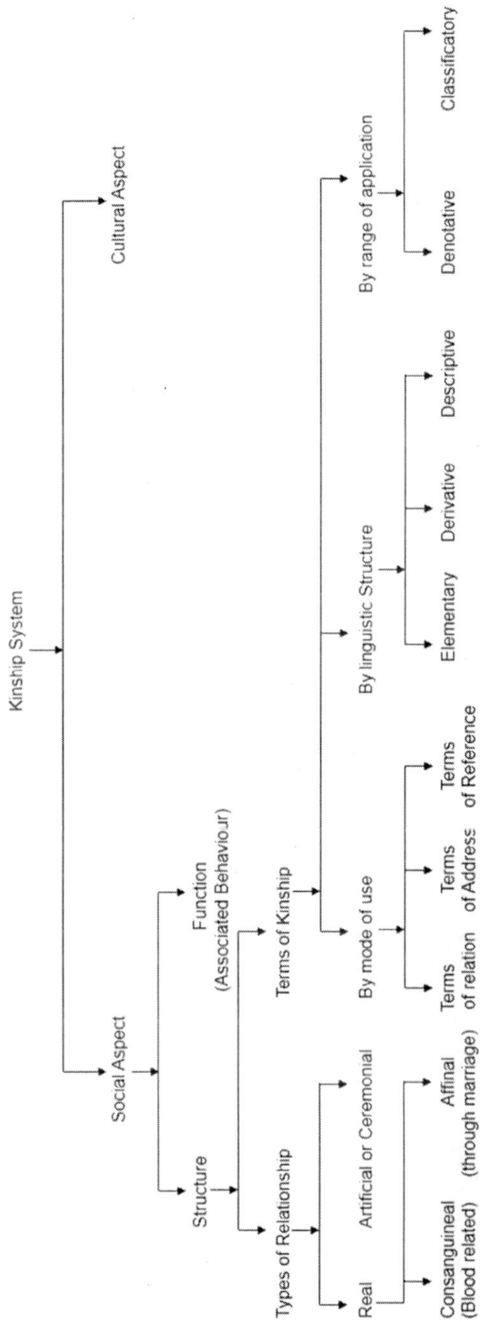
Kinship System
Social Aspect
Cultural Aspect
Structure
Function (Associated Behaviour)
Types of Relationship
Terms of Kinship
Real
Artificial or Ceremonial
Consanguineal (Blood related)
Affinal (through marriage)
By mode of use
By linguistic Structure
By range of application
Terms of relation
Terms of Address
Terms of Reference
Elementary
Derivative
Descriptive
Denotative
Classificatory

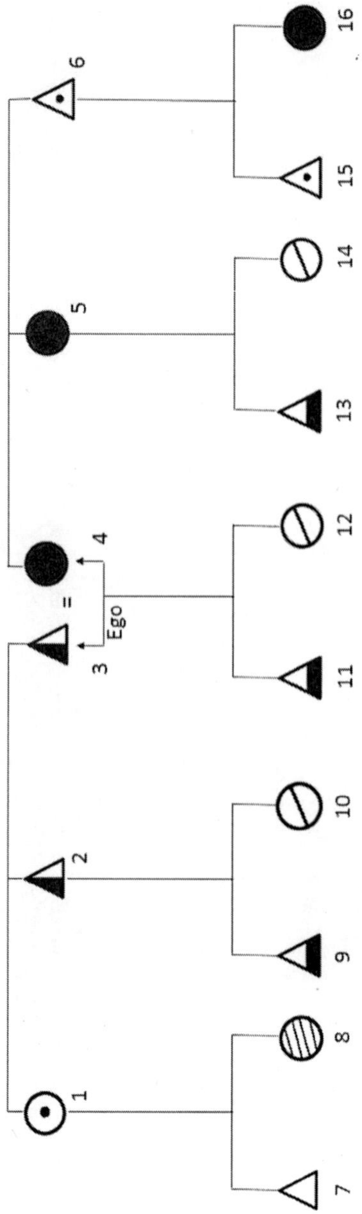


**Omaha Kinship Terminology System**

### B. Crow Kinship Terminology

Father's sister's daughter and mother's brother's daughter are called by different terms and terminologically differentiated from sisters and parallel cousins, but father's sister's daughter is terminologically classed with sister's daughter and mother's brother's daughter with mother's sister. A type of kinship terminology, usually found in conjunction with matrimonial descent. (Matrilineal descent; which assigns the child exclusively to his mother's kin group).

### C. Iroquis Kinship Terminology

Fa Si Da and Mo Br Da are called by the same terms but are terminologically differentiated from parallel cousins as well as from sisters ; parallel cousins are commonly but not always classified with sisters, i.e. Children of Fa Si and Mo Br have same terms which are different from what is used towards parallel cousins as well as their own siblings. A type of kinship terminology, also called bifurcate merging. (Bifurcate merging: Lineage system of descent groups tend to produce bifurcate-merging systems of terminology. Father's brother is merged with father, while both are distinguished from Mother's brother. Put in another way, father and paternal uncle are lumped, and maternal uncle is distinguished. Likewise, Mother and maternal aunt are lumped, and paternal aunt is distinguished. Members of the two descent groups are vigorously kept separate from each other).

### D. Hawaiian Kinship Terminology

All cross and parallel cousins are called by the same terms as those used for sisters and brothers. A type of kinship terminology, also called generational. (Generation: The emphasis in this type of system is on merging of all relatives on a given generational level. Thus, mother, mother's sister and father's sister are all lumped under a single kinship term. The same is true of father, father's brother and mother's brother).

### E. Eskimo Kinship Terminology

Fa Si Da and Mo Br Da are called by the same terms as parallel cousins but are terminologically differentiated from sisters; the terms for the two cross-cousins are usually, but not always, the same. Children of Fa Si and children of Mo Br and children of Fa Br have the same term but a different one form what they use for their own brother and sister. A type of kinship terminology, also called lineal, often found in conjunction with cognatic descent. (Lineal: This system emphasises the distinction between direct ascendant and descendant

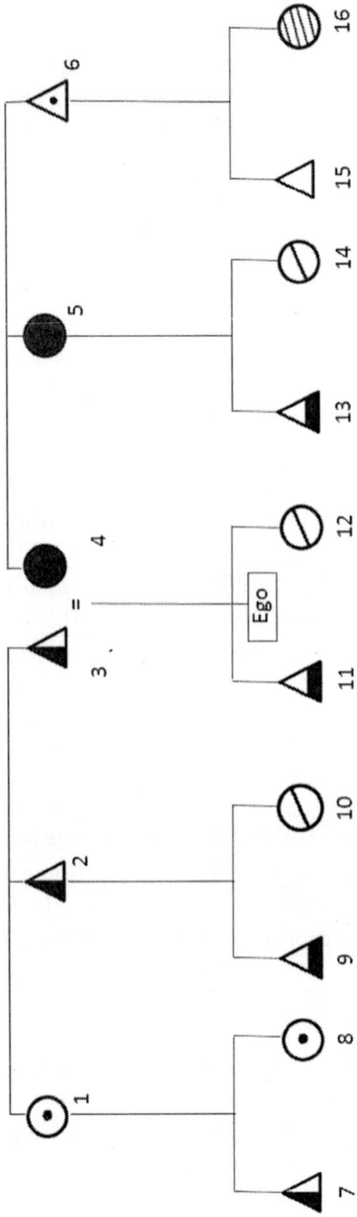


**Crow Kinship Terminology System**

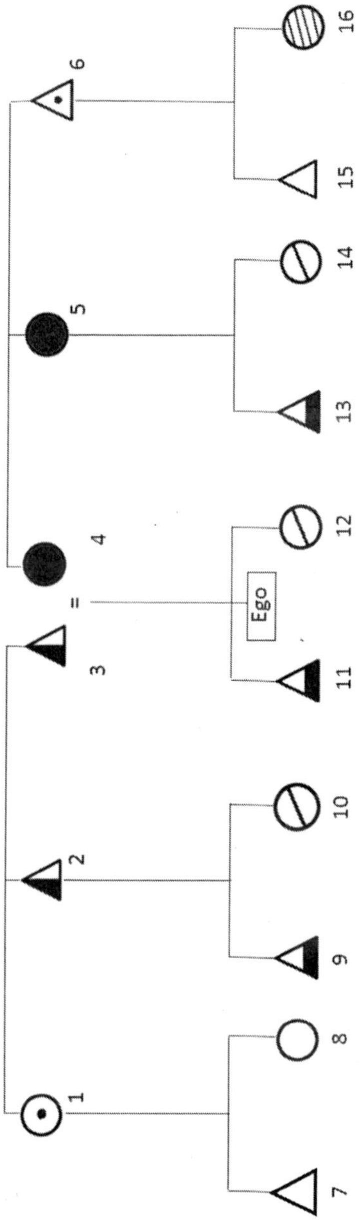


**Iroquis Kinship Terminology System**

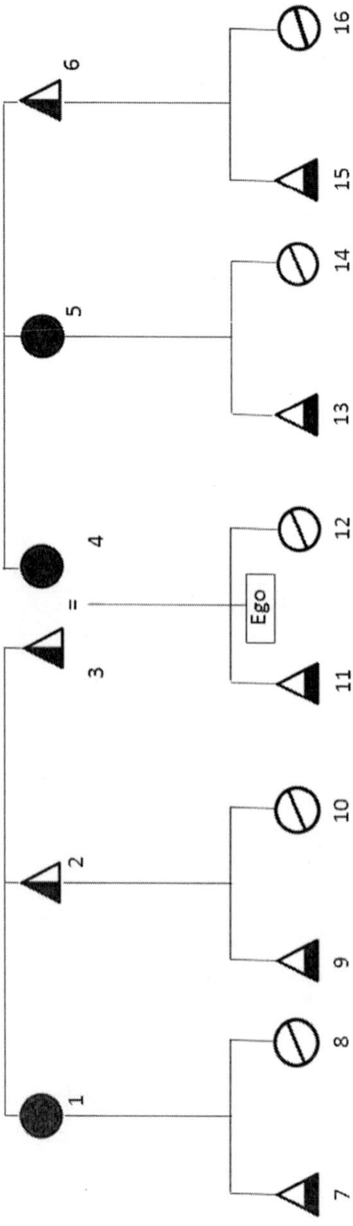


**Hawaiian Kinship Terminology System**

relatives as separate from mother's sister, and father's sister, who are merged as in English Aunt. The same holds for father and his collaterals, who are merged as in English Uncle. Lineal systems are also associated with bilateral system of descent groups.

Cognatic Descent–is formed of genealogical ties without particular emphasis on patrilineal or matrilineal connections.

Bilateral Descent. -When a person is affiliated with a group of close relatives through both sexes ; it limits the number of close relatives by excluding some of both the father's kin groups and mother's kin groups.

## F. Sudanese Kinship Terminology

Unlike the kinship terminological system, Sudanese system of kin terminology usually does not lump any relatives in the parents' and ego's generations. It is usually a *descriptive* system in which a different term is used to refer to each of the relatives as shown in the figure. Sudanese terminology is associated with relatively great political complexity, class stratification and occupational specialisation. It is a system of kin terminology in which each cousin is called by a separate term.

Now in the following lines some empirical examples from Indian context will be presented.

### (i) Birjia—a Particularly Vulnerable Tribal Group of Jharkhand

Kinship ties are maintained closely only among near kinds. This is a significant merging of affinal kins with kins of common blood as far as the fulfilment of kinship obligations are concerned. They call their blood relatives or consanguineal kins as *Kutumb* and affinal relatives or relatives through marriage ties as *sambandhi.* The Birjia kinship is an undifferentiated category into which kins of all kinds are merged, the predominant position is enjoyed by the paternal kins i.e., cognates. In seeking help or assistance, the kins from paternal side are first approached.

In an individual's life, the kinds fulfil their customary obligations on occasion of birth, name giving ceremony, marriage and death ritual. For example, the parents of a daughter visit her father-in-law's house for the first time after her marriage, with some presentation of *haria*, cereals and clothes after birth of the first issue of their daughter. It is known as *sambandhi milna* or *bihan dekhna*. During the name giving ceremony on the day of *chhetti*, for the new born child, the grand parents of either side (generally the father's side and in their absence,

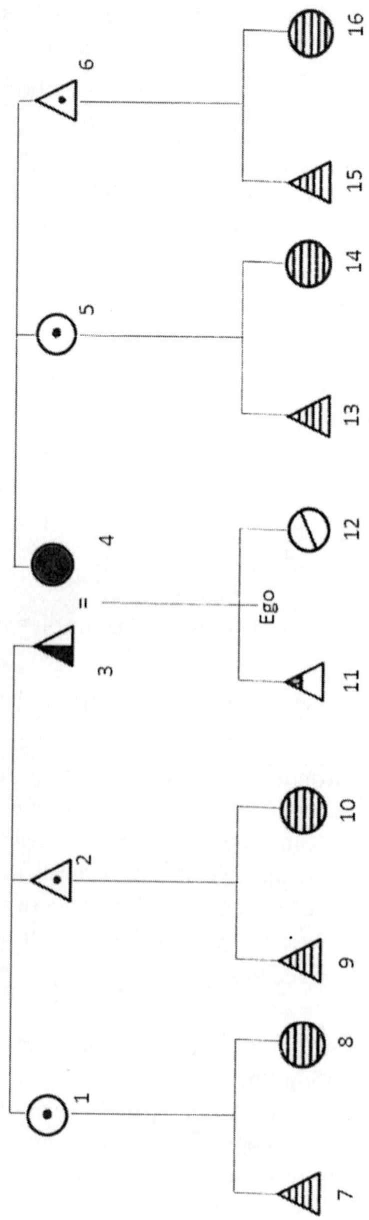


**Eskimo Kinship Terminology System**

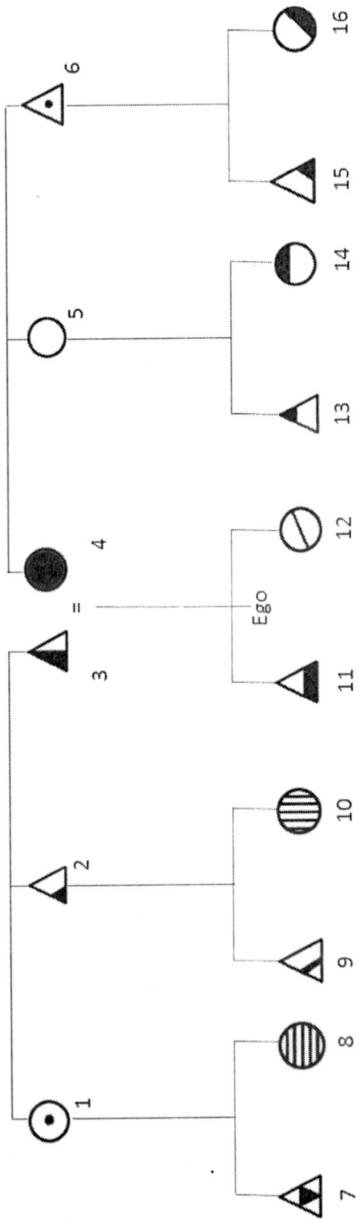


**Sudanese Kinship Terminology System**

of mother's side) keep the name of the child. *Mundan* (ritual shaving of hair) of the child is done by the *mama* (maternal uncle). At the time of *muhjutti* (first rice-feeding ceremony) the *mama* (maternal uncle) must give presentation of a new *sari* for his sister who is the child's mother and some cereals to the family. But kinship ties are maintained closely among near kins. There is strong evidence that beyond the immediate range of kin, individuals even do not remember the names of their relatives. Regular visits by kin are maintained among the immediate and most near kins. The affinal kins also visit except on important events in the family, when it becomes a moral obligation for them. Married daughters or sisters along with their children do visit at regular interval to enquire about the welfare of the members of the family.

The Birjia kinship terminology is characterised by a preponderance of classificatory terms. It is assumed that the Birjia have borrowed some of the kinship terms from Hindu neighbours in respect of certain kin. Altogether thirty one numbers of kin terms can be identified for eighty five number of kins. Among those twenty four are of classificatory type clubbing together sixty number of kin [A separate chart of classificatory terms (Table 4.2) is given after the description].

The kinship terms of the Birjia are shown in the Table 4.2.

It is observed from the analysis of the Birjia Kinship terminologies (Table 4. 2) that according to Lowie's model Birjia Kinship is of collateral type where the father, father's brother and mother's brother have different terms of reference and address. Here, the father is referred to by the term *appatte* and addressed as *baba*. Father's elder brother is referred and addressed as *badda* and the younger brother is referred and addressed as *Kaka* Mother's brother is referred and addressed by the term *mama/mamu*. In Murdock's model of Kinship, the Birjia use Iroquois system where the parallel cousins are called by different terms from cross cousins. Here the parallel cousins, that is, father's brother's sons and mother's sister's sons are referred and addressed as *badda* and their daughters are referred and addressed as *Baddi*. The cross cousins, that is, the father's sister's and mother's brother's elder sons are referred as *dadain* and addressed as *dada* and their elder daughters are referred and addressed as *dai*. The younger sons and daughters of both father's sister and mother's brother are referred as *bokoin* and addressed by name. Polygyny is prevalent among them and they have *miromin* as the term for co-wives. The term for husband's elder wife and elder sister is *dai* which indicates the existence of sororate. Existence of sororate is further supported by the fact that the

**Table 4.2: Kinship Terminologies of Birjia**

| *Category* | *Relationship* | *Terms of Reference* | *Terms of Address* |
|---|---|---|---|
| Second Ascending Generation | Fa Fa | Tata | Tata/Dada |
| | Fa Mo | Jiain/Aji | Aji |
| | Mo Fa | Nana | Nana |
| | Mo Mo | Nani | Nani |
| | Wi Fa Fa | Tata | Tata |
| | Wi Fa Mo | Jiain/Aji | Aji |
| | Wi Mo Fa | Nana | Nana |
| | Wi Mo Mo | Nani | Nani |
| First Ascending Generation | Fa | Appate | Baba |
| | Step Fa | Kath Bap | Baba |
| | Mo | Engate | Aya |
| | Step Mo | Kaki | Kaki |
| | Fa Br (el) | Badda | Badda |
| | Fa Br (Yo) | Kaka | Kaka |
| | Fa Br (Yo) Wi | Kaki | Kaki |
| | Mo Br | Mama/Mamu | Mamu |
| | Mo Br Wi | Mami | Mami |
| | Fa Si | Hatom | Hatom |
| | Fa Si (Yo) | Hatom | Hatom |
| | Fa Si Hu | Mama/Mamu | Mamu |
| | Mo Si (el) | Baddi | Baddi/Kaki |
| | Mo Si (Yo) | Kaki | Kaki |
| | Hu Fa | Hoinharin | Baba |
| | Hu Mo | Hunhari | Aya |
| | Wi Fa | Hoinharin | Baba |
| | Wi Mo | Hunhari | Aya |
| Same Generation | Br (el) | Dadain | Dada |
| | Br (Yo) | Bokoin | By name |
| | Si (el) | Dai | Dai |
| | Si (Yo) | Bokoin | By Name |
| | Fa Si So (el) | Dadain | Dada |
| | Fa Si So (Yo) | Bokoin | By Name |

| Category | Relationship | Terms of Reference | Terms of Address |
|---|---|---|---|
| | Fa Si Da (el) | Dai | Dai |
| | Fa Si Da (Yo) | Bokoin | By Name |
| | Mo Br So (el) | Dadain | Dada |
| | Mo Br So (Yo) | Bokoin | By Name |
| | Mo Br Da (el) | Dai | Dai |
| | Mo Br Da (Yo) | Bokoin | By Name |
| | Fa Br So | Badda | Badda |
| | Fa Br Da | Baddi | Baddi |
| | Mo Si So | Badda | Badda |
| | Mo Si Da | Baddi | Baddi |
| | Hu | Jaoain/Haramake | Orahor/Tyknonymy |
| | Wi | Kuri | Tyknonymy |
| | Hu Br (el) | Apuintiku | Tyknonymy |
| | Hu Br (Yo) | Deoarin | By name |
| | Hu Si | Dai/Daihanhar | Dai |
| | Wi Br (el) | Dada Hoinharin | Dada |
| | Wi Br (Yo) | Sarain | By name |
| | Wi Si (el) | Dai-hanhar | Dai |
| | Wi Si (Yo) | Sarin | By name |
| | Br Wi (el) | Hilli | Hilli |
| | Br Wi (Yo) | Bahuriya/Kimin | Bahuriya/Kimin |
| | Si (el) Hu | Teyang | Teyang |
| | Si (Yo) Hu | Bokoin-arain/Sarain | By name |
| | Hu Br Wi (el) | Jatea/Daihanhar | Didi |
| | Hu Br Wi (Yo) | Jatea | Bahen |
| | Hu Wi (el) | Dai | Dai |
| | Wi Br (Yo) Wi | Bokoin | By name |
| | So Wi Fa | Balaku | Samdhi |
| | So Wi Mo | Kudi Balain | Samdhi |
| | Da Hu Fa | Balaku | Samdhi |

| *Category* | *Relationship* | *Terms of Reference* | *Terms of Address* |
|---|---|---|---|
| | Da Hu Mo | Kudi Balain | Samdhi |
| | Co Wives | Miromin | Miromin |
| | Si Hu Br | Sangi | Sangi |
| | Br Wi Si | Sangi | Sangi |
| Second Descending | So So | Nati/Natiyan | Nati/By Name |
| Generation | So Da | Natin | Nati/By Name |
| | Da So | Nati/Pabu | Nati/By Name |
| | Da Da | Natin/Maiyu | Natin/By Name |
| First Descending | So | Hoponte | Babu |
| Generation | Da | Hoponte | Mai |
| | Step So | Katbeta | Babu/By Name |
| | Step Da | Katbeti | By Name |
| | Br So | Badda/Bhacha | By Name |
| | Br Da | Baddi | Baddi/By Name |
| | Si So (el) | Musbeta | Babu/By Name |
| | Si So (Yo) | Bada/Bhajina | Babu/By Name |
| | So Wi | Bui/Bahuriya | Bui |
| | Da Hu | Arain | Babu |
| | Hu Si So | Bhacha | Babu |
| | Wi Br So | Bhacha | Babu |
| | So Wi Br | Arain | Babu |
| | Fa Si (Yo) So Da | Bhatijin | Mai |
| | Br (el) Da | Bhatijin | Mai |

term for mother's younger sister and step mother is *Kaki*. The term for father's brother's (younger) wife is also *Kaki*. The term for mother's brother and father's sister's husband is *mama* or *mamu* which signifies the existence of marriage by exchange or *golat*. It is also found that the similar term *badda* is used for father's elder brother and brother's son and the term for mother's elder sister and brother's daughter is *baddi*. Besides these there are many other classificatory terms existing among them which are given later in the Table 4. 3. The term for sister's husband's brother and brother's wife's sister is *sangi* which perhaps indicate their joking relationship.

**Table 4.3: Classificatory Kinship Terminologies used among the Birjia**

| *Category* | *Relationship* | *Terms of Reference* | *Terms of Address* |
|---|---|---|---|
| Second Ascending Generation | Fa Fa | Tata | Tata/Dada |
| | Wi Fa Fa | Tata | Tata |
| | Fa Mo | Jiain/Aji | Aji |
| | Wi Fa Mo | Jiain/Aji | Aji |
| | Mo Fa | Nana | Nana |
| | Wi Mo Fa | Nana | Nana |
| | Mo Mo | Nani | Nani |
| | Wi Mo Mo | Nani | Nani |
| First Ascending Generation | Mo Br | Mama/Mamu | Mamu |
| | Fa Si Hu | Mama/Mamu | Mamu |
| | Step Mo | Kaki | Kaki |
| | Fa Br (Yo) Wi | Kaki | Kaki |
| | Mo Si (Yo) | Kaki | Kaki |
| | Fa Si (Yo) | Hatom | Hatom |
| | Mo Si (el) | Baddi | Baddi/Kaki |
| | Mo | Engate | Aya |
| | Hu Mo | Hunhari | Aya |
| | Wi Mo | Hunhari | Aya |
| | Fa | Appate | Baba |
| | Step Fa | Kath Bap | Baba |
| | Hu Fa | Hoinharin | Baba |
| | Wi Fa | Hoinharin | Baba |
| | Br (el) | Dadain | Dada |

| *Category* | *Relationship* | *Terms of Reference* | *Terms of Address* |
|---|---|---|---|
| | Fa Si So (el) | Dadain | Dada |
| | Mo Br So (el) | Dadain | Dada |
| | Br (Yo) | Bokoin | By Name |
| | Si (To) | Bokoin | By Name |
| | Fa Si So (Yo) | Bokoin | By Name |
| | Fa Si Da (Yo) | Bokoin | By Name |
| | Mo Br So (Yo) | Bokoin | By Name |
| | Mo Br Da (Yo) | Bokoin | By Name |
| | Wi Br (Yo) Wi | Bokoin | By Name |
| | Fa Br So | Badda | Badda |
| | Mo Si So | Badda | Badda |
| Same Generation | Br (el) | Dadain | Dada |
| | Br (Yo) | Bokoin | By name |
| | Si (el) | Dai | Dai |
| | Si (Yo) | Bokoin | By Name |
| | Fa Si So (el) | Dadain | Dada |
| | Fa Si So (Yo) | Bokoin | By Name |
| | Fa Si Da (el) | Dai | Dai |
| | Fa Si Da (Yo) | Bokoin | By Name |
| | Mo Br So (el) | Dadain | Dada |
| | Mo Br So (Yo) | Bokoin | By Name |
| | Mo Br Da (el) | Dai | Dai |
| | Mo Br Da (Yo) | Bokoin | By Name |
| | Fa Br So | Badda | Badda |
| | Fa Br Da | Baddi | Baddi |
| | Mo Si So | Badda | Badda |
| | Mo Si Da | Baddi | Baddi |
| | Hu | Jaoain/Haramake | Orahor/Tyknonymy |
| | Wi | Kuri | Tyknonymy |
| | Hu Br (el) | Apuintiku | Tyknonymy |

| *Category* | *Relationship* | *Terms of Reference* | *Terms of Address* |
|---|---|---|---|
| | Hu Br (Yo) | Deoarin | By name |
| | Hu Si | Dai/Daihanhar | Dai |
| | Wi Br (el) | Dada Hoinharin | Dada |
| | Wi Br (Yo) | Sarain | By name |
| | Wi Si (el) | Dai hanhar | Dai |
| | Wi Si (Yo) | Sarin | By name |
| | Br Wi (el) | Hilli | Hilli |
| | Br Wi (Yo) | Bahuriya/Kimin | Bahuriya/Kimin |
| | Si (el) Hu | Teyang | Teyang |
| | Si (Yo) Hu | Bokoin-arain/Sarain | By name |
| | Hu Br Wi (el) | Jatea/Daihanhar | Didi |
| | Hu Br Wi (Yo) | Jatea | Bahen |
| | Hu Wi (el) | Dai | Dai |
| | Wi Br (Yo) Wi | Bokoin | By name |
| | So Wi Fa | Balaku | Samdhi |
| | So Wi Mo | Kudi Balain | Samdhi |
| | Da Hu Fa | Balaku | Samdhi |
| | Da Hu Mo | Kudi Balain | Samdhi |
| | Co Wives | Miromin | Miromin |
| | Si Hu Br | Sangi | Sangi |
| | Br Wi Si | Sangi | Sangi |
| First Descending Generation | Br So | Badda/Bahacha | By Name |
| Same Generation | Fa Br Da | Baddi | Baddi |
| | Mo Si Da | Baddi | Baddi |
| First Ascending Generation | Mo Si (el) | Baddi | Baddi/Kaki |
| First Ascending Generation | Mo Si (el) | Baddi | Baddi/Kaki |
| | | | |
| First Descending Generation | Br Da | Baddi | Baddi/By Name |
| Same | Si (el) | Dai | Dai |

| *Category* | *Relationship* | *Terms of Reference* | *Terms of Address* |
|---|---|---|---|
| Generation | Fa Si Da (el) | Dai | Dai |
| | Mo Br Da (el) | Dai | Dai |
| | Hu Wi (el) | Dai | Dai |
| | Hu Si | Dai/Daihanhar | Dai |
| | Wi Si (el) | Daihanhar | Dai |
| | Hu Br Wi (el) | Jatea/Daihanhar | Didi |
| | Hu Br Wi (Yo) | Jatea | Bahen |
| | So Wi Fa | Balaku | Samdhi |
| | Da Hu Fa | Balaku | Samdhi |
| | Si Hu Br | Sangi | Sangi |
| | Br Wi Si | Sangi | Sangi |
| Second Descending | So So | Nati/Natiyan | Nati/By Name |
| Generation | Da So | Nati/Pabu | Nati/By Name |
| | Da Da | Natin/Maiyu | Natin/By Name |
| First Descending | Fa Si (Yo) So Da | Bhatijin | Mai |
| Generation | Br (el) Da | Bhatijin | Mai |
| | Da | Hoponte | Mai |
| | So | Hoponte | Babu |
| | Da Hu | Arain | Babu |
| | Sowi Br | Arain | Babu |
| | Hu Si So | Bhacha | Babu |
| | Wi Br So | Bhacha | Babu |
| | Si So (el) | Musbeta | Babu/By Name |
| | Si So (Yo) | Bhajina/Bada | Babu/By Name |
| | Da Hu | Arain | Babu |
| | So Wi Br | Arain | Babu |

**(ii) Abujh Maria—** a Particularly Vulnerable Tribal Group of Chhattishgarh

## Kinship

The objective of kinship study is to highlight the structural forms and principles, the systematic and typological classification of Kinship terms, some correlations between the terminological system and socio-cultural phenomena and analytical observation (Mukherjee, 1981). It also evaluates the structural principles and categories which directly or indirectly have some bearings on the development of kinship system.

Abujh Maria or the Hill Maria Gond are a very primitive tribe. They have a society where the persons are related with each other by tightly knitted network of social relation that is, through the kinship bondage. In fact they trace their kinshp or relationship from the Heavenly world where their Pens live. In the Heavenly or the celestial world, the Pens–the Abujh Maria clan deities have a large family and a larger group of kins. All the kins or relatives as stated earlier are related through *bhaiband* and *akomama* ties. They have followed a strict rule of marriage and they are all exogamous groups.

Following their rules of marriage exogamy and also the types of relationship, the Abujh Maria people at the terrestrial world enjoy the same type of relationship and at the same time they follow their Pens in performing the responsibilities that lie on each and every status of relationship. As for an example Pen –Tuler Raja or Pat Raja has seven sons and he is the head of the family and sole authority of his territory. Further he divided his territory among his sons who ultimately form separate nuclear families. Similarly, in the terrestrial world in a Abujh Maria family father is the head of the family and divides his share of land among his children who ultimately form their own individual families.

Now a list of kinship terminology is given. Prior to that it is mentioned that they have linguistic affinity with Dravidian group.

Now, it is revealed from the above table of Abujh Maria Kinship terminology that as per Lowie's (1929)clubbing pattern, it is bifurcate collateral system wherein they have separate terms for Father, Father's brother and Mother's brother. The kinship terms of Indian tribes have also been categorised as per Spier's (1925) and Murdock's (1949) typology based on cross cousin terminology. In Murdock's model of kinship, the Abujh Maria use Iraquois system where parallel cousins are called by different term from cross cousin. Here parallel cousin, that is, Fa Br So and Mo Si So are referred as *dada* while their daughters are referred as *didi.* The cross-cousin that is, Fa Si So, and Mo Br So are referred as *permo* while their daughters are called as *mandari.*

From the kinship analysis it is observed that they call their father-in-law and mother's brother, father's sister husband as *mama* and they call their mother-in-law and mother's brother's wife and father's sister as *ato* instead of addressing the father-in-law and the mother-in-law as *bawa*(father) and *awa* (mother) respectively though the relationship is actually of father and mother. Then a question automatically arises whether they have any cross-cousin marriage or not. After study it is observed that among their marriage types cross cousin marriage is preferred most by these people.

Among the Abujh Maria people father is referred and called by the term *baba* and *awa* is the term of mother. It is observed that in case of the step mother the term of reference is Bada *awa* (for elder) and *Udla awa* (for younger) and the term of address is *Pheri/Peri* and *Kuchi* respectively. It is further noted that the term of reference and the term of address for mother's elder sister is *Peri* or *Badaawa* and for her younger sister is udla awa or kuchi. Incidentally it is seen that they are allowed to perform sororate but junior, and probably due to this in their society the step mother (younger) and mother's younger sister are referred and called by the same term. Now the question arises whether in their society senior sororate is allowed or not. If not then why the term of reference and term of address are same in case of step mother and mother's elder sister. They say that in case of co-wives the younger one treats the elder one as elder sister and the elder one treats the younger one as younger sister and due to this the children also use the same term of reference and address for both the step mother and the mother's sisters (younger and elder). Nextly, the term of address and term of reference is Kaka for both Fa. Yr. Br. and step father. In their society junior levirate is allowed.

Again for the cross-cousin marriage another additional document is that son's wife's father or daughter's Husband's father are called as Eremto. Eremto is also a term for Hu. Si. Hu and Wi. Br. Similarly, Akka is the term for Da. Hu. Mo and Son. Wi. Mo. It is also a term for Wi. Bi. Wi. Which also gives a sign of cross-cousin marriage. Wife's younger brother and husband's younger sister's husband are called as Eowand. So there is a sign of marriage by exchange. Again, Hellor is the term for father's brother's daughter and wife's younger brother's wife which means a persons cousin sister is married with his wife's

## Table 4. 4: Abujh Maria Kinship Terminology

| Sl No. | Kin Name | Terms of Reference | Terms of address | Remarks |
|---|---|---|---|---|
| 1 | Fa | Baba / Bawa | Baba | Step father and Fa Br(Yr)are |
| 2 | Mo | Awa | Awa | referred and addressed by term |
| 3 | Fa Fa | Tado / Dado | Tado/ Dado | KaKa which indicates that junior |
| 4 | Fa Mo | KaKo | KaKo | levirate is prevalent in their the |
| 5 | Mo Fa | Akom | Ako | society. |
| 6 | Mo Mo | Dadi | Dadi | Step mother (el) and Mo Sis (el) |
| 7 | Step Father | KaKa | KaKa | are Bara awa or Pheri or Peri. |
| 8 | Fa Br (Yr) | KaKa | KaKa | Again step mother (Yr) Mo Sis |
| 9 | Fa Br (el) | Pepi / Bara Baba | Bara Baba | (Yr) are Udla awa or kuchi. |
| 10 | Step Mother (el) (Yr) | Bara awa / Peri/Pheri | Pheri /Peri | All these signify that there is the |
| 11 | Mo Si (el) (Yr) | udla awa / Kuchi | Kuchi | practice of sororate in their the |
| 12 | Fa Si (el) (Yr) | Bara awa / Pheri/Peri | Pheri/Peri | society. |
| 13 | Mo Br wi | UdlaAwa/Kuchi | Kuchi | Ato term denotes to both Fa Si |
| 14 | Mo Br | Ato | Ato | and Mo Br Wi, which indicates |
| 15 | Fa Si Hu | Udla Ato | Udla Ato | that there is marriage by |
| 16 | Mo Si Hu | Ato | Ato | exchange prevalent |
| 17 | Fa Br (Yr) wi | Mama | Mama | in in the society |
| 18 | Br (el) (Yr) | Mama | Mama | Mama term denotes both |
| 19 | Sis (el) (Yr) | Kaka | Kaka | mother's brother and father's |
| 20 | Mo Si So (el) (Yr) | Kuchi | Kuchi | sister's husband which also |
| 21 | Fa Br So (el) (Yr) | Dada | Dada | indicates that there is |
| 22 | Mo Si Da(el) (Yr) | Tamo | Tamo | marriage by exchange in their |
| 23 | Fa Br Da (el) | Akka | Akka | society. |
| 24 | Fa Br Da (Yr) | Hellar | By name | Kaka is a term used for the Fa Br |
| 25 | Fa Si So | Bara Dada (Bara) | Dada | (Yr) who may also be a step |
| 26 | Mo Br So | Udla Dada | By name | father and for the Mo Si Hu which |
| 27 | Mo Br Da | Dada | Dada | indicates that the Fa Br (Yr) can |
| 28 | Fa Si Da | Permo/Tamo | Permo/Tamo | marry the Mo Si, that is, two |
| 29 | Hu Fa | Akka /Didi | Akka / Didi | sisters can be married in the |
| 30 | Wi Fa | Pila/Kuchi | Pila | same family. |
| 31 | Hu Mo | Didi / Ange | Didi / Ange | Fa Br(Yr)wi, Step mother, Mo Si |
| 32 | Wi Mo | Hellor | Hellor | (Yr) all are Kuchi. It denotes that |
| 33 | Hu | Mario/ Permo /Marrior | Mario | Fa Br (Yr) wi may be step mother |
| 34 | Wi | Mario/ Permo/ Marrior | Mario | in case |
| 35 | Hu Br (el) (Yr) | Mandari | Mandari | of levirate and Mo Si (Yr) is also |
| 36 | Wi Br (el) (Yr) | Mandari | Mandari | Kuchi which signifies the junior |
| 37 | Wi Si (el) (Yr) | Mama | Mama | sororate. |
| 38 | Hu Br Wi (el) (Yr) | Mama | Mama | All of them are parallel cousin, |
| 39 | Wi Si Hu (el) (Yr) | Ato | Ato | get similar status with own |
| 40 | Hu Si Hu (el) (Yr) | Ato | Ato | brother and sister where marriage |
| 41 | Wi Br (el) (Yr) | Koito / Koitor (when below 50 yrs of age) | Tyknonymy | is prohibited due to incest taboo. |
| 42 | Wi Br Wi (el) (Yr) | Muitto (above 50 yrs of age) | Tyknonymy | All are cross consins |
| 43 | Hu Si (el) (Yr) | Arh (when below 50 yrs of age) | Dada | Hu Fa , WiFa , Mo Br , Fa Si Hu |
| 44 | So Wi Fa | Muitte/ Mutte (above 50 yrs of age) | By name | are Mama which indicates the |
| 45 | Da Hu Fa | Dada | Dada | prevalence of cross section |
| 46 | So Wi Mo | Ewand/Eondi | Permo | marriage. |
| 47 | Da Hu Mo | Eremto/ Eramtogh | Didi / Akka | Hu Mo , Wi Mo , Mo Br Wi , Fa Si |
| 48 | Son | Permo | Permo | all are Ato which also indicates |
| 49 | Dau | Akka/ Didi/Akoin | Dobki/ Akka | the prevalence of cross-cousin |
| 50 | Br So | Permo | Hellar | marriage |
| 51 | Si So | Akka/ Mutte/ Dobki | Dada | Hu Br Wi (el) and Si (el)are Akka. |
| 52 | Br Da | Hellar | Permo | The Hu Br Wi (Yr) & Si (Yr)are |
| 53 | Si Da | Dada | Dada | Hellar – indicates they get equal |
| 54 | Br So Wi | Permo | By name | status. |
| 55 | Si So Wi | Eremto/ Eowand | Dada | Wi Br (el), So WI Fa, Da.Hu. Fa, |
| | | Eowand | Permo | Hu Si Hu are Eremto. |
| | | Eremto/ Eramtogh | Akka | Wi Br Wi (el), So Wi Mo, Da Hu |
| | | Eowand/ Errandi | By name | Mo are Akka (as they get equal |
| | | Akka | Ange | status |
| | | Hellar | Hellar | with sister). All these indicate that |
| | | Ange | Eremto | there is cross cousin marriage in |
| | | Hellar | Eremto | their society. |
| | | Eremto | Akka | |

younger brother. Hence marriage by exchange is prevalent among them.

Therefore, it is seen from the kinship analysis among the marriage types cousin-marriage, marriage by exchange, levirate (Junior) sororate (Junior) etc. are prevalent. In all the types they have followed the verdict of their Pen deities. They have their own reasons and analysis behind all those marriages (which will be discussed afterwards). Except those in their kinship analysis some other points also come out. As for example, they say that co-wives treat themselves as sisters and due to this term of address and term of reference in case of co-wives are Akka/Didi (for the elder) and Hellor for the younger which is the same for the sisters. Again the children call their step mother's and Mo. Si. both elder and younger by the same term Pheri/Peri and Kuchi respectively.

Akka and Hellor–these two terms signify the elder sister and the younger sister. But these two terms are very commonly used for all the relatives who get equal status of sister such as co-wives (already written), mother's sister's daughter, father's brother's daughter, Husband's sister's (elder is called as Ange), husband's brother's wife, and wife's brother's wife. Wife's younger sister is called as Kokkar/Kohkari as with her he has joking term and she is not treated as sister.

Similarly, the term of address and the term of reference for wife's brothers (el) and (yr) and husband's sister's husband (el) and (Yr) are Eremto/Erramtogh and Eowand respectively. Eowand is the term for husband's younger brother also. It is told that they all get equal status and call by the same term. Husband's younger brother is also called as Eowand or Eowandi but the elder brother is called Dada, as he holds a very respected post and enjoys a similar status with his own elder brother. Wife's elder sister's husband also called as Dada but the younger one is Eowandi.

Each and every kin has his/her own status and according to the status they have their own duties and responsibilities.

### (iii) Kandh (ST) and Kui Domanga or Pano (presently SC) of Kandhamal, Odisha

### Kinship:

Kinship Terminology of Kui Domanga or Pano and Kuinga or Kui Kandh in the Studied 21 Villages

**Table 4.5: Kinship Terminology of Kui Domanga or Pano and Kuinga/Kui Kandhi**

| *Category of kin* | *Relationship* | *Terms of Reference* | *Terms of Address* | *Remarks* |
|---|---|---|---|---|
| Second Ascending generation | Fa Fa | Mai akke aba | Akke aba | |
| | Fa Mo | Mai attali | Attali/attaja | |
| | Mo Fa | Mai akke aba | Akke aba | |
| | Mo Mo | Mai attali | Attali | |
| | Wi Fa Fa | Akke aba | Akke aba | |
| | Wi Fa Mo | Attali | Attali | |
| | Wi Mo Fa | Akke aba | Akke aba | |
| | Wi Mo Mo | Attali | Attali. | |
| First Ascending generation | Fa | Mai aba | Aba | |
| | Step Father | Do | Do | |
| | Mo | Mai aiya | Aiya /ayiya /ajja | |
| | Step Mother | Do outsiders refer them as Wo san aja | Do/Wo san aja | |
| | Fa Br (el) | Mai/Nai deri aba | Deri aba | |
| | Fa Br (yo) | Mai kogge aba | Kage aba/kogge aba | Mai= in plural sense |
| | Fa Br (el) Wi | Nai drei/Deri ajja | Deri ajja/drei aja | Nai= in singular sense |
| | Fa Br (yo) Wi | Nai kogge ajja | Kogge ajja | |
| | Mo Br | Mai maama | Maama | |
| | Mo Br Wi | Mai amma | Amma | Signify for Marriage by exchange |
| | Fa Si | Mai amma | Amma | Do |
| | Fa Si Hu | Mai Maama | Maama | |
| | Mo Si (el) | Mai deri ajja | Deri ajja | |

| *Category of kin* | *Relationship* | *Terms of Reference* | *Terms of Address* | *Remarks* |
|---|---|---|---|---|
| | Mo Si (yo) | Mai ango | Mausi or mansi /ango | |
| | Hu Fa | Sasura abba/Patalenju | Abba/Patalenju | |
| | Hu Mo | Sasu ajja/Patali | Ajja/Patali | |
| | Wi Fa | Mai sasur abba/Patlenju | Abba/Patlenju | |
| | Wi Mo | Mai sasu ajja/Patali | Ajja/Patali | |
| Same Generation | Br (el) | Mai dada | Dada | |
| | Br (yo) | Mai babu /Apo | Ambesa/apo | |
| | Si (el) | Mai bai | Bai | |
| | Si (yo) | Mai budi /mai angi | Budi /Angi | |
| | Fa Si So (el) | Mai mrigi dada | Mrigi dada | |
| | Fa Si so (yo) | Mai mrigi babu | Mrigi babu | |
| | Fa Si Da (ol) | Mai mrigi bai | Mrigi bai | |
| | Fa Si Da (yo) | Mai mrigali | Mrigali | |
| | Mo Br So (el) | Mrigi dada | Mrigi dada | |
| | Mo Br So (yo) | Mrigi babu | Mrigi babu | |
| | Mo Br Da (el) | Mrigi bai | Mrigi bai | |
| | Mo Br Da (yo) | Mrigali | Mrigali | |
| | Fa Br So | Mai dada/mai apo/ambesa | Dada (el) and ambesa /apo (yo). | |

| Category of kin | Relationship | Terms of Reference | Terms of Address | Remarks |
|---|---|---|---|---|
| | Fa Br Da | Mrigi bai / mrigali / angi | Mrigi bai (el) and mrigali / angi(yo) | |
| | Mo Si So | Mrigi / Talisa dada /apo | Mrigi / Talisa dada (el) / mrigi/ talisa apo (yo) | |
| | Mo Si Da | Mrigi bai / Talisedi / mrigali | Mrigi bai / Talsedi (el) /mrigali / talsedi (yo) | |
| | Husband | Nai Jama | Tyknonymy ( prefix with son or daughter's name or prefix with village name and suffix with 'li') | |
| | Wife | Nai kuda / Aapi | Do | |
| | Hu Br (el) | Mai abba / Ajanaba | Abba | |
| | Hu Br (yo) | Mai Aapo/ Sejunju | Apo / baabu/ sejunju | |
| | Hu Si | | Bai (el) / Buddi / Para nanja(yo) | |
| | Wi Br (el) | Jahala | Jaahala | |
| | Wi Br (yo) | Missunju | Missu | |
| | Wi Si (el) | | Poora / Pora | |
| | Wi Si (yo) | Nanja | Missuli / Nanja | |
| | Br Wi (el) | | Bai | |
| | Br Wi (yo) | Kuda mida | Buddi / Kogge Api | |
| | Si (el) Hu | | Jaama Dada | |
| | Si (yo) Hu | | Jaama Apo | |
| | Hu Br Wi (el) | Jajeredi | Ejana Appi /bai | |
| | Hu Br Wi (yo) | Jajeredi | Buddi | |
| | So Wi Fa | | Samdi / Samdhi | |
| | So Wi Mo | | Samadedi | |
| | Da Hu Fa | | Samdi / Samdhi | |

| *Category of kin* | *Relationship* | *Terms of Reference* | *Terms of Address* | *Remarks* |
|---|---|---|---|---|
| | Da Hu Mo | | Samadedi | |
| | Co-wives | | Bodh (el)/and Samdli or Sandedi (yo) | |
| Second Descending Generation | So So | Anga mida | Angamida or by name. | |
| | So Da | Anga mida | Anga mida | |
| | Da So | Anga mida | Anga mida or by name | |
| | Da Da | Anga mida | Anga mida or by name. | |
| First Descending generation | So | Mirenjhu | Apo/Mirenjhu | |
| | Da | Budi/ Mara /Maaru | Budi/Maaru | |
| | Step So | Asan Mirenjhu | Apo/Mirenjhu | |
| | Step Da | Asan Maaru | Asan maaru/Maaru | |
| | Br So | Kogan Mirenj ( for Younger brother) and Deranju Mirenju (for elder brother) | Mirenj/Prenda | |
| | Br Da | Nai Maro Derang Maro for (el) and Kogan Maro /Peru for (yo). | Maro/Peru | |
| | Si So | Badenja | Badenja | |
| | Si Da | Badenji | Badenji /Baadenji | |
| | So Wi | Apotara Api/ Kuda mida | Kuda mida | |
| | Da Hu | Jaama | Jaama ,Maijaama | |
| | Hu Si Da | Badenji | Badenji | |
| | Wi Br So | Badenja | Badenja | |
| | So Wi Br | Apo/Babu | Aapo/Babu | |
| | Hu Si So | Badenja | Badenja | |
| | Wi Br Da | Badenji | Badenji | |

It is revealed from the terminology above that they practise marriage by exchange perhaps to reduce bride price. According to Murdock's model of kinship, the Kui Kandh and Kui Domanga or Pano both use and practise **Iroquois** system where the parallel cousins, that is fathers brothers son and mothers sisters son are referred to and addressed as Mai dada/mai apo/Ambesa and Mrigi/Talisa dada /apo and their daughters are referred to and addressed as Mrigi bai (el) and Mrigali/ Angior talsedi(yo). The blood related or consanguineal kin are known as *ro rakka* or *kutum* and affinal kin are termed as *begali rakka*. The **putative Kinship** is also observed in the studied vilages among both the Kui Domanga or Pano and Kuinga or Kandh which is termed as ***sahu domanga***.

## References

Banerjee. Biswanath and Amitabha Sartkar, 1996, *Fundamentals of Social and Cultural Anthropology*, Calcutta: Firma KLM Pvt. Ltd.

Dasgupta, Samira, 1994, Birjia: *Society and Culture (A Study in Cultural Ecological Perspective*), Calcutta: Firma KLM Private Limited.

Dasgupta, Samira and Amitabha Sarkar, 2005, *Reflection of Ethno-Science: Study on the Abujh Maria*, New Delhi: Mittal Publications.

Ember,Carol R and Melvin Ember, 1977, *Cultural Anthropology*, New Jersey: Prentice-Hall, Inc.

Mayer, A. C., 1960, *Caste and Kinship in Central India: A Village and its Region*, London: Rout ledge and Kegan Paul (Indian edition: Allied Publishers Pvt. Ltd.)

Murdock, G. P., 1949, *Social Structure*, New York: Collier Macmillan

Sarkar, Amitabha, Samira Dasgupta and Dhanjaya Senapati, 2015, *Birds of a Feather Flock Together: A Quest for Social Identity of Pano or Kui Domanga*, New Dehi: Mittal Publications.

Schneider,David, M., 1968, *American Kinship: A Cultural Account*, New Jersey: Prentice Hall, Inc.

Schusky, Ernest L., 1965, *Manual for Kinship Analysis*, London: Holt, Rinehart and Winston.

# 5

# Study on Social Organisations

## Prologue

In Presidential address to J. R. A. I, 1954 by Raymond Firth criticised vehemently one of his teachers –Professor A. R. Radcliffe Brown. In his classic address entitled on 'Social Structure', delivered before J. R. A. I., 1940, R. Brown defined social structure in terms of "a complex network of social relations"....... "actually existing relation". R. Firth pointed out that

(a) R. Brown did not concretely indicate what he meant by using the term 'network of relations'; whether these relations are intersecting lines or a meshed fabric held together by knots. We know that actually in case of a society relations usually emerge from certain units and the relations radiate; next within the unit, members are bounded by the cementing material of 'reciprocal relations', which in the conception from Nadel's view point is the 'role basis' exists. We must have no doubt that the ultimate content (components) of social structure is 'network of relations'. But the systematic patterning of the same is of two types; first, relations between persons within a group or unit and second, relations of persons belonging to two separate units establishes the link between two units. Radcliffe Brown might have not gone into so much detail but his idea of 'network of relations' puts the foundation of the present day analysis of relations into these patterns.

(b) Firth's second argument was that R. Brown had not mentioned whether these relations were permanent or temporary in nature. We hardly anticipate that R. Brown's intention of analysing the relations of persons in a society would be of temporary nature. Thus, in this report Firth's criticism of this sort is to some extent superfluous.

Firth criticised that Brown's definition of 'Social Structure' was all inclusive, he merged both permanent and temporary relations. But so far as our anthropological study is concerned we usually deal with the permanent groups and the interactions between men as a member of permanent groups. We also consider temporary relations in the form of institutions for it has a profound and to some extent durable implication on the part of a person.

(c) Third area of Firth's critical dimensions is that Radcliffe Brown, though he said that he meant to study "actually existing relations", had failed to make a clear cut demarcation between 'ideals' and 'practices'. Following R. Brown's definition of social structure Evans Pritchard had failed to picture the actual practices of the Nuer society and which is our prime area of concern. Naturally in this respect if we consider the 'ideals' as part of a social structure we will be in a static position but still we know that the law of dynamism has also an impact on social structure.

(d) Radcliffe Brown proposed to study the value-system basing on which actually the existing relations are practised. But with the introduction of new technologies, innovations and new development of out-look, the value system of society changes. So we should have to study both the 'ideal' and 'practiced' part of social structure in association with the dynamic aspects of structure and value system.

Now after these criticisms which also give an idea to the reader that one should have to start from Brown's structural part of view in order to get an overall idea of a society but this is not all for the further study, one would naturally be concerned with the social organisation proposed by R. Firth himself and change of a society.

In this paper what R. Firth has actually added to Radcliffe Brown's structure concept for understanding and observing communities social life is the idea or organisation which is an indispensable supplement for a rational estimation of Brown's structural concept. Structural principle gives an idea of a society for a static view at a particular time and space, while, the organisational concept points for dynamic understanding pointing out the assessment towards change. Therefore, organisational study means structural study as a whole along with change aspect, while structural study is ideal type study. Hence, methodology is structural (i.e. inter-relationship)—functional (i.e. interaction) analysis.

## Social Organisation of Abujh Maria of Tribal Bastar: Communion between Celestial and Terrestrial Life

### Introduction

The Abujh Maria, a primitive tribal group are found in Madhya Pradesh (now Chhattishgarh), India. They are one of many tribal groups of large Gond tribe. Gonds identify themselves as koitor; it means man in their Gondi dialect. Koitors are broadly divided into two groups namely the Dor Koitor and the Meta Koitor. The Dor Koitors are those who live in the plains and the Meta Koitors live in the hills. The Abujh Maria are Meta Koitor as they live in the Metabhum (hills/high land). The Abujh Maria name or identity is given to them by the neighbouring non-Gond communities and also by the neighbouring Dandami Maria and Muria, they are called as Madia or Maria. Those people live in the Abujh Marh (Abujh means unknown and Marh means hills) area and hence are called as Abujh Maria. Kurup (1963) wrote that the word Abujh means 'rustic' and in Gondi Marh is hills. So Abujh Maria are the rustic people living in the hills.

### Geographical boundary

Abujh Marh is a mountain mass, a continuous geographical area embellished with lofty hills and steep valleys, situated in the South-West Bastar District (presently Naryanpur district) of Chhattisgarh. The Abujh Marh is bounded by the Indrawati river on the south, on the north by the Antagarh plains. On the east it is bounded by the Jhoria country and the Gudra Valley from the Chota Dongar to the Mangnar near the Indrawati and Barsur and on the West by the Kotri river from Partabpur to its junction the Indrawati at Bhairamgarh in the Ahiri Jamindari of the Chanda district of Maharashtra (Grigson 1991, reprint). The whole Abujh Marh area is covered with extensive ranges of hills and deals with peaks varying from 2200 to 3160 feet in height (Kurup 1963). Abujh Marh is a natural division of Bastar district with no administrative division. It is divided by the people of the area in some territories. These are Barsur Marh, Orcha Marh, and

Kutru Marh. All these places are named after the nearest known place. Again for the administration of the tribal areas of the district, the district was divided into some Parganas. Each and every pargana was headed and controlled by a headman who was known as Pargana Manjhi. Each Pargana has some villages under its control. Again every village is headed by a headman called as Manjhi or Patel. All the village Manjhis come under the control of Pargana Manjhi. Some of the Abujh Maria inhabited Parganas are Padalibhum, Tapalibhum, Nurbhum, Mangnar, Behramar, Hukkagotal, Bardal, Farsal and Chote Dongar.

The land is undulated by the presence of high mountains and steep valleys, clothed by dense forest of sal (*Shorea robusta*), Saja or aden (*Terminalia tomentosa*), sagaon (Teak or *Tectona grandis*), Sulphi (*Caryota urens*), Mahua (*Bassia latifolia*), bans (Bamboo), dhaura (*Anogeissus latifolia*) etc. and other forest growth. Grasses of different varieties grow in plenty throughout the Marh. Wild animals such as tigers, wild boar, bear, bison, sambhar, chital, panther, wild buffalo, deer, and hare are found in plenty.

## Economic life

Hunting, gathering and shifting hill cultivation are their primary occupations. They do shifting cultivation by slash-and-burn method in the Abujh Marh area which is an unsurveyed zone, so there is no Government rules and restrictions in felling or cutting of wood.

They believe that the area covered by Abujh Marh hills is their own domain which is actually owned by their *pen* deities of celestial world. Again the *pen* deities divided and distributed the land among the Abujh Maria people of the terrestrial world, and those are distributed through the *kattas* (clan like social groups) to which the Abujh Maria people belong. As for example *Karmaikola Mutte* is one of their *pen* deities who is the sole authority of the village Ader. Among the *kattas* under her control, people of Jodi/Jugho/Jughalor/Karmai *katta* live in the village-Ader. They believe that the land and five hillocks under the control of *Karmaikola Mutte* are divided among the families of the Jodi *katta*, transmitted from one generation to the next. It is told that they are a group of shifting cultivators. They cultivate a piece of land not more than successive four years and after that the land is left abandoned for a long duration not less than twenty years. In these twenty years they generally shift from one place of land to another for four to five times and in this way they shift from one land to another and cultivate in those five hillocks rotationally one after another. Except hunting, gathering and shifting hill cultivation they also do settled cultivation in their permanent land which they have acquired as permanent land very recently.

## Social organisation

The Abujh Maria society is very unique and interesting in both its structure and function. Right from the origin of Abujh Maria society, they have various types of stories, tales and myths. They believe that the almighty Bhagwan, to please his wife, created two sets of brothers and sisters named Nelariya, Nelire and Bumeriya, Bumire and put them to live in the hills and forests of this area long long ago. As time passed, children grew-up. Nelariya was married to Bumire and Bumariya was married to Nelire. Gradually they have got children and formed two sets of social groups.

Each of these two groups is exogamous in nature and tied by *dadabhai* or *bhaiband* or *consanguineal* relationship that is, tied by non-marital ties. They are not allowed to marry within the group and have to do it outside their won social group that is in another group, members of which are referred by them as *akomama* or *saga* or relatives through marital ties or in a word affinal relatives. If one holds this mythical story as the main root of their social organisation then it can be said that the tribe has moiety division in their social organisation. Several scholars and researchers such as Jay (1970: 78), Hiralal (1932) were in favour of speaking of moiety organisation whereas there are authors like Grigson (1991, reprinted) who gave opinion in favour of phratry organisation instead.

Besides the mythical story of the two sets of brothers and sisters, the Abujh Marias believe that they have originated from certain deities who are called as *pen*. These *pen* deities have large families and a huge number of relatives of having both the affinal and consanguineal relations. Among these *pens* Pat Raja or Tuller Raja or Raja Dokra is the oldest and is the first *pen* deity among all the *pens* of the Abujh Maria people. They believe that the pens' original home is at the celestial world. They have come down to the earth to guide their Abujh Maria progenies. It is found that all of these *pens* have one or more *kattas* (clan like social groups) which are under their control. These *pen* deities are directly linked with the terrestrial world of the Abujh Maria people through the *katta* organisation. Kattas are nothing but social groupings of the Abujh Maria of the terrestrial world which regulate the marriage rules and are exogamous in nature. These are very similar to the clan organisation in a tribal society. Therefore, it is seen that in this way a linkage between the *pens* of the celestial world and the Abujh Maria people of the terrestrial world are related and a strong thread of linkage between the celestial and the terrestrial world is there which can never be ignored. This link monitors much of their social norms and practices.

The present study is done in the village Orcha and Ader of the Chote Dongar pargana of the Abujh Marh. Each of these two villages has its respective *pen* deity. In Ader the *pen* deity is karmaikola mutte and in Orcha the *pen* deity is Pirtin Dewan; He is also known as Wikir Kunga or Hunga Muitto and popularly known as Dewan Dokra. Among several myths, there is a myth about Dewan Dokra's family, his relatives, ancestors and friends. They believe that he is Pat Raja's son and married with Karmaikola mutte (See genealogical chart of the family–Figure 1).

The above genealogical chart shows that Pat Raja–the oldest deity of the Abujh Marh area, married Pat Rani and brought her to his own place at the Mohonar village of the Mangnar Pargana. His wife belongs to the Dandami Maria group. Pat Rani's borther's name is Modia who is the presiding deity of Kekhami Katta of Dandami Maria group of Ghotpal. There are several stories which tell that in ancient days the Abujh Maria and the Dandami Maria used to have marital relationship but afterwards due to some disputes between the two groups they were separated and stopped to have any such marital alliance.

According to Grigson (1991), Dewan Dokra or Paikal Deo is the younger brother of Pat Raja. During present field investigation it is found that Paikal Deo is not his brother but one of his sons. It is told by them that Pat Raja has seven sons. They are Burha Dokra, pandu Hunga, Parkal Deo/Paikal Deo, Pirtin Dewan/Wikir Hunga/Hunga Muitto (actually pirtin and Paikal-these are the presiding deities of orcha and it's neighbouring Gudari village; due to some disputes between the villagers of Orcha and Gudari on the issue to instal the deity in their own village, Paikal had to be born in another shape and at last the villagers of Orcha village brought the deity's stick as his emblem in their village and established the deity there as Pirtin Dewan. The villagers of Gudari village have established the deity in a new form and he is Parkal Diwan. In this way the deity is worshipped in two above mentioned villages in two separate forms, names and identities and regarded as two brothers though both are the same. All of the children of Pat Raja are married and they have their own family.

It is observed that each of these *pens* has one or more *katta* under his or her control. The *pen* deity of Orcha village–Pirtin Dewan has several *kattas*. Usendi is one of those and the people of Orcha belong to that *katta*. Similarly *Karmaikola Mutte*-the Jodi/Jugho/Jughalor/ Karmai *katta*. A list of some *pens* and the *kattas* under their control is collected and these are given below (Table 5.1) :

**Figure 1: Genalogy of Patraja - The Supreme Authority in Celestial World**

Informant : (a) Tonderamusendi, vill. Orcha. Male, 75
(b) Koriya Jodi, vill. Ader, Male, 70
(c) Senior Male members of Gudari Village

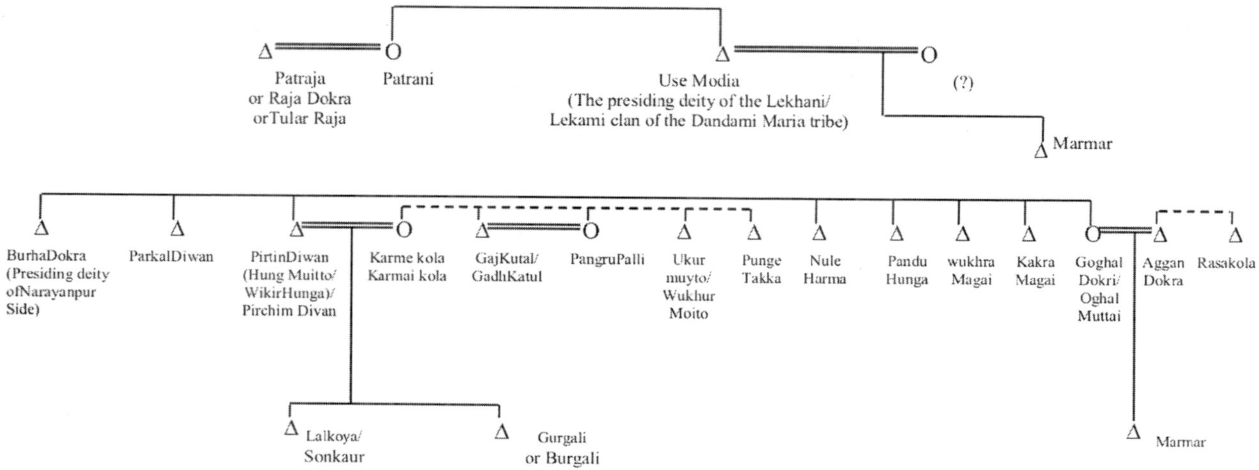

**Table 5.1: Kattas under control of the respective Pens (deities)**

| *Sl. No.* | *Name of the Pens* | *Kattas under Control* |
|---|---|---|
| 1. | Pat Raja | a. Jaterom/Jate (of Chote Dongar and Mangnar Pargana)<br>b. Hukur<br>c. Alami Mangnar Pargana<br>d. Nonde |
| 2. | Printin/Dewan Dokra Wikir Hunga and Parkal Diwan. (Pat Raja's son) | a. Usendi<br>b. Wadder/Vedda<br>c. Erme<br>d. Korami<br>e. Deda<br>f. Dodi<br>g. Dol<br>h. Gecha (Chote Tondabera village area)<br>i. Ahkal (Gudari village)<br>j. Demor |
| 3. | Nule Harma (Pat Raja's son) | a. Deda<br>b. Parsal<br>c. Ete (Kurmer village)<br>d. Boka (Kurmer village)<br>e. Koda |
| 4. | Pandu Hunga (Pat Raja's son) | Katlami |
| 5. | Wukhra Magai (Village Takveda) (Pat Raja's son) | Vetti/Wetti |
| 6. | Kakra Magai (Pat Raja's son) | Netam |
| 7. | Sonkuar (Pirtin and Karmaikola's son) (Chalcher village) | a. Parsak/Parsal<br>b. Kodlo |
| 8. | Karmaikola | a. Jugho/Karme<br>b. Jodi/Juri<br>c. Modor<br>d. Kohanaka<br>e. Ichami/Hichami<br>f. Badebako/Barbako<br>g. Nighaku<br>h. Dondaku<br>i. Korami |
| 9. | Reka mudia (Jatlur village) | a. Jatah/Potam/Poyami<br>b. Gota |
| 10. | Maramar | a. Marvi (Taktoli village in Mangnar Pargana) |
| 11. | Gogal Dokri/Oghal Muttai | a. Dhurwa<br>b. Dheorai<br>c. Dhodi<br>d. Vadde |

Now, Pat Raja or Tular Raja and his sons–all are *dadabhai* to each other or related trough consanguineal non-marital ties with each other and in this connection it can be said that the *Kattas* under the control of those *pens* are tied by similar *dadabhai* relationship.

In the genealogical chart (Figure 1) it is found that *pen*-Pirtin of Orcha village married the *pen* Karmaikola of Ader village. Now it is seen that each of these two *pens,* that is, the Pirtin Dewan and Karmaikola and the two above mentioned *kattas* under their control that is, Usendi and Jodi has two sets of relatives, that is, *pen* Pirtin Dewan and Karmaikola have several *dadabhai* and *akomama* relatives. Those are given in Tables 5.2(a) and 5.2(b).

Now, if the society has moiety organisation then all the *dadabhai* (non-marital relatives) and *akomama* (marital relatives) *pens* of the Pirtin Dewan and Karmaikola *pens* and all the *dadabhai* (non-marital relatives) and *akomama* (marital relatives) *Kattas* of Usendi and Jugho/Jughalor/ Jodi/Karmai *Katta* must enjoy the same and similar relations enjoy. But in reality the picture is different. As for example, in Figures 5:2(a) and 5:2(b) it is observed that *pen*–Kapatdar and *pen*-Kapatdar and *pen*-Warm Mari are *akomama* that is related by marital ties with both Dewan and Karmaikola. Similarly, the *Kattas* belong to these two *pens* are *akomama* with both Usendi and Karme/Jodi/Jugho/Jughalor *Katta.* In fact Dewan and Karmaikola belong to two separate groups related by marital ties and Usendi and Jugho/Jughalor/Jodi Karme similarly are related martially. If the Social devision is of moiety organisation then these *pens* and *kattas* should have marital relation with one of the two *pens*-Dewan or Karmaikola and non-marital relation with the other. Therefore, if differs from the concept of moiety organisation.

During field investigation it is found that, to Kapatdar, Waram Mari and Ukhra Magai are *dadabhai* and Dewan Dokra, Sonkuar, Karnwal, Rekamudia and Karmaikola all are *akomama.* But Waram-Mari and Ukhra Magai do not belong to the same group and are *akomama* with each other.

Therefore, the present study shows that the social organisation of the Abujh Maria can never be said as to have moiety organisation as the society has several smaller social divisions which are either martially or otherwise related with each other that is, related through *dadabhai* and *akomama* ties.

It has already been told that Grigson (1991, reprinted) also was not in favour of moiety organisation. He cited several examples in favour of his argument. Grigson also for his studies has taken the Usendi *Katta* of Orcha village. This Usendi *Katta* also has two sets of relations Fig. 4(b). One set is of *dadabhai* or non-marital relation and

**Table 5.2 (a): Formation of Agnatic Group through a Single Pen Pen or Deity–Pirtin Dewan/Dewan Dokra/Wikir Hunga/Katta-Usendi Wonga Muitta/Hunga Muitto/Phungar Deo**

| *Dadabhai/Bhaiband (Consanguineal kins)* | | | | *Akomama/Saga (Affinal kins)* | | | |
|---|---|---|---|---|---|---|---|
| *Katta* | | *Pen* | | *Katta* | | *Pen* | |
| 1. | Usendi | 1. | Wikir Hunga | 1. | Mador | 1. | Karmaikola |
| 2. | Vetti/Wetti | 2. | Ukhra Magai | 2. | Kohanaka | 2. | -do- |
| 3. | Netam | 3. | Kakra Magai | 3. | Gumelor (Barsur Marh Area) | 3. | Verma Muitto |
| 4. | Poyami/Potam/Jatal | 4. | Reka Mudia/Rekha Mudia | 4. | Jugho/Jodi/Juri/Karmai | 4. | Karmaikola |
| 5. | Salem | 5. | ? | 5. | Barbak | 5. | -do- |
| 6. | Sodi | 6. | Tul Mutte | 6. | Nighaku | 6. | -do- |
| 7. | Ahakal | 7. | Phungar Deo/Hunga Muitto/ Wikir Hunga | 7. | Dandaku | 7. | -do- |
| 8. | Duggal | 8. | -do- | 8. | Badebaku | 8. | -do- |
| 9. | Wadder/Vadde | 9. | -do- | 9. | Dhurwa | 9. | Oghal Muttai/Gogal Dokri |
| 10. | Katlami | 10. | Pandu Hunga (Yr. Br. of Wikir) | 10. | Kohami | 10. | -do- |
| 11. | Jaterom | 11. | Pat Raja/Raja Dokra/Tular Raja | 11. | Dheorai | 11. | -do- |
| 12. | Demor | 12. | Pankola Deo | 12. | Vedda | 12. | -do- |
| 13. | Deba (of Kurmer village) | 13. | Nule Harma (Yr. Br. of Hunga Muitto) | 13. | Marvi | 13. | Hunda Kosa/Maramar/Maramagh (Dewan's sister's son) |

| *Dadabhai/Bhaiband (Consanguineal kins)* | | | | *Akomama/Saga (Affinal kins)* | | | |
|---|---|---|---|---|---|---|---|
| *Katta* | | *Pen* | | *Katta* | | *Pen* | |
| 14. | Erme | 14. | Hunga Muitto | 14. | Karangalor | 14. | Unable to collect |
| 15. | Korami | 15. | -do- | 15. | Dughalor | 15. | -do- |
| 16. | Parsak/Parsal | 16. | Sonkuar/Nule Harma | 16. | Farsal | 16. | -do- |
| 17. | Kodlo | 17. | Nule Hurma | 17. | Bardal | 17. | -do- |
| 18. | Alami | 18. | Pat Raja | 18. | Ghotal | 18. | -do- |
| 19. | Nonde | 19. | -do- | 19. | Unable to collect | 19. | Maramar |
| 20. | Tokalor | 20. | -do- | 20. | -do- | 20. | Naratma |
| 21. | Hukur | 21. | -do- | 21. | -do- | 21. | Visarma |
| 22. | Parlo | 22. | Unable to collect | 22. | Gaitta, Gaitachu, Mukhla, Irkal, Temor/Timor | 22. | Kapatdar |
| 23. | Kohka | 23. | -do- | 23. | Kahari | 23. | Waram Mari |
| 24. | Ark | 24. | -do- | | | | |
| 25. | ? | 25. | Karnwal | | | | |
| 26. | Dodi | 26. | Wikir Hunga | | | | |
| 27. | Dol | 27. | -do- | | | | |
| 28. | Gecha | 28. | -do- | | | | |

**Table 5:2(b): Formation of Agnatic Group through a Single Pen**

**Pen or Deity–Karmaikola; Katta–Jodi/Juri/Jugho/Jughalor/Karmai**

| *Dadabhai/Bhaiband (Consanguineal kins)* | | | | *Akomama/Saga (Affinal kins)* | | | |
|---|---|---|---|---|---|---|---|
| *Katta* | | *Pen* | | *Katta* | | *Pen* | |
| 1. | Mador | 1. | Karmaikola | 1. | Parsak/Parsakodlo | 1. | Sonkuar |
| 2. | Kohanaka/Kohanak | 2. | -do- | 2. | Netam | 2. | Kakra Magai |
| 3. | Barbako/Badebako | 3. | -do- | 3. | Poyami/Potam/Jatal | 3. | Reka Mudia/Rekha Mudia |
| 4. | Nighaku | 4. | -do- | 4. | Gaitta | 4. | Kapatdar |
| 5. | Dondaku | 5. | -do- | 5. | Gaitachu, Mukhla, Irkal, emor/Timor | 5. | Kapatdar |
| 6. | Jodi/Juri/Jughalor | 6. | -do- | 6. | Vedda/Wadder/Damor | 6. | Pankola (Wikir Hungo) |
| 7. | Karmai | 7. | -do- | 7. | Wetti | 7. | Ukhra Maghai |
| 8. | Hichami/Ichami | 8. | -do- | 8. | Mahari | 8. | Waram Mari |
| 9. | Marme | 9. | Unable to collect | 9. | Demo/Demmo | 9. | Pankola or parkal Deo |
| 10. | Visharma | 10. | -do- | 10. | Usendi | 10. | Dewan Dokra |
| 11. | Naratma | 11. | -do- | 11. | Erme | 11. | -do- |
| 12. | Bodaku | 12. | Maramar | 12. | Vardaku | 12. | Karnwal |
| 13. | Gochaku | 13. | -do- | 13. | Gotaku | 13. | -do- |
| 14. | Dhurwa | 14. | Oghal Muitte/Gogal Dokri | 14. | Mallor | 14. | Waram Mari |
| 15. | Kohami | 15. | -do- | 15. | Kohla/Kola | 15. | Mahimakola |
| 16. | Yete | 16. | Unable to collect | 16. | Tokanar | 16. | Waram Mari |
| 17. | Dolwar | 17. | -do- | 17. | Gume/Gumelor | 17. | Verma Muitto |
| 18. | Marme | 18. | -do- | 18. | Farsal | 18. | Unable to collect |
| 19. | Ahaka | 19. | Ponga Takka | 19. | Bardal | 19. | -do- |
| 20. | Marvi/Mandvi | 20. | Maramar | 20. | Gotal | 20. | -do- |

**Table 5.3 (a)**

| i. | *Pen-Dewan Dokra* | | |
|---|---|---|---|
| | Bhaiband/Dadabhai/non-Marital relationship | Akomama/Marital relationship | |
| | Pat Raja and All his sons Sonkuar, Wukhra Maghal | Kapadar, Waram Mari, Karmaikola | |
| ii. | *Pen-Karmaikola Mutte* | | |
| | Bhaiband/Dadabhai/non-Marital relationship | Akomama/Marital relationship | |
| | Karmaikola, Maramar, Oghal Muitte/Gogal Dokri, Ponga Takka | Reka Mudia, Karnwal, Kapatdar, Waram Mari, Dewan Dokra | |
| iii. | *Pen Kapatdar* | | |
| | Bhaiband/Dadabhai/non-Marital relationship | Akomama/Marital relationship | |
| | Again these are *akomama* to each other<br>↑<br>Waram Mari Ukhra Magai | Sonkuar, Reka Mudia, Karnawal<br>Dewan Dokra → Marmaikola | These two are *akomama* to each other, while Karmaikola and Karnwal are *akomama* to each other but, Karnwal and Dewan Dokra are *dadabhai* to each other. |
| iv. | *Pen-Waram Mari* | | |
| | Bahaiband/Dadabhai/non-Marital relationship | Akomama/Marital relationship | |
| | Kapatdar | Wukhra Magai | |
| v. | *Pen-Wukhra Magai* | | |
| | Bhaiband/Dadabhai/non-Marital relationship | Akomama/Marital relationship | |
| | Kapatdar | Waram Mari | |

the other set is of *akomama* or marital relation. He could identity six *dadabhai* and fourteen whether the social organisation is having moiety organisation or not. To Usendi, Gume *Katta* of Barsur Marh and Jugho *Katta* of Chote Dongar Marh of Ader village are *akomama* or related by marital ties. Jugho is further identified in the present research as Jodi or Karmai or Jughalor *Katta*. In the concept of moiety organisation both

Jugho and Gume *Kattas* should be in the same group having a *dadabhai* relation with each other as both of them are *akomama* to Usendi *Katta*. But in reality they have marital relation that is *akomama* relation with each other.

**Table 5.3 (b)**

| | | |
|---|---|---|
| i. | *Katta-Usendi* | |
| | Bhaiband/Dadabhai or (Non-Marital relation)<br>Usendi | Akomama or (Marital relationship)<br>Gume, Jugho/Jodi |
| ii. | *Katta-Jugho/Jodi* | |
| | Bhaiband/Dadabhai or (Non-Marital relation)<br>Jugho/Jodi | Akomama or (Marital relation)<br>Gume, Usendi |
| iii. | *Katta-Gume* | |
| | Bhaiband/Dadabhai or (Non-Marital relation)<br>Gume | Akomama or (Marital relation)<br>Jugho/Jodi, Usendi |

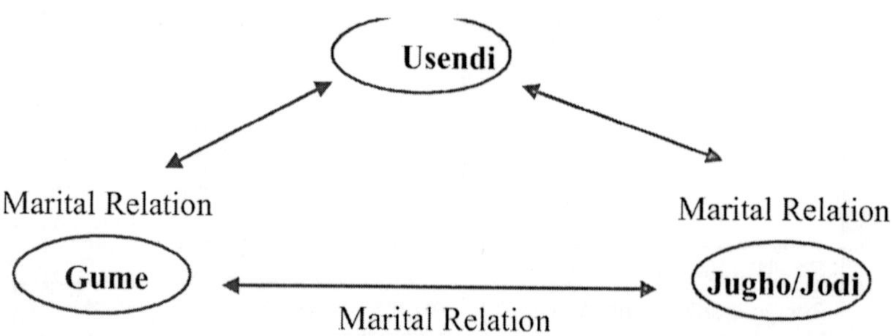


Next, there is the example of the Jate *Katta* of Mohonar village of Mangnar Pargana. It has a *dadabhai* relationship with Tokalor and Hukur *Kattas* of Erpanar village. Jate takes wife from Gumelor like an Usendi. Now Gumelor takes wife from marvi of Taktholi village of Mangnar pargana. So Marvi should be in the same division with Jatelor, Tokalor, Hukur of Mangnar Parganas . However, it is seen that the Jetelor, Tokalor, and the Hukur of Mangnar Pargana are also in *akomama* relation with the Marvi *Katta* of the Takholi village of the Mangnar Pargana.

**Table 5.3 (c)**

| i. | *Katta-Jate* | |
|---|---|---|
| | Bhaiband (Non-Marital relation)<br>Jate, Tokalor, Hukur, Usendi | Akomama (Marital relationship)<br>Gumelor, Marvi |
| ii. | *Katta-Gumelor* | |
| | Bhaiband (Non-Marital relation)<br>Gumelor | Akomama (Marital relation)<br>Marvi |

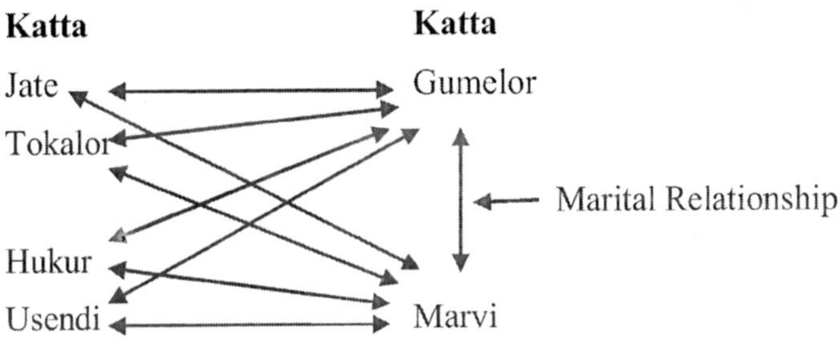


(⟷ Signifies marital relation)

Again, Dhurwa *Katta* is *dadabhai* to Jugho/Jodi or Jughalor *Katta* regarded as the elder brother of Karme and intermarries with Usendi and also with Gumelor. If it is a moiety Organisation, then Dhurwa should be in *dadabhai* or non-marital relation with Gumelor as *Usendi* has the *akomama* or marital relationship with Jodi and Gumelor but the case is different.

**Table 5.3 (d)**

| i. | *Katta-Dhurwa* | |
|---|---|---|
| | Bhaiband (Non-Marital relation)<br>Jugho/Jughalor/Jodi | Akomama (Marital relationship)<br>Usendi, Gumelor |
| ii. | *Katta-Usendi* | |
| | Bhaiband (Non-Marital relation)<br>Usendi | Akomama (Marital relation)<br>Gumelor,<br>Jodi/Jugho/Jughalor |

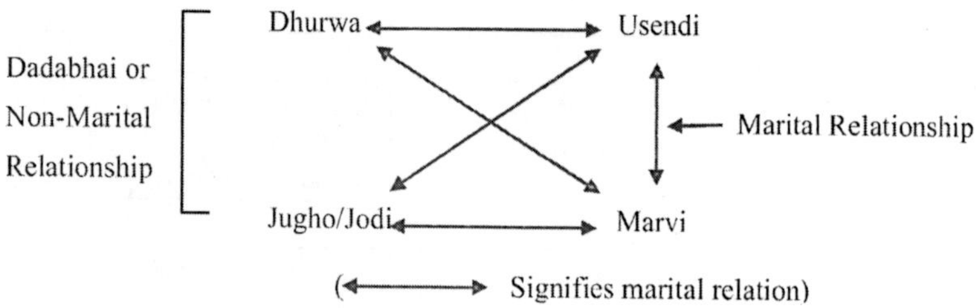


The Farsal, Bardal and the Gotal or Ghotal *Kattas* are *dadabhai* with each other, and they have *akomama* or marital relationship with Jughalor, Usendi and Waddar *Kattas*. But Usendi and Jughalor are always in *akomama* relationship, that is having marital relationship with each other.

**Table 5.3 (e)**

| i. | *Katta-Farsal* | |
|---|---|---|
| | Bhaiband (Non-Marital relation)<br>Farsal, Bardal, Gotal/Ghotal | Akomama (Marital relationship)<br>Jughalor, Usendi, Wadder |
| ii. | *Katta-Usendi* | |
| | Bhaiband (Non-Marital relation)<br>Usendi | Akomama (Marital relation)<br>Jugho/Jodo/Jughalor |

Usendi of Kiringalor and Dughal Parganas are *akomama* or with marital relationship with Karangalor and Dughalor *Kattas*. Karangalor and Dughalor *Kattas* are *dadabhai* or has non-marital relation with Farsal, Bardal, Gotal *Kattas* form a group. They are *akomama* to Usendi of Kiringalor and Dughal Pargana and also to the Jughalor *Katta*. But Usendi and Jughalor are never included in the same group with *dadabhai* relation.

**Table 5.3 (f)**

| i. | *Katta-Bardal* | |
|---|---|---|
| | Bhaiband/Dadabhai (Non-Marital relationship)<br>Karangalor, Dughalor, Farsal, Bardal, Gotal, Nugoti, Tape, Hichami | Akomama or (Marital relationship)<br>Usendi, Jugho/Jodo/Jughalor |
| ii. | *Katta-Usendi* | |
| | Bhaiband/Dadabhai (Non-Marital relation)<br>Usendi | Akomama (Marital relation)<br>Jughalor |

**Table 5.4: Marital Inter-relationship between Kattas**

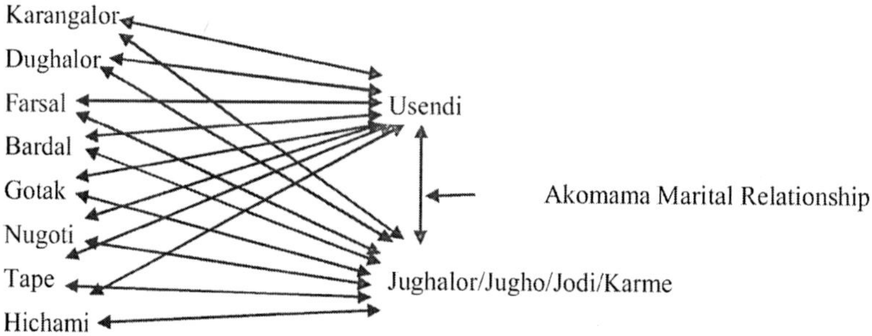


It is seen that both Jughalor and Usendi are treated as *akomama* or relatives through marital ties with many *Kattas* mentioned earlier but no one can club these two in the same group with *dadabhai* relation with each other. These two are completely separate from each other and are only related through marital relation. . With all these examples it can be said that the Abujh Maria social system can never be said to have moiety organisation as it is divided into several divisions instead of two equal halves. We may call it Phratry Organisation, which is also the opinion of Grigson (1991. Reprinted).

There is an observation among the Kolam (Hazra, 1983) that the tribe is divided into four divisions, each one is affiliated to a number of Gods, namely 4 *dev* (God), 5 *dev*, 6 *dev*, 7 *dev* and each one is exogamous. These divisions, in most of the cases are called as *Kur, Kuri, Katta, Katte* etc. These small divisions are necessarily exogamous in nature.

This situation is also found among the Gonds and allied tribes of Central India. Hazra (1970, 1983), Jay (1970), Singh (1980 and 1986), Thusu (1968, 1970) et. al., on the basis of field information, tried to explain the relationship among the three systems: the supernatural or celestial world, the division within the tribe belonging to the terrestrial world and the marriage systems.

Similarly, the Lalung tribe of the plains of Assam are divided into atleast 31 clans, each of which is known as *Khul*. These 31 clans are divided into eleven (11) clan clusters while the 31st clan 'Lorom' is not included in any cluster. The clans belonging to a cluster are considered as sister clans and they cannot marry with other clans of the same cluster. Each cluster is called *mahari* which offers the character of a phratry. It is also seen that the clan 'Mithi' is included in two separate clusters; even then they can not marry with each other lest that affects their consanguineous character. Side by side with this clan clustering, one can find that each clan is affiliated to 12 *bhani* (sister) vis-a-vis each *mahari* is not clear in the minds of the Lalung but it can be observed that this affiliation to the traditional group of sister also has an important role to play in ascertaining the alliance system.

## Conclusion

It can be said from the present study that the social system of the Abujh Maria people is controlled by some deities called *pen* whose actual abode is a at the celestial world. Each of these *pens* has two sets of relative namely *dadabhai pens* and *akomama pens*. The *dadabhai pens* are those with whom they have non-marital relations; These *dadabhai* and *akomama* relationships are overlapping; that is; one *pen* has *dadabhai* relation with a group of *pens* and *akomama* relation with another group. But all of that particular *pens*. *Dadabhai pens* are not necessarily *dadabhai* to each other. Some of them may have *akomama* relation instead of *dadabhai* relation and in many cases have *dadabhai* relation with the *pens* of other group. Now, under each of these *pens* there are a number of *Kattas* which directly control the Abujh Maria people and their society at their terrestrial world and in this way communion between celestial and terrestrial world is maintained. These *Kattas* are again exogamous in nature with two types of relatives–*dadabhai* and *akomama* and their agnatic relationship is traced under the banner of their own *pen* and known as *dadabhai* group and thereby marriage within such group is strictly prohibited. Considering the above data in mind it can be said that perhaps a kind of exogamous band cluster prevails among them and in no way it supports the concept of moiety organisation.

In the villages of Orcha and Ader from where the data have been collectyed, two distinct *Kattas* are identified namely *Katta* of Usendi and *Katta* of Jodi/Jugho. The former comprises 28 *dadabhai Kattas* which are considered as fraternal clans of Usendi and with whom marriage is prohibited. Similarly, the other *Katta* Jodi is composed of 20 *dadabhai kattas* with whom inter-marriage is prescribed for Usendi. If the whole Abujh Marh tract is thoroughly covered, one may locate some more *Kattas* which obviously would have the character of phratries. These *Kattas*, apart from having social function of regulating marriage also operate as corporate unit because it also performs some economic functions.

The Abujh Maria are shifting hill cultivators. They cultivate land by slash-and-burn method and after cultivation of a land for consecutive four years they shift to another batch of land in the Abujh Marh hills.

It is believed that the land in the Abujh Marh hills is under the control of their *pen* deities who are held as the actual owners. Then the land is mythically divided by the *pens* among the *Kattas* under their control and those are ultimately owned by the Abujh Maria progenies of those *kattas*. Therefore, the Abujh Maria territory have been demarcated in terms of *pen* whose affiliation with the *Kattas* is more or less clear and obvious. Each *pen* has one or more villages under his or her control or has a particular territory, and the members of the said *pen* enjoy the right to utilise the land, in which their economic need for sustenance is operating and in view of maintenance of sustenance, the *Kattas* under a *pen* (which Grigson referred as phratry) of a particular area or a territory of Abujh Marh act as a corporate group.

In this context it may be observed that among the lalung of Assam similar exogamous sister clusters play a significant role in the social organisation and also in their economic life. The Lalung term for such sister clusters is *mahari*. Incidentally, any such nomenclature is absent among the Abujh Maria territory. In the absence of detail data of the total Abujh Marh territory each exogamous *Katta* can be termed as exogamous band cluster.

In the case of Abujh Maria the authors are naturally interested in highlighting the *'Katta-pen'* relationship where it is found that each *katta* is affiliated to one *pen* or the other. At the same time the Abujh Marh hills are also marked out in terms of *Katta* and *pen*. This has reminded the authors of a cognitive relationship between the *Katta* and the *pen* (that is the terrestrial world and the celestial world) in the organisation of the Abujh Marh society.

*Acknowledgement:* We express our sincere regards and thanks to Dr. B. K. Dasgupta, Ex-Dy. Director of Anthropological Survey of India and Shri Bageshwar Singh, Ex-Anthropologist of Anthropological Survey of India for their valuable observations and suggestions on the manuscript.

## References

Chattopadhyay, K. P. 1946. Korku marriage customs and some changes. *Journal of Royal Asiatic Society of Bengal;* pp. 43-70.

Dasgupta, Samira and Amitabha Sarkar 2005. *Reflection of Ethno-Science: Study on the Abujh Maria*, New Delhi: Mittal Publications.

Elliot, C. 1856. Deputy Commissioner's notes. Unpublished manuscript, Jagadalpur Record Room, Bastar District, Madhya Pradesh (Document Index: XXXVIII, Office Head quarter and Tashil, No. 25, 25/1).

Firth, Raymond 1954 " Presidential Address", in Journal of Royal Anthropological Institute, Vol. 84.

Fürer-Haimendorf, C. V. 1952. The Cult of Ayaks among the Kolam of Hyderabad, *Weiner Beitrage Zur Kultur-Geschichte und Linguistic,* Vol. 9, pp. 108-123.

Glasfurd, C. L. R. 1862. Reports on the Dependency of Bastar (Record Room Jagadalpur, Bastar).

Grigson, Sir Wildfried 1991. *The Maria Gonds of Bastar,* Oxford University Press, Delhi, (Reprinted).

Hazra, D. 1970. *The Dorla of Bastar,* Anthropological Survey of India, Memoir No. 17, Calcutta.

Hazra, D. 1983. *The Kolam of Yeotmal,* Anthropological Survey of India, Member No. 49, Calcutta.

Hiralal, Rai Bahadur 1932. *Inscriptions in the Central provinces and Berar.* Nagpur.

Jay, Edward, J. 1970. *A Tribal Village of Middle India,* Anthropological Survey of India, Memoir No. 21, Calcutta.

Kurup, A. M. 1963. People of the unknown hills, *Vanyajati* Vol. X: 38-41.

Rakshit, H. K. 1975. Understanding caste for demogenetic studies. In *Bio-Anthropological Research in India,* ed. By H. K. Rakshit. Anthropological Survey of India, Memoir No. 46, Calcutta.

Razeq. K. A. 1967-1968. "Korku" (unpublished report); Field work carried out during 1967-68 from Anthropological Survey of India, Nagpur.

Singh, Bageshwar 1980. The marriage and its wider implication: The case of the Kodaku of Sarguja district, M. P. *Indian Science Congress Association, Anthropology and Archaeology Section.* Abstracts No. 7.

Singh, Bageshwar 1981. The Bhil are not a single tribal whole, *Man in India,* 61, No. 1.

Singh, Bageshwar 1985. Marriage among the seven tribes of india: A comparative approach *Eastern Anthropologist,* Vol. 38, No. 4.

Singh, Bageshwar 1986. *The Kodaku of Sarguja.* Anthropological Survey of India, Memoir No. 70, Calcutta.

Singh, Bageshwar and Samira Dasgupta 1987. Caste: How much tradition involved. *Man and Life,* Vol. 13, Nos. 3 and 4.

Syam Chaudhuri, N. K. and M. M. ·Das 1973. *The Lalung Society: A Theme for Analytical Ethnography,* Anthropological Survey of India, Calcutta.

Thusu, K. N. 1968. *The Dhurwa of Bastar,* Anthropological Survey of India, Memoir No. 16, Calcutta.

Thusu, K. N. 1980. *Gond Kingdom of Chanda.* Anthropological Survey of India, Memoir No. 53, Calcutta.

# SOCIAL ORGANISATION OF BIRJIA OF NETARHAT PLATEAU OF JHARKHAND

## Social Organisation

The Birjia are an endogamous group of people of Netarhat plateau with two traditionally endogamous *koms* (sub-groups) namely the Sinduriya and the Telia or Telha. Among these two sub-groups, the Sinduriya claim superior status over the Telha or Telia sub-group as they believe that the Telha eat cow which is regarded as a sin to the Sinduriya. The Sinduriya eat bullock and even carrion (these are also taken by the Telha group of people) but never a cow. Due to this reason, they claim superiority over the Telha or Telia sub-group of people. Each of the *Kom* (sub-group) is divided into some exogamous totemistic sirtha or gotar (clan) such as Lakra, Bir, Kujur, Tetenga, Baghwar, Sher and Induar etc. It is observed that they do not follow the rules of marriage such as *Kom* endogamy and *sirtha* exogamy. According to them after migration they have settled very dispersedly and in a very small number in a particular village. So due to geographical isolation they faced a lot of problems to arrange a marriage. They could only keep connection with the people of closer proximity. In this situation, they are forced to arrange marriage sometimes in the same *sirtha* and sometimes even outside their own *Kom* and ultimately decided to follow *Kodaku* (lineage) exogamy as the rule of marriage.

It is told that on the way of their migration the lineage members gathered together at a place and kept some symbol of their *Kodaku* (lineage) and after that they dispersed. It has helped to identify a lineage member even after generations. Each of the lineage has separate symbol. The symbol is known as ***hargori***– the parental abode, and the place, where it is established is known as Baigaasthan. As for example, in Tusrukona tola of Range village among the Birjia, a group of people have their *hargori* near Jamtoli, at western portion of Netarhat plateau. It is nothing but a vertical stone slab which is named as Sarna Dohar. In Netarhat plateau also there are some Birjia living in Jamtoli and Nayatoli hamlets who belong to the same *hargori*. So marriage between the Birjia of these two villages is strictly prohibited as they possess the same *hargori*, that is, belonging to the same *Kodaku* (lineage).

After the implementation of the new rule of *Kodaku* exogamy, the *kom* and *sirtha* have got less importance and as a result most of them have now forgotten their own *sirtha*. But they are very much aware of their own *kom* as there is a particular marriage ritual through which the specific *kom* still preserve identity. This will be discussed later while describing marriage rituals.

The Birjia are unable to remember their ascending genealogies beyond their upper third generation. The parental grand father is usually remembered by name but not always the grand mother. They hardly are able to tell the names of maternal granddfater. It is probably due to this fact, that the Birjia say that the parternal relationship or *kutumb* (aganatic kins) is the real one while the maternal relation or *sambandhi* affinal kin) is of secondary importance.

The patrilineal descent of the Birjia homestead of the nucleus is of an extensive system of partilineages which palys an important part in the organisation of their social life. As with the descent group of the homestead, only men are full members of this system, and descent is traced through the male line to a common ancestor. Several related homesteads, whose male members are descendant of one grand father, recognise themselves as a single group or lineage members or *kutumb* on particular occasions.

The smallest unit among the Birjia is *paribar* (family). Their families are patrilocal in residence.

Though customarily the Birjia families are of nuclear type, yet, it is told by the Birjia informants that they like to live in the extended type of family along with parents and married brothers as they do not want the fragmentation of their little land. Moreover they prefer to live in the extended type of family because of their *Ora-bhitar*–the room for their ancestors, where their souls are established after their death. They say that they live in the hills and forests whee there is a fear of ferocious animals and many unpredictable hazards. They think that in the hills and jungles evil spirits roam here and there and whenever get a chance, they cause harm to a person. In such a condition their ancestors are believed as their guard-deities. So they treat their ancestors as their family deities who protect them from all kinds of evils. The ancestors are propitiated time to time when all the family members gather together to get the blessings for a peaceful and prosperous life. When a family breaks down into smaller units, the *Ora-bhitar* remains with the original family. Those who are separated have no right to establish another *Orabhitar* during their life time. (The may prepare a *kothli* or chamber in their own houses for future use; that is; when they die, their children may establish their souls called *mua* inside the *kothli* forming a new *Ora-bhitar*though it is not compulsory. Their souls also may be established in the original household). They have to join the rituals performed in the *Ora-bhitar* jointly with others in the original family when their parents die, their *mua* are also established in the *Ora-bhitar*. This religious aspect of their life, caused partly by ecology, forces them to live together. They like to live in the original family where the protecting deities reside and among the studied 66 families 30 (45.45 per cent) are extended type of families.

The tables show that the numbers of nuclear families are not so less; that is, 26 (39. 39 per cent) of the total families are of nuclear type.

According to them an extended family breaks down due to maladjustment in the work load, scarcity of food etc. They suffer from scarcity of food during most part of the year. It brings quarrels in an extended family. A person who does hard labour than other persons in a family, always wishes to get a bigger share of food for at least his children which ultimately leads to quarrels in a family and as a result the family breaks down into smaller units. Therefore, it can be said that ecology is partly responsible for the breaking down of an extended family.

Now, if one notes carefully the composition of the extended families, one can see that among 30 extended families 18 are of vertically extended type of which 7 are composed of nuclear families with some dependents.

Horizontally extended families are only 2 in number. Rest are the mixed extended type which are mostly composed of parents, their unmarried children, married sons, their wives and children. Therefore, from the above analysis and discussion it can be said that the Birjia families are mostly of nuclear type.

It is found that, in all the cases, the average family size is small. It is told by them that due to less availability of resources, they suffer from scarcity of food. So they think it better to have a small family so that they suffer less from the scarcity of food than to have a large family where the suffering due to shortage of food may be more. This is also supported by the point that the Birjia live in a village in a small cluster forming a hamlet. Due to less availability of resources it is not possible for them to live in a large cluster. Therefore, it can be said that ecology is partly responsible for the preponderance of smaller families.

The allocation of role and interpersonal relationship observed among the family members are marked. Relationship between the husband and wife is that of mutual help and co-operation which is noticed in each and every sphere of their daily life. The husband is the chief earning member and wife's primary duty is to maintain the household chores. But a wife's activities in economic sphere of their life cannot be ignored. She, along with her household chores, always keeps herself busy in collection, labour in various sectors. In this way, they jointly earn their livelihood.

During infancy, the child's relationship is that of affection on the part of father and respect on the part of the son. It gradually turns into strictness on the part of father, especially in a bid to make his son successful in life economically and socially. When the son becomes matured enough to maintain a family, the father handa over most of the responsibilities to him and gradually becomes dependent upon the son in his old age.

Father-daughter relationship is of same kind as a father and son during childhood of the daughter, this gradually leads to restraint on both sides as the daughter grows older. Affection on the part of mother for both the son and daughter is noticed. The daughter helps the mother in household chores. During old age, like father, mother also becomes dependent on the son.

Relationship with early playmates leads to co-operation which in economic and other spheres of life makes brother to brother relation. Similarly during childhood brother-sister relationship is marked as early playmates. Brother's responsibility is to protect the sister in each and every sphere of life. Early relationship among sisters is that of playmates. This leads to intimate friendship and an attitude of co-operation.

In case of a household where there are grandparents, the relationship between grand parents and grand children is less formal in nature. They joke with each other, love and respect in the part of grand children and affection in the part of the grandfather is noticed.

When the married brothers live together with their wives and children together with their parents in the same household, it is seen that the relationship between the father-in-law and daughter-in-law is formal. The father-in-law usually behaves with the daughter-in-law as a father and the daughter-in-law as a daughter. They can talk, gossip, quarrel with each other but the father-in-law is not allowed to call her by name. the relationship of a married woman with *apuintiku* (elder brother-in-law) is of some kind of restriction and avoidance. It is lessened after performance of a custom known as *jum mandi* which means eating rice, held after marriage. Before performance of the ritual they are not allowed to talk with each other, they will not serve rice-beer or rice to each other. This is generally performed on some occasions like Sarhul, Fagua, Kharwaj. On that day the *apuintiku* first invites his younger brother's wife to his house along with other members of the family. After her arrival, both of them sit face to face and the *apuintiku* offers her rice-beer in a leaf cup after ceremonially wishing her feet, knees and shoulder by touching those with rice-beer by his own hands. Then the woman drinks. . Then she serves him cooked rice and *haria* (rice-beer). After a few days the woman invites him on similar occasion. In this way *jum-mandi* is performed and taboo rules are partially relaxed. But they do not talk with each other except when needed. The *apuintiku* never calls her by name.

The relationship between the mother-in-law and the daughter-in-law is of mutual co-operation. A married woman seems to be friendly with her younger brother-in-laws and sister-in-law, especially with the younger brother-in-law with whom she has a joking relationship.

Relationship between the brothers' wives living together is friendly with mutual co-operation in the household chores.

Property of a father is generally inherited by his sons. His wife has no claim over it. Generally the daughters have no claim over the property. When a man has no son, then he generally allows the married daughter with her husband to stay in his family/house and in that case property is inherited by them. Even in some exceptional cases, in spite of having sons, a married daughter may live with her husband in father's family. In such cases, the property is inherited by them equally. When a man has no child then the property is inherited by his brother or brother's son. The person who will inherit the property will look after the wife of the deceased. In most of the cases the property of a person mainly his cultivable land is inherited by the sons where the eldest son gets aslightly bigger share known as *jethans*.

In case of succession, according to rule the eldest son gets the authority to do the ancestor worship of the family. After marriage, if the eldest son builds his separate household (because of lack of space or due to maladjustment with others in the house) then he makes a separate *kothli* in the house as a place of ancestors. Generally the youngest son lives with his parents even after marriage. But he usually does not perform any ritual for the ancestors. In his death, his eldest son becomes responsible to do the same.

## Reference

Dasgupta, Samira 1994 Birjia: Society and Culture (A Study in Cultural Ecological Perspective) Calcutta: firma KLM Pvt. Ltd.

# 6

# Social Stratification of Bastar Tribes

The concept of stratification refers to unequal rewards that are attached to position. According to Talcott Parsons "social stratification is regarded here as the differential ranking of the human individuals who compose a given social system and their treatment as superior and inferior to one another in certain socially important respects". (Parsons, 1954, p. 59). The idea towards Indian tribes is that it is an egalitarian society but practically it is only a myth. Changing scenario of social landscape may be observed through social stratification angle. When social scientist's study the society from conflicting print of view of unit of observation is usually. Recently Marxists Social Scientists focus their arena of study from agrarian relations which is again a stratification point of view.

The tribal social stratification is altogether different from caste stratification of Hindu fold. Among caste system there is ranking or hierarchic system, purity and pollution concept and moreso, caste are considered as a system functionally related together while in case of tribe, the picture is altogether different. Each tribal group is endogamous and ranking in the tribal group, therefore, is done interms of individual, family and clan as structural unit.

Now-a-days the tribal society like any other society is not homogenous because of changing scenario where modernisation and industrialisation plays a key role. It reveals from ICSSR Survey report on Sociology and Social Anthropology from 1969-79 that nothing was mentioned about tribal stratification. However in the middle of 70's R. K. Prasad (1975) discussed some aspects of stratification and interaction among Parhaiya of Palamou District of Bihar. Prasad (1975) also informed that the tribal group have adopted a kind of caste like jajmani system. Shah (1976) has also infored stratification found among tribal groups of Broach and Panchmahal Districts of Gujrat. He said that due to forces of modernisation and development schemes initiated by the government, tribal society has ceased to be homogeneous and egalitarian. Sem Topno (1970) discussed stratification among Munda, in terms of impact of Hinduis and Chrisianity on the choice of names of children. Singh (1985) also mentioned that social stratification exists among the West Bengal and Bihar tribes. He opinions that there has been internal differentiation among them and it was due to colonial transformation. He observed that tribal society has been changing his status towards peasant caste pole.

## II

Some of the aspects of social stratification are related to question of theory, structure and processes. The study of stratification in Indian society has mainly two orientation viz. (a) parameter of purity-pollution concept, sacred and hierarchy etc., while (b) the second orientation to stratification is dominant in economic and political sphere. In these fields there are several studies in our country but sincerely speaking there is a lack of study on Tribal Stratification.

To understand tribal stratification it must be said that in Indian situation we must define and identify the structural unit of our study. This unit whether a person, a group viz., caste or a tribe has to be related to the basic questions of theory, structure and process of change.

Yogendra Singh (1985) in his report on Indian stratification observed that the theoretical and substantive studies concerned in India are oriented to the methods of: (a) Structural-Functional, (b) Structuralist, (c) Structural-Historical and (d) Historical-Materialist or Marxist.

The studies on social stratification based on the Structural-functional method, treat caste as a hierarchial system. Caste system is viewed as a system of co-operation. While the structuralist approach to the study of social stratification may be characterised by the studies of Dumont (1970)–Homo Hierarchicus. In social anthropology studies purely on tribal stratification is meager. Social Anthropologists who have followed Dumont's structural approach are Leach (1960), Bailey (1968), Desai (1948), Vidyarthi (1965, 1970, 1971) and Sachidananda (1964). The main focus on such tribal studies has been to provide an ethnographic aspects of the tribes belonging to different ecological niche of the country. These studies have mainly restricted to the analysis of clan, kinship and religion, which reveals that their theoretical orientation was towards structural-functional and structural.

The third orientation in the understanding of India social stratification is structural-historical where structuralism has over looked historicism. Singh (1985) observes on this approach: such studies has two dimension viz. (i) Non-Marxist and (ii) Marxist. The Non-Marxist historical studies are again differentiated. Under the structural-historical approach a huge impirical data have been generated and is used by socio-cultural anthropologists. Within this theoretical frame work most studies are primarily on caste and class. But now-a-days it's horizon is extended towards the study on agrarian structure and peasantry. History interms on non-marxism has been extensively used by both Indian and foreign anthropologists posted in different parts on our country (like Risley, Dalton, Thurston, Croocks etc. ) worked extensively on various communities of our country like tribe, case in peninsular India. They used non-Marxist history to present a detail anthropological profile of the communities of our country.

Fourth orientation to the study of social stratification is Marxist approach which is characterised by its features, dialectics, structure and historicism. It locates historical forces in the mode of production and production relations. The production relations and production forces are related to certain dialectics of history.

Desai (1977) who is a Marxist sociologists observed that the members belonging to this category of tribal groups were uprooted from their mode of production in the same way as were millions of cultivators and artisans living in the multitude of unmitigated villages of pre-British India from their self-sufficient, self contained village community setting. During British period under the impact of new administrative, political and economic measures there tribesmen lost their moorings from their traditional age-old socio-cultural settings. A large section of them became pauper which ultimately force them to live in the status of bonded labour or serfs to the Zamindars, Contrators or money lenders.

Pathy (1984) has carried out researches in the tribal agrarian stratification. He argues that he tribals are a peasantry and working on this hypothesis he applies Marxian frame work of analysis and finally identifies following agrarian strata: (i) Landless, (ii) rich peasant, (iii) middle peasant, (iv) small peasant and (v) farm worker.

## III

In Indian caste system rank concession is one of the parameter of purity and pollution. It rests on ideas and values. In short, the essence of caste system is that it is based on co-operation and rests on a system of hierarchy. According to Marriott (1965) caste ranking is determined on the basis of collective opinion concerning the placement of ethnic group as corporate wholes, higher or lower that one another in precedence.

In the following lines tribal stratification needs a little clarification. There is nothing like tribal system as has been observed among caste system. Each tribal group is strictly endogamous. They provided specialise service from within their own specialists.

In tribal stratification ranks are not differentiated at the level of two or more tribal groups. On the contrary in the caste system ran differentiation is observed. In case of tribal stratification we would only observe the inequality among the individual properties of tribe, that is, the properties of individuals in terms of achievements, in education, economy, elite status etc. By tribal stratification we mean differential rank groups such as native groups, economically well off groups, vegetarian, non-vegetarian group, pure-impure blood of origins that is, inter caste marriages signify impure blood of origin, wearing of sacred thread etc. When the members of a tribal group attain specialisation, differentiation in rank, there emerges social stratification. In the Indian context when we discuss tribal stratification, we rank the position held by individual members within the endogamous frame work of the tribes.

## IV

Bastar district of present day Chhattisgarh is dominated by numerous tribal groups, has long been isolated due to geographical barriers and lack of proper communication from the mainstream of India civilisation. Of the total population 72. 77 percent are tribals in the district which includes various sub-groups of the Gond tribe, who possesses their distinct socio-cultural identity. The forest clad Bastar district is the homeland of tribes like the Abujh-Maria, Dandami Maria, Muria, Dorla, Dhurwa, Bhatra and the Halba. According to Grigson (1991 reprinted) the Gond high land are known as meta-koitur and low land as Dor-koitur which indicates this classification is based on geographical situations.

## Muria

It has been observed that the Muria near Jagadalpur are somewhat different in their socio-economic behaviour from Kondagaon-narayanpur area to whom they consider superior in status. Even they try to avoid marital alliance with the Muria of Narayanpur area; perhaps, reason behind such is that the Muria Jagadalpur area are more exposed to modern world that their fellow brethren of Narayanpur. It is also noticeable that here is no Ghotul (youth dormitory) system among the Muria of Jagdalpur area while it is an identifying feature among the Muria of Narayanpur–Antagarh and parts of Kondagaon region. If we consider the social parameter to understand rsocial hierarchy among tribal people o bastar, it is revealed that the Muria occupy the highest position. The indepth study will show that the Muria of Jagadalpur are simply advanced section of the Dandami-Maria or Bison-Horn Maria and use of the Muria identity is simply a process of Sanskritisation or upward social mobility. In gondi Murias are called as koitor. Again, among the Muria there is one section known as Jhoria Muria who are confined usually to northern part, i. . e., south of Kolur pargana, Narainpur, Benur pargana, Kurangal and the plain area villages of Chota Dongar pargana of Antagarh tehsil. Since they have a phratry (bash) system, the alliance takes place only among akemama (wife' clan) group of themselves. It is also observed that though they have a ghotul (Youth dormitory) system but they are very much akin to the Hill Maria in respect of their appearance, clan system (i.e. their clan have their own territory in which clan shrine resides) and clan gods are similar to Hill Matia (or Abuj-Maria), even their festivals are almost similar to these of the Hill Maira. On the contrary, their agricultural practise is highly advanced that that of the Hill Maria. It is also reported that some of their dadabhai (brother's clan) and akomama clan are similar to those of the Hill Maria, they may intermarry with the Hill Maria akomama as per their customary rule but in practise it is not possible due to geographical barrier like hilly terrain. Due to their closeness with the Hill Maria their rank is below that other Muria. The name Jhoria is not ordinarily used now-a-days. It is also found that all koitor in Bastar call themselves as the Muria and raised their social ranks above the Maria.

## Maria

Marias are divided into two halves, viz, whose who like in the hilly terrain are known as the Marhes or Abuj Maria and those who lives in plain area (usually river Indrawati makes the boundary) and south of Indrawati, are known as the Marias/Madias/Dandami Maria (or Bison-Horn Maria). Among these Maria groups Dandami Maria occupy the highest position by virtue of their developed technology of agriculture and absence of ghotul system among them. The emic view of the Hill Maria to the men of plains (including Muria, Jhoria, Muria, Dandami Maria etc. ) or low land are known as Koitor.

### Bhatra

Usually the Bhatras are confined mainly at the north-east corner of Jagadalpur which is adjacent to Jeypore (Orissa). Many among them wear sacred thread, and this right was achieved by their ancestors in the past from the Raja of Bastar in whose feudatory state, Jeypore was also included. The tribe is becoming Hindu caste and divided into three groups, based on purity of their blood, that is, during marriage when one takes women from other tribes, he is regarded as impure. According to their social hierarchy these groups are: (a) Amnit Bhatra or Bade Bhatra, (b) Sargimundi or Majhli Bhatra and (c) Batamundi-Masnimara or Pit Bhatra or Shan Bhatra. Among them Amnit hold the supreme status. The Shan Bhatra holds the lowest status among them and are derogatively called as the Muria Bhatra. Again, on the basis of economic criteria the Sargimundi (who used to depend mainly on Sal tree and its products) and the Batamundi (who used to make bata, that is, reed baskedts, mats etc. ) are differentiated. Each of such group has a number of exogamous tetemistic clans (Sarkar and Dasgupta, 1986). According to their religious faith they are again divided into Jagatlok (those who are followers of traditional religion) and Bhagatlok (those who are converted into bhagar cult and wear saffron colour cloth, eat vegetarian food, devoid of taking liquor and overall lead a simple life). This is a kind of social mobility. The emic view of this section of Bhatra is consumption of vegetarian food has acquired higher social rank that non-vegetarian food among their brethren fellow.

### Dhurwa

The majority of them live in south-east of Jagadalpur. The Dhurwa are originally a section of Parja community, who claims separate identity by abstaining from taking beef from the beef eating Parja. The Bastar Parja beyond the Kolab-Sabari river in Sukma Zamindari Estate and around Mount Tulsidongri in Sukma and Jadgalpur tehsil bordering Jeypore-Koraput of Orissa now identified themselves as the Dhurwa and recend being called the Parja. Infact the name Parja is corrupt Aryan term Praja (means subject) which differs from Raja or ruler. The Dhurwas are bsket makers and their habitats are located in such places where bamboo groove is abundant. Grigson (1991) observed that there was another section of parjas who he termed as peng parjas, were supposed to come with first Raja of Bastar from Warangal but confined to Jeypore Zamindari estate of Orissa which is very adjacent to the present settlement area of Dhurwas of Bastar; infact the river Kolab-Sabari forms the boundary between Orissa and Bastar District of Chhattisgarh

### Dorla

The Dorla is a corrupt form of Dor-Koitor which means the Koitor with low lying habitat. Koitor is a term used by most of the sections of the Gond tribe and this people are also a section of it. The Dor Koitor are regarded as inferior to the Metakoitor or hill koitor, and due to this reason the Dor Koitor changed their name fro Dor Koi to Dorakoi or simply Dora or Dorla. The Telegu Dora means Chief or lord and it is the singular form of Dorlu (Hazra, 1970). They are also identified as Koya in adjacent Andhra Pradesh. They are strictly endogamous with exogamous pratries or bash or gatta.

### Halba

In Bastar they are mainly concentrated towards northern and Central part. It is believed that the Halba are the descendents of old paik militia (Shukla, 1992). It is also believed that they migrated from Warangal of Andhra Pradesh along with first King of Bastar.

It has been observed that they claim superior status over the Ghasia, Mahara, Maria and Gadaba and some other communities. During field investigation it is found that they are divided into two endogamous and territorial divisions namely, Chhattisgarhi and Bastaria. The Bastaria halba are again divided into two endogamous groups viz. Purit or Jat Halba and Surit or Nani Halba. The Purit claim superior status over other, which is based on purity concept, that is, pure blood while the other is admixture of blood of other community. It has been observed that in some occasion at Madhota village the Purit Halba are Sanskritised their way of life by wearing sacred thread.

## V

With the passage of time the tribes are becoming class structures. With the adoption of agriculture by the tribal people for their subsistence, class formation is becoming the only major avenue of social stratification. Agricultural capitalism got accelerated after independence. Simultaneously, there increased the growth of commercial market economy, which is competitive in nature. The subsistence sector among the tribal groups has been changing towards market economy for which they are now inclined towards production of cash crops. The economic disparity among these tribes often creates rank determination.

Both Marxist and non-Marxist-Weberian scholars have analysed the process of tribal stratification. According to non-Marxist approach the process of social differentiation among the tribal groups continuum from tribe to caste. By adopting the attributes of Sanskritisation the tribal groups are achieving the corresponding status of caste (Aurora, 1972; Bailey, 1960, Bose 1947 etc. ).

The Marxist approach on the other argue that the process of tribal differentiation is from tribe to class mainly peasantry. According to them homogeneity of the tribal society is a myth and not reality. The tribe always had some kind of primordial infrastructure of social differentiation. During British regime the feudal India there was gross uneven land distribution among tribes. Therefore, tribal differentiation is not from tribe to caste, rather it is from tribe to class.

From the above discussion it may be concluded that tribal social stratification makes clear that the structural unit of a tribe in our country is altogether different from the structures of caste or class. Conceptually both caste and class are considered as system of groups. On the contrary, tribal groups do not possess any system. Each tribe is an autonomous, endogamous, commensal–kin oriented–clan group. The direction of social stratification among the tribal groups as reported by Singh (1985), Jan Breman (1979) and Pathy (1984) clearly show the induction of agrarian modernisation appears to have taken a firm base among the tribal people. The present authors personally feel that they (i.e., the Bastar tribes) are still in the scale of peasants (Wolf, 1966) but nor farmer. Gradually with the process of modernisation their status from tribal pole to peasant pole is becoming witnessed at the moment. It is also expected in due course that after introduction of massive industrialisation and communication system they will give rise to class structure (in terms of economic point of view) as found among the Dhodias of South Gujarat (Punalekar, 1980).

## References

Aurora, G. S. 1972 *Tribe-Caste-Class encounters,* Hyderabad: Administrative Staff College of India.

Bailey, F. G. 1960 *Tribe-Caste and Nation: A Study of Political Activity and Political Change in Highland Orissa*. Manchester: Manchester University Press.

Bailey, F. G. 1963 "Closed Social Stratification in India, *European Journal of Sociology*, Vol. 4, No. 1.

Bose, N. K. 1947 "Hindu Method of Tribal Absorption", *Man in India*, Vol. 27.

Bose, P. K. 1981 "Stratification Among the Tribals of Gujarat", *Economic and Political Weekly*, February 7, 1981.

Bose, P. K. 1985 *Classes and Class Relation among Tribals of Bengal*, Delhi: Ajanta Publication.

Breman, Jan 1979 *Patronage and Exploitation, Changing Agrarian Relations in South Gujarat* Delhi: India Berkely.

Breman, Jan 1985 *Peasants, Migrants and Paupers*, Delhi: Oxford University Press.

Desai, A. R. 1948 *Social Background of Indian Nationalism*, Bombay: Popular Book Dept.

Desai, A. R. 1977 "Tribes in Transition", in *Tribe Caste, Religion in India* (ed. ) R. Thaper, Delhi: The Macmillan Co. of India.

Grigson, Sir Wilfred 1991 *The Maria Gonds of Bastar*, Calcutta: An. S. I., Memor No. 17. (Reprinted from 1938)

Hazra, D. 1970 *The Dorla of Bastar*, Calcutta: An. S. I., Memoir No. 17.

ICSSR 1985 *Survey of Research in Sociology and Social Anthropology* (1969-1970), 3 Volumes, New Delhi: Satvahan Publications.

Leach, Edmund, R. 1960 (ed. )*Aspects of Caste in South India, Ceylone and North-West Pakistan*, London: Cambridge University Press.

Marriott, Mckim 1965 *Caste Ranking and Community Structure in Five Regions of India and Pakistan*, Poona: Deccan College.

Parsons, Talcott 1954 "An Analytical Approach to the Theory of Social Stratification"., *Essays in Sociological Theory*, Glenco: The Free Press.

Pathy, Jagannath 1984 *Tribal Peasantry: Dynamics of Development*: New Delhi: Inter-India Publication.

Punalekar, S. P. 1980 *Migration and Social Stratification: A Study of Dhodias of Surat City, Surat: Centre for Social Studies* (Mimeographed).

Prasad, R. K. 1975 "Some Aspects of Stratification and Interaction among the Parhaiya of Palamou", *Journal of Social Research*, Vol. 18, No. 1.

Sachchidananda 1964 *Culture Change in Tribal Bihar*, Calcutta.

Sarkar, A. and Samira Dasgupta, 1996 *Spectrum of Tribal Bastar*, Delhi: Agam Kala Prakashan.

Shah, Ghanshyam 1976 *Stratification among the Scheduled Tribes: In the Bharuch and Panch Mahal Districts of Gujarat*, Surat: Centre of Regional Development Studies.

Shah, Ghanshyam 1984 *Economic Differentiation and Tribal Identity*, Delhi: Ajanta Publication.

Sharma, K. L. 1980 *Essays on Social Stratification*, Jaipur: Rawat Publication.

Shukla, H. L. 1992 *History of the People of bastar*, Delhi: Sharda Publication House.

Singh, K. S. 1985 *Tribal Society in India*, New Delhi: Manohar.

Singh, Yogendra 1977 *Social Stratification and Change in India.* Delhi: Manohar.

Singh, Yogendra 1985 *"Sociology of Social Stratification", in Survey of Research in Sociology and Social Anthropology*, Vol. II, ICSSR, Delhi: Satvahan, pp. 43.

Topno, Sem 1970 "Changing Pattern of Munda Personal name", *Eastern Anthropologists*, Vol. 22, No. 2.

Vidyarthi, L. P. 1965 *Cultural Contours of Tribal Bihar*, Calcutta: Punthi Pustak.

Vidyarthi, L. P. 1970 *Rise of Social Science in India: An Anthropological Orientation*, Bombay: Asia Publishing House.

Vidyarthi, L. P. 1971 *Notes on Andaman and Nicobar Islands*, Totus Home.

Wolf, Eric, R. 1966 *Peasants*, New Jersey: Prentice Hall, Inc.

# 7

# Anthropology of Culture of Space among Indian Tribes: Application of Anthropological Knowledge for Community Development

## Prologue

Ever-widening global communication facility often confronts many urbanites as well as country/town planners and architects with task beyond their own cultural environment. This often creates significant problems, since what is accepted in one's own field might be entirely different in other's cultural domain.

The anthropological notion of use of space shows that–in terms of cultural history–the homogenous space concept is varied according to the value system of the community. Now-a-days the country and urban planners have become increasingly aware of the importance of the fact that different cultures show different attitudes in this regard to space.

A set of beliefs, emotional attitudes etc. when practised by a group of people in order to cope with the unknown and unseen problems of his surroundings otherwise termed as Supernatural power, —is identified as religion. Experiences of certain day to day unusual incidents of life in action, disease, death and the unexplainable happening compelled the tribal people believing into other than the material visible world, that is, invisible world of spirits which is idolised by them as Supernatural power. They have established a kind of close relationship between themselves and this power by adjusting themselves to it, chiefly in two ways—first, by overpowering the spirit by some ritual activities and enchanting *mantras* and secondly, by offering puja to placate the power of celestial world for their desired goal.

To our mind *'religion is a phenomenon of social articulation followed by ritual and practices and by practising it one have to feel security from uncertainty as well as feeling of an in-group social bondage, which differs from others. The intricate dependence upon various benevolent and malevolent spirits, which becomes the part and parcel of survival strategy in a particular ecological niche, signifies a kind of belief and dependence towards Supreme Being in the celestial world'*. (Sarkar and Dasgupta, 2011).

The belief system among the tribal people occupies a definite cultural space which is value loaded and deeply enmeshed with the intricate system of social organisation. Space is a physical domain where some action, activities and institutional rites and rituals are performed. The cultural space of religious activities may be termed as '**Inscribedspaces**' (i.e. fundamental relationship between human and environment, Lofgren (1984), again this cultural space is defined by socio-economic status where, one can secure mental and physical stability. According to Radcliffe Brown (1935) religion has been originated just as a means for social survival that is, out of a sense of dependence on it. Singh and Sinha (1991) have observed 'the tribals(the Santal have significantly lower theoretical, political and economic value, they are well-endowed with social, aesthetic, religious and moral values, and their deficiency in scientific zeal and aptitude—the ingredients of theoretical value—are attributed to inherent traditionality, superstitions and orthodoxy'.

Application of this sort of anthropological knowledge is fruitful for community development in rural India.

## Concept of Culture of Space among the Tribes

Increasing global communication facility often confronts many urbanites as well as country/town planners and architects with task beyond their own cultural environment. This often creates significant problems, since what is accepted in one's own field might be entirely different in other's cultural domain. Actually in architectural and planning domain is space, that is to say fundamental differences in the interpretation of space by the planner and urbanites on one side and by the marginalised group of people on the other.

Western architects have firmly established on the modern enlightened concept of homogenous space within certain limits, it can be used freely by the architect/planner. Buildings and other planned elements are often conceived in some geometrical matrix following pragmatically estimated basic human needs.

The anthropological notion of use of space shows that–in terms of cultural history–the homogenous space concept is varied according to the value system of the community. Now-a-days the country and urban planners have become increasingly aware of the importance of the fact that different cultures show different attitudes in this regard to space. But this trend only concerns the acceptance of fundamental cultural differences (due to cultural pluralism) and consequently, emphasises the adaptation of conventional type with its immediate niche. Therefore, one has to take care of value system of the particular ethnic group and only then developmental strategy can be framed. That is, all sort of developmental activities to these marginalised groups should be culture-friendly.

In the light of the discussion above, the present paper highlights on the empirical study on the tribal groups of Bastar of Chhattisgarh and eastern India, consisting of both Chhotanagpur plateau and West Bengal. It suggests that documents of local settlement history in each situation contain codes of structure of settlement, where some earmarked space are expressed on a meta-language level or with some signs-symbols, known as culture of space and it is very much value loaded in one's own culture.

## Empirical Observation

Toto–a mongoloid tribal group of West Bengal living in Totopara village of Madarihat Police Station of Jalpaiguri district. The village is situated at the foothills of the Himalayas and is adjacent to Bhutan border. They are declared as one of the Particularly Vulnerable Tribal Groups (PVTG) by the Government of India

Most of the Toto live in bamboo huts (*sha* or *naiankosa*) built on raised platform (*dui*). One has to climb a single log or tree trunk (*kaibei*) with notches for getting a grip, to reach the platform (*dui*). The log is removed during night. They have only one room in the hut or *sha* and the room is earmarked for some functional cultural space, namely,

(a) Siri–used for sleeping purpose of family members;

(b) Diachiko–siri–This portion of the room is used for guest's sleeping purpose;

(c) Chima–This place is marked for their ancestral deities.

Till date, Toto believes that their god *oda* and *pisu* live in *chima* where they keep a pitcher of *eu* (home brew liquor) and wooden stool as a symbol of their god. The outsiders are tabooed to enter in this sacred area of hut. There is a separate cooking place (*merring*) for *siri* and *daichiko–siri*. The portion below the *siri* and *daichiko–siri* of the house is covered with bamboo and wooden splits and their pig, fowl and other livestock are kept there. Outsiders are not allowed to go to *siri* or touch the *merring* in *siri*. The room is generally 12′ to 15′ in lenghth and 8′–12′ in breadth. Sometimes a small square window is also found in one of the walls. The doors, which open on the bamboo platform, are about 4′ to 5′ high and 2′ to 3′ wide. The projected bamboo platform is about 8′ to 10′ wide running along the whole length in the front. . This serves as their parlour where fuels, domestic utensils etc. are kept as family requirements (Das, 1969, Sarkar, 1993). This platform also functions as a place for gossip, a small family meeting etc. (Sarkar, 1993).

Similarly, Birijia–a least known Particularly Vulnerable Tribal Group (PVTG) of Jharkhand live in forest and for whom environment has a direct bearing on their occupation and consequently on economy. They are chiefly basket weavers, slash and burn cultivators (*beonra*) and collectors and distributed in the hilly and forested terrain of Gumla and Palamou districts of Jharkhand.

According to Dasgupta (1994) the Birjia believe that in very ancient time they used to live in caves. Gradually they have got the idea to live in constructed shelter. They prepared a semi-circular space covered with bamboo splits and thatched with *mahulain* creeper; there was no window or door; it is called *dhako*. The height of *dhako* was so low that one had to crawl to enter. Infront of *dhako,* the open space was used for cooking purpose.

Now a day they construct their houses on the *pat* (table land), *ghat* (hills slopes) and valley of the hills. For making a hut a piece of land is selected and cleaned by removing bushes and the suitability of land for the purpose is ascertained by a supernatural means. Family head or any adult male of the family does this. A small hole is dug in the middle of selected plot that is filled up with water and some rice grains are put to it and the performer utters some *mantras* and observes them. If the rice grains move anti-clock wise or settle down then the indication is negative and thus they reject the spot. If *the* rice grains move clock wise then they think that the place is suitable for making hut.

There is another method of selection of plot. A small hole is dug in the plot and water is poured in it and the place is left for one night. Next morning, if the hole remains wet they think the plot is suitable for making hut. During the tests for selection of plot women are not allowed to stay there. In case of second test also it is done either by the adult male members of the family concerned or by the sacred specialists.

A Birjia house consists of a rectangular shaped main room with a small chamber or *kothli* inside the room. In front of the room, in most of the houses there is a covered or partly covered verandah, which is attached with the main room. There is a cattle shed in a comer of the verandah.

The main room is at least 7 feet to 8 feet high. It has no window. The entrance, in some cases especially in the village of Holang, is generally without door but in some cases is provided with door. The entrance is generally attached to the verandah. An adult with a standard height has to bend down to enter into the room. The low height and slanting frontal part of the roof of the house probably protects themselves from the hot wind. In one comer of the room there is a small chamber or *kothli* separated by a half partition wall with an entrance. This *kothli* is known as *ora bhitar*. The entrance of the verandah attached with the main room is open.

The walls of the houses are constructed either by fixing branches of trees or narrow bamboos in a row. Sometimes the walls are plastered by mud at the outside. Recently, constructed houses have thick mud walls. The walls are plastered time to time by cow dung and black soil paste. The wooden pillars on the verandah support the roof of the house. The structure of the roof is made of split wood or bamboo splits and thatched either by the *kher* (a kind of jungle grass) or *khapra* (burnt tile) made by them from local soil are placed over the frame. If there is any door, it is in most cases made by neatly woven bamboo splits in a frame. It is known as *chata*. But in Harup and Range villages there are a few houses having wooden doors attached with the entrance. In case of *chata* it is either locked with the thread made of grass fiber or some wooden piece. The entrance of a house usually faces either east or south. There is a provision to lock the door both from inside and outside. The floor of the hut is built with mud.

Mostly the main room of the house is usually used for sleeping and relaxing purposes. They also keep their clothes, grains, implements etc., in it. The *ora bhitar* is a sacred place, as there is the altar for their ancestors. It is the place for ancestor worship. No outsider is allowed to enter into *ora bhitar.* They also keep their stored grains in *ora bhitar.* A person has to pass through the verandah to enter into the main room. A corner of the verandah is used for cooking purpose. They a1so keep musical instruments, fire-wood, basket making implements in the verandah. The place is a1so sometimes used for sleeping purpose. If there is no verandah attached with the main room, they cook their food either inside the room, or outside, in front of the room.

The articles required for the construction of a house are collected from jungle. The male members collect wooden log and bamboo from jungle. The women collect the *kher*. During construction of a house a used burnt *handi* (pitcher) is kept upside down on the newly built wall. They believe that it protects the home under construction from evil eyes of the spirits. The men do the heavy jobs in the construction of a house while the women do light jobs like carrying mud and water. They water the newly built walls.

The Birjia neighbours and kins, helping a Birjia family in constructing house, are fed by two meals daily till the end of work. They are also offered *hanria* (ricebeer). No other remuneration is given to them. This mutual cooperation among them is usually practised.

Behind a house, a kitchen garden, known as *bari* is common among them. The area is fenced by bamboo split and dried up prickly herbs. Generally maize, mustard, vegetables etc., are grown here.

Before entering into a newly constructed house they perform *ora puja.* The date is fixed after they can arrange the money for the puja. On the day of *ora puja* they bring a new *ghalia* (an urn made of clay). After taking bath they keep the *ghaila* turning up-side down. A small quantity of *aroa* (sundried) rice is kept upon it, which is allowed to consume either by a black *chengna* (chicken) or a piglet. They then sacrifice that chicken or the piglet offering to the ancestors telling them 'Oh my forefathers, we are entering into the new house. We are living in the way, which you have shown to us. We observe all the rituals and customs of our own. So be pleased with us and protect us from all the evil spirits. By the blood of the sacrificed animal a *tika,* (mark) is put on the forehead of the wife of the head of the family. The members of the house perform the puja. The women cook the rice and the meat separately. The sacrificed animal is eaten only by the male members and married women of the family. The assembled kins, neighbours and their unmarried and married daughters take food in their house, which is cooked separately outside the *ora bhitar.* The sacrificial meat and rice is known as *sirni.* The male members and the married women of the family eat entire sirni. The place where the *sirni* is taken is cleaned and plastered with mud. All persons then come out of the house and drink *hanria* sitting in front of the house. After performing *ora puja* they can start to live in the new house.

The empirical data collected from Bison Horn Maria or Dandami Maria of Bastar, Chhattisgarh also reveals that in comparison to Abujh Maria or Hill Maria of Bastar, the Bison-Horn Maria villages like Bastarnar, Kilepal, Burnmpal and Bada Bachali are thickly populated. . Each villager likes to have a large *bari* or kitchen garden enclosure at the back of his house where he can grow tobacco, maize, chillies, tomatoes, sesamum and can also pen his cattle for the sake of manure. The each *parish* (phratry) among the Bison Horn Maria is still said to be the *bhum* (earth) of the clan who first settled there, though there are also other clan members' houses and wife-clans (*akomama* group of clans) from whom the first settlers and their descendents have taken wives. (Grigson, 1991, reprinted). Their houses instead of parallel to the village street are usually at right angles to it and a double row houses, one on each side of the street which resulted the houses are too close to each other to allow each house to have its *bari* land behind it due to such some householders must have their *bari* opposite them across the street. Each *bari* is fenced with bamboo wattle work. The houses of the clan in the village are usually all together in one group, i.e., in clusters while there are separate clan groups in other parts of village with whom marital alliance can takes place. It is also observed that there is no separate *kurma-lon* or menstruation hut among them like Abujh Maria tribe of their neighbour.

**Rough Ground Plan of a Bison Horn Maria House**

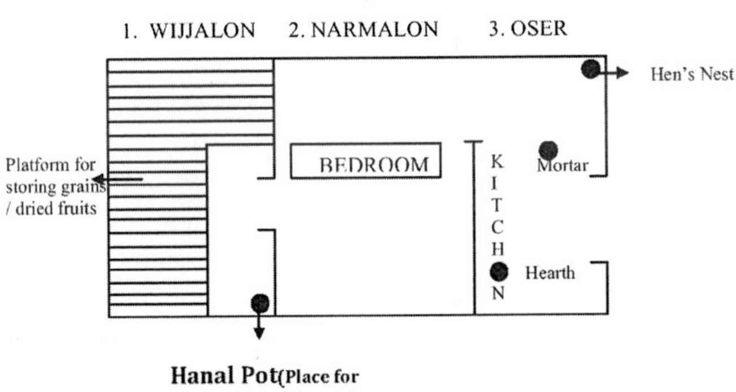

From the above rough sketch of Bison Horn Maria House ground plan it is evident that it is chiefly divided into three halves–(a) *wijja-lon* (Seed house) in the rear and the middle of the house is used as bedroom known as *narma-lon* which is made first and then the *oser* (verandah) is constructed with low height. They thatch the house with forest grasses or pieces of small stone slab, which are locally available (Sarkar and Choudhury, 2013 ).

The *narma-lon* is a sleeping room for women and small children and household goods and utensils are usually kept there. Oser is the place for the cooking hearth and *ahki* mortar holes in which grains is husked with *musal* pestle, hen's nests, water pots, leaves for plates etc. It was also found that when intoxicating *landa* (an intoxicating gruel made from rice and millet (*Eleusine coracana*)) gruel is under brew, it is kept usually in the cooler and darker portion of the house, that is, either at *narma-lon* or *wijja-lon*. In the *wijja-lon* area there is a place for *hanal* pot, which is very sacred to them where outsider's entry is strictly tabooed and it is sacred place for ancestral soul.

**Discussion**

It appears from the empirical observations stated above from various tribal situations that such portrayals are accurate. In each situation it is found that as per value system they have not only constructed their houses but some spaces are earmarked for specific cultural function. The widespread occurrence of this pattern i.e. cultural space, points to the considerable symbolic significance of the culture distinction. It is also observed especially among Bison-Horn Maria of Bastar that wherever their society is divided into social classes, the upper ranks of the hierarchy appropriate to themselves symbols of disembodiment, thereby separating themselves from the physical set-up while, they leave the lower ranks of the hierarchy in varying degrees of association with corporality and nature (Barrett, 1991). It is also observed that tribal people are very much involved and associated with signs and symbols known as meta language and that too are applied in their house architecture and functional space of the house according to their value system. This type of application of Meta language level is identified by Victor Turner as "**Social Outsiderhood**" (Turner, 1974).

With the help of actor oriented perspective or emic approach the main thrust for tribal housing development is to understand the native categories of thought process and to know how the natives divide up their social-natural universe. Here the anthropologist tries to peer inside the culture to determine how that world appears from the native's eye. Malinowski (1922) expressed, "this goal is, briefly, to grasp the native's point of view, his relation to life to realise his vision of his world". Such a goal is reflected beautifully in Evans-Pritchard's (1937) account of Azande Witchcraft in which the author skillfully translates native taxonomy and worldview into the language of his audience. Therefore, it can be concluded that for any development programme in the tribal area one should consider native's cognition and value system.

## References

Barrett, Richard A. 1991 Culture Conduct: An Excursion in Anthropology, California: Wadsworth Publishing Company.

Das Amal K. 1969 The Totos, Calcutta: Scheduled Castes and Tribes Welfare Dept. Govt. Of West Bengal.

Dasgupta Samira 1994 Birjia: Society and Culture, Calcutta: Firma KLM Pvt. Ltd.

Evans–Pritchard, E. E. 1937 Witchcraft, Oracles and Magic among the Azande. Oxford: At the Clarendon Press.

Grigson, Sir Wilfrid 1991 The Maria Gonds of Bastar, Delhi: Vanya Prakashan and Oxford University Press (reprinted).

Lofgren, Orvar 1984 The Sweetness of Home: Class,Culture and Family life in Sweden, Ethnologica Europea, XIV: 44-64.

Malinowski Bronislaw 1922 Argonauts of the Western Pacific, New York: Dutton.

Radcliffe Brown, A. R. 1935 On the Concept of Functionalism in the Social Sciences', American anthropologist, Vol. 37.

Sarkar, Amitabha 1993 Toto Society and Change: A Sub-Himalayan Tribe of West Bengal, Calcutta: Firma KLM Pvt. Ltd.

Sarkar, Amitabha and Samira Dasgupta 2011 Mal Paharia Culture at the Crossroad, New Delhi: Agam Kala Prakashan.

Sarkar, Amitabha and Pijush Choudhury 2013 "A Study of Traditional Wisdom among Bison Horn Maria of Bastar", in Traditional Wisdom and Sustainable Living: A Study on the Indian Tribal societies (ed) by Hrishikesh Mandal and Amitabha Sarkar, New Delhi : Anthropological Survey of India and Gyan Publishing House.

Singh. L. B. 1991 "The Tribal Pattern: A Case Study of and the Santals", in Tribal Thoughts and Balanand Sinha Culture:Essays in Honour of Surajit Chandra Sinha, ed. Baidyanath Saraswati, New Delhi: Concept Publishing Company.

Turner, Victor W. 1974 Dramas, Fields and Metaphors: Symbolic Action in Human Society. Ithaca: Cornell University Press.

# 8

# Conceptual Approaches to the Study in Cultural Ecology

Culture and environment plays a significant symbiotic role for human adaptation. Majority of Indian tribes are nurtured in forest environment. The wild flowers blossom infusing the air with their sweet enchanting smell. The tribals are born in the forest, grow in the forest and also die in the forest. Infact forests govern their way of life and culture. Quite naturally indigenous ecological knowledge system is embedded in such human population who is working out his survival strategy and existence from such ecological niche for his sustenance. The ecological survival of the Indian subcontinent is ultimately linked to the preservation of forest; more than 80 million tribal people of India are still dwelling in the forest.

Before going into detail let us describe the development of the school of cultural adaptation through ecological anthropology.

## II

Human ecology, broadly speaking as the study of human interactions with the environment.

In this discussion alternative conceptual models of human relations with the environment are being described in the historical order in which they have appeared in the scientific literature.

Although largely described among social scientists, classical and early modern theories of environmental influence on human affairs i.e. **determinism**and **possibilism**, are often employed by historians like Arnold J. Toynbee, who advocates a possibilist stance in his book—-*A Study of History*.

The **model of Cultural ecology** proposed by Julian Steward is still the guiding paradigm for many among us but in recent years it has been challenged by the **Ecosystem-based model** first proposed by Andrew P. Vayda and Roy A. Rappaport.

The individual making characteristic is the focus of **Actor-based model** of human ecology and the **systems model of human ecology** stresses investigation of interaction between human social systems and ecosystems based on their reciprocal exchange of energy, materials and information (i.e. the human social system is seen as being linked to its ecosystem through the interchange of energy, materials and information).

**III**

## Origin of Human Ecology

- Since early days there have been many attempts to explain events in terms of environmental influences on human behaviour. Astrology represents one early system of thought relating impact of environmental forces i.e. stars/planet, to human actions.
- With modern scientific thought the ancient Greek Philosophers recognised that man was both influenced by nature and a force for change in the environment. It was suggested, for example, that the different forms of political organisation of the Greek city states and the eastern empires reflected the influence of climate on the personalities of their citizens.
- This theme later was developed by **Montesquieu** and other French writers of the Enlightment and advocated in recent times by the American Geographer **Samuel Huntington**.
- The ecological **Catastrophe writing**during **1880's by George P. Marsh, entitled 'Man and Nature or, Physical Geography as Modified by Human Action'.**
- It was only with the development of geography and anthropology as scientific disciplines in the later part nineteenth century that human/cultural ecology became the subject of systemic study. The first theoretical approach is Environmental determinism.

## IV

Ecological anthropology may be defined as the study of the relations among the population dynamics, social organisations and culture of human population and the environment which they live in (Orlove, 1980). "It presents the development of ecological anthropology, not as a smooth accumulation of information and insights, but as a series of stages" (Orlove, 1980). "The first stage is characterised by the work of Steward and White, the second is termed neo-functionalism and neo-evolutionism and third one is called processual ecological anthropology" (Orlove, 1980).

The German-Austrian continental diffusionists are considered superior to British School in their outlook, methodology and ideology. Freidrich Ratzel was one of such scholars in German School. He was basically zoologist but soon he turned towards geography and then to anthropology. He wrote many volumes on anthropo-geography. German School of diffusion owes its origin to Ratzel. He made a clear-cut distinction between territorial geography and social geography, which he called as anthropo-geography. According to him, environment plays an important adaptive role. He was nevertheless convinced that people were more influenced by one another than by factors of climate and terrain.

"Anthropologists in America led by Boas questioned the unilinearity of the evolutionary thought and the assumption of progress inherent in evolution". (*ibid*, 1980). The American diffusionists received the idea from their German friends and, therefore, it is said that in the American Culture Area Theory of diffusion was influenced by the Museum Methodology of German School of Diffusion. Boas, the father of American ethnology, was born and educated in Germany. German diffusionists were followers of Cultural Circle School or Cultural Historic School, talked about complex form of diffusion of culture but they failed to explain as to why diffusion took place. Here American diffusionists attempted to solve this question. On the basis of empirical researches, they discredited the universal sequences established by the classical evolutionists. They were of view that the empirical researches were evident to refer to that give and take of culture traits and culture complex had taken place through the medium of transport and communication. In order to show the diffusion of cultural traits and complexes, the American diffusionists devised a methodology known as culture area approach. They did not analyse cultural diffusion prevalent all over the world at the same time; instead, they divided the world into different cultural areas on the basis of geographical regions. They were of the opinion that geographical aspects of culture could not be ignored in the study of culture area. Thus, according to them, the concept of culture area reveals geographical area of cultural similarities. Under the influence of geographical categories, the

American Museum of Natural History, New York and the Field Museum, Chicago decided simultaneously to use geographical categories instead of evolutionary trends in the museum, in order to get better insight by the museum visitors. The teachers of Boas were trained physicists and mathematicians from whom he learnt many theoretical concepts and applied them in anthropological field. He joined an arctic expedition of Baffinland, North America, as a geographer in 1883-84. With the passage of time, a definite central theme "historical particularism" has come to be associated with Boasion period.

The scholars accepted the interest in cultural process and change but looked more prudently for details of each case of cultural change, examining whether traits were diffused or independently invented and how they were reworked by each culture that adopted them. The school that they formed was named historical particularism. In fact, ecological anthropology emerged from the Boasian School of Historical Particularism.

Steward's work in ecological anthropology due to contact with noted geographer Carl Sauer led him to examine the effect of environment on culture. His method of cultural ecology signifies materialist emphasis. This method entails the study of the relation between certain feature of the environment and certain traits of the culture possessed by the people living in that environment. Within the environment, Steward emphasised the quality, quantity and distribution of resources. The aspects of culture that he examined most closely were technology, economic arrangements, social organisation and demography, although he also included other aspects. Steward stressed the fact that the environment influenced only certain elements of a culture, which he termed the 'culture-core'.

"Leslie White's relation to Boasian tradition was somewhat different. White shared Steward's emphasis on culture as the unit of analysis and his interest in cultural evolution, his partitioning of culture into technological, social and ideological components gave him a materialist stance generally similar to Steward's. White was more concerned with the broad details of evolution than with specific adaptations, however, he also directed relatively little attention to the influence of environment on particular cultures. Instead he emphasised levels of energy use as the determinant of cultural evolution" (Orlove, 1980).

There are certain fundamental differences in the approaches of White and Steward. The former may be called universal evolutionist who defined cultural evolution culturally (and not biologically) while the later was a multilinear evolutionist who adopted a functional approach to comprehend the interrelationship of ecology, technology and other aspects of culture. White's primary thrust has been on 'technology' whereas Steward's major emphasis has been on 'ecology'. Nevertheless, both represent an American trend to reconsider the importance of evolutionism in the post-1935 era.

In the second stage of ecological anthropology there are two main trends: (i) the neo-evolutionists claiming both White and Steward's to be correct and (ii) the neo-functionalists claiming that they were both wrong.

The neo-functionalists established a series of evolutionary stages and used the notions of specific and general evolution to accommodate Steward's method of cultural ecology to White's work on unilinear evolution (*ibid*, 1980).

Marvin Harris and the early work of Andrew Vayda and Roy Rappaport represent the neo-functionalist school. The term 'neo-functionalism' signifies "the social organisation and culture of specific populations as functional adaptations which permit the populations to exploit their environments successfully without exceeding their carrying capacity" (*ibid*, 1980). "In general, neo-functionalists explain specific aspects of social organisation and culture in terms of functions which they serve in adapting local populations to their environments" (*ibid*, 1980).

Both neo-evolutionists and neo-functionalists have examined the mechanisms which link social structure and culture to the environment.

Apart from the neo-evolutionist and neo-functionalist schools, a different approach in the arena of ecological anthropology has begun to emerge. This work will be called "processual ecological anthropology". The use of the term "process" refers to the importance of diachronic studies in ecological anthropology and to the need to examine mechanism of change. The term "processual ecological anthropology" signifying current developments in the field does appear to be new. Important trends are: (a) the examination of the relation of demographic variables and production system, (b) the response of populations to environmental stress, (c) the formation and consolidation of adaptive strategies which follow Barth's early work on the use of the concept of the niche, and (iv) new work in Marxism, including the emerging interest of anthropologists in political economy and structural Marxism (Orlove, 1980).

A number of comprehensive treatments of environmental thinking in anthropology and the environment vs. culture controversy have been compiled by cultural anthropologists who have found that an ecological approach is fruitful both in research and teaching (Anderson, 1973; Hardesty, 1977, Vayda and Rappaport, 1968). The framework for these reviews has been provided by some contrasting major schools of thoughts or conceptual approaches, viz., environmental determinism, environmental possibilism, cultural ecology of Steward, and current ecological anthropology including actor-based model, eco-system-based model, ethno-ecology and systems-ecology model, etc.

### Environmental Determinism

In this concept, it is said that environment of a particular area determines its culture directly. The founders of this concept are Ratzel (1889), Semple (1911), et. al. They all believed that humans were completely the product of their environment that is, human culture and behaviour were caused directly by environmental influences. For example, the British were a nation of seafarers because they were an Island dwelling community surrounded by seas; the Arabs were monotheistic Muslims because living in the vast empty desert turned their minds towards a single God; the Eskimos were primitive nomads because the harsh conditions of their arctic habitat forbade their development into a complex civilisation and so on.

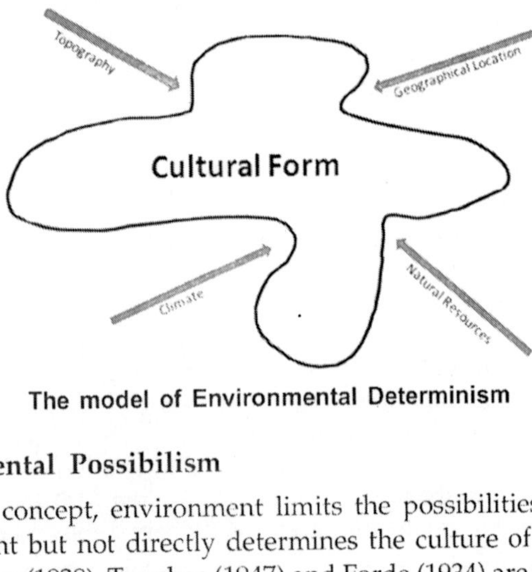


**The model of Environmental Determinism**

### Environmental Possibilism

In this concept, environment limits the possibilities of cultural development but not directly determines the culture of a particular area. Kroeber (1939), Toynbee (1947) and Forde (1934) are the believers of this thought.

Its proponents asserted that while the environment did not directly cause specific cultural developments, the presence or absence of specific environmental factors placed limits on such developments by either permitting or forbidding their occurrence. Thus Island peoples could be seafarers but residents of Inner–Mongolia could not be ; inhabitants of temperate regions might practice agriculture, but those living in arctic latitudes could not. The value of the possibilist approach was perhaps best cited by the American Anthropologist A. L. Kroeber who showed that the Indians of northwestern North America could not adapt maize cultivation from their southern neighbours because the frost-free growing season in their region was shorter than the four months required time for the maize plant to attain maturity. Their environment thus limited the ability of their culture to evolve into an agricultural direction.

The British Anthropologist Daryll Forde concluded in his book – *Habitat, Economy and Society (1934)*,which was perhaps the last major scientific exploration of Possibilism, "between the physical environment and human activity there is always a middle term, a collection of specific objectives and values, a body of knowledge and belief, in other words, a cultural pattern".

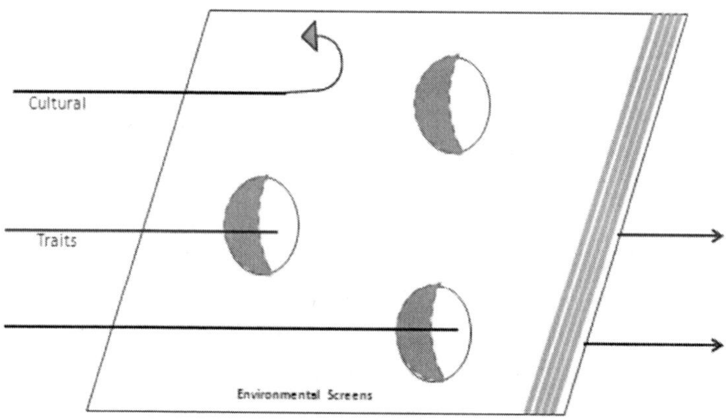


**The Model of Environmental Possibilism**

## The Concept of Culture Ecology

The founder of the concept is Steward (1955). Ecological anthropology emerged from Boasian school of historical particularism. According to Steward, the interaction between environment and technology is related with the core of culture, which includes the population structure, economy, and socio-political structure. Before Steward, all the scientists used to limit their concept on the material culture. Geertz (1963) and Harris (1966) also followed the model of cultural ecology developed by Steward.

(**According to Steward *Culture Core means those feature of a culture that are most closely related to subsistence*).

Steward's experience of field work among the shoshone hunters and gatherers in the Great Basin of North America had led him to recognise that ecological adaptation had played at least as significant a role as diffusion in the formation of Shoshone culture. It was Steward's view that not all aspects of Shoshone culture, could be explained in ecological terms –many traits were present as simply the accidental result of diffusion from neighbouring tribes—but that only some elements, which he labeled as 'Culture Core', had adaptive significance. He gave special emphasis to the relationship between technology and the environment in his model of Cultural ecology.

The implicit feed-back conception in this concept –"how the adaptation to the physical environment had an influence on other features of culture and to determine whether similar adjustments occur in similar environments and to trace these historically through a succession of very unlike periods".

Therefore, the method of cultural ecology then involved the analysis of :

1. The inter-relationship between environment and exploitative or productive technology.
2. The inter-relationship between "behaviour" patterns and exploitative technology.
3. The extent to which those "behaviour" patterns affect other sectors of culture.

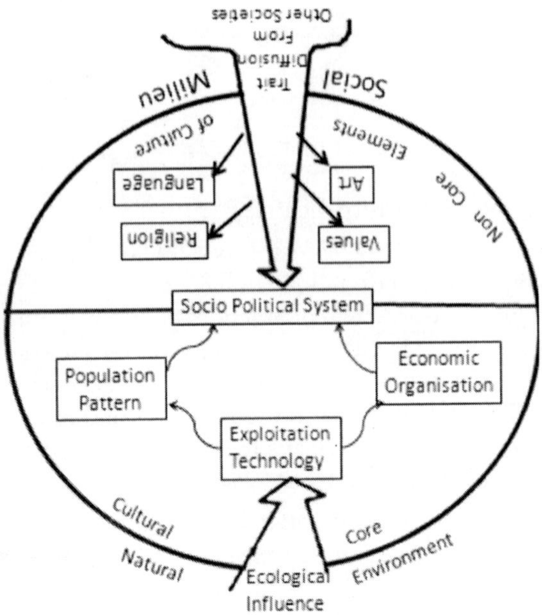


**The Model of Cultural Ecology**

Andrew Vayda and Roy Rappaport (1968) while recognising the importance of Steward's contribution, have criticised his approach as being inadequate.

Cultural Ecosystemicism by Geertz, Clifford (1963) influenced many cultural ecologist and prehistory. Here interdependence of culture and physical factors is the primary postulate.

Cultural Ecosystemicism by Geertz, Clifford (1963) approach influenced many cultural ecologist and prehistory. Here interdependence of culture and physical factors is the primary postulate.

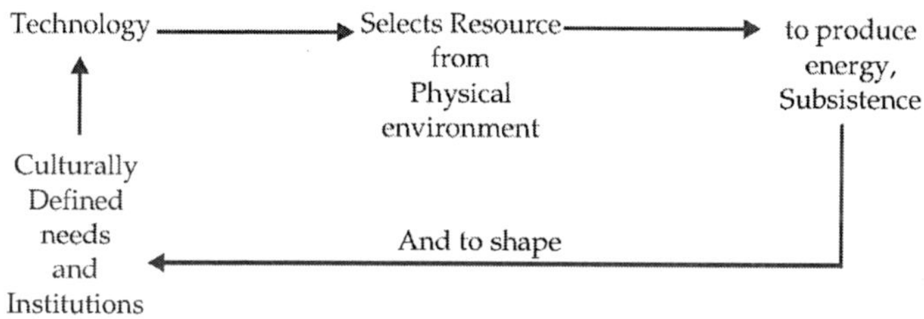


The fundamental weakness of the concept of the cultural ecology is revealed in the work of Marvin Harris—an American anthropologist who has incorporated this approach into studies of what he refers as ' techno-environmental determinism', meaning, technological means of adaptation to the environment is the prime mover of cultural evolution. In his paper "The Cultural Ecology of India's Sacred Cattle" (1966). Harris argues that, contrary to the accepted view that Hindus keep excessive numbers of useless cattle because of their religious belief that cattle are sacred, these cows are actually extremely important to the economic welfare of the poor peasants, helping them to make maximum use of the scarce resources of their environment. Therefore, he concludes, the religious beliefs must have been caused by techno-environmental factors.

## Ecosystem-based Model

Vayda (1968, 1969) and Rappaport (1968) suggested that instead of studying how cultures are adapted to the environment, attention should be focused on the relationship of specific human population to specific ecosystem. In their view, human beings constitute simply another population among the many populations of plants and animal species that interact with each other with the non-living components (climate, soil, water) of their local ecosystem. Thus, the ecosystem, rather than culture, constitutes the fundamental unit of analysis in their conceptual framework for human ecology.

**Ecosystem-based Model**

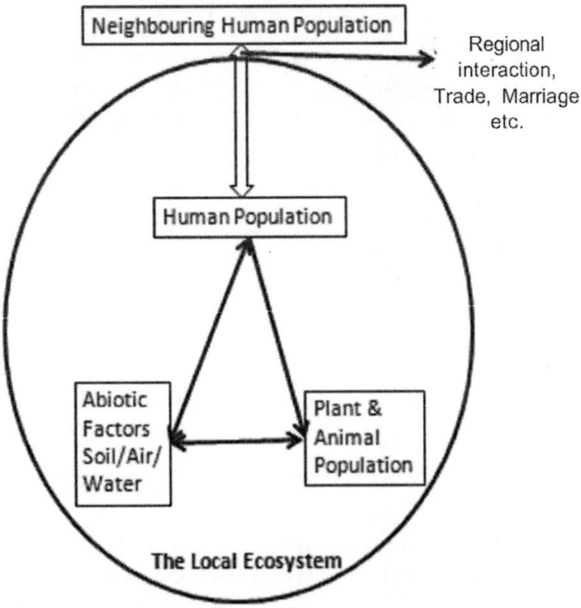


The ecosystem based model of human ecology is illustrated by Roy Rappaport's well known book— *Pigs for the Ancestors* (1968) in which he attempted to demonstrate how the religious rituals practiced by the Tsembaga tribal group of New Guinea functioned to maintain their population in balance with the available resources of their environment. Religion, an institution that Steward had largely excluded from his concept of ecologically adaptive cultural core, was seen by Rappaport as playing a key regulatory role in relations between the Tsembaga population and the other components of their eco-system.

## Actor-based Model

The adaptation occurs primarily at the individual level rather than at the level of group, population and social system. The founder of this model is Benjamin Orlove (1980). This model emphasised the process by which the people make decision about how to interact with their environment.

In the case of human society, environmental adaptation is seen as occurring not as the result of natural selection on the cultural or social system level but rather as the result of the thousands of individual decisions about how best to interact with the environment. Individuals are assumed to be making choices constantly about how to exploit available resources while coping with environmental hazards. Those who make the "correct " choices will survive and prosper ; those who choose less wisely will be selected against.

**Actor-based Model**

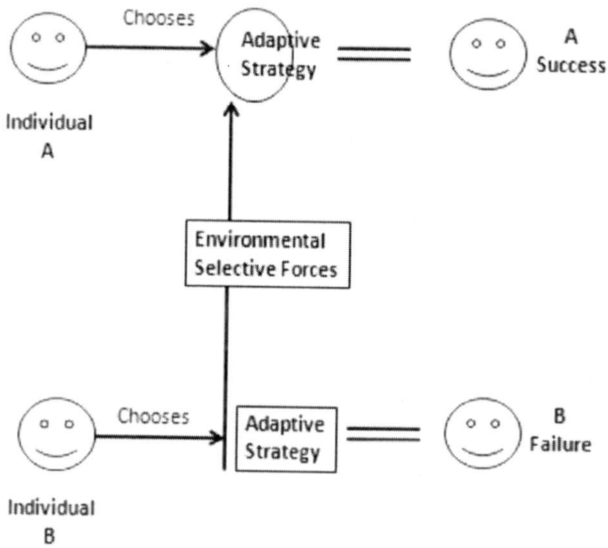


The actor-based model of human ecology is thus one of limited applicability. It can reveal a great deal about why individuals within a particular social system make the particular choices about interactions with the environment that they do, but cannot explain why their social system presents them with particular choices it does. Hence, System Model of human ecological approach emerged.

## System Model

A major scientific development in recent years has been the formulation of "General System Theory", which is concerned with the general properties of the structures and functions of systems as such rather than with their specific contents; adaptation and selection through interaction between ecosystem and social systems (Greetz, 1963; Rambo, 1983). Ecosystem includes water, soil, climate, flora, fauna, fish, pet livestock, crops, trees etc, and social system includes social organisation, nutrition, health, population, technology, economy, religious values, language etc. In the system model of human ecology, both the social system and the ecosystem with which the population interacts retain their integrity as systems, with each changing its structural configuration according to its internal dynamics.

## System Model

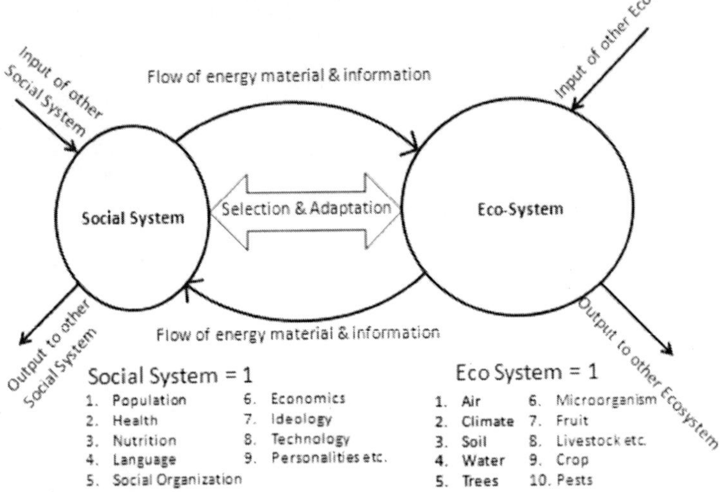


Geertz believes that the concept of the ecosystem or ecological system is the constant interplay between culture, biology, and environment. Theoretically, the ecological system is a dynamic set of relationships between living and non-living things through which energy flows and materials cycle and because of which other problems of survival are worked out.

Thus, System ecology is the study of systemic relationship between living and non-living things.

### Ethno-ecology

The differences between the approach and philosophy adopted by ethno-ecology and by systems ecology orientation in anthropology are so great as to make it appear, perhaps, inappropriate to discuss them under the same heading. Ethno-ecologist has produced detailed and excellent data on how people in different societies categorise their environment (Conklin, 1954; Frake, 1962). Vayda and Rappaport (1968) also are in favour of an ethno-ecological approach. Ethno-ecology is essentially a research strategy and a number of anthropologists who have used an etic and systematic theoretical orientation have sought to introduce rigour into their fieldwork by adopting in part an ethno-ecological approach (Knight, 1974).

### New Ethnography

In the post-1950 era, the anthropologists have been more interested in cognitive anthropology or structural anthropology or new ethnography. The major thrust has been to understand the structure of the culture and to know about the cognitive structuring of the culture. In the formation of culture or the structure of the culture, geography has influenced immensely and therefore, a thorough assessment of cognitive aspect of ecology has been found to be useful for the study of culture. In this, the new ethnography has relied more on the insiders cognition than an outsiders interpretation. This often is called as ethno-science.

## References

Ellen, Roy 1982 Environment, Subsistence and System:: The Ecology of Small Scale Social Formation, Cambridge: Cambridge University Press.

Hardesty, D. L. 1977. Ecological Anthropology, New York: John Wiley and Sons.

Rambo, A. Terry 1983 "Conceptual Approaches to Human Ecology", Research Report, No. 14, Honolulu Hawaii: East-West Environment and Policy Institute.

Sarkar, Amitabha and Samira Dasgupta, 2000. Ethno-Ecology of Indian Tribes: Diversity in Cultural Adaptation, Jaipur and New Delhi: Rawat Publications.

# 9

# Anthropological Research in Ethnosciences—The Indian Scenario

## Prologue

The indigenous ecological knowledge system is embedded in such ethnic groups who are eking out their survival strategy and existence from such ecological niche for their survival and sustenance. Majority of Indian tribal groups are nurtured in forest environment and their life and culture is accordingly fostered by it. Indigenous ecological knowledge is more focus-oriented New ethnography where cognitive aspects of structures of culture in relation to its environment is understood, that is, folk taxonomy where application of traditional knowledge system is acquired over generations, one of the tools becomes of survival strategy. The present discussion highlights the Sundarban situation where Chhotanagpur tribal groups,the immigrant ethnic groups, adapted to the local condition for survival. It also closely focuses on a tribal group—Abujh Maria of Bastar, presently in Chhattishgarh state, have depended upon their immediate geographical environment not only for livelihood but also for various aspects of their life. For example, to recover from illness they make use of environmental resources, the knowledge of which ia a gift from their time-honoured interaction with nature.

## Introduction

Culture and environment plays a significant symbiotic role for human adaptation. Majority of Indian tribes are nurtured in forest environment. The wild flowers blossom infusing the air with their enchanting sweet smell. The tribals are born in the forest, grow in the forest and also die in the forest. Infact, forests govern their way of life and culture. Quite naturally indigenous ecological knowledge system is embedded in such human population who is eking out his survival strategy and existence from such ecological niche for his survival and sustenance. The ecological survival of the Indian subcontinent is ultimately linked to the preservation of forest; more than 80 million tribal people of India are still dwelling in the forest.

## II

It is already stated earlier that indigenous ecological knowledge is more focused oriented new ethnography where cognitive aspect of structure of culture in relation to its environment/geography is understand, that is, in other words folk taxonomy is the major thrust of understanding, where the traditional knowledge is embedded which is acquired over generation and here lies the adaptive strategy for survival. Now in the following lines examples from Indian situation is being presented.

### Sundarban situation

It is reported that in the Sundarban forest –every moment is full of insecurity and uncertainty. Even then the people of Sundarban are not afraid of going into the forest for collection of honey and cutting of fuel wood. It is astonishing to observe that tribal people like the Munda, Oraon, and Bhumij from Chhotanagpur plateau or Mayurbhanj of Orissa have not only adapted their life and culture but also acquired such wisdom, which are the distinctive trait for the Sundarbans region only.

### Application of Indigenous Ecological knowledge for sustenance

It is reported that honey collection is a seasonal operation that starts from the month of *chaitra* (March-April) and continues atleast for three months. With the end of the season of neem flower it is the time when the beehives are steeped in honey, as all the flowering trees are full with bloom. The *mouleys* locate the beehives, tracing the velocity of the northerly wind. Mauley is a group people specialised for honey collection. They collect *hental* (*Phoenix paludosa Roxb*) leaves to use as broom and put on *chappals* and shoes during collection. For collection of honey, they set fire to the mixture of the dried and fresh *hental* leaves and the smoke of the burnt leaves drives the bees are driven away. After setting fire they hold it in favour of wind. The rising smoke reaches the honeycomb, and drives the bees off to make it easy for the mauleys to collect the honey.

Whenever they dig out any tuber from the earth, they do not uproot the whole portion of it. They always leave the stump to grow and sprout in future again.

**Use of Traditional Knowledge for Fishing**

| *Name of the fishing net* | *Name of catches* | *Nature of water etc.* |
|---|---|---|
| 1. Benti Jal | Chapra Prawn, Small fish (chuno fish) | Found in low water near sand-bank |
| 2. Char pata Jal | Bhetki, Phansa | Coastline of mangrove and sand bank |
| 3. Khal Pata | Chapra prawn, Chuno fish, Betki, Datney, Kan fish, Payra toil | Where estuary of river becomes dry |
| 4. Kumo Jal | Kan, Payratoli, Bhetki, Koibhol | Different trees twigs are used in covering the area for catching fish |
| 5. Kalsi Jal | Bhetki, Jawa bhetki, Payra Datney | Nets are tied with big tree on both sides of creeks or rivers. |
| 6. Monofil Jal | Khayra, Parsey, Prawn (big size) | With the help of bamboo fishing nets are spread over the creeks and canals and rivers |
| 7. Galsa Jal | Sheley, Jawa, Bhetki, Bhola (big size) | Nets are spread in the water with the help of *gorapi* (made of iron and used as anchor) where current in the river is found. |
| 8. Bhesal Jal | Chapra Prawn, Parsey, Phansa. | Use search light in the boat that attracts shoal of fish. Nets are then spread from inside water. |
| 9. Khepla Jal | Prawn, Parsey, Phansa and various small fishes (chuno fish) | Nets are thrown from ground in knee deep river water. |
| 10. Don Barsi Jal | Thorny fishes like Mochan, Medh, Kan, Sheley, Murali etc. | For deep water. Use bait in fishing hook, where prawn, loteh or nereh, sita pati etc. fishes are used as baits. |

It is observed that young bamboos shoots are a delicious item to them. Often they cover the young bamboo shoots with an earthen pitcher, locally known as *handi*. The bamboo shoot grows in circular fashion inside the *handi*, which looks like a cabbage. Though it is a delicious item even then they avoid taking it as it hampers in the growth of bamboo.

During our field investigation it is found that the fisher folk of the Sundarbans use various kinds of net depending on: (a) nature of catch, (b) depth of water, (c) colour of water and (d) bubbles created by a shoal of fish in the water etc. It is reported by the groups of fisher folk at Gosaba of Sundarban that following nets are used for various types of catches.

During both full moon and new moon day, the intensity of tide and ebb is very high. The tide on these two days is called *kotal*. The *kotal* on the full moon day is regarded as a *madi* or female *kotal* and that of the new moon day is called as *madda* or male *kotal*. The force or intensity of the male *kotal* is more than a female *kotal*. There is a myth behind it. It is told that the female *kotal* wants to run away from male *kotal* who runs behind to catch hold of her. The effect of the *kotals* is continued till next three to five days. After that it gradually wanes to a minimum. The tide with lesser force is called as *marani* tide and *marani* ebb. Catching of crab also depends on nature of *kotal*. The crabs come with the tidal water towards the bank of the river, locally called as *khari* and they take shelter in the holes of the riverside. After sometime during the ebb they dig out the crab by an iron stick. Often it is observed that they hang a small fish (*chunomach*) tied in a thread, attached with a stick or a branch of twig by the side of the river, very close to a hole. When a crab gets attracted and comes out of hole, it gets caught. There are various types of crabs depending on nature of *Kotal* as well as *tithi* (determined through almanac), such as *tele, chiti, nona and hero* etc. Among these *chiti* crabs grow more in summer, the *tele* variety is found during monsoon while *nona* and *hero* crabs are available throughout the year in the rivers.

According to the inhabitants of Sundarban villages there are chiefly three seasons, namely, *garam* (Summer), *varsa* (Monsoon) and *thanda* (Winter). It is told by the Munda and Oraon tribal people that with the performance of *Sarhul* they feel that the summer season is approaching. Again with the blooming of flowers like *khalse*, mango and *neem* trees they are confirmed about the days of scorching heat are very close. During summer season when they observe that the ants, especially the black ants are moving in rows towards a safe and comparatively high land from a low lying place with eggs in their mouth, they recognise it as the signal of the rainy season. Again, the frog's croak is the confirmation of the rains. It is also informed that if there is a plenty of mango production, they get assured that the sufficient amount of rainwater will help them in cultivation for a bumper crop. When they see the tamarind production is high, they become afraid of 'excessive rain' and that may lead to a flood like situation. Similarly, when they observe that the crabs crawl on plants and snails are seen to climb on plants and trees, it is definite that there will be flood.

When they observe that there is wind blowing from the northern direction, the date palm trees are ready with juice in the morning there is mist and there is a feeling of cold, they say that winter season has arrived. According to them, during winter season if the wind blows from the southern direction, they are confirmed that next day in the morning there will be fog.

## Bastar Situation

It is also believed that indigenous ecological knowledge is a pivotal factor for empowering the communities. Each aspect of life and culture of a community lives in rural, hilly forested clad area or in a riverside possesses a body of knowledge as a means of their survival strategy which are intricately interwoven and inextricably linked with the sustenance of their pattern of living. In the light of modernisation and diversity and cultural pluralism in Indian culture, their rich indigenous knowledge embedded with cultural and technical knowledge and bio-diversity, is now being given importance on priority basis by global community.

Under the backdrop of this theoretical framework some empirical observations are now made. From time immemorial the people of India irrespective of their cultural and technological achievement, have depended upon their immediate geographical environment not only for livelihood, but also for various aspects of their daily life (Sarkar and Dasgupta, 2000). The knowledge to utilise the local environmental resources their ailments is mainly dependent upon their age-old interaction with the local environment for sustenance over generations together and often this essence of knowledge is highly confined to particular persons. It is also widely accepted that most ethnic groups are exploiting their environment through hunting, collection, gathering for consumption, sale or exchange of forest produce within the same geographical niche or outside (Haimendorf, 1943; Bhowmick, 1989). Apart from these they also exploit such resources during their ailment. It has also been observed that due to prolonged association with forest environment the tribal people eke out also some medicinal herbs, plants, roots and tubers for cures to their ailments. But to detect and diagnosis the actual disease they are dependent on some specialist, in case of Bastar situation the medicinal men are known as *sirha* or *leske* who has the expertise in detecting diseases by reading the pulse beat. In case of Abujh Maria or Hill Maria–a primitive tribal group of

Bastar, Chhattisgarh, it has been keenly observed that "situation has compelled them to find out way through which they may recover or survive from any illness. As a result they often use their local resources to cure their ailment"(Dasgupta and Sarkar, 2005).

The study of indigenous beliefs and practices regarding health and disease in different cultures is of great significance in understanding human behaviour. An in depth study of folk medicine from an emic point of view will help in understanding the cultural symbols and meanings and their integration with the culture (Tribhuwan, 1998). Anthropological data on ethno-medicine is instrumental in understanding the health related beliefs of the Abujh Maria tribal people as well as mechanism adopted by them to preserve and conserve the surrounding bio-diversity of their habitat. They utilise the resources of a particular territory for their ailment over generation and also protect the resource base to sustain their future generations; this is ensured though certain cultural stigma which is religious value loaded like presence of sacred grove known among them as *tallur*. This knowledge also ensures the means adopted by them to enable the members of the future generation to be benefited by the natural resources. Thus, ethno-medicine is belief and practices relating to health and disease, which are products of indigenous cultural developments and not derived from the knowledge taught by the modern medicine (Dasgupta and Sarkar, 2005).

The abode of Abujh Maria, a little known primitive tribal group, is luxuriant with vast tract of forest resources. The Abujh Maria depends on their specialist like *leske* (medicine man) and *sirha* (sorcerer) who possesses a thorough knowledge of plants, herbs and roots of their territory. The *leske* or *sirha* through his magical performances try to identify the actual cause of the sickness. If the *leske* or *sirha* gets some hints through their magical power that some has performed some detrimental activity through black magic or sorcery to do harm of a person who ultimately becomes ill, the *leske* or *sirha* prescribes remedies. If they fail to identify the actual reason or culprit, they take the help of 'log god' or *pen* deity (clan deity) who by his/her divine power identifies the witch or wicked person responsible for the mischief and also prescribe remedy in their dreams which frequently may include some forest leaf or root with some magical quality. But in almost all cases a ritual offering to the deities is obligatory.

Hence the present treatise is confined on the Abujh Maria tribe of Bastar who exploit their immediate natural resources for their ailments. In the following lines a list of locally available herbs, plants and seeds with their curing power are presented.

**Indigenous Knowledge Being Health Care Practice***

| *Sl. No.* | *Use of local herbs/ plants/ seeds* | *Name of the Disease* | *Method of use* |
|---|---|---|---|
| 1` | 2 | 3 | 4 |
| 1. | Turguma fruit, Katta or Kota fruit | Headache and Stomached | Boil the fruit in water then consume the fruit or fry the fruit and consume |
| 2. | Harra (Terminalia chebula) | Cold, Cough and fever (Local Name : *Mutapasinta*) | Grind it in water then keep it soaked in water for at least 2 hours; then drink the water. It is taken 2 to 3 times in empty stomach |
| 3. | Kohka or velva seed (Semi carpus anacardium) | Headache and wound (Local name : *Talanaunta*) | The seed is slightly broken and heated. The oil of the seed comes out and is applied on the forehead/wound. The wound will be healed. |
| 4. | Beng podia tuber | Blood dysentery (Local name : *Neturpota*) | Grinded and soaked in water overnight, taken in the morning. |
| 5. | The root of duli tree | Diarrhoea (Local name : *Tatti/ pet darna*) | It is grinded and soaked in water overnight. It is drank early in the morning |
| 6. | Pendra root | Body pain (Local name : *Mendur nainta*) | Grinded and taken |
| 7. | Pittereka fruit (green small sized) | Eye trouble (Local name : *Kondang putingta*) | The fruit is taken as a medicine which is available in forest. |
| 8. | Tora seed oil (Mahua seed) | Cold, cough and crackes in the skin | At first the oil is heated then the warm oil is massaged all over the body |
| 9. | Karanj Seed (Pongamia glabra) | Skin disease | Extracted oil is applied on the affected parts of the body |
| 10. | Chiratia (Swerita chirata) | Malaria, blood purifier | Grind it and soak in water overnight and the water is taken. |
| 11. | Sannhemp seed (Crotrolaria junea) | Barrenness (Local name : Banj) | It is taken after grinding |
| 12. | Balbairang or Babreng (Embelia ribes) | Wormicide | Root of the plant is ground and taken |
| 13. | Mud of ant hill | Sprain | Collect the mud and it is heated and then anointed at the place of sprain. |
| 14. | Bark of neem tree (Azadirachia indica) | Irregular menstruation | Bark of *neem* tree is ground and soaked in water for few hours and then the water is drunk. |
| 15. | Arjun bark (Terminalia arjuna) | Chest pain | Bark is soaked in water overnight and water is taken. |
| 16. | Gunchee (Abrus precatorius L.) | Skin disease | The seeds are pounded with water and the paste is applied. |
| 17. | Iswarmul (Aristo lochia indica) | Snake and rat bite | The whole plant is ground and consumed. |

*Source:* Reflection of Ethno-Sciences: Study on the Abujh Maria, 2005.

The above data on indigenous health practices by the Abujh Maria clearly reflects that their own concept of diseases and their way of treatment are directly influenced by local herbs, plants etc. of their abode. The *sirha* or *leske* who actually knows the medicinal plants always try to conserve it in their ecological niche by imposing certain norms and values. Since these medicines are the products of the forest, there is no degenerating effect. Moreover, it is also revealed that use of herbal medicine is curative rather than preventive. Therefore, this kind of vast indigenous knowledge should be properly documented in the light of not only globalisation but also for the interest of future generation.

Apart from the health care practices in indigenous way the Abujh Maria socio-economic life is also guided by indigenous knowledge where myth plays a key role. Abujh Maria are traditionally *penda* (slash and burn) cultivators. Ownership of land here is firstly on the village basis and then on the clan deity basis. It is learnt that sometimes the village site is abandoned for various superstitious reasons such as death, disease or any calamity. After cultivating a land for two to four years, they shift to another plot of land leaving the previous land fallow for its regeneration and nitrogenous balance is re-acquired in this way.

They move from one hill to another hill, when all the land of that particular hill are cultivated and exhausted, they leave the total hill and shift to another hill, which is also under the control of same clan deity. In this way they used to shift from one hill to the other for cultivation and again come back within 15-20 years to the old site, that is, first *penda* plot in rotation. As they have to move from one patch of land to another in an interval of four years, they have a requirement of a vast land but there is a sharp territorial demarcation of each and every *pen's* (clan deity) area and again each *pen*'s territory is divided among the Abujh Marias according to their *kattas* (clan). (Each *pen* consists of a number of *kattas* which are considered as *dadabhai* or *bhaiband* group and marriage within the same *dadabhai* group is strictly prohibited). Under this backdrop the *katta* members are bound to cultivate within their own territory that ultimately results in a land limitation and it indirectly has an impact on their family size. The empirical data from studied villages of Abujh Maria (mainly uni-ethnic villages) suggests that average family size of the Abujh Maria is 4. 92 members. From the aforesaid discussion it is revealed that how myth has penetrated the economic life which in turn affects their family size. Practice of *penda* cultivation and movement of one patch of land to other in an interval of four years clearly suggest that in their indigenous knowledge they are highly aware that the fallow land will be rejuvenated with nitrogenous balance.

## Discussion

It is evident from the aforesaid discussion that Indigenous Ecological Knowledge and Natural Resource Management examines how traditional ecological knowledge (TEK) is practised today among Native communities. The indigenous ecologicalknowledge based traditional practices, especially the primary health care system offers great potential for sustainable development. Poor and rural people would be initial beneficiaries. Moreso, it is cheaper and easily reachable-cum-affordable. Local people are of opinion that indigenous knowledge based practices can be improved or even blended with mainstream modern technologies. The conservation of indigenous knowledge, biodiversity, and natural heritage should assume paramount importance in face of the relentless pressures resulting in the vanishing of species, loss of genetic diversity, the disappearances of indigenous knowledge and destruction of livelihood. The age-old traditional health care system can also partly fill this gap if biodiversity and indigenous knowledge is preserved even in the current of globalisation of the present day; the sweep of such wave may also even reach the remote corner of the Indian subcontinent.

It can obviously be concluded that the life and culture of the Sundarban people and Abujh Maria tribe of Bastar are deeply enmeshed in forest environment. The cognisance of each and every sphere of their livelihood is embodied with the brackish water and forest environment respectively, in which their personal attributes are socialised. All these indigenous knowledge help them to preserve their immediate bio-diversity with the help of taboos, beliefs and practices, which ultimately help them to maintain a sustainable living condition. The role of Physical environment of the area, which has control on the formation of culture, is understood in cognitive way and helpful for sustainable living.

## References

Bhowmick, P. K. 1989 The Chenchus of the Forests and Plateau: A Hunting-Gathering Tribe in Transition, Calcutta: Institute of Social Research and Applied Anthropology.

Das, Amal Kumar 1981 "Trend of Population" in *a focus on Sundarban*, ed. Amal K. Das and et. al., Calcutta, Editions Indian. pp. 17-29.

Dasgupta, Samira and Amitabha Sarkar, 2005 Reflection of Ethno-Science: Study on the Abujh Maria, New Delhi: Mittal Punlications.

Dasgupta Samira and Amitabha Sarkar 2013 "A Study on Traditional Wisdom among the Munda and Oraon of Sundarban", in traditional

Wisdom and Sudtainable Living: A Study on the Indian Tribal Societies, (ed) by Hrishikesh Mandal and Amitabha Sarkar, New Delhi: Anthropological Survey of India and Gyan Publishing House.

Haimendorf, C. V. Furer, 1943, The Chenchus: Jungle folk of the Deccan, London: Macmillan and Co. Ltd.

Mondal, Asim K. 2003, *The Sundarbans of India: A Development Analysis.* New Delhi: Indus Publishing Company.

Saha, Bikash Kanti 1999, *Mangrove Tigerland: Sunderban*, Calcutta: Intelsoft.

Sarkar, Amitabha and Samira Dasgupta 2000, Ethno-ecology of Indian Tribes: Diversity in Cultural Adaptation, Jaipur: Rawat Publications.

Tribhuwan, R. D. 1998, Medical World of the Tribals, New Delhi: Discovery Publishing House.

# 10

# Culture and Adaptation

## Prologue

Cultures are human adaptations (Marshall Sahlins, 1969). Human beings have sufficient capacity to adapt with the ecology for the sake of their existence. The hypothesis of adaptation of man to environmental conditions through socio-cultural institutions and behaviour has been widely employed (Frake, 1962, Harris, 1966, Sahlins, 1964, Steward, 1955) with interesting interpretations. This is a kind of dialectic interplay between culture and environment. According to Anderson (1973) cultural change is a part of adaptation.

### (a) Impact of Environment on Culture: Adaptation being the survival strategy among the Sundarban Tribes

Sundarban is one of the largest deltas in the coastal Bay of Bengal. The historical record reveals that to clear the forest and reclaim the marshy lands to make it habitable, a large number of labourers were engaged (Mukherjee, 1981). These labour force are mostly from Chhotanagpur plateau of Jharkhand, tribal areas from West Bengal and Bangladesh. These early settlers were gradually outnumbered in latter decades by the population of other sectors who migrated to this area in varied strength and successive waves in quest of livelihood (Das, 1981). After partition of India in 1947, the influx of immigrants at this place was further added from East Pakistan (now Bangladesh). In course of time, they also settled at Sundarban; now it became a place of culture mosaic.

The people of this area are multi-ethnic having different occupational pursuits with pluralistic religious belief. They settle in common ecological set-up, has been forced to practise some common religious ritual activities due to their survival and sustenance. In such hostile environmental situation (i.e. due to presence of cunning and most intelligent Royal Bengal Tiger) criss-cross, brackish river water with tide and ebb twice in a day plays a key role in regulating their whole economic life. The forest of Sundarban also plays a predominant role for sustenance among the local inhabitants who know fully well that any kind of danger and mishap is awaiting for them in such a habitat of clever tigers and crocodiles.

Against this backdrop each community maintain their ethnic boundary through their social-religious behaviour. However, during mere profession-oriented activities of life struggle in such locale, the ethnic boundary is not taken into account. The environmental limitation has forced them to adopt the local folk behaviour in order to maintain their livelihood. The present paper intends to highlight about the uncertainty of life of inhabitants of Sundarban vis-à-vis their dependence on various folk deities as rescuer which makes cohesive agent of mutual co-existence between different ethnic groups even belonging to of different religious dogma.

## History of Sundarban and People

Sundarban, one of the largest delta in estuarine phase of the river Ganga–is an unique bio-climatic zone on a tropical geographical situation in the coastal Bay of Bengal. It consists of about 102 low lying islands out if which 54 are inhabited with an area of 5366 sq. km. . The total area of Sundarban region is 9630 sq. km. Sundarban is located between $21^0 32'$ and $22^0 40'$ north latitude and between $88^0 05'$ and $89^0$ east latitudes bounded by Dampier-Hodges line. It stretches for about 120 km. from Hooghly river to the Haribhanga river and runs in land up to 125 km. covering the greater part of North and South 24 Parganas districts of West Bengal.

The history of reclamation of land in Sundarban dates back to 1770 when the than collector general Claud Russel planned for utilisation of forest land for agriculture. In 1785, the commissioner of Jessore–Tilman Henckell with the permission from Warren Hastings, distributed land among cultivators. It took 40 years for the *ijardars,* who held plots of land, to reclaim land in areas such as Sagar Islands in the south and Canning in the east. In 1814, the East India Company decided to distribute land directly to the cultivators and for this in

1816 the post of Commissioner was created in Sundarban. Scott–the first Commissioner, observed that the company has not received revenue from the *ijardaras* and *zamindars* for a long time. In consequence there upon the land of sundarban was declared government property in 1817.

During 1822-23, the part between the rivers Jamuna (East Pakistan, now Bangladesh) and Hooghly was surveyed by Princep with the help of a map prepared by Morrison, who divided the area into smaller blocks called lot. During 1829-30 the entire forested area was surveyed by William Dampier, the then Commissioner and Hodges, the then Surveyor, who divided Sundarbans into 236 lots. In 1830 the Company framed a policy to distribute forest area among European settlers in India. Later in 1832-33 the Princep line was officially accepted by Dampier to demarcate the area of Sundarbans from rest of the country. During 1878-79, 4856 sq. kms. of area was declared as protected forest area.

In 1903 Sir Daniel Mackinan Hamilton, a Scotch national, came to Sundarbans and established his *Zamindari* with the purchase of 9000 acres of land in Gosaba island (Lot No. 143) comprising the villages Gosaba, Arampur, Dulki and Sonargaon; and Rangabelia island (Lot No. 149) consisting of the villages Rangabelia, Pakhirala, Bagbagan and Uttardanga. These two islands were separated by narrow tributary of Bidya and Gomar rivers. Later on when the river was embanked, these two formed a common island. The first to come in these islands were the tribal groups mainly the Bhumij and the Munda from Chhotanagpur plateau to clear off the forest. They were followed by the Bengali Mahisya population and the Muslims from the Midnapur district in pursuit of agriculture. Only a handful of Malo and Rajbanshi, the fishermen, immigrated to this island as refugees from East Pakistan (now Bangladesh) during 1948-49 and later in 1952-53 as a result of political exodus during the post-independence period. They encroached over barren lands and occupied plots of land near the river Bidya and the settlement strictly restricts these two population groups in these twin islands. Forest of Gosaba (Lot No. 143) was cleared earlier than Rangabelia (Lot No. 149). Rangabelia allowed the people to settle down by 1920s, especially to those who came from Midnapur district of West Bengal in search of a prospective future.

In 1920 Sir Hamilton procured the islands of Satjelia and Lahiripur comprising 13000 acres of land, lying across the river Gomar on the eastern side. These twin islands were separated by a narrow stream of Dutta river, which has been later embanked, the area now being called Banitala, as Bani/Baen (Avicennia officinalis) tree is found in abundance here. This island was totally inhabited during 1948-49 as a result of influx of refugees from East Pakistan (now Bangladesh) and also later on during 1965-66 and 1971-72 as post war consequences. The first to settle in this land were sat (seven) jeles (fishermen-all Rajbanshi by caste) from whom the name of the island, Satjelia has come. This island constitutes the population all being Hindus, entirely from East Pakistan (now Bangladesh) except the Bhumij and the Munda who came here earlier to clear off the forests. Incidentally, till date, this island is the last inhabited island on the eastern side after which there are a couple of islands totally covered under forest (being core area of tiger reserve of Sundarban biosphere), and under government control, and across the river Raymangal, lies the country of Bangladesh. .

The history of reclamation of land in Sundarban with special reference to the trend of settlement is the fundamental guideline in understanding the process of cultural syncretism or cultural synthesis that is under operation here . To get a viable picture of this, the present authors have selected the islands of Gosaba-Rangabelia and Satjelia-Lahiripur as these two sets of islands encompass population from two different countries namely, India and Bangladesh.

Contrary to the situation above, the area of Raidighi of Mathurapur-II block of South 24 Parganas was reclaimed much earlier, sometime during the middle of nineteenth century, that formed a part of the feudal estate of the *Zamindar* Baroda Prasad Roy Choudhury. Five villages namely Khari, Kashinagar, Barasi, Sovanagar and Panchpukur, alongwith adjacent areas including Raidighi, were studied for the present research work. This area, lying under Mathurapur-II Block mainly accommodates people who have come either from Midnapur district or from Ranchi and Hazaribagh areas. The tribals mainly belong to the Oraon and Munda groups and the Hindus comprise of Poundra Kshatriya, Mahishya, Bagdi and so on, all being indigenous to South 24 Parganas. Apart from them there are Muslims and Christians, the latter one belongs to the Catholic Mission.

The islands lying under Gosaba Block were reclaimed within the past 100 years that formed a part of the feudal estate of Sir Daniel Mackinan Hamilton. In the Gosaba–Rangabelia island empirical studies were conducted in the villages of Gosaba, Arampur, Rangabelia and Pakhirala, and in the island of Satjelia field studies were carried out in the villages of Dayapur and Satjelia villages as mentioned earlier.

The area of Raidighi was reclaimed much earlier, sometimes during the middle of nineteenth century, that formed a part of the feudal estate of the Zamindar Baroda Prasad Roy Chowdhury. Five villages namely Khari, Kashinagar, Barasi, Sovanagar and Panchpukur, alongwith adjacent area including Raidighi, were studied for the present research work.

## Sundarban people

The scheduled castes and scheduled tribe of Sundarban region play a vital role in composition of its population. These scheduled tribes of this area are mostly the descendants of those who were once brought over to this area, from their original homeland of Chhotanagpur pleteau of present day Jharkhand state and adjoining Odisha state, for clearing the forest and making the land cultivable (Das and at all, 1981).

There are altogether 6 major scheduled tribes in the Sundarbans who are numerically dominant tribe group in the region; they are Bhumij (88.8 per cent), Munda (82.3 per cent), Oraon (63.3 per cent), Santel (65.7 per cent), Kora (91.9 per cent), and Mahali (89.5 per cent) etc. (These data are based on 1971 census). Their pressence also reported in Gosaba, Sandeskhali, Hasnabed and Canning while Oraon are found in Mathurapur, Basanti, Sandeskhali, Canning etc. police station of 24 Parganas district (undivided).

## History of Migration

The history of present habitation in Sundarban goes back to the early eighteenth century. The labourers were engaged for cleaning jungles and for reclaiming lands, criss-crossed by rivers and rivulets and often inter connected by cables. The basic labour force was drawn mostly from Chhotanagpur (at present Jharkhand state). With the gradual settlement of different ethnic groups into a close tie in the new habitation, there emerged a new society with a heterogamous culture.

Because of estuarine feature of this area, the periphery of those habitations is protected by bunds or dykes which almost always run along the village boundary, to keep out salt water of the tidal rivers and interconnecting channels. Often the dykes are used as roads by the inhabitants of villages.

Both textual and empirical situation speaks that the Oraons (often called locally as Uran/Dhager) original inhabitants of Jharkhand trace their origin from Chhotanagpur plateau but none can remember the exact place name of their origin of migration. Historical information speaks that they immigrated at Munda area of Chhotanagpur who had already settled there for a long time. The Oraon with a comparatively superior material condition and with a better knowledge of agriculture spread their dominance over the land and gradually occupied the territory (Das and et al., 1981).

During British period when reclamation by the Jamindars at Sundarban was in progress, the Munda, Oraon and others were brought as labourers from Ranchi area for clearing of forest tracts. Most of the tribes of present day Sundarbon are the descendants of those early settlers. It is also reported that on reclaiming Sundarbon these people changed their settlement from one place to other in quest of their livelihood. The present young generations who are born and brought up in this situation are having a culture which is not in tune with their traditional abode of Chhotanagpur. They have lost their original/traditional culture behaviour and present day Sundarban has become the traditional homeland to them. It is also reported that their forefathers left their ancestral village in Chhotanagpur under advance economic pressure. During present field investigation it is observed that some of them trace their clan name from of their ancestral place name like tamariya and silli etc. though they do not possess any idea about where Tamar and Silli area are situated at Ranchi district of Jharkhand.

## Cultural Mingling

The effect of cultural mingling of different ethnic groups is well evidenced in the Bengali language which is current in Sundarban. This further unfolds a long history of migration and settlement of different categories of population in that area. At the beginning of settlement and reclamation the big landowners came from Calcutta, Midnapur and Jessore-Khulna region of Bangladesh. Along with this came the tribals. The habitations grew up there with the Hindus, Muslims and Tribals. Subsequently, Christianity spread among the people particularly among the population belonging to the lower strata of society due to influx of missionaries and formation of churches. In course of time, two distinct Bengali speaking population became dominant in that area–the western side was influenced by Midnapur district dialect while the eastern part of this area of Sundarban was affected by the dialects of Jessore–Khulna of Bangladesh. In this forest-clad and estuarine area the typical habits and habitations of the population concerned helped in adopting terms and terminologies which characteristically left imprints on the local Bengali dialect.

Now with the gradual settlement of different ethnic groups into a close tie of new habitations there emerged a new society with heterogeneous culture. With the passage of time gradual transformation and synthesis has started which ultimately left marks of change on the societal and cultural affairs of the people concerned.

## Economic Profile

The economic profile of Sundarban region has its own distinctive features. Once they were dependent on forest resources like collection of honey and wax by *mauley* (honey collector) and wood cutting by *bauley* (wood cutters). However, with the passage of time gradually this forest based economy was replaced by settled agriculture, wage labour and *meen dhara* (collection of shrimp or prawn seedlings). In fact, collection of prawn seedlings by villagers from early morning to till evening is a regular phenomena and it is a lucrative earning source for many of them and the livelihood of many families. Out of such economic pursuit each family earns Rs 400 to Rs 500 average in a month. It has been observed that in each and every household in the studied villages chiefly women members of family and children (age group 8 to 16 year) are involved in meen dhara profession and surprisingly these children are non-school going.

At the tribal hamlet of studied villages there are Munda and Bhumij who have immigrated from Chhotanagpur plateau of Jharkhand State as labourer. Now-a-days during our field investigation their chief economic pursuit are agricultural labour work, wage earner as well as *bagda* (a variety of prawn) collection from deep rivers of Sundarban. It is also observed that the Muslims and Christians are primarily agriculturists but they often visit Sundarban forest for catching of fish or collection of honey and wood etc. These people are now usually *saidar* (moneyed gentry).

It is also reported that a few Muslim families in earlier day were *mauley, bauley* and were regular visitor to forest for mere subsistence. Due to fear and uncertainty of life at the Sundarban forest, (for the presence of cunning Royal Bengal Tiger), most of them have now left the jungle based profession.

The villagers at this region are chiefly dependent on the surrounding natural resources for maintaining their livelihood. Due to such the traditional wisdom as well as cognisance of environment possessed by the inhabitants of Sundarban region are also shaped according to the local niche and it has been adopted by all including the immigrants tribal people of Chhotanagpur, refugee settlers (of Bangladesh) and plain land people from the District of Midnapur and Hooghly. The major resources are forest and surrounding brackish water of river. They catch various kinds of fishes and crabs in the creek and rever which depends on the movement of moon locally known as *gan*. Those who are involved in fish and crab catching in deep river, or in various creeks and nalahs of Sundarban river, also often collect wood, honey and wax from deep forest after obtaining necessary permit from the Forest Department. The collection of honey and wax is completely seasonal; it starts from *Chaitra* (March-April) to Vaisak (April-May). Collection of honey from forest is locally known as *mahal* and during this time the chance of tiger attack upon human is maximum. Forest entrants during *mahal* consists of 7-8 members who are highly aware of the area of occurrence of good quality honey and obviously these are in the core areas of Sundarban Tiger Reserve. According to *mauley* informants of both Hindu and Muslim that best quality honey they procure from Khalsi (Aegiceras cornicalatum (L)) flower which is followed by keora (Sonneratia apetala) and Bani (Avicennia offieinalis) flower. Therefore, it is observed that Sundarban forest play a dominant role for sustenance among its inhabitants.

## Adaptation towards various folk deities

It has been observed that all the jungle goers irrespective of their ethnic identity are primarily the devotees of Banbibi–the Sylvan Goddess, Shajangali and Dakshinrai. They are mainly dependent and find refuge in the blessings of the deities. She is regarded as the presiding deity at Sundarban forest. Prior to the journey into deep forest or *Khari* (creek) area of Sundarban, the honey collectors, wood cutters, fishermen of Hindu, Muslim, Christian and Tribals pay offerings and propitiate Banbibi for blessing to avert dangers. In many Hindu, Muslim and Tribal households there is an alter or than meant for the deity.

Here is a list of deities in which all the residents of Sundarban have a strong faith which they have accordingly adopted into their own cultural milieu.

**Name of the Deities Propitiated by Tribals, Hindu, Muslim and Christian of the studied area and purpose of worship**

| *Sl. No.* | *Area* | *Name of the Deities* | *Purpose of worship* | *Associated with* |
|---|---|---|---|---|
| 1. | Gosaba | Banbibi | Safe return from forest | Sylvan Goddess or Tiger Goddess |
| 2. | -do- | Dakshin Roy | -do- | Tiger God |
| 3. | -do- | Shajangali | -do- | -do- |
| 4. | -do- | Kalu Rai | To appease crocodiles | Water God |
| 5. | -do- | Badar Pir | For safe journey in deep sea | Water God – A Muslim Saint |
| 6. | -do- | Chandi | -do- | Water God (Head of the boat is regarded as Chandi) |
| 7. | -do- | Manik Pir | Welfare of domestic cattle | A Muslim Saint |
| 8. | Gosaba and Mathurapur-II Block | Gazi Saheb/ Bara Khan Gazi | Protector of jungle goers, he is also appeased to cure diseases and eradication from barrenness. | A Muslim Saint. |
| 9. | Kashinagar (Mathurapur-II Block) | Maibibi/ Bibima | Welfare of family, business. | Family, Business etc. |
| 10. | Sovanagar, Raidighi (Mathurapur-II Block) | Naibibi/ Sathbibi | To get rid of various diseases like Cholera, Diarrhea etc. | Cure of various Tropical diseases. |
| 11. | Kashinagar (Mathurapur-II Block). | Naryani | Welfare of family. | Welfare of family and safe return from forest. |
| 12. | Gosaba and Mathurapur-II Block. | Manasa | Appease her for safe from snake bite. | Snake deity. |
| 13. | Mathurapur-II Block | Ateshwar | Worship to get missing article, prevent tiger or robber from entering the village and cause harm. | Welfare deity. |
| 14. | -do- | Basanta Roy | He is considered as lord of the region. | -do- |
| 15. | -do- | Sitala | Save from epidemic diseases. | -do- |
| 16. | -do- | Gopal/ Krishana | Welfare in family and expect his blessing. | -do- |
| 17. | -do- | Kali | Protector of unnatural events. | -do- |
| 18. | -do- | Panchananda/ pachuthakur/ Dharma Thakur. | Worship to get a child. | Fertility cult (Buddhist cult may have influenced in it). |
| 19. | -do- | Panchanan | Blessing son of Lord Siva. | Welfare Deity. |
| 20. | -do- | Jarasur | To get rid of high river. | -do- |
| 21. | -do- | Santoshima/ Bishalakhi | Protection from all unnatural events. | -do- |
| 22. | -do- | Andamuni | Cure from blindness and eye trouble | -do- |

**Banbibi:** The goddess Banbibi is represented by a stone slab or by a pot vessel or by an icon with two hands seated on the back of tiger and dukhe (a child) in her lap or close to her left feet. In some places instead of tiger as mount it is deer as observed in Khari village or fowl as in Panchpukur village. In the **'Bon Bibir Jahurnama'** it is found that Banbibi was nourished under the lap of a deer and her milk, during her infancy.

The case histories also suggests that before the entrance of forest or jungle the Banbibi and Shajangali in particular are propitiated by *saidar, patni* (boatman), *mauley, bauley* and fisherman. There is no role of Brahman priest to conduct the ritual. Those who enter in the jungle in search of forest produce or those who fish in khari or creeks of riverine Sundarban, require the blessings of the deity. Banbibi through her supernatural power only can protect the life of the people from all sorts of evils. It appears from close observation that the devotees irrespective of their ethnic identity and religion pray before Banbibi–the 'guardian of the forest'–the native's perception, that "mother we are going to your kingdom for our mere sustenance, kindly protect us; please keep vigil for our safe return so that we do not fall prey under your tiger's paw. We have no other alternative other than to enter your kingdom. Please keep us alive and protect us and thereby save our family and children and also save our wife's fortune; only you can protect us."

The offerings made to the Banbibi is known as *hajat*, which consists of fruits, *batasa* (sweet cakes), parched rice and puffed rice. Both Hindu, Muslim and other communities accept the offerings as prasad. Either in annual worship or in daily ritual no sacrifice is made in honour of the deity. Only fowls are offered as vow and they are set free in the forest. When this puja or ritual is performed before the entrance in forest the hajat is simple. The main thing of annual worship of Banbibi during *Pous Sankranti* (the last day of Pous month, that is during middle of January) or Basant Panchami–the day of Saraswati Puja during Falgun (January-February), is to read 'Bonbibir Johurnama' as *panchali* (reading ritual text) from back side to front side like Urdu literature.

**Shajangali**–Along with Banbibi in the same altar there is a place of Shajangali who is a brother of Banbibi, on costume Banbibi icon appears to be a Hindu idol and usually in her left side Shajangali stands with a *gada* (club) in his hand with which it is believed he drives away the tiger. From his personal attire it appears that he is from Muslim gentry. Through participant observation it can also be said that both the deities of Banbibi–Shajangali faces towards west because west is pious and sacred side among the Muslim since Macca is to the west of India.

The most striking observation as per Muslim religious dogma is that they do not believe in any anthropomorphic icon while Banbibi is not only an anthropomorphic icon but it is equally worshiped by Hindu, Christian and tribals. The Muslim priest read *panchali* of Banbibi in front of the deity.

Therefore, it can be said that situation force them to compromise and adopt the cultural traits–the ritual of Banbibi in view of their mere subsistence in such environment.

**Dakshinrai**–The another important deity of Sundarban tiger infested area is Dakshinrai. The effigy of Dakshinrai is a male figure sitting on a tiger. He is regarded as a malevolent deity. When they go to forest or creeks to collect forest produce or to catch fish he is worshipped by people of any caste, creed and religion. He is appeased by Brahman priest as observed in Kashinagar, Khari, Chhatrabhag villages. Sacrifice is also made provided there is any vow. In South 24 Parganas Dakshinrai is widely adored and its influence and popularity are keenly noticed there. He in many respects surpasses the influence of other local folk deities especially in the region of south-west part of Sundarban, that is, Raidighi, Mathurapur, Namkhana, Patharpratima, Sagar areas etc. Dakshinrai has the full form of a soldier, either in a standing or seated position: In places he is without a carrier or often seated on a tiger or horse. This powerful tiger cult/deity is conceived in the fringe area also as cure deity. It is also reported that once this part of Sundarban was ruled by king Mukut Roy and Dakshinrai was his Senapati (military general). Due to his bravery he became a historical figure and gradually turned into a legendary deity (Chattopadhyay, 1981). All these certainly indicates how a howling and roaring cruel tiger deity has become a cure deity and also a fortune deity along with the change of relationship between the deities and the devotees in different ecological situations (Niyogi, 1996).

In Bon Bibir Jahurnama (1388 B. S. ) Dakshin rai demands human sacrifice directly -

*"Yabat na daya more narabali puja"*
(so long as human sacrifice is not offered to me)
*nahi diba mom-modhu-dekhaiba maja*
(will not give honey or wax and I'll make you pay)
*Jodi tumi narabali puja para dita*
(if you can offer human sacrifice)
*sat-dinga-mom-diba tomar dalite*
(will give you seven boat–load of wax)

in this way everywhere Dakshinrai image has become cruel and dreaded.

The thirst for human blood, desire for human sacrifice and chopped bara head manifest the primitive character of Dakshinrai. It is estimated through the *Raymangal Kavya* (a narrative poem in Bengali literature) of Krishnaram Das (1686) (Bhattacharya, 1957) that in the battle with Gazi, Dakshinrai's head fell and that chopped head was worshipped as *baran*:

*"Bada khan hanilo khanra galay tahar*
*Maya munda kshiti pode emoni prokar*
*Virodh bhangiya dilo ashiya eshwar*
*Tarpar dostani pailo dohey bar*
*Kata munda bara puja sei haite kare*
*Kono khane divya murti bagher upare".*

In this manner, there was an acceptance of worship of godly image by the side of chopped head. It is also pointed out that animal sacrifice is present in almost all deities in the Sundarban region especially in South 24 Parganas. During *jatal* puja of Dakshinrai, animal sacrifice is significant. Now one can infer that the worship of *bara* head image might have originated in ancient religious belief and primitive magic, belief etc. It might also derived from the custom of human sacrifice.

Now, it is revealed that at times the different religions and cultures confront each other through various events and try to accommodate or adapt through various social rites. More so, perhaps in this way primitive belief systems and folk gods and goddesses are raised from its social position towards universalisation. In the historical–dialectical process of co-ordination and contradiction the worship of human chopped head which may have traced its root in the primitive belief system, perhaps transformed into Dakshinrai at a particular time and space. In course of time during the collection of wood, honey, wax, fish and other forest produces from Sundarban and spread of human habitation at this niche where in each and every step there is dreaded fear of Royal Bengal Tiger (or mama), the story of tiger came to be linked with the worship of human head—the folk-magic belief in fertility cult aiding procreation.

It can be stated that the etymological meaning of Dakshin Rai is the 'over lord of South'. The main basis of identifying Dakshinrai as the Tiger God, probably is the form of tiger as carrier in the *Rayamangal Kavya*. **It is also inferred that metamorphosis of Zoomorphic image**

**of the tiger–god into the modern anthropomorphic image through the influence of various cultural waves in the ocean of time.**

Lastly, it can be said that myth of Dakshinrai, the episode of *Rayamangal Kavya* and *Bonobibir Jahurnama* after the advent of Islam in this part of Bengal, strongly suggest a compromise among the faiths of both Hindu, Tribal, Christian and Muslim catalysed by the Super powers like Dakshinrai and Barkhan gazi of that period.

### Muslim Pir/Saint

Barkhan Gaji/Gaji Saheb is another presiding deity–of tiger at Sundarban. He is also regarded as pir or saint. He is considered as the protector of jungle goers who have regular concern with the forests. The Gaji is the mighty lord of the Sundarban forest, he can save the unfortunate entrants in the forest from any unavoidable misfortunes like attack of the tiger, and he can also assure the undisturbed trip and safe return from the forests. He is also appeased to cure the diseases and approached for eradication from barrenness.

In short, according to villagers one's desire is fulfilled if Gaji is pleased and appeased. He is officiated by Muslim Fakir as found in Khari village of Kashinagar, of Mathurapur–II Block where a tomb like *makbara* also exists. It is also observed that rarely casual devotee–mostly Hindus, do offer *hajat* to Gaji through the Muslim Fakir. It is also reported that people from far away come to offer their *hajat* to Gaji and it is performed at Khari village before and after their entrance and exit respectively from the Sundarban forest. Broken brick chips or small earthen balls are found hanging in the window or ceiling of the room which indicates vow of barren women (both Muslim and Hindu) as reported by fakir of *Gaji than (makbara)* at Khari village.

The *than* of Gaji at Khari village is a little bit uncared, where the icon Barakhan Gaji sits on horse back. He is out and out a Muslim religious preacher and due to his various supernatural deeds, ultimately is converted into a deity like figure in the folk belief of this part of South Bengal. The Fakir became Gaji and with the passage of time took the shape of a deity. He blessed every one like Tribal, Hindu, Christian and Muslim by his charismatic supernatural power and it is widely accepted by the rural folk of South Bengal.

### Nai bibi/Sath bibi–Cure deities

They are very common Muslim propitiated local folk female deities of South 24 Parganas. The than (altar) of these group of deities in a village is either seven or nine. Each of these deties is responsible for cure of one tropical disease in tropical country like cholera, diarrhoea etc. Most of the diseases are communicable and its out break is at summer season and due to this the deities are worshipped (annually) at the onset of summer during the month of Magh, Falgun in villages. During early part of Falgun (later part of the month February), these are worshipped at *kachari more* of Raidighi, Mathurapur–II Block, while at Sovanagar village close to Kashinagar, Mathurapur–II Block it is worshipped at the end of Magh. Usually a Muslim Fakir officiates the ritual. It has been observed that among the devotees both Muslim, Hindu and Christian participate actively and most of the devotees are woman and majority among them is Hindu. The Hindu devotees offer *prasad* consisting of fruits, cocoanut, *batasa*, while Muslim devotees offer *hajat*. In both cases Muslim Fakir officiates the ritual. The nine or seven *bibis* are sister and are held to be responsible for different diseases and their respective curatives. The name of nine *bibis* are–*Asan bibi, Ola bibi, Tola bibi, Jholabibi, Kurenibibi, Maribibi, Jharibibi, Darbaribibi, Jhentuney bibi*. Of these *Asanbibi* is regarded as the most powerful among all and if she is pleased then there will be no harm as is believed by devotees. One striking observation is this at Muslim dominated area the personal attire and faces of icon look like Muslim girls while at Hindu dominated area the icon are closely akin to Goddess Lakshmi, Saraswati etc. At Sovanagar village the altar of *naibibi* is at the outskirt of village.

During our field investigation at Ateshwartala*than* of Raidighi Dakshinpara it is noticed that in one side of the *than* there are Hindu deity like Ateshwar, Narayani etc. officiated by Brahman while the other side of the same than is the place of Muslim deities like *nai bibi* which is worshipped by Muslim Fakir and Shri Srimanta Sau, Age–50 yrs sing the song of bibima. The almost same picture is also found at kacharimore of Raidighi.

## Process of Adaptation and Assimilation

Ecological and demographic features coupled with the history of reclamations of land lay the foundation for understanding sundarbans in terms of its spatial and cultural growth. It was during the colonial period when reclamation of land started to make islands habitable for human settlement. For the purpose of the present study the thrust area was delimited to two locales: (1) forest area, and (2) non-forest area. In the forest area two islands of Gosaba Block were taken under the purview of study and in the non-forest area Raidighi lying under Mathurapur–II Block was considered for empirical observation.

In the forest area the demographic map of the said two islands depicts a polar picture. Whereas the island of Gosaba–Rangabelia was inhabited by the people belonging to the faiths of Hinduism, Islam, Christianity and tribal pantheon from areas which remained parts of the mainland of the state and country, namely, the district of Midnapur lying in the Western part of West Bengal and the districts of Ranchi and Hazaribagh etc. of Chhotanagpur plateau in Jharkhand (formerly Bihar); the Satjelia island population immigrated to this soil mainly from East Pakistan (now Bangladesh) as a result of political exodus during the partition of our country and achievement of national independence and also later on during the successive wars in 1965 and 1971.

The area of Mathurapur–II Block mainly accommodates people who have come either from Midnapur district or from Ranchi and Hazaribagh areas. The same ethnic composition of Hindus, Muslims, Christians and tribals are found here.

The factors of human settlement in this part of the country coupled with the crises of survival have brought people together under a common canopy of synthesis to syncretism, which borrows a myth from the twin faiths of Islam and Hinduism. The resultant force of this mythical spread has formed a common folk cult in this part of Gangetic delta, which has taken roots in all societies irrespective of their religious faith and occupation. However, there have been a differential rate of the degree of acceptance in different societies, if observed individually but the uniqueness of this mythical spread is that it lies at the cognitive dimension of the people. Empirical findings suggest that this common cult may have originated in and around this region during the last century or so and had a sacred bond, which now takes the shape of a secular feature where the religious sacraments are guided in the principles of sacred-secular continuum.

The folk cults that dominate in Sundarbans are Banbibi, Dakshinrai, Shahjangali, Gazi Baba, Nai Bibi, and so on. Whereas some are placated for survival strategy, the others are venerated for warding off evil diseases like pox, cholera etc.

Cognitively the people of Sundarbans conceive of the landmass as low area (*nicher dik*) and high area (*oporer dik*). Whereas the former category takes into cognisance of the areas under islands and forests, the latter category includes areas attached to the mainland of south Bengal.

Ban bibi is the predominating cult here, who is considered in lower Sundarbans by the people of *atharo bhati* (area of eighteen low tides) as the daughter of a Muslim saint who became the sole protector of all the people living here irrespective of their religious affiliation. The parallel cult is Dakshinrai, the male counterpart of Ban bibi, who along with her has formed a mythical background that lays the foundation for common religious belief, socio-economic environment and a historical signal of trans-cultural overlapping.

The text of *Raymangal* also refers to Gazi Baba along with Dakshinrai. The legend says that Bara Khan Gazi took to preaching of Islam leaving behind his father's wealth. As a saint he enters the *bhati* (Sundarban area) where he gets confronted with Dakshinrai. However, the dispute is settled and in consequence of that both the communities of Hindu and Muslim here come closer for propitiating Dakshinrai and Gazi Baba in a common *than* (altar). The tradition still continues.

The legend of Ban bibi is current among all the people who live in Sundarbans. If one looks into the core issues associated with the legend, she/he will find that it is the story of class struggle where a woman, deserted daughter of a commoner, makes the society free from a tyrant ruler. There is a probability that this was a struggle for encroachment of territorial existence in terms of social, cultural and religious supremacy. Dakshinrai was an indigenous cult here who has been overpowered by an encroacher. The settlement pattern and development of the area in term of historicity of people's rehabilitation here has a link with the story of Ban bibi.

Earlier ethnographic records noted during the period of reclamation of land and first human settlement from the tribal areas of the neighbouring state and the fringe areas of West Bengal, do not show any reference to Ban bibi. The process of acculturation got accentuated in this part of land after the immigration of Muslim population and the people of East Pakistan (now Bangladesh). It is an acculturation of two predominant faiths, Hinduism and Islam, mainly through direct contact and through the easy accessibility of *Darbesh*, *Fakir* and *Pir* (all Muslim Saints).

The idol of Ban Bibi has been manifested in manifold manner. She has been seen sitting over a roaring tiger in general, but at times she has also been seen sitting over a deer, and on rare occasions, over a wild fowl. In this part of land there are a host of people who are directly or indirectly associated with their immediate environment, the forest and the river. People who are directly associated with the forest and river are called *jungle kara lok* (forest goers) and they include *jele* (fishermen), *mauley* (honey collectors) and *bauley* (wood collectors) obviously for livelihood. Cognitively if a person goes to the interior areas by their only mode of conveyance, i.e. boat, he is referred to as *jungle karte gechche* (gone to the forest). So, to them, forest is the most important aspect of their life. Hence, the cult of Ban bibi stands as the most undisputed savior of Sundarbans, irrespective of one's religious affiliations. Some idols of Bon Bibi show a male child sitting in the lap of a woman. Worshipping of a female cult with a child in lap directs one's thought towards fertility cult and productive economy. One may presume here that agriculture developed in this part of land at a quite later stage.

All the characters mentioned above have a legend of their own, which sometimes overlaps mythical characters and sometimes historical characters. Almost in all cases no sacred text is identified. However, the day of annual worship always overlaps important festive days of Hindu calendar like *Makar Sankranti* (for Hindus and Muslims) and *Basant Panchami* (for tribal). The entire phase of acculturation as a continuous process was although routed along such a path where the carrier agents were divine or semi-divine human characters like sufis and saints. The form of Islamic faith which entered India following the tradition of Sufism differ largely with greater Islamic canopy interms of sacraments prescribed and proscribed in Islam. Hence, the folk tradition borrows a little from established Islam. The same has been reflected in Hindu belief system too. An is interesting part of the legend of Ban bibi is that today She is "worshipped" as a Hindu deity by a Muslim priest where she is offered *hajot*, instead of *prasad*. Unlike other Hindu Gods and Goddesses she sits facing the east and the priest obviously faces the west while 'worshipping' her, a tradition that is prescribed in Hindu faith. Moreover, the very term ' worship' of an idol does not fit in the normative pattern of Islamic mode of religious sacrament. The acceptance of a Muslim girl, daughter of a Muslim parenthood, as a Hindu deity comes under the purview of the process of syncretism that took birth under the canopies of acculturation and assimilation (Niyogi, 1996).

It is, however, felt that the performance of this sort of folk tradition in a localised pocket is an attempt to justify supremacy of good over evil, struggle for territorial existence, where myth, legend and imaginary characters are the carriers of belief system and once this belief system gets a footage, the forces of synthesis as well as syncretism process in the religious axis gets strengthened.

Similarly, local belief says that Nai Bibi (nine deities) were born out of the sweat of the forehead of Allah. These nine Bibis are siblings where the eldest one is Asan Bibi, named after *asan* (meaning easy access). This set of deities also gets their share of sacred offerings in the form of *hajo*t by the Muslim priests, who sits facing the West to worship these deities. The cult of Nai Bibi has got a wide spread appellation in this part of rural Bengal who are appeased for either warding off epidemics like Cholera, Pox, Dysentery, etc. or for protection of children from the said deadly diseases. It is learnt that rural Bengal was once prone to epidemics for which people developed faith on these folk deities who may have entered this soil and got wide acceptance through the preaching's of Fakirs, Pirs and Darbes where religious faith and belief played no bar at all. The Muslim saints also had easy access to folk medicine/ethno medicine which otherwise helped all to cure the diseases. Probably this seems to be the potential reason to identify a disease against a particular deity, called Bibi and a way to get rid off it. The amalgamation of people's belief system and the encroaching ideas probably formed a system that was different from either of the two original cultures. This probably laid the stage for the process of formation of synthesis to syncretism in this part of lower Bengal.

From the above note it is apparent that there was a tendency or effort to reconcile and unite various systems of philosophy or religious opinion on the basis of tenets common to all and against a common enemy. This fusion of two or more inflectional forms, which were originally different as of two cases of religion, has taken a root under the canopy of syncretism. The form of synthesis/syncretism as is seen in Sundarban is an attempt for blending, harmonising of different or antagonistic elements, which were clearly understandable in terms of the peopling of Sundarbans, habitational pattern, composition of folk songs, belief in saints (particularly Muslim saints) myths and legends that are current among people professing different religious, practising varied occupational pursuits and from the pattern of immigration to this soil.

From the foregoing discussion with empirical field observation it appears that each community maintains its ethnic boundary through social structure, ritual and festivals etc. but during profession oriented activities or life struggle activities the ethnic boundary is not taken into account due to survival in such a niche. The local ecological factors forced them to adopt the local or folk cultural behaviours in order to maintain livelihood which ultimately led to the process of religious synthesis as well as syncretism but it is restricted only among jungle goers. The religious factors centering around Ban bibi–Dakshinrai–Gazi–Nai bibi etc. makes cohesive agent between caste-creed and religious sects. Whether a saint of a god is Hindu or Muslim is not a crucial importance, in Sundarban it is the land itself that gives its Saints and its people their wisdom, their power and their peace. The Gazi Saheb is a fakir–a Muslim Shaman. His powers are believed to be so effective that they can clear an entire section of forest of danger, allowing the fisherman, wood cutters, or honey collectors in his company to work there safely. Therefore, he is in great demand in Sundarban. His powers are unequivocal and work equally well both among Hindus and Muslims, as believed by jungle entrants of Sundarban. Therefore, it is assumed that under compulsion of the dreaded niche of Sundarban and for maintaining subsistence the jungle entrants as well as villagers of Sundarban area are adopting local cultural behaviour, where caste, religion and ethnic boundary is no barrier. For the sake of their smooth livelihood they maintain a peaceful and harmonious co-existence in this environment.

Considering the mythical textual data i.e. from Mangal Kavya (Bhattacharya, 1957), Banobibir Jahurnama (Munshi, 1388 B. S. ), Gaji-Kalu-o-Champabati (Munshi, 1388 B. S) as well as present empirical observation it can also be said that it is a kind of conflict between two Hindu-Muslim religion for domination over each other. Dakshinrai was Military General under Mukut Roy Kingdom and vehemently in opposition of Islam faith but his surrounding states accepted subordination under Islamic impact. Perhaps, due to this situation there arose a myth where Gazi-Kalu-Banbibi-Shajangali etc. characters appeared with power and respect due to their welfare activities to people at this delta region. It is assumed Dakshinrai was an expert in war on the water as this area is known as *'Bhatir desh'* (land of low tide are) and his power matched that of a ferocious tiger of Sundarban (the empirical data reveals that in some places Dakshinrai is worshipped in icon where his face is alike to roaring tiger while body is alike to human). It is also thought that Gazi can control the wrath of ferocious tiger and hence is considered as a religious preacher, which also indicates that the Gazi due to his soft and saintly behaviour and charismatic welfare activity among Sundarban people was able to control a cruel personality like Dakshinrai and who in turn accepts his subordination which certainly indicate a kind of mutual co-existence between two groups. This behaviour of mutual co-existence is reflected in various cultural spheres among Sundarban people and the present treatise is one such example.

**Discussion**

Now the empirical data cearly suggests that the people of Sundarban Biosphere has contributed to the formation of a syncretic platform through the process of cultural synthesis where all the communities contribute to the acceptance of certain deities which ultimately leads to harmonious co-existence between different social and religious ethnic groups.

It has also been observed that the people of this locale (i.e. Sundarban) are struggling primarily for survival and their subsistence and in the second category there are cure deities all of which are deeply enmeshed with the local people. The hierarchy of local pantheon is at first category–the deities associated with survival and subsistence, which is followed, by the cure deities, which often cut across and overlap the ethnic boundary. Tribals of this region who were immigrated chiefly for forest reclamation work here also adapted to the local belief and pantheon in view of their survival and existence in this island environment. In course of time it becomes a part and parcel of their life and culture.

## References

Bhattacharya, Asutosh, 1957, Bangla Mangal Kavyer Itihas, Calcutta: A. Mukherjee Sons.

Bose, N. K. 1941, "The Hindu Method of Tribal Absorption. " *Science and Culture*, Vol. VIII.

Chattopadhyay, Tushar Kumar, 1981, "Dakshinrai Cult", in *A focus on Sundarban,* ed. A. K. Das., et. al., Calcutta: Edition Indian

Das, Amal Kumar, 1981, "Trend of Population" in *A Focus on Sundarban,* ed. A. K. Das et. al., Calcutta: Editions Indian.

Mukherjee, Sankarananda, 1981, "Historical and Geographical Background", in *A Focus on Sundarban,* ed. A. K. Das et. al. Calcutta: Editions Indian.

Munshi, M. Khater, 1388 (B.S.), *Bonbibir Juhurnama,* Calcutta: Gaosia Library.

Munshi, A. Rahim 1388 (B.S.), *Gaji–Kalu–o–Champabati,* Calcutta, Gaosia Library.

Niyogi, Tushar K., 1996, *Tiger Cult of the Sundarbans,* Calcutta: Anthropological Survey of India (Memoir No. 95).

Singh, K. S., 1992, *People of India: Introduction.* Calcutta: Anthropological Survey of India.

## (b) Culture and Adaptation among Hilly Terrain Inhabitants of Odisha

Kandhamal district of Odisha is a forest clad with hilly terrain; chiefly this area is largely covered with deciduous forest with a number of perennial water sources. The chief inhabitants are the Kandh–a ST and its inalienable neighbour the Pano or Kui Domanga–a SC. They practice *podu* (Shifting hill) cultivation and their major cash crops are turmeric and ginger. Till date the major part of the district is covered with forest and with hilly terrain.

Khondmals sub-division is a wild hilly tract intersected in all direction by streams and torrents, which run dry after the rains. The area of arable land is small. The uplands and the slopes leading down from the foot of the hills are periodically cleared for raising dry crops and the low paddy lands have been permanently cleared and cultivated every year. The rest of the country is covered with thick forest. Kalinga ghat is the main gateway to Balliguda and Khondmals sub-division from the Ganjam side. After climbing continuously for about 11 km. one arrives at Kalinga, a height of 701 metres, from where a road leads to Phulbani and another goes to Balliguda via G. Udaygiri. The entire sub division of Balliguda is a plateau and lies at a height varying from 300 to 1100 metres above the sea level. The hills of the sub division are a part of the Eastern Ghats and lie within the Deccan plateau. Owing to its higher latitude, the climate is tempered to a considerable degree (Gazetteer of India: Orissa, Boudh—Khondmals, 1983 ).

The present study was carried out at Kandhamal district of Odisha especially centering around Balliguda block. We have carried out our research investigation in a number of villages of various panchyats and blocks. All of them are located in erstwhile Kandhamal Sub-division of Phulbani district of Odisha. Among all the villages, we have made intensive study at Budrukia village of Balliguda block.

The villages where we have carried out our field investigation have a distinctive form, with rows of houses, joined under a continuous roof, one row on each side of a whole road—very much different from other tribal inhabited villages, where households are usually dispersed. In the centre or in a corner of the village there stands sacred places of *darni penu, soru penu, burha penu,* and *kor koba* where buffalo sacrifice is made during *merriah* or *kedu puja (yatra)* in the month of March, prior to agricultural season.

### Methodology

We, the researchers, employed the following tools for generating empirical data. Firstly, we would like to submit that it is primarily an extensive survey work. To substantiate primary data we have carried out survey work in a number of villages in order to understand the variation and the area of operation of particular cultural attribute or attributes for both the communities. The data were collected from the Kui Domanga or Pano and the Kuinga or Kandh/Kondh community who are living in all the villages together. Group interviews with case studies were employed. The key informants were from panchyat level, village and community's elites and the *laka gatanju or* priests and *kepagatanju/clega* or gunia(i.e. sorcerer). In some cases 'observer participant' technique was also employed in case of data collection on *'merriah yatra'*(to appease earth deity they made human sacrifice in earlier days. Apart from those, genealogy, structured questionnaires and focused interviews were also made. In all the studied villages the Pano and the Kandh are kui speakers. The field work was carried out from March, 2014 to May, 2014 at various villages of Kandhmal district of Odisha. After completing 1st draft of the report the researchers again visited the field area on last week of June, 2014 and the draft report was read before the informants and was taken necessary observation from them and finally the same are incorporated in the final report.

**Name of the Studied Villages (Kandhamal District, Odisha)**

| *Name of the Village* | *Block / Panchayat* | *Ethnic Composition (with approx. number of families)* | *Infra-structural facilities available in the village* |
|---|---|---|---|
| 1. Budrukia | Balliguda block | Kui Kandh or Khand (200), Kui Domanga or Pano (30), Goura (1), Guru (1) | Electricity, Dish TV, Tube well, Well, Anganbadi, Primary School |
| 2. Dandapadar | Balliguda block | Kui Kandh or Khand (3), Kui Domanga or Pano (37), Brhaman (1) | Electric, Dish TV, Tube Well, Well, Kachha road, Pr. School (2), Upper Primary (1), Anganbadi (3). Having 05 hamlets. |
| 3. Borikiya | Balliguda block | Kui Kandh or Khand (50), Kui Domanga or Pano (50), Gouda (1) | Electricity, Anganbadi, Chua for drinking water and bathing, Upper Primary School upto class VIII, kachha fair weather road. |
| 4. Kurtamgada | Tumudi-bandh block | Kui Kandh or Kuinga or Khand (30), Kui Domanga or Pano (9) | Electricity, Anganbadi, pr. School, Tube well, nearest health centre is 18 km. away, from village to nearest bus stop is 22 km. away. |
| 5. Masedikia | Raikia block | Kui Kandh or Khand (32), Kui Domanga or Pano (60) | Electricity, well, motorable road, Dish TV, School, Anganbadi |

*contd. . .*

*contd. . .*

| *Name of the Village* | *Block / Panchayat* | *Ethnic Composition (with approx. number of families)* | *Infra-structural facilities available in the village* |
|---|---|---|---|
| 6. Solakia | Balliguda | Kui Kandh or Khand (37), Kui Domanga or Pano (33) | Electricity, Church, No dispensary, Anganbadi, School (I-V) |
| 7. Solabadi | Simanbadi GP, Daringbadi block | Kui Kandh or Khand (42), Kui Domanga or Pano ( (22). | Electricity, Tube well, Church, Dish Tv, Pucca road, Pr. School |
| 8. Dasingbadi | Daringbadi block | Kui Kandh or Khand (158), Kui Domanga or Pano (200), Oriya Patnaik (1) | Pucca road, Electricity, Anganbadi, Panchayat office, School: High, Middle, Primary, Auxilary Nursing Midwifery. |
| 9. Kandi Banda | K. Nuagaon block | Kui Kandh or Khand (21), Kui Domanga or Pano (7), Gauda (1), Oriya (3) | Electricity, Dish TV, Chua for drinking water, Church, Kachha road. Non Kui speaking people identified here as 'Sashi'. |
| 10. Midiakia | Balliguda block | Kui Kandh or Khand (200), Kui Domanga or Pano (74), Oriya and Paik (200) | Electricity, Fair price shop, Kachha road, Anganbadi, Primary School, High School, Auxillary Nursing Midwifery. |
| 11. Dombuli | Daringbadi block | Kui Kandh or Khand, Kui Domanga or Pano | Kachha road, Well, electricity, Anganbadi. |
| 12. Kumbar Munda | Daringbadi block, Kirkuti Panchayat | Kui Kandh or Khand, Kui Domanga or Pano | Kachha road,chua for drinking water |
| 13. Sadaa Panga | Daringbadi block, Tilori Panchayat | Kui Kandh or Khand (12), Kui Domanga or Pano (25) | Electricity, well, Pr. School, Anganbadi, Kachha road |
| 14. Kampada | Balliguda block | Kui Kandh or Khand (15), Kui Domanga or Pano (32) | Electricity, Anganbadi, Tubewell, well, Situated on the metalled road. |
| 15. Badagaon (Madapada) | Balliguda block | Kui Kandh or Khand (20), Kui Domanga or Pano (20) | Electricity, dish TV, Anganbadi, Tube well, Well, Patakhanda temple |
| 16. Gumikia | Balliguda block, Bataguda Panchayat | Kui -Khand (15), Kui Domanga or Pano (27) | Electricity, Pucca road, Tube well, Church, Pr. School. |

*contd. . .*

*contd. . .*

| *Name of the Village* | *Block / Panchayat* | *Ethnic Composition (with approx. number of families)* | *Infra-structural facilities available in the village* |
|---|---|---|---|
| 17. Sakusabali | K. Nuagaon block | Kui Kandh or Kandh (30), Kui Domanga or Pano (13), Oriya (8). | Electricity, Anganbadi, kachha road, Well, tubewell |
| 18. Tiangia | G. Udaygiri block, Katingia Panchayat | Kui Kandh or Kuinga or Khand (45), Kui-Domanga or Pano (80), Khandait (4) | Electricity, Tubewell, well, Anganbadi, Church, Road inside the village is of concrete, Dish TV, grocer's shop, matha (temple). Here Kui Domanga or Pano are weavers. |
| 19. Barakhama ( Badasahi) | Balliguda block | Kui Kandh or Kandh, Kui Domanga or Pano, Ghasi (8),Oriya Patra | Electricity, Kuchha road, Well, Anganbadi. Entrance road of the village is of metalled. |
| 20. Sonaponga | Chakapada (Tikabali) block | Kui Kandh or Kandh (34), Kui Domanga or Pano (55), Gauda (4), Gudra (4). | Electricity, Anganbadi, Tubewell, Well, internal road of the village is of kachha, nearest health centre is 8 K.M. away at Tikabali. |
| 21. Pabingia | Phiringia block, Pabingia Gram Panchayat | Kui Kandh or Kandh (150), Kui Domanga or Pano (80), Hadi (4), Patra (4). | Electricity, Tube well, Dish TV, Post office, internal road of the villge is Kachha, Church, Mahila Samity, High School and Primary School, Veternary dispensary, Angan Badi. |

Presently the Kui Domanga and Kandh are primarily cultivators. Along with cultivation, they also do collection from jungle. Some among them also work both in skilled and unskilled sectors. Now a days, hunting as an occupation is not pursued, instead both *podu* and plough cultivation are done by them. Hunting or *plambu*-Now-a-days hunting as an occupation is not taken up by them. . In the jungle the preys are rarely found. It is done occasionally. It is connected with some rituals such as kedu. After *kedu* festival is completed, they arrange for hunting. Before going to hunting they (both Kandh and Pano or Kui Domanga together), arrange for the puja of *Beta penu* or *Budeli laka devi.* It is performed during day time by the male folk at the village boundary.

**Map of Odisha**

**Focussed Area**

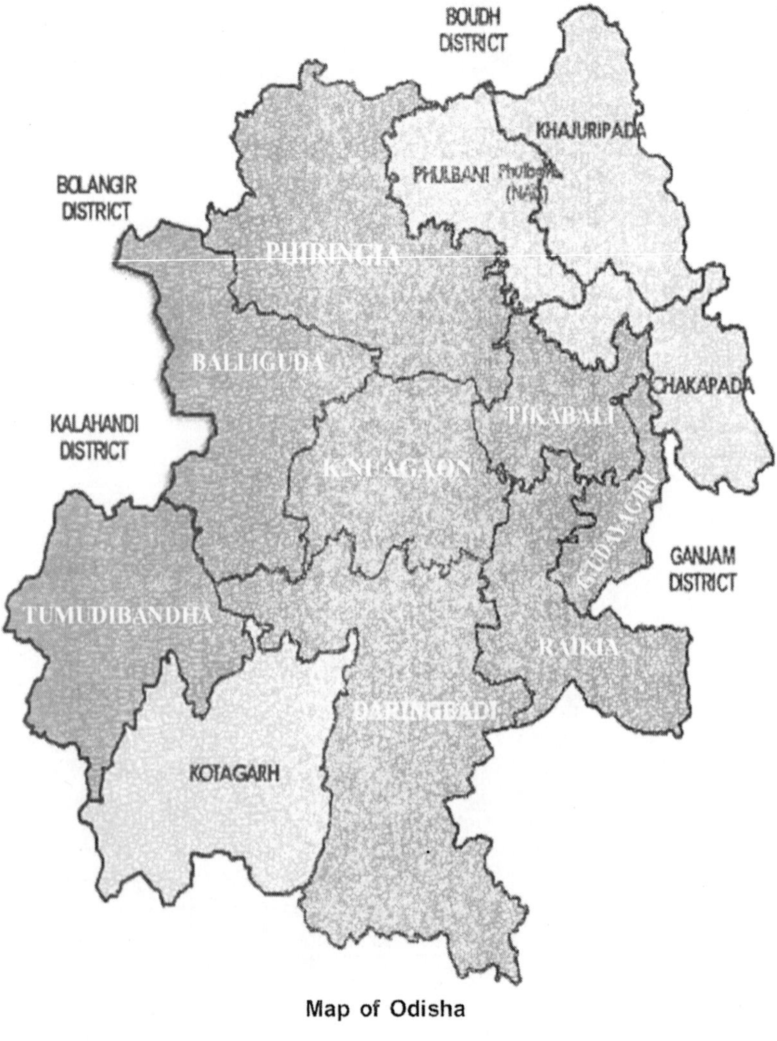


**Map of Odisha**

**List of Minor Forest Produces for Sustenance for both Pano or Kui Domanga and Kandh or Koenga**

| Season | English. equivalent. | Oriya equivalent | Collected Items |
|---|---|---|---|
| **Pijudeli** | (June-Sept) Rainy Season. (September is lean season for them.). | **Kamakara (Varsa Rutu)** **(Kamakara means earn food by work. Kama means work and Kara means food.)** | Pa-dasi (jackfruit), La-sengi (fruit), Na-ndru (blackberry), Jrakie (Kadam flower), Terka (bamboo shoot), Ka-sami (kusum seed and flower), Bda-haa (fruit), Musadi (fruit), Pudra (pumpkin), , Paeraka (siari leaves to make plates and bowls), Da-rka (bark of darka tree to make rope), Kadakanga (a kind of pulses of hills), Jurgakanga (amla or aonla), Tdasukanga (fruit), Sralikanga (tamarind), Mundru (cucumber), Kareka (bitterguard), Jae-Ika (maize), G-anda (crop), Jadi (crop}, Jargi-aka (sal leaves), Sadali (resin), Sani (gum), Katreka (jungle kundru), Beteka (fruit), Napanga (fruit), Patinga (tuber), Jargi Pananga (sal leaves to make plates and bowls), Paeri pananga (piari leaves bowl), |
| **Peni deli** | (Oct-Jan) Winter | **Enda Kraha (Sito Rutu)** (Endakraha means time for playing, dancing, merry making; it is the time for harvest). | Kudinga (paddy), Masanga (green gram), Dedi (mandia), Kueri (kusla), Arka, Katranga (seed of kangu), Kaulka (kalika?), Kadanga (kulthi- pulses), Kanga (pulses), Mara (seed to prepare vegetables), Tilaka (oil seed), Sarsa kusa (sarso sag), Sainga (seem), Kadakanga (jurunga pulses), Rasika (til), Sarsa (mustard), Sambukunanga (aram tuber), Medakunanga tuber), Rajikunanga (root and tubers), Kambakunanga (sakalu), Tdasukanga (harra seed), Lasakanga (Bahera seed), Nedi (tamarind), Kamla (orange), Alu (potato), Pudranga (pumpkin), Mundruka (kakri), Mula, Bdakaka (similar type of vegetable like kakri), Paredi betaka (a kind of fruit), Pajaka (small sized brinjal with medicinal value for respiretory problem), Paerikanga (siari fruit), Bdumbeka (a type of fruit). |
| **Kara deli** | (Feb-May) Summer | **Plambu-beta (Grisma Rutu)** **(Time for forest activities like hunting, collection of MFP and marriage season).** | Irpi (mahua flower), Pdia (green mango), Taga (fig), Pipali (papal ), Baandangi (fruit of banyan tree), Sreka (fruit), Maha (mango), Bdaha (fruit), Sindikanga (khejur), Kendu (fruits and leaves), Garinga (mahua seed), Paerikanga (piyari fruit), Maradaka (sal seed), Kapukasa ( a type of leafy vegetable), Patakalu ( a type of red coloured flower), Puki (honey), Nisu (honey), Nedilguts fruit), Alu–ulu (A type of onion).Lesudi, Patalguta (tomato), Dua (tobacco), Sainga (seem), Sambukusa (leafy vegetables of aram), Beska aka (fuel wood), |

Mushroom or *kutka* –These are collected in rainy season. Names of some mushrooms are given below:

Mandelanga, Patruka, Mendang kutka, Pisaka, Daloka, Lugamorenji, Pusilipka, Sekadanga, Nandru kutka, Sroi kutka, Joger kutka. Except the last one all the *kutkas* are edible. In the hills they practice *podu* or shifting hill cultivation. The area is common land.

Each individual family is used to do *podu* in the area of hills that they could clear for thatcultivation. No outsider is allowed. Later the village headman, after several meetings with the villagers, settles the boundary of land for each family.

Indigenous peoples have rich and diverse cultures based on a profound spiritual relationship with their land and its natural resources. Dichotomies such as nature vs. culture do not exist in indigenous societies. Indigenous peoples do not see themselves as outside the realm of nature, but as part of it, and they have their own specific attachment to their land and territory and their own specific modes of production based on a unique knowledge of their environment. In many indigenous cultures, social and political institutions are part of the cosmic order, and it is on the basis of their worldview, beliefs, values and customs that indigenous peoples define their own forms of governance, as well as their customary laws and norms. Another salient characteristic of indigenous cultures is that they are based on a collective perspective. In the same way that indigenous peoples consider their lands and resources to be collective assets, they see their cultural values and activities—their identity—as a function of the group, not of individuals. This also applies to the ownership and custody of their cultural heritage, which is collective. Indigenous communities have kept their cultures alive by passing on their worldview, their knowledge and know-how, their arts, rituals and performances from one generation to the next.

The salient observation in these blocks among the Pano or Kui Domanga is that they are animistic (*pdadhisaja* in kui dialect) in nature (i.e. no anthropomorphic images are worshiped, on the contrary they are nature worshipper), no Brhamanical services are also required in their life cycle rituals which are very much closely akin to their immediate neighbour–the Kandh, especially in customary laws.

The religious life of both Kandhand Pano are very similar to each other. They primarily are nature worshippers. They believe that god is there in the hills, jungles, rivers, and streams. Their ancestors are their deities who protect them from all evils and dangers. They invoke their souls and install them in their house. To them, Bura penu is the creator of the earth, Piter Penu is his wife, Pideri Pita is their ancestor, Ijam penu is the inner room where they store their harvested grains, Jaker penu is another name of Darni penu.

Penu is the term for both male and female deities Again *penu* are of two types such as *negipenu* or benevolent *penu* and *da-e penu* or malevolent *penu*. Some of them are described in the following lines:-

**Darni Penu:** She is the supreme Deity. She is their mother goddess and earth godedess. In each and every new harvest, they offer her fruits and flowers. In case of breach of the norm which is an insult to her, they believe that tiger will come in the village and is sure to do some harm. . Generally she is installed in a place of the village which is called as Darni or Jakeri. In this place there are three boulders. The two large boulders are named as badawali regarded as one of the deity who protects hills. Next is jakerbali. She protects Jaker or Darni. The smallest one is siribali/milawali who are the children of badawali. Together they are called Darni. These apart, there are three wooden pillers in the village in the directions of east and west and third one is established in the centre. The pillers of east and west protect the village from any type of evil from outside. These two pillers are known as *ota koba* and the piller of the middle is known as *karu kaba.* It protects Darni penu from all evils. Media is her puja or ritual and it is the most important festival in their life held once in a year during March-April before the starting of cultivation. Both Kandh and Pano of a village perform it together.

**Saru or Soru penu:** He is regarded as mountain god. He is also their protector from all evils. He is specially worshipped as he protects them from all disasters such as heavy rain, storm, and thundering etc. Saru penu always gives them support in their crises. When a woman has no child, or a person is sick or suffering from fever or any other disease, they call the penu with a vow of worship and offerings of chicken or goat. At the time of keeping vow they take some sundried rice and a small chick. The chick eats the rice grain and is freed at the boundary of their homestead. It is then not sacrificed. It grows and after the request is fulfilled, it is sacrificed before two days of merriah.

**Piju penu:** He is rain god. He is worshipped with a prayer for plenty of rain which is necessary for cultivation. He is worshipped during the month of Jaishth/Jestha.

**Tada penu:** Another name of Darni penu. She is worshipped for plenty of harvest. She also protects them from all ghosts and evils.

**Birma penu:** In the month of April he is worshipped in a place outside their village under a tree where a boulder is placed or in the hills before seed sowing. After his worship they sow seed for a successful cultivation. It is believed that if they worship her then they will get a rich harvest and the penu will guard his cultivable land. She is not worshipped on Tuesday, Thursday and Saturday.

**Linga penu:** He is responsible for building structures along with figures of all living creatures. Except ferocious animals/creatures in the forest they used to prepare effigy of deer, elephant etc. of hollow-metal cast dokra and place those on the *chhatta* of Darni to appease linga penu.

**Jo-Ra penu:** She is also called as Jara penu. She gives protection to the children from their birth from all evils. It is told that she takes a newborn on her lap as soon as the child is born. If she leaves the child, it will die immediately. Again it is told that she protects all the living creatures from all the evils from their birth till death. If she leaves anybody he or she will die immediately. To worship Jo-Ra, they call **gunia** who takes a thread, turmeric paste, sundried rice and a chicken. He anoints the thread with turmeric paste, then cuts a portion of the feet of the chicken and ties it with the thread. The **gunia** or **kuutagatanju** or **tlamba** then ties knots in the thread and sprinkles sundried rice on the child with chanting of *mantras*. In this way they worship Jo-Ra penu for the child's protection.

**Badi penu**-Her sacred place is situated close to the place of Darni or Jaker. During Media/meria festival or *kodu laka*, after the buffalo sacrifice, it's ears, lung etc. are kept in that place. Then those are set fire to burn alongwith the dead body at the time of cremation. Then they sprinkle all the crops and cereals harvested throughout the year in the fire. All the villagers both Kandh and Pano dance encircling the fire. She is the mother goddess who protects the village from all evils. It is called as *baditrapa*.

They have some *penus* who are not benevolent but have power to do harm. Because of this, they worship also to appease them so that they will not do any harm.

According to their religious pantheon they considered following hills are the abode of their ancestors, namely, *Dimbuli* (a female deity, her area is extended from Koraput → Kalahandi → Kandhamal border), *Srambuli* (a female deity, her area is from east of Dimbuli), *Aseri* (west of Dimbuli, that is, Daringbadi, K. Nuagaon, Balliguda and Kotoguda blocks) and *Goseri* (border area of three blocks namely, Daringbadi, K. Nuagaon and Kotoguda blocks). Accordingly both the ethnic groups appease them in the beginning of each ritual activities.

Since they are animists in their faith and in their ancestral worship and also in other ritual activities they chant in the beginning *'nagela, bondela, kula, doha dimbuli, srambuli, aseri* and *goseri'* which are the names of their ancestors.

Information of their yearly religious cycle as collected from field is given below—

**Annual Ritual Calendar**

| *Month or danju* | *Meaning of the local term used as month* | *English equivalent* | *Rituals and festivals* |
|---|---|---|---|
| Ka-eri danju (Pous) | Ko-eri means when all cereals, crops etc. and food are plenty in house | Dec.-Jan. | Dangar puja, Diali puja |
| Kanga danju (Magh) | Kanga is a kind of dal or millet. | Jan.-Feb. | Kanga laka |
| Irpi danju (Fagun) | Irpi means mahua | Feb.-Mar. | Kanga ka-eri ritual |
| Pdiha danju (Chaitra) | Pdiha means green mango. | Mar.-April | In this month they perform merriah or kedu laka When they worship Darni, after that they perform Budeli laka when they worship Budel penu also known as Beta penu. Raha balo (within March to May) |
| Maha danju (Vaisakh) | Maha means ripen mango | April-May | They worship birma penu (they perform the ritual at village boundary except on Thursday and Saturday. Wednesday and Tuesday are the best day, Raha balo (within March to May) |
| Mata danju (Jaistha) | Sowing month | May-June | No ritual except Raha balo |
| Uha danju (Ashad) | Plantation of maize and specially paddy. | June-July | |
| Ganda Danju/Gurji Danju/Sakki Danju (Sravan) | Gurji or suji type millet | July-Aug. | Malangi laka |
| jueli danju (Bhadro) | Maize | Aug.-Sept. | No ritual. |

| *Month or danju* | *Meaning of the local term used as month* | *English equivalent* | *Rituals and festivals* |
|---|---|---|---|
| Bika/Biko danju/ Sakki Danju (Aswin) | Lean season | Sept.-Oct. | Kudi koeri (Naya khani- When they offer first ripened crop/cereals to Darni and consume), Saki penu laka. |
| Enda danju Kartick | Dancing and harvesting season | Oct.-Nov. | No ritual |
| Mogsiro (Oriya language) danju/ Kueri danju (Aghran) | Sugi like grain | Nov.-Dec. | No ritual. |

Some rituals are observed at the family level; that is; performed separately by the families individually and separately. All these rituals are performed by both the communities.

Now, at a glance we may see the chief cultural attributes of the Kui Domanga or Pano and Kuinga or Kandh in the studied area:

**The Salient Characteristic features in terms of Cultural attributes between the Kui Domanga/Pano and Kuinga or Kandh**

| *Sl. No.* | *Cultural attributes: Parameter* | *Kui Domanga/Pano* | *Kuinga/Kandh* |
|---|---|---|---|
| 1. | Language | Kui | Kui |
| 2. | Clan; Practice exogamy | Totemic like-- Kumbhar (earthen vessel), Kushala/ Kusaliya (a kind of ragi-cereal), Kuldipa (lamp), Bagh (tiger), Kuer (a kind of cereal), Surjal (sun), Basiya, Beda, Urma etc. | Totemic like— Mallick, Jani, Kahara, Jhankara, Majhi, Pat majhi, Bhoi, Sona majhi, Basinga, Manglanga, Jatolanga, Benaranga, Kundunga, Sonudanga etc. |
| 3. | Dress, Ornaments and Tattoo marks on the face and forehead | These are same with the Kandh and one cannot differentiate from other. | These are same with the Pano and one cannot differentiate it from the other. |
| 4. | House type and internal lay out | These are same with the Kandh and one cannot differentiate from other. | These are same with the Pano and one cannot differentiate from other. |
| 5. | Rites-de-Passage or Life cycle rituals. | These are same with the Kandh and one cannot differentiate from other | These are same with the Pano and one cannot differentiate from other |
| 6. | Kinship terminology | Iraquois type | Iraquois type. |

*contd. . .*

*contd. . .*

| *Sl. No.* | *Cultural attributes: Parameter* | *Kui Domanga/Pano* | *Kuinga/Kandh* |
|---|---|---|---|
| 7. | Putative Kinship | Existence of *Sahudomanga* with the Kandh only. | Existence of Sahu domanga with the Pano/Kui Domanga only. |
| 8. | Cultivation | The empirical data also speaks that the primitive or pre-literate section of Kui Domanga or Pano and Kuinga or Kandh are largely in the studied area of the district are *podu* or shifting hill cultivators—one of the remarkable trait of primitiveness.<br><br>Even the folk taxonomy of land classification on the basis of retention of water in the land are equal and same with Kuinga/Kandh. | The empirical data also speak that the primitive or pre-literate section of Kui Domanga or Pano and Kuinga or Kandh largely in the studied area of the district are *podu* or shifting hill cultivators—one of the remarkable trait of primitiveness.<br><br>Even the folk taxonomy of land classification on the basis of retention of water in the land are equal and same with Pano/Kui Domanga. |
| 9. | (a) Religious belief and Practices | They are nature worshipper, their belief in various spirits, hills etc. are very much similar with the Kandh.<br><br>Both the endogamous groups believe in Darni - the earth goddess and the Supreme being. She is not only powerful but the highest among all deities in their religious pantheon. She is also responsible for the growth of vegetation and other produce of land. | They are nature worshipper, belief in various spirits, hills etc. which are very much similar with the Kui Domanga/Pano.<br><br>Both the endogamous groups believe in Darni - the earth goddess and the Supreme being. She is not only powerful but the highest among all deities in their religious pantheon. She is also responsible for the growth of vegetation and other produce of land. |
| | (b) Appeasement of hills | Distinct belief systems in following hills which are considered as the abode of their ancestors namely, *Dimbuli*, *Srambuli*, *Aseri* and Goseri – to appease them in the beginning of all ritual activities. | Distinct belief systems in following hills which are considered as the abode of their ancestors namely, *Dimbuli*, *Srambuli*, *Aseri* and Goseri – to appease them in the beginning of all ritual activities. |

*contd. . .*

*contd. . .*

| *Sl.No.* | *Cultural attributes: Parameter* | *Kui Domanga/Pano* | *Kuinga/Kandh* |
|---|---|---|---|
| 10. | Spirituality and belief system:<br>Annual lineage festival or brotherhood of clan festival | In an insecure forest environment, festival such as *merriah* or *kedu* emerged as a celebrated festival. It ushered in a time for sharing with one another; a time for rekindling and strengthening community bonds on which depended their very survival.<br>This is chiefly a festival to appease earth deity–*darni*, performed prior to agricultural season in the month of *Irpi danju* (March). | In an insecure forest environment, festival such as *merriah* or *kedu* emerged as a celebrated festival. It ushered in a time for sharing with one another; a time for rekindling and strengthening community bonds on which depended their very survival.<br>This is chiefly a festival to appease earth deity –*darni*, performed prior to agricultural season in the month of *Irpi danju* (March). |
| 11. | Priest are custodian of village welfare/shrine/village people/cattle etc. | Among both the ethnic groups the same person—*Tlamba* or *Kutauguru* or *Kutagatanju* performs the duty as and when required. | Among both the ethnic groups the same person—*Tlamba* or *Kutauguru* or *Kutagatanju* performs the duty as and when required. |
| 12. | Magical rites specialists | The person responsible for black magic is *Clega* or *Kepagatangu* and performs his duty as and when required for both the community. | The person responsible for black magic is *Clega* or *Kepagatangu* and performs his duty as and when required for both the community |
| 13. | Belief in transmigration of soul | Same belief with the Kandh and perform ritual after delivery of a new born. | Same belief with the Kui Domanga/Pano and perform ritual after delivery of a new born. |
| 14. | Typical political Organisation | They are part and parcel of Muttah organisation as a member of the village. | They are part and parcel of Muttah organisation as a member of the village. |

## V

## Observation and Conclusion

Adaptation is a behavioural process that seeks satisfactions for present needs, with greater or lesser concern for the future. Human social systems are all adaptive; some are more dynamic than others. In the preceding pages the empirical situation clearly suggests how the cultures of the indigenous people in hilly-forest area are influenced with the physical environment for a sustainable living condition. They have adapted to the specific natural environment since the hoary past. The culture and environment of this indigenous population are so closely fused into each other which clearly remind us Harris (1968) observation on 'Cultural Materialism', which he defines as "similar technologies applied to similar environments produce similar arrangements of labour in production and distribution and that those in turn call forth similar kinds of social groupings, which justify and coordinate their activities by means of similar systems of values and beliefs" (Bennett, 1976). Thus, it appears that in the struggle for survival, interaction with the nature for sustenance, there is a mutual inter-dependence with the socio-economic-system in one hand and the religious belief systems on the other which are mutually inter related. in the particular niche referring to the observation made by Morab (1981) among the Soliga of Biligiri Rangana Hills of Mysore district.

## References

Anderson, J. N. 1973, "Ecological Anthropology and Anthropological Ecology", in handbook of social and Cultural anthropology, (ed.) J. J. Honigman, Chicago: Rand McNally.

Bennett, John, W. 1976, The Ecological Transition: Cultural Anthropology and Human Adaptation, New York: Pergamon Press Inc.

Frake, C. O. 1962, "Cultural Ecology and Ethnography", American Anthropologist, Vol. 64.

Harris, M. 1966, "The Cultural Ecology of India's Sacred Cattle", Current Anthropology, Vol. 7, pp. 51-61.

Harris, Marvin, 1968 The Rise of Anthropological Theories, New York: Crowell

Morab, S. G. 1981, "The Soliga: A Study in Ecology, Society and Religion of a Hill Tribe in South India", in Nature Man Spirit Complex in Tribal India (ed.) R. S. Mann, New Delhi: Concept Publishing Company.

Sahlins, Marshall, D. 1964, "Culture and Environment: The Study of Cultural Ecology", in Horizons of Anthropology, (ed.) Sol Tax, London: Allen and Unwin Ltd.

Steward, Julian, H. 1955, Theory of Culture Change, Urbana: University of Illinois Press.

# 11

# Study of Traditional Knowledge

## Prologue

Indigenous or Traditional Knowledge (I. K. or T. K. ) refers to the unique, traditional, local knowledge existing within and developed around the specific condition of women and men indigenous to a particular geographic area. The development of TK/IK systems, covering all aspects of life, including management of natural resources have been a matter of survival to the people who generated these systems. It is based on experience, often tested over centuries and adapted to local culture, environment and dynamics. Other names for TK/IK are local knowledge, folk knowledge, indigenous technical knowledge and traditional ecological knowledge.

Rural people have an intimate knowledge of many aspects of their surroundings and their daily life is governed as per the dictum of such knowledge. Over centuries, people have learned how to grow food and to survive even in difficult environments. They possess knowledge of varieties of crops to cultivate in a same plot considering the nature of soil and its water retention capacity, when to sow and weed, which plants, tubers and mushroom are poisonous and which can be used for medicine, (i.e. particular part of the plant), how to cure diseases and how protect or preserve their environment in harmonious manner and in sustainable fashion.

This TK/IK covers a wide range of subject such as agriculture, food preparation, education, institutional management, natural resource management, health care and many other allied disciplines.

IK is stored in people's memories and activities and is expressed in the form of stories, songs, folklore, proverbs, dances, myth, cultural values, beliefs, rituals, community laws, local language and taxonomy agricultural practices, equipment, materials, plant species and animal breeds. IK is shared and communicated orally by specific examples and through culture. It may be noted that IK is not confined to tribal groups or the original inhabitants of an area; it is not even confined to rural people, rather any community may possesses indigenous knowledge –among the rural/urban/settled/nomadic/and migrants too.

Learning from IK can improve understanding of local conditions and provide a productive context for activities designed to help the communities. Yet IK is still an underutilised resource in the development activities. Special efforts are needed to understand, document and disseminate IK for preservation, transfer or adoption elsewhere.

The holders of indigenous/traditional knowledge and initial conservers of biodiversity in rural India remain marginalised and poor while on the other hand those who use their heritage knowledge bank and material in commercial way through biotechnological enterprises are not only rich but well established in society. Now time has come to recognise the primary conservers of biodiversity for possessing and maintaining this knowledge bank over generations.

In order to understand the difference between IK and TK, the working definition following Kamal. K. Misra (2007) is taken into consideration. . While defining indigenous knowledge, he has listed the following characteristics:

Indigenous knowledge is local and culture-specific; it is orally transmitted through imitation and demonstration; it is the consequence of practical engagement in everyday life and is constantly reinforced by experience, trial and error and deliberate experiment; it tends to be empirical and empirico-hypothetical rather than theoretical in the strict sense; it is 'people's science' and is asymmetrically distributed in a population; the organisation of indigenous knowledge is essentially functional, denotative 'know-how' geared to practical response and performance; and it is holistic, integrative and situated within broader cultural traditions.

Traditional Knowledge and indigenous knowledge are often used as synonyms. However, indigenous knowledge is more confined to a group or locality, while traditional knowledge can be indigenous or non-indigenous for the practicing community. Hence, we would prefer the term Traditional Knowledge. Knowledge, which is collectively held from experience and transmitted inter-generationally is defined as TK. It is expressed through environmental knowledge:

a. Knowledge on the natural environment,

b. Knowledge on human modified environment.

Knowledge on social environment includes knowledge on self and others including knowledge about social organisation and conflict management (legal knowledge), agricultural knowledge, knowledge on health and hygiene, Traditional Technical Knowledge (TTK) religious knowledge, cultural interpretations of landscape etc. Some of this knowledge remains secret to their custodians, while many other forms of knowledge are expressed in public domain and shared within and beyond the boundary of the community. Thus, traditional knowledge is holistic, comprehensive, context sensitive, culturally compatible, environmentally viable and located within broader cultural traditions of the practicing communities. It is generally transmitted orally and through body centric performances and conservation ethics are often part of traditional knowledge.

## (A) FOR SUSTAINABLE DEVELOPMENT: TRADITIONAL KNOWLEDGE FOR SUSTENANCE AMONG THE ASUR

Human society is dynamic and it's culture is expressed through tangible and intangible forms. In the tangible forms of culture one can observe and even touch the objects while the intangible forms of culture can be felt through one's empathy and expressed through folklore, myth, riddle, and also through performing art forms etc. These are all included in intangible expression of a culture. Through all those tangible and intangible forms the indigenous knowledge and traditional knowledge are described.

Though apparently the term Traditional Knowledge (TK) and Indigenous Knowledge (IK) are synonymous to each other but in course of our empirical study among various communities of India it has emerged that there lies very subtle difference between these two. Traditional Knowledge (TK) is a holistic Knowledge of a community for his sustainable living while Indigenous Knowledge (IK) is usually very much local knowledge embedded in the community of a particular geographical terrain and very much unique to specific cultural group.

"Since the early 1990's, IK has been a fertile ground for research, exploring the ways in which it is stored in peoples memories and activities and expressed in stories, songs folk lore, proverbs, dances, myths, cultural values, beliefs, rituals, community laws, local languages and taxonomy, agricultural practices, equipments, materials, plant species and animal breeds etc. Attention is also being paid to how it is shared and communicated orally with specific examples and through culturally accepted ways of communication." (Misra, Kamal Kant; 2007).

Perhaps the most important outcome of the research on IK is to document the best practices and to replicate them in other places and communities. But there are many inherent problems in this exercise in this age of patenting, bio-piracy and Intellectual Property Rites (IPR). (*ibid*, 2007).

It is important to study indigenous knowledge as it is the local knowledge and the people (both permanent settlers and migrants) of a particular place have their own traditional knowledge. Now how the people of that particular region are adjusting to the local ecological condition responsible for growing of socio-economic life of that particular region applying either of or both traditional knowledge and indigenous knowledge suitable to a particular situation, is to be exnaustively examined.

In the present study the authors have done their work among the Asur-a primitive tribe of Chhotanagpur area of Jharkhand state of India. They live in the Netarhat Plateau, in the midst of forest of Gumla and Latehar Districts at 3600 feet height above sea level, where it is very difficult to reach. Among their villages some are Jovipat, Lodapat, Amtipani, Chhattasarai, Bhatthi Pat/Bhatipat, Naoatola, Kujam, Chapakona, Chotongpat, Kone, Komepat, Gorapahar, Khairipat, Sakhuapani, Polpolpat, Ramjharia, Pirhapat, Chakdipa, Kotia, Sonaitangar, Garhatoli, Kulhukona, Tiluwari, Dokapat, Lopungpat, Bijapat Bhariapat, etc. These are all situated in Gumla District. In Latehar District, Husumbu is the only one village where Asurs live. Here the investigators are interested to see how far the Asur are adjusting to their local niche with the help of local or indigenous knowledge even after they had to shift to other economic pursuits leaving their own traditional callings of iron smelting and slash and burn cultivation. Here it is necessary to mention that they have not totally forgotten or abandoned their own traditional knowledge rather they also apply it when and where it is necessary, applicable and also suitable.

There are several opinions on the term Asur. Leuva (1963: 3) was with opinion that they have similarities with Ashur in Assyria mean 'powerful people'. There is mention of Asur in several places of Rigveda, Upanishad and even in the epic Ramayana where they were mentioned as great builders. They also opine that they are the descendants or children of Asur of Ramayana who were cursed by Ravana originally their forefather and the king of Lanka to become dull and worthless as they fought against Ravana taking the side of Ram and also for killing their own brother, who was with Ravana. They are sure that due to his curse they are in the present state without any progress in a miserable condition.

Roy Bahadur S. C. Roy (1926) wrote that the Asur are divided into three sections namely Soikia Asur or Agaria, Birjia and Asur (Dasgupta; 1994). They also introduce themselves as Bir Asur. They claim that they are superior among the three groups and very strong and well-built just like Hanumanji and they call Birjias as Bandar whom they give a very low status. They told that they were originally the inhabitants of Patan of Sarguja district of Chhattishgarh. They used to do iron smelting work as their traditional calling where they used young Sal trees to generate heat (about 1500 degree Celsius) to melt stone containing iron-ore. One-day the king of Patan got irritated with the smoke of that burning wood and ordered his chiefs to drive out all the Asurs from his, state. As a result, they were forced to leave the place and migrated to nearby Gumla and Palamau region and ultimately settled to the Netarhat Plateau of the region.

The Asur informants told that once upon a time they were in dispute resulting to fight with their Oraon neighbours in the issue of their land. As a result they were defeated and had to leave their land and habitat and ultimately forced to leave Sarguja and settle in their present habitat at Netarhat Plateau.

According to 1991 census the Asur are 10712 in number and their literacy rate is 10. 66. Traditionally they are iron smelter. Along with iron smelting, they also used to do slash and burn cultivation. Hunting and collection from jungle were also very much important. Gradually they had to shift from iron smelting and slash and burn cultivation to settled cultivation. They had totally left iron smelting but could not totally stop slash burn cultivation. Hunting became an occasional and primarily a festive phenomenon. At present along with settled cultivation they do collection of various edible roots, fruits, tubers, mushroom, seeds etc and several non-edible items for their material use.

They are an endogamous community having atleast sixteen exogamous totemistic clans. Some of those are Indwar, Beng, Toppo, and Tiyigo etc. The tradition of child marriage in the community is presently replaced by adult marriage. As usual like their other neighbouring tribes they are very much afraid of the malevolent deities roaming in their vicinity. To keep them quiet theyresort to several rituals and magical performances. Along with those, several benevolent deities are also there who they believe are their protecting deities. Though they have totally stopped iron smelting work but could not stop *Sansikutasi* ritual attached with their iron smelting work.

The present in-depth empirical study was carried out at Sakhuapani village of Bishunpur block of Gumla district, Jharkhand. It is a more or less uniethnic Asur village. In the northern outskirt of the village there are bauxite mines where a few villagers are involved as wage earners. On the east of the village, there is a village named Jovipat, in west Dumberpat and at the south Amtipani and Ramjhoria villages are situated. Infact all the mentioned villages are situated in Gumla district. For substantiating our empirical observation we also collected quantitative data from Dodhikona tola of Husumboo village; it is a multi-ethnic village under Mahuadanr block of Latehar district. In addition to this, we also collected data from Ramjhoria and Jovipat villages.

The Asur villages are found situated either on *pat* or table land area or in *garha* or gorge area, such as Ramjhoria village is situated at gorge. There are altogether 25 Asur villages with a total 755 families in Bishunpur block of Gumla district and found chiefly in Jovipat, Dumberpat panchayat. It is also reported that altogether 1188 Asur families live in Gumla district and they are distributed in Ghaghra, Bishunpur, Chainpur, and Dumbri and Raidih blocks of the district.

The village Sakhuapani is about 35 km away from Netarhat-the base camp of our present investigation. The village roads are jeepable but kutchha. There is no electricity. For drinking water they depend on well and a tube well. There is one *anganbari* school and a residential secondary school, which is purely for tribal boys. There is one Asur teacher in the school who hails from this village, named, Tipun Asur. On the southeast corner of the village hillock there is *sarna* (Sacred grove). Apparently the soil condition of the village is full of laterite. There is no primary health centre in the village while these are available in Netarhat and in the block headquarter of Mahuadanr, and Bishunpur block. The nearest hat or weekly market is at Dumberpat on Saturday, it is hardly 4 km. away on foot through forest and hill slopes, and at Netarhat on Wednesday, which is about 35 km. away. Jovipat village hat is on Thursday, about 22 km away and Banari hat is on Monday and Friday which is at the foot hills of Netarhat and is about 30 km away. The bus stoppage from the village is about 10 km. away.

## Methodology

The investigators employed standard anthropological techniques in collecting the empirical data, that is, door-to-door approach for household survey, which is followed by collection of genealogies. This not only helped them to have a good rapport in the village but also to get authentic data from the informants who enthusiastically, curiously and very joyfully without any hesitation gave data on change of occupation, marriage distance, nature of marital alliance and impact of developmental programmes. All these are easily ascertained through this method. Apart from this, group interviews as well as focused interviews were done along with verification and authenticity of collected data. Fieldwork was carried out from December, 2008 to January 2009.

A demographic profile among the Asur of Sakhuapani village is presented in order to understand the Sex Ratio, level of Literacy, family Size, nature of their families, marital status and Economic pursuits of Asur which clearly give significance of instability in their economic life and till date forest plays a key role in their subsistence activities. Inspite of the total change over from traditional economic pursuit of iron smelting work to settled agriculture in this plateau it does not provide their bare subsistence throughout the year and they are compelled to involve themselves in other locally available subsidiary means of livelihood and this is clearly depicted in the table of economic pursuit.

It appears that main economic pursuits among the Asur are Agriculture, Collection. Wage labour, Service, Household work, and Cattle herding. But not a single economic pursuit is sufficient for their subsistence and therefore they are compelled to involve in other economically gainful activities as subsidiary economic pursuits. Infact occupational opportunity in this plateau plays a major role among the Asur for their survival. It is also revealed from the above Table 6 that collection still plays a key role in their economic life. Of the total population 376, only 133 (35.38 per cent) persons are involved in various economic pursuits for maintaining their livelihood. It is also observed that only 43 (11.43 per cent) persons are involved in local bauxite mines as wage earners and from this avenue they earn cash directly.

## Tangible heritage: Use of traditional knowledge for sustenance by using local resources

The Asur are a tribe living in forest environment. Their cultural life is styled in relation to their local environment, that is forest environment. In each and every aspect of their life forest has some contribution. They use Sal or Karange twig as toothbrush. According to them it helps to keep the teeth clean and healthy. If there is any toothache, carries or any gum trouble and even bad smell in mouth the bitter tasted sap of the twig helps to get rid of all the troubles.

They use locally available mud called as *gilli hans or nakra hans* as soap to clean their body and head hair. If the scalp is affected by the attack of lice (*siku*) or dandurf (*chitu*) then this mud is very useful to get rid of all these problems. They clean and wash their clothes and utensils with ash of sal twig. They use plates and bowls made of sal tree leaves along with metal utensils.

### (i) Their traditional knowledge in Preparation of Haria/Hadia

Haria is part and parcel of their life and culture and for preparation of *haria* they primarily depend on local resources, and the knowledge they acquired from their forefathers.

At first they cook rice. Then it is spread on floor with dense starch till it gets cold. After it gets cold, they mix powdered *ranu* with it and keep the rice mixed with *ranu* in a mud handi and close the opening tightly with sakhoa leaves for seven days during cold season and for three days in hot summer season. Then they open the pitcher and verify whether the rice got fermented. After it is fermented they pour water, stir the whole substance and take it for consumption. According to them haria sometimes works as a substitute of food. They do not feel hungry quickly, get energy and it reduces the exhaustion of their hectic daily work. As it is prepared by rice it is full with carbohydrate.

Ranu is a substance used to help in fermentation. It is prepared with fruit of Koriya plant. It also works as digestive. To prepare *ranu*, according to some of them they collect a variety of shrub called as *jhilmilia* along its roots, then grind the whole shrub and dry it. Then they mix the substance with rice powder. In this way they prepare *ranu*.

### (ii) Folk Classification of Soil (hans)

According to them there are several varieties of soil with their different works found in their vicinity. Those are as follows:

**Safed hans**-It is white coloured glazy soil also known as *chuhi hans.* They collect it from jungle, and use it to anoint the floor and walls of house after plastering.

**Karia hans**-Black coloured soil collected from jungle and *don*-1 type of land. They use it in construction of floor and wall.

**Jarra hans**-It is yellow in colour used in house construction collected from *don*-1 and *tand*-1 type of land. It is told that after its collection they shatter/smash it with feet. After it is satisfactorily smashed they mix cow dung with it and then plaster the walls and floor with the mixture. After an interval of two to three days when those become dry, they paint those with black soil. This process helps to strengthen the construction, and they claim that their construction is stronger than cement.

**Gilli hans/Nakra hans**-Described earlier, used as soap.

### (iii) Traditional knowledge in House construction

They construct their houses at a higher place on uneven rock, sometimes at a slope, after selecting the place through some magical performances. Wooden log, bamboo, *khapra* of local soil, unbaked brick, (sometimes replaced by Bauxite), different types of *hans* and cow dung are needed. The central pole of the house is necessarily a fully matured thick *sal* wooden log. According to them their practical experience, taught them that the central pole should be strongest as it is responsible to keep the house structure totally balanced and carries the maximum weight of the roof. They prefer *sal* wood and if not then *gambhar* wood and bamboo poles as other supporting poles. They keep some holes at the base of the house just at the point of maximum slope. It is told that as the land is slanting, sometimes there may be some seepage or accumulation of water there inside the room. To take out the water from the room, they keep holes at the base of the hut at the slanting from where automatically water comes out. Otherwise the construction will get weak. They prefer to construct their houses either east facing as at the eastern side Sing Bonga–their supreme deity rises every day early in the morning, or south facing, as they believe it should keep connection with their own original kingdom at the southern direction as they have learnt from their ancestors. Actually the cause behind it is probably to get fresh air that got linked with the myth.

### (iv) Source of water

To dig well they select a place with big trees. They follow the direction of the roots. They are of opinion that the roots of a tree always go towards the water sources. In this way they ascertain the water source in the village. It is their source of traditional knowledge to find out the level of underground water in the village. Moreover, there are persons among them who possess a unique technique to identify underground water source through two bamboo sticks holding by their hands. The two sticks are tied together at one end. The open end of the two sticks are kept on both sides of the shoulder and hold by hands on two sides and the tied portion is kept in front of him and he proceeds forward. He says that during his walk, once he feels some vibration and in further proceeds, the sticks are attracted towards the ground and comes very close to the ground where he stops. This is the point where water is available. When such a person was asked how he identifies the place. He answered that he feels vibration just like the waves of water. Again, the sticks points out the actual point of water source, and never he failed. He is very much in demand also by the neighbouring villages.

### (v) Folk Classification of forest based on need for survival:

1. **Reserve Buru:** Government reserve forest; villagers are not allowed to collect any MFP (Minor Forest Produce) from this area.
2. **Bakash Buru:** The forest areas outside the reserve forest from where collection of fuel wood and cattle grazing are allowed.
3. **Ghanghor Buru:** It is a deep forest and some portion of which is declared as reserve forest. In this forest they generally go for collection of edibles, medicinal plants and materials of daily use. In this forest there are several *sarnas* (sacred grove) such as *Kadleta Sarna, Sarhul Sarna, Kara Sarna* etc. Kadleta Sarna is a small reserve forest, while *Sarhul Sarna* is a bigger one. There is another *sarna* named *Kara Sarna.* In all the *sarnas* they go for rituals associated with the *sarna* such as in twelve years they perform Kara festival when they offer a *kara* (buffalo) to the spirits (both malevolent and benevolent) to appease them. After the ritual is performed, they leave the buffalo in the forest and return. They are tabooed to fell wood and collect even dry wood in the *sarnas.* They are allowed to do collection outside the *sarnas.* In this way their beliefș helps in conservation of their forest.
4. **Patdara Pat:** It is also a very big reserve forest.

### (vi) Survival Strategy:

Folk Classification of neighbouring hillocks in terms of availability of water (their traditional knowledge):

1. **Dnari Kona**–At the eastern side of the village Sakhoapani the hill is situated. Their own Sarna is situated in this place where their own deities reside. They fell wood in this jungle leaving aside the place of their own Sarna and it's surroundings. They very often go to this hill for collection, as it is full with several varieties of tubers and other edible items.
2. **Gurdari Dnari**–It is situated at the western side of the village. Here also several of their benevolent and malevolent spirits reside. One of those is Barham bhut. Its shadow is also dangerous which brings diseases and sometimes-even death. In this hill one very interesting thing is that there is a point where water is available throughout the year but due to the fear of several bhuts they hardly go to the place only except certain rituals and worships.
3. **Icha Dnari**–Situated at the northern direction. Here in this pahar, water is available throughout the year. They are not tabooed to fell wood in this area.
4. **Burha/Mandav Dnari kona**–It is situated at the southern side of the village. Here a very dangerous evil spirit named Kara darha resides. They are tabooed to fell wood in this hillock.

## Adaptive Strategy for Maintenance of Livelihood: Use of Traditional Knowledge in Economic Life

Traditionally they are iron smelters and slash and burn cultivators. Hunting and collection were the subsidiary occupations.

**Iron Smelting**–They had their own traditional knowledge for identification of particular stone (rich with iron) and also of extraction of iron. They used to extract iron from a special type of stone having two varieties. These were collected from the area named Banstoli. The name of those two varieties of stone are *bichi tuku* and *karia tuku*. Bichi *tuku* is deep chocolate/brown/liver coloured and of best quality very rich with iron content. Another variety of stone is *karia tuku,* which is black in colour. It is told that for iron smelting their traditional knowledge taught them to fell and burn green young *sal* trees to generate heat for melting of stone. (This particular variety of fuel is needed to extract iron because it can generate 1500 degree Celsius temperature that was essential for iron extraction.) They used to construct mud *bhatti* (furnace) near water sources, as after melting, water is needed to cool the melt. Agricultural implements, domestic articles, and tools of daily use were prepared with that iron.

**Traditional Knowledge for Slash and burn cultivation**-They used to clear a vast patch of land and fell wood not from the base but leaving atleast two feet from the base. The felled woods were then kept in that land for drying. After drying those were burnt into ashes. Then they used to wait till shower comes. After shower the land is ready for broadcasting and they used to spread seeds. Sometimes some holes were dug in that land and a few seeds were sown in each of the dug holes. After three to four months when the crop were ripen those were harvested. It is told that generally they used to do slash and burn cultivation for three successive years in a particular patch of land, then leave it as fallow land for a long time, atleast fifteen to twenty years, to replenish nutrients and by this time the land regains its fertility and there are again big trees grown and the land gets ready for slash and burn cultivation.

At present they have totally abandoned Iron smelting. Slash and burn cultivation is done in insignificant form. Among Hunting and collection, hunting became an occasional event.

Now Plough cultivation became their primary occupation. Collection has got a very important position in their life.

**Hunting and collection**: They have different types of traps such as *sim funda* to catch jungle fowl, *kutunga funda*–a variety of noose trap to catch hare and porcupine. They have knowledge about how an animal will be attracted towards a trap and easily will be caught. As for an example, hares are very fond of salt, to trap it they dig a hole at the side of the road and fit a trap there. The villagers who pass by the side of the hole urinate there. The salt of urine is accumulated in the hole. Being attracted by it's smells hares come to taste the salt and fall down in it and are automatically trapped.

There are several indigenous techniques to catch birds where traditional knowledge, which they have acquired over generation is also applied.

Collection is done primarily by women They are efficient to detect the place from where they will get various types roots fruits and tubers. Their traditional knowledge taught them to identify the place from where *kanda* (tuber) is available observing it's plants/creepers grown on the soil. They do not dig up the whole portion but leave a portion of it for growth for future.

**Table 11:1: Annual Calendar of Collection of Minor Forest Produce (MFP) required for sustenance among the Asur**

| *Month in Local dialect (E.E.)* | *Collection of Forest Materials* | | | | | | |
|---|---|---|---|---|---|---|---|
| | *Root/Tubers* | *Shoot* | *Leaves/Vegetables* | *Flowers* | *Fruits* | *Seeds* | *Mushroom* |
| 1 | 2 | 3 | 4 | 5 | 6 | 7 | 8 |
| Chait (March-April) | - | - | Munga Sag | Mahua | Ber | - | - |
| Vaisakh (April-May) | Gethi, Nakoa, Pitharu, Daru, Kulu, Baiyaug, Baser | - | Koenar Sag, Amit Sag, Munga Sag, Jirkan Patta, Futkal Sag, Tend Patta* | Moreja, Mahua | Amba, Jamun, Kathar, Papra, Piyar, Tend, Chihar, Mahulain, Pethu, Kachnar | - | - |
| Jaith (May-June) | Do | - | Fudina Sag, Chirkani Sag, Rote Sag, Munga Sag, Jirkan, Patta, Koenar Sag, Tend Patta* | Moreja, Mahua | Dumbar, Amba, Gular, Kathar, Kusum, Jamun, Porhu, Tut | Sakhoa, Dori, Karanj | - |
| Ashad (June-July) | Do | - | Munga Sag, Matha Sag, Katai Sag, Boro Sag, Futkal Sag, Koenar Sag | Mahua | Satalu | Do | Various types of edible mushroom |
| Sawan (July-August) | Do | Karil | Munga Sag, Boro Sag, Kena Sag, Seliar Sag, Dal Sag, Futkal Sat | - | Karonda Satalu | - | Do |
| Bhado (August-Sept.) | Do | Do | Do | - | Do | - | Do |

contd. . .

contd. . .

| *Month in Local dialect (E.E.)* | *Collection of Forest Materials* | | | | | | |
|---|---|---|---|---|---|---|---|
| | *Root/Tubers* | *Shoot* | *Leaves/Vegetables* | *Flowers* | *Fruits* | *Seeds* | *Mushroom* |
| 1 | 2 | 3 | 4 | 5 | 6 | 7 | 8 |
| Aswin/Kuar (Sept.-October) | Do | Do | Munga Sag | - | Do | - | - |
| Kartick (October-Nov.) | Sakhina/ Sakar Kanda | - | Kohra Sag, Laua Sag, Munga Sag | - | Kohra, Gongra | - | - |
| Aghan (November-December) | - | - | Munga Sag | - | - | - | - |
| Pus (December-January) | - | - | Munga Sag | - | - | - | - |
| Magh (January-February) | Pitharu, Nakoa, Gethi | - | Do | Jirkan Kachnar | Bayer | - | - |
| Fagun (February-March) | - | - | Do | Mahua flower | Ber | - | - |

They also collect wood *moreja patta* (by which they used to prepare string), Mahulain Patta and Juru Patta (for preparing rain coat and Chopi or hat) Khajur leaves (to prepare mat) and Kher grass (for thatching) throughout the year.

## Application of Traditional knowledge: Folk Taxonomic classification of MFP being edible items:

They have several types of tubers of various taste and edible value. Some of those such as *gethi* and *pitharu* are of bitter taste. To remove the bitter taste they keep it in a basket after slicing it in a flowing water source overnight. Next day they take it, boil atleast for two to three times changing water and then after washing in fresh water they cook it.

They identify the *putu* (a variety of tuber taste like potato) in the forest by observing the upper surface of soil in naked eye; If it is broken then there are chances to get *putu* either *jait putu* (black) and *chhaira putu* (white). These grow in forest and hills. The colour of young *chhaira putu* is white and when it grows old becomes black in colour. They take the young one. Jait *putu* is tastier and they cook it with chicken. They eat several varieties of *jait putu* and among those *mani putu* is very tasty.

They have varieties of leafy vegetables (sag) such as *koenar sag* (collected from jungle), *bathua* (in cultivable land), *futkal* (in the homestead land), *kado/losar sag* (in jungle), *puru sag* (in jungle). They sometimes cook the *sag* only by boiling in water. They take it adding salt only. Puru sag is very tasty and they take it mixing with *dal* (pulses).

Varieties of *khukries* (mushroom) grow in their vicinity such as *sarki lom, utur, bharwali, patka* (of bitter taste), *burbhu, ad,* and *bans khukri.* Those grow in forest and hills. They can easily identify what type of mushroom they can consume and which one is poisonous.

## Indigenous Knowledge in view of perception of time as well as picking up of mahua

The *mahua* flower is available during the summer months. Everyday it starts falling from tree early in the morning and it is continued till 12 noon to 1 p.m. by which they identify the time. The flower falls under the tree where throughout the day leaves are fallen and accumulated, from where it is difficult to pick up the flower. To avoid the difficulties, at night they do control firing so that they can easily pick up the flower fallen on the ash, early in the morning. Mahua is a precious and important item in their daily life and culture.

Traditional knowledge to use local natural resources for economic activities:

### Grass

They have identified several varieties of grass growing in their vicinity. (a) Among those *kher* grass is very necessary which grows on the contour bunding in the cultivable land, on the pathway of the hillocks and slopes or tarai. They use those to make cattle shed, poultry and piggery. Some of those are used to shed their huts also. These are used as fodder for the cattle. (b) Another variety is *kash* grass. These are also grown in the contour bunding. Their cattle eat the smaller, younger one while the larger one is used to prepare *kumni* (fishing trap). (c) Where there is soft and wet mud, *dub* grass is grown there. Their cattle are fond of this. (d) *chhiner*–another variety of grass when it is young, their cattle consume it otherwise it has no use. (e) They have another variety of grass known as *kush* grass used for preparation of broom.

### Bamboo (*mand*)

Two varieties of *mand* are there. Those, which they collect from jungle, are known as *jungle bans/mand* and the other one is *gaon mand*. It is told by them that they prefer *gaon mand* to jungle *mand* because of its strength and durability. They use jungle *mand* as a substitute for *gaon mand*

### Fishing

They do fishing in garha river-a streamlet in the western side and dhardhari nadi (streamlet) in the eastern side. They say that fishes are available in good quantity in the month of Bhado (Aug-Sept). During winter they get fishes of smaller size and also large headed hamru fish (hanku). During summer, they get prawn of smaller size, lathi or puti, bhumig and aind hanku. During rainy season they set varieties of traps such as dander to catch large and kumbi for small fishes. They can locate path and signature of movement of fishes in water beside the land. It helps them to understand whether there is fish or not in the water. Sometimes they take manjhua, a variety of leaves, dry it and then grind it; then the powder is mixed with molasses and after binding a portion of it for at least two days put the substance in a streamlet where they have identified the presence of fish. The fishes get intoxicated and float on the river and become easy to catch. They use fenka jal or danra jal in this fishing. They buy the thread of net from the market and in fenka jal they attach 100 to 150 weights of led at the net's open portion to increase its weight, which is necessary during fishing to keep it stable in water after throwing. The increase in number of weight and closer fitting of those is advisable and helpful for fishing.

They tell that where they get large fishes, small fishes are not available as the bigger ones swallow the smaller ones.

## Cultivation

Settled plough cultivation is their primary occupation now. Primarily they have two varieties of land namely *tand* (dry or non-irrigated) and *don* (wet) land. These two are again divided into several divisions depending on their quality (whether even or uneven), position, irrigated or non-irrigated, water retention capacity etc . As for example, a portion of land of the *tand* variety situated at slope is known as *telengtar.* A brief chart is given where a structure of their land holding along with their choice of cereals production is given in order to understand their embedded knowledge in this regard which they have learnt from their neighbours like the tribal group–the Oraon, Munda and Nagesia.

**Ploughing:** They start cultivation with ploughing. They plough a land for four times. They refer it *char chas and* each of such *chas* has its own significance as per theirwisdom. Those are as follows:

When a cultivator observes lightning at the southeastern side of the sky he understands that the time of ploughing has come and he gets ready to go to the field for first ploughing. The first ploughing is known as *chairabu* or *farin*. It is done just before or after first shower. The first ploughing is done to crack the hard soil and to break the lumps and also to uproot all the grasses grown in the field. In this ploughing, the land is cracked through which the cold air and the water pass from surface to the lower portion of soil to make it soft and wet.

After first ploughing, they leave the land for two to three days

The second ploughing is known as *dograibu* or *dobar*. If one has done first ploughing from east to west, then second ploughing is done from north to south.

Third ploughing is known as *tibrai abu* or *teghar*. They plough to prepare land thoroughly. All the weeds are uprooted and those are ultimately decomposed, the insects are killed. The land is loosened and made ready for cultivation. During ploughing lumps of cow dung are broken and mixed with land.

## CLASSIFICATION OF CULTIVABLE LAND AS PER WATER RETENTION CAPACITY IN THE LAND

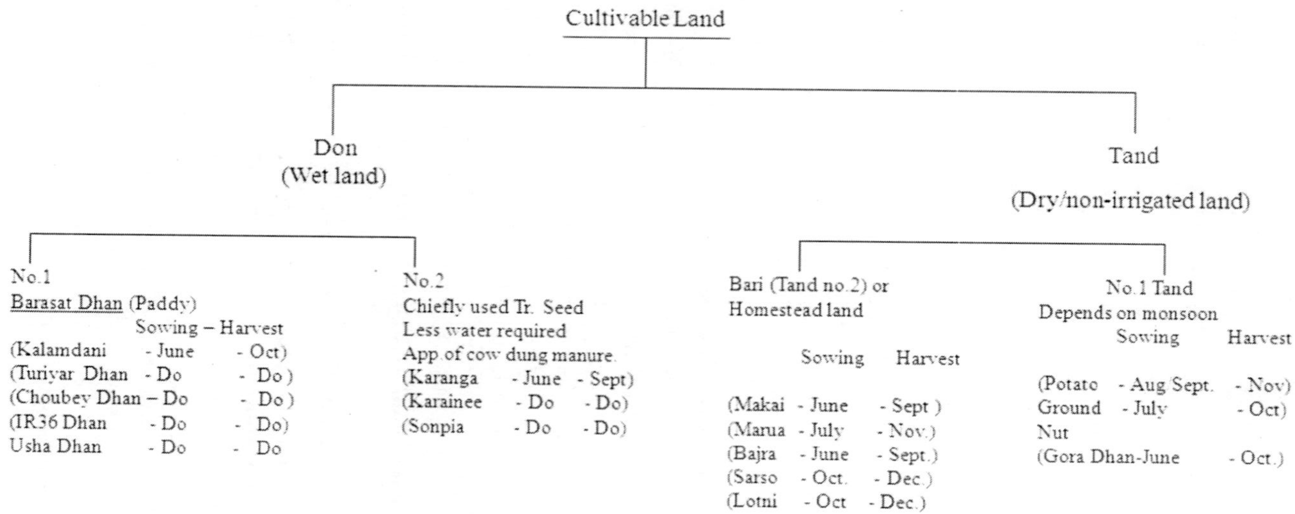

The fourth ploughing is known as *choukhaibu* or *chanbar*. In this ploughing broadcasting or spreading of the seeds is done. After each and every ploughing they leave the land for three to four days to give time for decomposition. Through ploughing the soil gets loosened so that air, water and sunlight easily can penetrate. The rotation of the soil of upper level to lower level and the soil of lower level to upper level along with the grasses, decomposed insects and cow dung is done which are also very necessary to increase the fertility of the plot.

After rain, they again do ploughing to prepare the muddy, cultivable land ready for transplantation. This is known as *paltai abu*. In cultivation through transplantation, more water is needed and for retaintion of water according to their wisdom *paltai abu* is needed. It is told that they get more products in the method of transplantation than broadcasting.

## Their Traditional Knowledge in Storing of Seeds

They store the seed either in an earthen pitcher or prepare a container by *juru* leaves called as *potom* and after keeping seeds in it; it is tightly covered with straw. According to them till the next summer season, they are tabooed to touch the pot. Otherwise, they believe that, the seeds will be damaged or spoiled by insects. The pot is kept inside the *ora-bhitar* (the room where the souls of their ancestors, regarded as their guardian deities are established), where the outsiders are not allowed to enter. In case of earthen pitcher, they plaster cow dung outside the container. Sometimes they store seeds in bamboo baskets. The inner and the outer portion of the container are plastered with cow dung. The mouth of the basket is open. It is told by other informants that sometimes to protect the seeds from damp and insects they bring out the seeds in open space of the courtyard in sunlight. The seeds eaten or half eaten by insects are fanned away and the unaffected are stored again. They prefer to use their traditional seeds but those cannot fulfil their need. So they are compelled to purchase seeds such as *chobe, karenga, sita, kaveri, kalinga* and *sita* etc. from block.

## Traditional Knowledge involves in preparation of land for sowing

Prior to seed sowing, they add fertiliser in their land. Among the fertilisers cow dung is preferred. To prepare cow dung as fertiliser they have to decompose the cow dung. At first they dig out big holes and accumulate cow dung in those holes till those are completely filled up. It is done in the month of May and kept till it gets rotten. After that they dig out all those and add to the cultivable land. They also use D. A. P. and other inorganic manures during transplantation. They also use urea for quick growth of plant.

## Traditional Knowledge for Irrigation in the terrace land

Generally their lands of *tand* 1 and 2 and *don* 1 are completely dependent on rain. Irrigation from nearby streamlets is done in don-1 type of lands by preparing canals. Again it is told that as the villages are situated at the hilly slope there is no need to channalise or drain out the village wastewater, which also carries a lot of organic materials and a good source of fertility. Generally don-1 and sometimes tand-2 type of land gets such water. Excess water in case of plots of lands separated by contour bundings flows from one plot to its immediate next plot situated at slightly lower level. To channelise the excess water from one plot to its next plot at lower level they keep hole on that side. In this way all the plots from upper level to lower level are automatically irrigated and at the same time excess water cannot harm the crop.

## Traditional Knowledge to protect the plant, soil erosion and various phases of cultivation

When a plant grows above 6 inches of water level, there are chances of its getting infected by insects. Upto 6 inches the insects cannot climb or stay on the plant. So they always are careful in this issue. In case the insects affect a plant; they apply D. D. T. and other insecticides purchased from shops.

Boundary is needed especially in Bari land attached to their homestead land to check the loss of soil or soil erosion. They plant different types of fruit giving plants such as *papita* (papaya), *tamrash* (guava), *kathal* (jackfruit), jojo (tamarind), in the boundary to check soil erosion and at the same time it gives them a little economic support adding to their food chart. Again the biodegradable wastes from homestead land comprising of vegetable waste, poultry waste, piggery waste and the waste water from kitchen and other places of hut are accumulated in the bari land which ultimately are decomposed and very useful for the increase of fertility of the land.

Weeding or *hnerera* is done during rainy season after transplantation. They say that if weeding is not done in proper way and there are weeds, then the paddy will not grow properly. When they see that the paddy grains are black in colour they understand that the crop did not get sufficient food in the form of juice and as a result this is ill nourished because the weeds along with the cultivable items share the nutrients of the land. To avoid it and to give sufficient nourishment, weeding is compulsory. In paddy cultivation, they plant a bunch of plant consisting of three to four plants in a same hole in transplantation. They avoid planting more as the plants then will be also week as from a single area they have to extract their food. The crops and cereals produced in the lands are mentioned in the chart/table.

**Mixed cultivation**-They cultivate *makai* and *bajra at* the same time in the same plot of *bari* land. They sow the seeds of *makai* in lines and at the same time they broadcast the seeds of *bajra* in that land. The plants of both the varieties grow simultaneously but grow with separate identity of plant, fruits etc.

When they cultivate *arhar* with urid/marua/kurthi or surthi they plant arhar in between the other plants. The *arhar* plants grow taller than the other plants so one can easily identify it.

**General characteristics of some plants**-It is told that *marua* can also grow in rough rocky area, if the chemical fertiliser is added but for it's cultivation muddy soil is preferred. They broadcast *kurthi* in a much dispersed manner, as they do not want thick growth of the plant, as this is a creeper. If they grow thick in a plot then the creepers will grow clumsy and interlocking with each other. As a result the product will not be sufficient. Kurthi can grow in non-irrigated, rocky area full with pebble. Its roots are very strong, can pass through the rocky substance. Gondli cannot grow on rocky area instead soft muddy soil is needed. But *arhar* can grow in both the conditions in *tand*-1 and *tand*-2 types of land. Jatengi grows in *tand* land by broadcasting method. A large quantity of seeds is broadcast. As the grains are very small in size, to get more product they broadcast in such a fashion that the plants grow in bunch and very dense. The paddy of smaller size ripens quickly. In *bari* land they cultivate *jinor* (*makai* or maize) and after it's harvest they cultivate *sarso.* Along with *sarso* at the same time in the same plot they cultivate *alu* (potato) and *muli.* They cultivate these in broadcasting method.

After the crop and cereals get mature, they do cutting. Each and every item has it's own time for cultivation. After cutting they keep the harvested crop in the field in the sun for drying. After those become dry, they take the grain /cereal from the whole plant by threshing or beating the harvested crop/cereal.

During harvesting, they do not cut from the base or uproot the whole plant but cut leaving at least 10 inches to 1 foot from the base in the land. These are left in the plot for natural decomposition and transformation to fertiliser. These are dried in sun, decomposed in rain and ultimately get mixed with the mud. Their cattle that graze in the land after harvest also feed on these. When the cattle graze in such a land it is profitable for a cultivator by thir droppings, which ultimately become manure and add to their land. In this way the cultivator is benefited. All these add to the soil fertility.

The straw is a very important item used as fodder for their cattle. They separate *pual* (straw) by a wooden stick with spikes. Those are stored in a side of their field and in rainy season are stored in a corner of living room.

The husk is mixed with fodder of their pigs. And some are burnt into ashes to manure the field.

**Traditional Knowledge for Extraction of oil from jatengi-**They extract oil from *jatengi*, which is used to cook vegetables. To extract oil from *jatengi*, at first they grind the grains. Then those are kept in a bamboo basket, and then the opening of the basket is tightly closed with a fine cloth. After that they keep the basket turned upside down on a container. The container has a small opening and it is filled with water. The water is then boiled and when it reaches the boiling point, the vapour comes out and passes up to *jatengi* through the cloth. After sometime when the vapour comes out from the basket they understand that the seeds are ready for oil extraction and immediately they bring out the jatengi and press to extract oil.

## Folk Classification of their domesticated animals and birds being tangible heritage

Along with their other movable and immovable properties, domesticated animals and birds give a family a very important position not only in their society but also as necessary and compulsory items in their daily life and in their ritual occasions. Among those the most important to them is chicken, as it is needed not only for their consumption but also as a compulsory and necessary item as an important offering for their rituals. Next to chicken, pigs are very important. A person's economic condition is judged by his pig holdings. In fact it is needed in any feast associated with their life cycle and other festive occasions. Next position is hold by goat-specially the he goat. They can earn a good amount by selling them. They also consume the meat and in some of their rituals it is sacrificed. Cow and bullock holds the lowest position among them. It is told that bullock is only needed in ploughing. Rest of the time these have no utility but they have to fed and taken care of throughout the year. To them, cow is only important for the rearing of it's calves. They do not drink milk as it is regarded as the gift of Heavenly father as food for its calves. They are tabooed to milk the cow. They do not eat beef and it has no importance in their ritual life.

## Conservation of forest

There is much scope for utilising traditional knowledge for sustainable development. TK has an important role to play to restore and conserve the biodiversity of village forests. They have several ideas for the preservation and conservation of bio-diversity of flora and fauna. Some of those are given below:

Whenever they fell trees in the jungle, they do not cut it from its bottom but leaving at least 2 feet height. They do not cut it straight but oblique or slanting. They say that in straight cutting, the tree cannot survive but when it is cut in a slanting way it definitely survives and after rains more than one tree grows from the same tree along the original one. Again in felling of trees, they always use axe instead of saw as saw damages the tree and it dies.

They never uproot the roots and tubers totally but leave at least a small portion beneath the ground for future growth.

Their cattle graze in jungle. The cow dung and droppings of other animals are transformed into manure, which is very useful and necessary item for forest growth.

Their customary laws tabooed them to fell several trees especially of sacred groves locally known as *sarna*, which are regarded as the abode of their deities. Their deities stay there, play, sing, swing in the trees. Always they have to keep the place pure with sanctity. They are tabooed to spit or urinate and their women are never allowed to visit a sacred grove. The male members can visit there but nobody is allowed to fell wood even the dry one and to cut a branch or pick up a flower or fruit or even a small twig fallen on the floor. If anybody does it even by mistake, their deities will be very angry and will send tiger or any jungle animal or an evil spirit to cause harm to the guilty person and his family. They perform several of their rituals in the *sarnas*. Rest of the period they do not disturb the place. They have several *sarnas* in several hills and forests of their vicinity Under Gurderi Panch; there is their biggest *sarna*, named as Gurderi Sarna. Expect this there are several other smaller *sarna* such as Raiyat Sarna, Deheri Sarna, etc. As mentioned earlier there are several *sarnas* in different hills and forests and are named as per the name of the place or mountain. Several economically valuable trees and plants such as Sakhoa, Durri, and Bel etc. are found in those *sarnas* but felling of those is not allowed. If a person cuts a tree in a *sarna* (to them this is an offence to the deities as they stay there) they are sure that within a few months the man will die and several persons of the village may also die. Those places are strictly kept undisturbed and sanctity is maintained as those places are only the abode of their deities. In this way by their customary laws and ritual bindings, conservation of forest is done.

They have several evil spirits roaming in the jungle. There are places meant for those. They go to the forest but avoid visiting those places so chances of collection and felling of trees there are nil and as a result conservation of forest is done.

They are tabooed to eat new fruits of the season and harvest before offering them to their deities and ancestors through rituals. They have to wait till the performance of the ritual on a particular date, fixed for it. Otherwise they have a belief that tiger will come out of the jungle and kill the offender or the person will suffer from stomachache or any stomach problem within this period of time and by this time the product gets fully matured and ready for further growth of new ones.

They are tabooed to consume or even kill the animals of their totems, which also help them for their protection of those animals.

**Intangible heritage: Cognisance of environment and their beliefs**

1. They understand that summer season is coming with the singing of *Kuhi Charai* (cuckoo).
2. When new leaves come in the Sal trees, it signifies that summer is coming.
3. With the falling of *pipal* leaves and coming of new leaves they get indication that summer is coming.
4. The blooming of flower of jackfruit, mango, *mahua, and palash* and with the performance of *Basant Panchmi* (aritual-newly introduced through village residential school) also indicates that the summer is approaching.
5. With the performance of *Basant Panchmi* they believe that the season of cold has come to its last phase. Haria gradually willbecome very tasty.
6. When they see that soft Sal leaves became large and hard then they understand that summer is at it's last stage and rainy season is coming.

7. When Daona/Daonaha-a bird sings then they believe that rainy season is coming.
8. When *jhingur* (a kind of insects) cries or the drone of the cricket is loud in jungle–generally in May, they know that within a few days rain will come.
9. Frog's croaking also indicates for heavy shower. .
10. If there is lightning at the southeastern side of the sky, then a cultivator understands that rain is coming and he gets ready with his plough to go to his field.
11. Heavy sweating also is an indicator of rains.
12. Black ants locally known as *sunumuig* or *lormui* (bigger variety of ant) with their food and eggs going in a line is a very good indication of rain.
13. When Sarai/Sal seeds get fully matured and fall from tree, it is an indication of end of summer season.
14. With the performance of Sohorai in the month katic (Sept-Oct) winter season comes.
15. Haria becomes tasteless, as cold climate is not suitable for fermentation.
16. They feel the change of climate with the change of wind.
17. If there is *badri* (cloud) at the east, then there are chances of rains. If badri is seen at the west side, then rain will not come quickly but it will take time. If *badri* is seen at the southern side then rain will come from south. It is told that it hampers the crop; it is believed that the rain from south brings salty water and it damages the plant and the produced cereal will be tasteless. The rain from north is good news to the cultivators as it is favourable for production of crops. If rains from south occur during katic, then immediately the cultivator cuts the crop to prevent the damage.
18. If wind blows from west to east, it is not good for their health and disease comes with it. Wind from east to west indicates that rain may come. Wind from north to south is very good for their health but wind from south to north brings rain and after that the weather will be very hot and they may be attacked by *loo* (heat wave). Their crops and cereals will be damaged.
19. When sun sets in a very red colour then there will be no rain and *thuribing* or rainbow stops rain.
20. They adjust time by observing shadow. During night they adjust time by noticing *Charhha Tara* (star) or *Harjuwari Tara* (star) or

*Tin Tara* (star). Tin Tara rises in the eastern sky and with the approach of time it moves towards west.

21. When they see *jono chanu* (comet) they get afraid that there will be no rain and there will be famine and they will face hard time.
22. If they see that the colour of *sakhoa* leaves is red and there are several elevated portions just like boil are found on the leaves, it indicates that there will be pox in their village.
23. They locally call whirlwind as bandro bhut. If any body falls within it, they get afraid that the evil spirit will do harm to him. They spit on it and do some magical performances to neutralise the evil effect.
24. Kohora or *dhund* or fog is according to them nothing but the water vapour, which is harmful for potato and lac cultivation.
25. Patthal or *pani sila*–the hailstone is harmful for mango and crops.
26. When sun rises slightly from south-eastern side then the days are small and cold days are coming but when the situation is just reverse that is the sun rises from north-east side then the days are long and hot.
27. If they see there is a circle-encircling the moon, it gives indications of rain. When the circle is found close to the moon, the rain will happen in places far from their village and when the circle is away from the moon, they believe that there will be rain in and around their village.
28. Eclipses are known as *garhan.*
29. In case of successful production of mango they know that there is no hailstone fallen on mango and the honey drops fall on the buds, and flowers of mango tree (which sticks on the mango bud and flower and hampers the growth of the flower into fruit and as a result these becomes dry and fall down), the honey is washed out.
30. According to them jackle, squirrel, chiti snake, hare, crow are considered as bad omen. During their journey if any of these is seen, then definitely there will be some disturbances.
31. An elephant, jara snake, dhaman snake etc. are good omen.
32. If anybody stumbles, he postpones his journey.

## Ethno-medicine: Traditional Knowledge in health and Hygiene

The term ethno medicine generally gives emphasis on the study of belief and practices related to illness of an individual of a particular community. The tribal communities of the country are distributed in the different eco-settings. Till date most of them are dependent on nature, utilising their environment, natural resources with the help of their traditional technology. Even to day they combat their ill health and other crisis situation with their indigenous methods of utilising their natural resources. In the study of ethno medicine primarily it is important to see that what their conceptionis regarding disease and ill health - whether it is caused due to some physiological disorder or due to malevolent act of some outward agencies is to be mentioned. Next, who will ascertain it - a doctor or a medicine man or sorcerer of their tribe or any of the local communities. If he is a doctor then why they go to him leaving their own traditional one. If he is a medicine man or a sorcerer, then how he detects the disease. Is it through some ritual or magical performances or understood through symptoms or by holding pulse bit of the patient? When the medicine man or sorcerer detects the disease, than what the process of treatment is - only by application of medicine or along with that they perform some ritual or magical performances. When the disease detected is supposed to be caused only by the malevolent act of a spirit or if it is caused due to some deity's anger or if the deity is displeased, -then what process of treatment to cure the patient may be taken. When a medicine man or a sorcerer fails, then where they should go? In his success what is his remuneration? It should be ascertained what they think about death. It is known that the herbal medicines have important role in village situation, especially among the tribal. Now how they get the knowledge about the medicine, their process and application. If there is any social or religious obligation, restriction or taboo associated with collection, preparation and application. How the knowledge is transmitted from one to another generations.

The Asur habitats in the Netarhat plateau are sporadically distributed in various hilly terrain of this plateau and are completely devoid of any primary health centre. Therefore, situation compelled them to depend on the mercy of tribal medicine men who are primarily herbal practitioners. The empirical data also suggest that Asur tribal medicine man, named Raghunath Asur of Sakhuapani village not only treats medically the patients of the village but also he receives request from neighbouring villages for attending patients who are even the Oraon, Hill Korwa and the Nagesia tribe of this plateau. Now, primarily when he was asked that how he detects a disease, he answered that he keeps his keen observation on the patient and side-by-side takes the case history in relation to the disease from his/her parents and also from the patient to detect the actual disease and causes behind it. He also applies his magical power to detect whether any supernatural power has any act behind the disease. Raghunath told that not a single cause is responsible for a disease. He thinks in all the cases act of supernatural power is there. He cited some examples.

In their village there are causes of falling from tree and getting fracture of body part. In such cases he is expert to cure his patients by fitting properly the broken part and plastering with herbal medicine in addition with oral medicines. But he argues that, a person generally falls due to the mischievous act of any of the malevolent spirit, which pushes and throws a person sitting on climbing a tree. Again in stomach pain or disorder, along with medicines needed to cure the disease, he identifies through magical performances, whether there is any other reason behind it. In several cases he comes to know through his magical power that the patient has taken the season's newly harvested item or fruit prior to the performance of the ceremony of offering of season's new food to the deities and ancestors which is an offence to them. As a result, for which they are displeased and felt insulted and caused that suffering to the person. So side-by-side along with medicines, he arranges for some rituals to satisfy the spirits and ancestors.

Traditionally among the Asur the post of medicine man is hereditary. Raghunath informed that he has inherited the post from his father who got it from his father. They believe that it is the god's gift to a person. His one of the forefathers acquired the power as a blessing from god and it is transmitted through generations up to him. But none of his sons are efficient to acquire the post. So it will be transmitted to efficient people who are keen to get the knowledge and it will be decided by their own jati panchayat. On the other hand the Asur are very keen to learn the magical performances. He told that they live in an uncanny atmosphere full with fear of some malevolent spirits. To overcome the fear it is very common to the Asurs to know several magical performances as protective measures. Generally the sons get the knowledge from father who very slowly transmits the knowledge to only that son who stays with him in the joint family. As soon as a son forms his own family separately, he gets no further knowledge. Due to this, there are several extended families found among the Asur community. They are very much afraid to talk about death. Death to them, as usual like others, is a very sorrowful event and the reason behind it as suspected by them is magical performance of a *dain* (witch), or of any malevolent spirit. When a sick person gets well, a ritual is performed as thanks giving to appease their deities and ancestors. The medicine man, sorcerer and the magical performer who is responsible to cure the patient is remunerated as per his demand and the patient's family's economic ability.

When Raghunath fails to cure a patient, then they consult other medicine men or shift the patient to nearby health centre at Netarhat which is faraway (i.e. 35 km.) from the village.

Here in the following lines the name of some of the herbal plants and its use are given:

**Table 11.2: Folk Treatment among the Asur**

| *Sl No.* | *Name of the Disease* | *Symptom* | *Use of herbal plants* |
|---|---|---|---|
| 1. | T.B. | Cough with blood | Lightly burn the leaf of *nagpheni* plant and then remove its upper layer with thorns and then consume it for a month. |
| 2. | Gelatonai (Leprosy) | Prolonged wound with loosing of flesh | Root of *tinpatti* (Desmodium polycarpurn) with cocoanut oil, *sakar kanda*, root of *bhuiprash*, *math kanda* (nodes of bamboo shoot) and stool of *lambha* (hare) are mixed and applied in the affected place. |
| 3. | Pet dukhe | Stomachache. | The root of *kedar* plant is grinded and consumed. |
| 4. | Sarap kata | Snake bite | The root of *chirdhoa/chauthdhoa* and its leaf together are ground. The paste is applied in the affected part and then the sorcerer chants mantras to extract poison from the patient's body. They do not have belief in tying up the affected part to resist the poison to spread out through the patient's body. |
| 5. | Boils | - | Collected anthills are ground softly and applied. |
| 6. | Khojli (Eczema) | - | The seed of *bara sengal* flower (which is sweet in taste and favourite of children) is burnt into ashes and mix with karanj oil or cocoanut oil and heated in lamp and applied in the affected part. |
| 7. | Gout/Gethia (Rheumatism) | Pain in joints | Tuber of *saru janam*, root of *tin patti* (Desmodium polycarpurn), root of *bandal aura*, sarkar kanda, root of *jabla siliyari*, potato, root of *bhaiparash*, root of *bhui kumbhi*, root of *dubri* or bark of *dubri* are altogether grounded and made paste with water and consumed as well as applied in the affected parts. |
| 8. | Bukhar/Jwar/Jendra (Fever) | Temperature in body | a) The bark of *karam* (Adina cordifolia) tree is crushed and soaked in water. It is then boiled in water, added with some salt and then taken.<br>b) Bark of *gethi* (Dioscorea bulbifera) tuber, which tastes bitter is crushed and taken with water. |
| 9. | To start mahinwari of a mother delivered a child recently | Pain in abdomen. | Gethi tubers are cut into pieces and then burnt into *chulha* (hearth) and added with *mahua* (Bassia latifolia) taken by new born's mother then menses is started. |

*contd. . .*

*contd. . .*

| *Sl. No.* | *Name of the Disease* | *Symptom* | *Use of herbal plants* |
|---|---|---|---|
| 10. | Protection from snake | - | The root of *kaniwyat* is ground and sprinkle into their hut, if there is any snake it will leave the place because of its repelent smell. |
| 11. | Sardi Jukham (Cough and cold) | Running of nose and conjetion | a) The root of *tin Patti* plant (Desmodium Polycarpurn) is taken with water.<br>b) Kali marich with salt are ground and consumed with water. |
| 12. | Phara Yatuna (Rough Skin) | | Tomato (indigenous or deshi) is consumed. |
| 13. | Ghao (Toe eczema) | | Harra (Terminalia Chebula) is heated and pasted. Then the paste is applied to the affected toe. |
| 14. | Anpachh (Indigestion) | | Ashes of the fuel wood is mixed with water and consumed. |
| 15. | Lahiksen (Dysentery/ blood dysentery) | | The root of *kedar* with wild grasses are ground and consumed with water. |
| 16. | Samang hasutana (Headache) | | a) Root of *putri* (Croton rox-burghii) tree is rubbed and applied on the forehead.<br>b) Garlic, mustard oil and *doob* grasses (Dog grass/creeping cynodon) are ground and the paste is applied. |
| 17. | Datahasua (Toothache) | Pains in gum and tooth | Bark of fruit of *putri* (Croton roxburghii) is ground and the paste is applied. |
| 18.. | Rangbaz/Masipisi (Measles) | Several red allergy type rashes found all over body | Leaf of *chakkoar* tree (Hibiscus sabdariffa) is pasted and rubbed in the body. |
| 19. | Menstruation Problem with pain in stomach | | Brak of *kumar amba* (the mango tree which is not yet flowering), bark of *piyar* (Buchanania latifolia) and *jovala kanda* tuber are mixed and grounded and then consumed. |
| 20. | Jwar (High Fever) | High body temperature | The root of *satawar* (Asparagus racemosus) and *putri* are mixed and added with water and consumed. |
| 21. | Malaria | Occurrence of high fever frequently. | The root of *parhi or Pathar kumrah* (Pueraria tuberosa) is ground with water and consumed. |
| 22. | Haddi tuta (Bone Fracture) | | The tubers of *datram singhi* (Vitis tomentosa) and turmeric are mixed into paste and applied. |
| 23. | Jalan/ jalni (Burn) | | The latex of *baghrandi* (Jatropha curcas) is mixed with salt and applied in the burning area. |
| 24. | Gethia dard (Gout pain) | Pain in the joints or joints pain | The bark and root of koreya (Holarrhena antidysenterica) are mixed into paste and applied in the affected part. |

In all cases before application of herbal medicine they perform some rituals with chanting of mantras. It is also reported that before collection of the herbs from forest they usually perform following things–

(a) Strictly avoid cohabitation with wife during night,

(b) Leave the house before sunrise silently in empty stomach,

(c) Prayer for *sing bonga,*

(d) When they collect tubers, roots etc from forest, some portion are kept there for future rejuvenation.

They have knowledge of some diseases and their treatments of their animals. Some of those are given below:

| *Sl. No.* | *Name of the animal* | *Name of the disease* | *Symptoms* | *Treatment to cure* |
|---|---|---|---|---|
| 1. | Murga (Fowl/Chicken) | Rangbaj (contagious disease) | Swelling of throat, keeps mouth open salivates, continuous swinging of head and white coloured loose motion, red coloured boil like swellings found on the body | Cauterisation by red-hot *hansua* (iron sickle) on the boils when the disease has just started. They burn incense in honour of diseased ancestors. |
| 2. | Merom/Chhegri (Goat) | Rangbaj (contagious disease) | It lies down, several red coloured swellings like boils found on the body | Cauterisation by red-hot *hansua* (iron sickle) on the boils. Along with this they prepare medicine by the leaves and roots of a (variety of herb) known as *saramdiring* collected from jungle. They smash those in total by hands and mix with the fodder and let the sick one take it. It gets well; otherwise they bring it to nearby veterinary hospital at Bishunpur.) |
| 3. | Suoar (pig) | Gilti Rangbaj (contagious disease). If such a pig is consumed by men, then they may get loose motion or itches | Similar symptoms are noticed as found among the goat. | They collect the excreta of kundru (an animal of water probably turtle) from the river side Then this is mixed with *bhusa* (straw) It is a very effective medicine and only one dose is enough to control the disease and three doses are enough to cure the affected pig completely |

*contd. . .*

*contd. . .*

| *Sl. No.* | *Name of the animal* | *Name of the disease* | *Symptoms* | *Treatment to cure* |
|---|---|---|---|---|
| 4. | Gai (cow), Bail (bullock) | Gilti Rangbaj | All over the body it gets red boils. In this disease swelling of throat is found the cow or bull cannot breath properly and suffers from cough and cold, the colour of the tongue gets black, keeps mouth open, salivates, stops taking food. | Cauterisation with red-hot *hansua* (iron sickle) on the boils. With it as a medicine they prepare a mixture of Dhan (paddy), *bahera*, *bandarlatha* seeds and *chirchitta* plant. All these are mixed and ground together and let it be consumed with fodder. |
| 5. | Do | Khurha | Ulcer or wound .occurs on the boot of the animal. | They wash the ulcer with water of battery cell or boil Velva seed or bark in water and wash the place for several times, and the wound gets cured. |
| 6. | Do | Chapka | Ulcer on tongue | The bark and seeds of kohora plant are ground together and let it to consume it. Generally the cattle do not want to take it. So they keep it on a leaf along with some tamarind and salt. |
| 7. | All types of cattle | Bouraha | There is a variety of grass, locally known as *matoasi ghash* and they call it as *bulbar ghash*. During grazing, sometimes those take this variety of grass with other grasses. Immediately such a cattle becomes mad. | Within 24 hours it should be given *kohora pani* (seeds of kohora plant mixed with water). Otherwise it dies. |
| 8. | Do | Dingtoatadiyaye | Sometimes during grazing, there is a poison less snake named *sarudin* which suddenly bites. The exact spot gets swelling. | They prepare a band of straw and ignite it and cauterise the particular place with burning straw on the affected place. |
| 9. | Do | Jwar | Fever | Cauterisation by a red-hot *hansua* (iron sickle). |
| 10. | Do | Ghao | Wound due to the attack or bite of any animal. | Apply *dimak mitti* (mud of anthill) at the wound. |

From their natural habitats, which provide them an enormous range of indigenous medicinal plants, they utilise and conserve these for future use. Thus, the tribal medicine man in this area play a significant role in catering the health care needs of their locality at this Netarhat plateau. They provide plants centered culturally appropriate personalised healthcare that meets the needs and expectation of the patients in their vicinity. Encouragement should be given to tribal SHG (Self Help Group) for training, management and maintenance of medicinal herbal gardens, training should be imparted on processing, store, packaging and marketing and accordingly suitable amendments are required in Indian Patent Act.

Thus, the rich wealth of knowledge and associated practices regarding indigenous exploitation of natural resources by the tribal communities in our country should be properly documented in order to have potential industrial application leading to pharmacological developments that could help many people across the country. Therefore, we cannot afford to lose this natural resources and its associated indigenous knowledge.

### Transmission of Indigenous knowledge to next generation through process of socialisation

Today their children are going to school to get formal education, which they think are not sufficient for them as they live in such an area where they always are scared with uncertainty and thus feel very insecured. To get confidence in mind they have several social customs and taboos. To cope up with the local ecological condition, from their very childhood they are enculturated and given training. Whenever they go for hunting and collection in forest, their children accompany them. In case of hunting their boys from 10 to 12 years of age accompany them. They drive the game close to the hunter by creating sound with *hurla*. They are taught to throw arrow on a particular object. Prior to that they practice to hit the aim by throwing of *gulel* (catapult). Children of both the sexes, especially the girls accompany them in collection of jungle products. They learn how to identify the places where the roots fruits and tubers can be found, what type of *putus* and *khukhries* are edible or poisonous, how to take out the tubers that grow beneath the soil, and also to preserve their food items for future use. They are taught to identify the path even in dense forest and where to go or not. In forest there are various evil spirits whom they should avoid and through several rituals and magical performances they keep those quiet. They are taught to identify if there is any animal on their way. They identify those by their half eaten fruits, their excreta and footprints. Each and every animal's footprint is different from other. They can identify when the animal pass through the path, by observing the freshness and temperature of the excreta. They are taught how to fell wood, what types of implements are necessary for it. They accompany their elders to identify the plants used as herbal medicine. Where there is a jungle of *putus* tree with blossom and where there are anthills, there are chances to meet a beer.

They have several riddles, myths, songs associated with their life and culture and through which one can understand their dependence on nature and also the conservation and preservation of forest in which their life is enmeshed.

## Conclusion

In the emerging global knowledge economy a country's ability to build and mobilise knowledge capital is essential for sustainable development (World Bank, 1997). One of the components of any country's knowledge system is its indigenous/traditional knowledge bank. It encompasses the skills, experiences and insight of people applied to maintain or improve their livelihood. Many traditional knowledge systems are at risk of becoming extinct because of rapidly changing natural environment and fast pacing economic, political, and cultural changes on a global scale due to impact of globalisation, electronic media and so on even into the depth of the secluded rural area of the country.

Through on going process of globalisation the traditional cultural elements are rapidly vanishing. The cognisances of environment among the Asur in which the crust of cultural elements are embedded for their existence in such ecological niche is highly threatened. The sacred groves (*sarna*) among the Asur are rich in terms of biological wealth. There are number of *sarnas* in and around the studied village which not only provide various environmental, socio-cultural, religious and economic benefits to them but these also act for the preservation of natural local resources, climatic actions, ground water level etc.

Perception of time, season, and climate are only understood by means of natural phenomena which they have observed since their birth as well as learnt from their earlier generation. It is the only means for their survival in such ecological niche in order to cope up with their life in action with surrounding natural environment. Forest provides a great cultural space in their livelihood. They pick up the elements from forest not only for their ailment but also for their livestock and for other economic and socio-religious occasions.

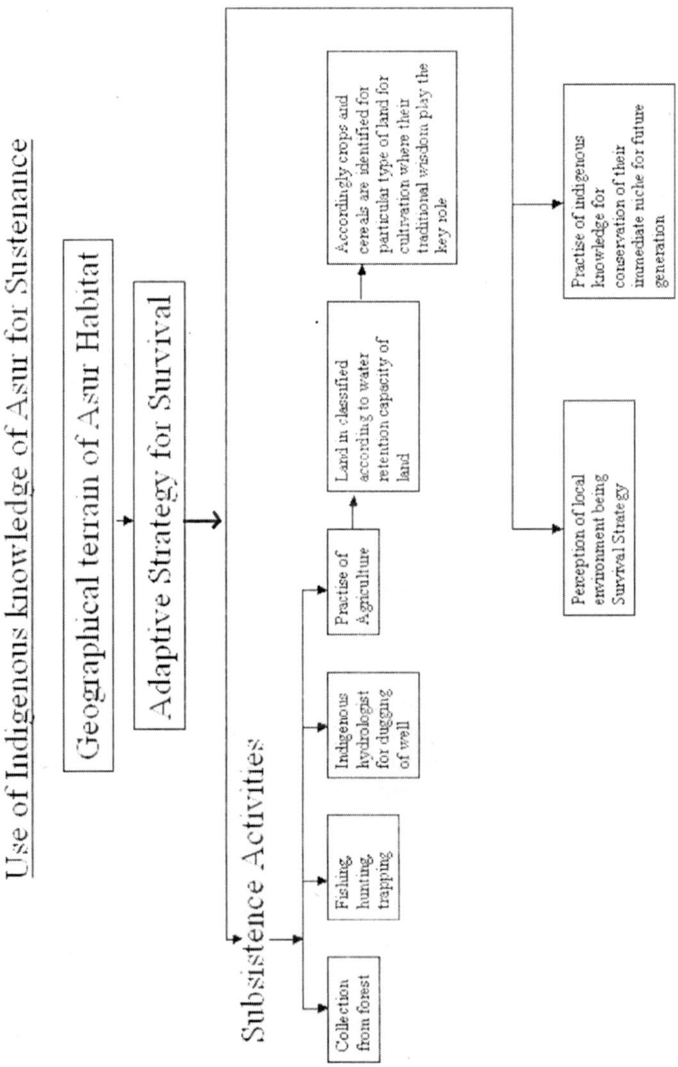
Use of Indigenous knowledge of Asur for Sustenance
Geographical terrain of Asur Habitat
Adaptive Strategy for Survival
Subsistence Activities
Collection from forest
Fishing, hunting, trapping
Indigenous hydrologist for digging of well
Practise of Agriculture
Land in classified according to water retention capacity of land
Accordingly crops and cereals are identified for particular type of land for cultivation where their traditional wisdom play the key role
Perception of local environment being Survival Strategy
Practise of indigenous knowledge for conservation of their immediate niche for future generation

Thus, in common parlance the indigenous knowledge is the knowledge, which originates locally from people, their perception and day-to-day practical experiences in an environment. It finds expression through many cultural practices of the Asur, which are mentioned in the above chart as being a survival strategy. Asur—once famous for iron smelting work, now a PVTG group as well as indigenous people of the country constitute the rich repository of TK because of their nourishment and for being cherished under forest environment for generation.

## References

Altman, Iruin and Martin M, Chemers, 1980, Culture and Environment; California: Brooks Cole Publishing Co.

Bates, Marston, 1953, 'Human Ecology', in Anthropology Today: an Encyclopaedia Inventory (ed.), A. L. Kroeber, Chicago: Chicago University Press.

Benneth, John, W., 1976, The Ecological Transition: Cultural Anthropology and Human Adaptation, New York: Pergamon Press, Inc.

Dasgupta, Samira, 1994, Birjia: Society and Culture (A Study in Cultural Ecological Perspective), Calcutta, Firma KLM Pvt. Ltd.

Leuva, K. K., 1963, Asur: a study of primitive iron smelters, New Delhi: Bharatiya Adimjati Sevak Sangh.

Prasad, Narmadeshwar, 1961, 'Asur', in Land and People of Tribal Bihar, Ranchi, Bihar Tribal Research Training Institute.

Misra, Kamal Kant, 2007, "Indigenous Environmental Knowledge Today: The Context and Relevance", in Traditional Knowledge in Contemporary Societies–Challenges and Opportunities, Edited by K. K. Misra, Bhopal and Delhi: IGRMS and Pratibha Prakashan.

**Collection of bans karil as food item during monsoon**

Collection of bark for rope making

Asur-agricultural land

## (B) STUDY OF ETHNO-MEDICINE

### Prologue

To the tribals, health, disease and it's treatment, death etc. everything has different meanings but it is interestingly noticed that each and every tribal community has belief on both benevolent and malevolent supernatural powers who are responsible for all these. The fate of a community and its members depend on their relationship with unseen forces which guide and intervene in all of their matters like day-to-day life sickness, disease and death. It is thought that if a man offends any of them, the mystical power punishes him by ill health, disease, and misfortune and even by death. Then at first to detect the actual cause of sickness, disease or death they go through magical performances, which tell them the name of the particular mystical power responsible for the misfortune and cause for its anger. To appease the power they pray for its forgiveness, seek kindness, and those are done through several prayers, offerings, sacrifice, magical performances. Along with these the sick person is treated with their own traditional or indigenous medicines, it may be any kind of inorganic or organic substance available in their particular niche. To perform all these, they have specialised persons of their community and in theirs failure they do not hesitate to go to the medicine man even of other community oralso of a neighbouring village.

The cultural cognition of illness etiology and at the same time application of herbal therapy among the tribals of Indian continent can be understood through three major components like environment, social system and cultural values. To understand the health behaviour none of these structural loci can be ignored.

### Environment

The influence of environment that includes altitude, temperature, topography, flora and fauna, strongly bears upon not only the livelihood or economic activities but also on health system. The environment also determines the types and shapes of shelter, use of raw material, dress, transport, *food* and *drinking habit, economic pursuits* as well as *occupational opportunity* and *collection of minor forest produce for sustenance* etc. Together they also exert substantial influence on the social system as well as on human biology. Here, not only that the notions, perception and cognition of the people but also the empirical studies that provide for understanding of causal relations between the natural elements and diseases/ailments in specific ethnic group, becomes an area of investigation. Such as, lesser incidences of heart diseases among the hill people, perhaps, have much to do with the natural habitat and biology of the people (Rao, 2007).

## Social System

Various social factors such as *family type and size* and *rate of literacy*, gender inequality, gender relation, economic status in terms of importance attached to *earning and non-earning members, sickness*, pressure from family members, *political and social freedom practices* etc. also do determine the *conceptions of ill health*, responsibilities of caretakers and application of treatment through their cultural practices followed by herbal therapy with the help of traditional medicinal specialist like *bhagat* (among the Dhodia of Gujarat), *sirha* (among the Bison-Horn Maria of Bastar, Chhattisgarh), *jhankri or pau* (among the Toto of Jalpaiguri, west Bengal), *ojha* or *jan-guru* (among the Mal Paharia of Santal Pargana, Jharkhand) etc. So, interaction of different institutions intersecting political, economic and religious systems can also be noticed operating at a micro level.

## Cultural Values

The *perception* of *good and ill health* and maintenance of good health are rooted in one's own prescription loaded with cultural values. These are developed and nurtured on the basis of people's conception and *relationship with the celestial world, human being and natural physical environment*, under this context, Man in terrestrial world is looked upon with by God and Spirits in celestial world and their relationship with nature, *the total world view provides a cultural repertoire that guides the individual and direct the family to adopt a particular strategy for dealing with ill health* or implications of curative measures according to one's own cultural prescription.

## Illness Ideology

Every culture has its own beliefs and practices regarding health care practices and its ailment, it often does not work in a logical fashion. Every system of culture tries to treat diseases in its own prescribed manner and here lies the cognitive way of understanding of health behaviour practices of the studied group. Interpretations of the cause of a given diseases depends much on the native's perceptions of the pathogenic agent or force responsible for the cause, the cultural situation (i.e., socio-economic backdrop, local environment, age old belief practices etc) or context in which the condition of ill-health has occurred and the degree of disruption of a patient's relationship with the pathogenic agents.

**Concept of cause of Disease**

The causes of different ailments among various tribal situation of the country are as follows :

1. Possession of evil spirit
2. Evil eye
3. Witchcraft and Sorcery
4. Disruption of human relationship with ancestral spirits
5. Violation of any social taboo
6. Sexual intercourse with menstruating women
7. Failure in performing any divine duty
8. Breach of social pollution (i.e. pollution during rites-de-passage rituals)
9. Maintenance of cultural space in construction of house and within its area
10. Irregular combination of diet
11. Maintenance of purity-pollution in view of performing rituals, sacred groove etc.

**Ritual Healing**

To an anthropologist the ritual healing aspect have a number of connotations which is purely a cognitive grammar. These are as follows:

(a) rituals encourage cohesion, strength, a kind of psychology to overcome all problems

(b) enhance individual and group autonomy

(c) help to achieve actors' goals

(d) help to resolve conflict

(e) rituals also define conceptual categories

(f) ritual function as symbolic modes of communication.

(g) Ritual actions express and communicate shared socio-cultural meaning which are symbolically transacted through the medium of ritual action (Munn, 1973).

It is reported that of the total population of our country (India) there are 8 per cent tribal groups (as per 2001 Census). Among the total 461 tribal groups (Singh, 1994), majority of them are in hilly terrain and dense forest (402 in number). Their cultures have developed in a particular ecological setting and for sustenance they fully utilise their natural resources even for their ailment.

### (i) Use of Herbal Medicine Among the Mal Paharia

Mal Paharia is one of the tribes who live in a geographically difficult area where they always have a feeling of insecurity and uncertainty or less predictability. In fact, Mal Paharia is a separate group of the tribe Paharia. Paharia is a blanket term for three separate tribes namely, Sauria Paharia, Kumbharbhag Paharia and Mal Paharia. All of the three are endogamous groups and are confined in their habitat in Damin–i–koh (a Persian word means skirt of the hills) area of erstwhile Santhal Pargana district, which is now divided into Dumka, Pakur, Deoghar, Sahebgunj, Godda, and Jamtara districts.

In the Damin-i-koh area all the three groups of Paharia are distributed in the Rajmahal hills, which covers the entire Damin area. It consists of the upland, undulating, long ridges and depressions along with some fertile lands, which are intensively cultivated. There are three lofty peaks among which Massanjore is situated in Dumka subdivision.

The present study was carried out among the Mal Paharia of Gopikandar and Dumka block of Dumka district of Jharkhand. Mal Paharia hamlets are situated in the denser portion of the forest at the higher altitude of the village. As they live in such a geographical atmosphere where they have an uncanny feeling of unseen spirits that is in an adverse situation, to get strength in mind, to combat with the mysterious events by getting hold of the supernatural power, which are solely responsible to shape their culture and give them protections from all evils. Hence, their life is very much oriented by the belief of supernatural power and propitiation of spirits holds an important position in their religious life.

To begin with the religious life of the Mal Paharia, it is necessary to mention that they have their own priest or religious practitioner who is known as *Deohar* or *Pujar/Pujahar*. The post is hereditary. He has his assistant called *Fuljharia*. Along with them there is a messenger called Gorait who informs and invites all Mal Paharias to attend and participate in the rituals and festivals. He also collects contributions from the villagers in case of any ritual and festival organised by the community or by the whole village.

Beside them they have an *Ojha/Ojha guru* - sorcerer of their own community who is consulted in the crisis such as disease and death etc. To be an *Ojha* it is thought that one should have knowledge to detect and tackle the malevolent spirits and to neutralise their acts with suggesting the remedies. In addition to these in most cases the

*Ojhas* also act as medicine man. If one *Ojha* fails to cure a person then they consult Jan guru– the sorcerer of the Santhal community who is believed as more powerful than their own *Ojha*. They have a faith in number of malevolent and benevolent spirits, whom they appease in various occasion. The details of such are described in chapter – 'Anthropology of Religion'.

They have belief in *Dayen* (witch). In case of any mishap or sickness they suspect that either any malevolent spirit or a *Dayen* is responsible for that. They cannot touch the spirit but can catch hold a woman suspected as *Dayen* and torture her brutally even sometimes kill her only out of suspicion.

The traditional knowledge (i.e. oral tradition) in regard to health care practices, which the tribal have acquired over generations, is the key source of inspiration of maintaining their livelihood in such forest environment (Dasgupta and Sarkar, 2005). Due to close association with forest the tribals are well aware of treating ailment through various local herbs, plants, roots and tubers and their various uses and parts of uses. The knowledge to use various local herbs and plants, fruits, roots and barks as medicinal value is very much restricted among a few members of the community which they have acquired from their ancestors and at present they are the living custodian of that great intangible cultural heritage. Thus, this knowledge is very much local and it is very unique for a particular community for their sustainable living in such forest environment. This knowledge bank of rural India is gradually dwindling and shrinking due to rapid expansion of globalisation.

From our empirical study it is revealed that Mal Paharia also possesses a good knowledge of the vegetation wealth of their vicinity and also of use of various herbs and plants for their daily diet chart, which possess a good calorie and vitamin value. They are highly aware of their forest wealth, which they use, in their traditional rituals and ceremonies and in ailment in a sustainable manner and on the basis of their great traditional wisdom they also conserve the bio-diversity of their niche. Interestingly, their economy, cultural behaviour, religious beliefs and practices, norms and morals are all the product of traditional and intimate knowledge about the nature, natural product and natural phenomena (Dasgupta and Sarkar, 2005).

The knowledge among Mal Paharia to get rid of ailment through local herbs, plants, tubers, roots and barks etc. clearly suggests that their beliefs and practices relating to health care and diseases, are products of completely indigenous cultural developments. The present treatise is confined upon the Mal Paharia of Dumka district, Jharkhand, who exploit their immediate natural resources for their ailment. It is also observed that before application of medicine the *ojha* or *janguru* (sorcerer-cum-medicine man) try to understand the problem of patient through the feeling of pulsebeat of the patient and which is followed by some magico-religious performances since Mal Paharia have a strong belief and cultural sentiment about various malevolent spirit of their vicinity usually believed to be responsible for various health problems. However, regarding application of herbal medicine they only depend on their *biro piyao* (baid) who is aged about 99 years at Madhuvan village.

**Application of Local Herbs through Traditional Knowledge for Ailment**

| *Name of the Disease (Local Name/English Name)* | *Use of Local Herbs* | *Application* |
|---|---|---|
| 1. Penjon or Anatarba (Irregularity / or delay or pain in Menstruation | (a) Kalihari jaghdai (*Gloriosa superba)* or, | It's tuber is grounded and applied in the forehead for at least seven days. |
| | (b) Kala datura/umman (*Datura fastuosa)* | Flower of it is grounded and mixed with molasses or honey and taken twice in a day. |
| | (C) Malkangni, kajuri/ chiron (*Celastrus paniculata)* | It's tender leafs are cut into pieces and fried in mustard oil. One teaspoon of such is taken twice in a day for 15-20 days. |
| 2. Shet Pradar (White discharge) | (a) Baer fruit/ilantha (*Zizyphus jujuba*) | It's fruit is grounded and mixed with molasses and taken twice in a day. |
| | (b) Bark of neem tree (*Azadirachta indica)* | Bark is grounded into paste and mixed with honey and taken one tea spoon twice in a day for a period of 10-12 days. |
| | (c) Seed bark of imli (Tamarindus indica) | The outer coat of *imli* seed is grounded and mixed with sugar candy and taken ¼ tea spoon twice daily for 7 days. |

*contd. . .*

*contd. . .*

| *Name of the Disease (Local Name/English Name)* | *Use of Local Herbs* | *Application* |
|---|---|---|
| 3.Sthan-Rog (Lactation Problem) | (a) Tuber of satawar (*Asparagusraccmosus)* | Tuber of satawar is gounded and mixed with cow milk and then it is boiled for some time and taken twice in a day |
| | (b) Root of erand (*Ricinus communis*) and tuber of satawar (*Asparagus racemosus*) | Both the items with equal proportion is grounded and prepared a small pea size two tablet and mixed with sugar candy and taken twice in a day |
| 4. Khasi (Cough) | Leaf of ishwarmul (*Aristolochia indica)* | Its leaf are grounded with honey and taken. |
| 5. Rangbandh (High temperature with red rashes in the body) | (i) Root if bindhi/ lal bherenda (*Jatropha gossypifolia)* | Root of bindhi is grounded and applied in the affected region of the body. |
| | (ii) Root of anantamul/ dudhilata (*Ichnocarpus frutescens*), root of bhui champa (*Kaempferiarotunda*), root of gharundi sag (Alternanthera sessilis) and root if kantha bhaji/ acch adro (*Amaranthus spinosus)* | All are mixed with ghee of cow and boiled for a long time. Paste is applied as well as taken for 3 to 4 times in a day |
| | (iii) Flower of goalichi/gulanch (*Plumeriaacutifolia*), root of chirchiti/ chirchira (*Achyranthes aspera*) and leaf of gritakumari (*Aloe vera*). | All the three are mixed and grounded and paste is applied and also taken. |
| 6. Ghav in new born's crown of the head (wound in newborn's crown of the head which is delightfully soft) | Dried Bones of tortoise and dried bark of *barka nimbu* (Pomelo) | Both are mixed and grounded into paste and applied on the surface of head of new born. |
| 7. Udri (Dropsy) | Root of erandi/ castor oil plant (*Ricinuscommunis*), *bansim* (wild variety of bean) and lime of the oyster | These are mixed and grounded and consumed. |
| 8. Nak sinjra (Cold) | Juice of velva/ bhilawa seed (*Semecarpus anacardium)* | The extracted juice of *velva* seed (unmatured) is applied inside the nose. |

*contd. . .*

contd. . .

| Name of the Disease (Local Name/English Name) | Use of Local Herbs | Application |
|---|---|---|
| 9. Pilhoi (Malaria) | Root of *tijubala*, tuber of *tiput*, root of *ishwar muli* (*Aristolochia indica*) | These are mixed with *gondh* and grounded and prepare tablet; and taken twice a day. |
| 10. Lahu ghav (wound) | Root of chibal and palash (*Buteafrondosa*) | (a) Roots of both are grounded and paste is applied.<br>(b) When the said paste is heated and applies on the wound, immediately the bleeding is stopped. |
| 11. Pet dukhai ( stomach-ache) | Root of champa (*Michelia champaca*), ban kursa and rakti. | Root of the three plants are grounded with *Ishwar muli gadh* and prepared tablets (*goli*) which are dried in Sun ray and taken two *golis* at a time for a period of one month. |
| 12. Sarpa bish (Snake bite) or Bichhu katna (Scorpion bite) | (a) Root of nagbael/sarpa gandha (*Rauwolfia serpentina*) or Ishwar mul (*Aristolochia indica*) | Root of this plant is grounded and consumed and paste of such is applied on the wound. |
| | (b) Bark of palash (*Butea frondosa*) | Bark of *palash* and pieces of ginger are grounded and consumed. |
| | (c) Bark of charai gorba simkata/ nagpheni (*Vitex peduncularis*) | Bark of this plant is grounded into paste and consumed as well as applied on the body. |
| | (d) Seed of kursi (*Mucuna nivea*) | About 6-8 pieces of seed are grounded with water and taken. |

Moreover, in order to protect their (Mal Paharia) houses from snakes, which are situated either in hill slopes or in the forest, they usually plant *airi* (*Pedilanthes tithymaloides*) and *kebamba sangha/kewa kanda* (*Costus speciosus*) in their *vitto* land.

| *Name of the Disease (Local Name/English Name)* | *Use of Local Herbs* | *Application* |
|---|---|---|
| 13. Bichhu kata (Scorpion bite) | (a) Latex of Papita (Papaya) ( *Carica papaya*)<br>(b) Juice of aonla (Phyllanthus emblica)<br>(c) Leaf of sakarkanda (*Ipomoca batatas)*<br>(d) Seed of karanj (*Pongamia glabra)*<br>(e) Tuber of kali musli (*Curculigo orchioides)* | Latex of *papita* is applied on the wound.<br>Juice of aonla is applied on the wound.<br>Juice of leaf is applied and consumed.<br>Seed is crushed into paste and consumed<br>Tuber is grounded with slight water and applied on the wound as well as consumed. |
| 14. Paychese (Dysentry) | (a) Young leaf of phutkal (*Ficus infectoria)*<br>(b) Bark of sal tree (*Shorea robusta)*<br>(c) Leaf and fruit of kukurbicha or seta bili / kucho bati (*Grewia hirsuta*) | Young leaf of *phutkal* is boiled and it's water is consumed and also boiled leaf are taken three to four times in a day<br>Bark of *sal* is grounded and about one teaspoon of such powder is made into paste on the hearth/oven and taken three times a day. It is alsoapplied during blood dysentery.<br>Both leaf and fruit are crushed and boiled and a thick substance prepared, which is consumed three-four times a day. |
| 15. Kukur Khasi (Whooping cough) | (a) Leaf of ishwarmul (*Aristolochia indica*) | At the initial stage its young leaf as well as dried leaf are grounded with honey and taken four times in a day. |

*contd. . .*

contd. . .

| Name of the Disease (Local Name/English Name) | Use of Local Herbs | Application |
|---|---|---|
| 16. Kashra (Missals) | Thorns of semal (*Bombax ceiba*) | Thorn of *semal* is grounded with water and consumed. |
| 17. Bukhar (Fever) | (a) Fruit and root of barhanta/ Indian night shade (*Solanum indicum)*<br><br>(b) Leaf of harsinghar/ night jasmine (*Nyctanthes arbor-tristis)* | Both root and fruit of *barhanta* are grounded and boiled with water, and a thick substance is prepared (*karha*) and taken about two tea spoon at a time for two times a day for five to seven days.<br><br>Young leafs are boiled into *karha* and taken about two tea spoon at a time for twice in a day. |
| 18. Haiza (Cholera) | Bark of jamun (*Enginiajambolana*), liquor of mahua* (*Bassia latifolia*)<br>(*Phulli liquor is required which is of high alcohol concentration; during distillation of mahua flower for liquor, the first 20 minutes distillation is known as *phulli*). | Both are mixed and grounded and taken one teaspoon at every hour till recovery. |
| 19. Sar dard (Headache) | (a) Bark of chilbil / churla (*Holoptelic integrifolia)*<br><br>(b) Dried up twigs of akhwan/ akanda/barangobali (*Calotropis gigantea*). | The fresh bark of *chilbil/ churla* is tied on the forehead.<br><br>Dried twigs are lighted and inhaled like *bidi*the smoke through nostrils. |
| 20. Moch (Sprain) | (a) Latex of akhwan/ barangobali (*Calotropis gigantea)*<br><br>(b) Bark of pojo/baglal (*Litsaeapolyantha*) and oil of kujuri (*Celastrus paniculata*). | Latex of *akhwan* is mixed with salt and applied.<br><br>Both are mixed and grounded into paste and applied. |

contd. . .

*contd. . .*

| *Name of the Disease (Local Name/English Name)* | *Use of Local Herbs* | *Application* |
|---|---|---|
| 21. Dama (Asthma) | (a) Leaf of ishwar mul (*Aristolochia indica)* | Firstly, young tender leafs are half-dried in the sun ray and taken after food by chewing one leaf like betel leaf for a period of 12-15 days. |
| | (b) Root of lajwanti/ chui mui (*Mimosapudica*) and fruit of loto/mainphal (*Randia dumetorum*) | Both are mixed and crushed into powder and mixed with honey and taken about one teaspoonful twice a day. |
| 22. High blood Pressure | (a) Fresh kunduri fruit (*Cephalandra indica*) and garlic | Fresh *kunduri* fruit is cut from middle put there a piece of garlic and chew the same in empty stomach at early morning. |
| | (b) Yellow leaves of sahijan or drumstick (*Moringa oleifera*) | Yellow leaves of drumstick are cooked with molasses and taken in empty stomach at early morning. |
| 23. Low blood pressure | (a) Leaves of charaigorba | Young leaves are boiled and consumed like tea. |
| | (b) Noni Sak (*Portulaca quadrifida*) | Leaves of it are prepared like a soup and taken twice a day. |
| 24. Masuro ka dard (Gum problem) | (i) Bark of kumbhi (*Carea arborea*) or Bark of amarbel (*Cuscuta reflexa)* | Bark is mixed with water and prepared a *karha* by boiling and the pour into mouth for rinse. |
| | (ii) Root of bhui champa (*Kaempferia rotunda*), kamraj (*Butteneria herbacea*) and bhengraj (*Eclipta alba*). | All the three roots are mixed and grounded and then as a paste applied. |
| 25. Danth dard (Toothache) | (a) Root and Bark of koreya (*Holarrhena antidysenterica)* | After grinding of both with water it is applied to the affected tooth. |
| | (b) Root of ishwarmul (*Aristolochia indica*) | Fresh root is washed and chewed in the mouth and juice with saliva is applied on the affected tooth. |

*contd. . .*

*contd. . .*

| *Name of the Disease (Local Name/English Name)* | *Use of Local Herbs* | *Application* |
|---|---|---|
| 26. Khujli (Eczyma) | Chirata/ kalmegh/mahamage plant (*Andrographis paniculata*). | The whole plant is soaked in water and water is consumed. |
| 27. Khujli,boil and pimple with pain | Fruit of *pitrin* tree | The fruit is rubbed in a stone slab and the paste applied. |
| 28.Piliya (Jaundice) | Seed of the fruit of *pitrin* tree | In case of *piliya* (or jaundice) the seeds of the fruit are used to make a wreath and wear it as necklace. |
| 29. Ban bish gethia bath (Joints gout) | Leaves having twelve nodes,fruit of *ralli*, root of *ralli*, bark of *patnopa*, bark of *ashariya*, bark of *rohin*, *goalki* (black pepper-procure from local market),*anantamul*,bark of *chatni* and *jaiphal* (procure from market) | All these are cut into pieces and pounded and consumed one teaspoon twice in a day. |
| 30. Raat kana (Night blindness) | Ghogol (dove bird) available in the agricultural field | The sap collects from the anal region of *ghogol* and applies 6 to 8 drops in the eye for 3 to 4 times in a day. |
| 31. Jhala pardho/ badhak (Irregular menstruation) | Bark of *rohini*, bark of *patnopa*, *semul* flower, *akhwan/akanda* flower, *mach kuda* fruit, *jabaphool* (china rose), root of *raipan* , *ashariya* and *kedar rahet*, seed of *kanoyek jang* (it is a creeper), *himsagar* (looks like a yellow leaf), root of *kendmahakkal*, *bansim*, *ban kapas* and *majur jhuti* root, flower of *parat*. | All these are mixed and cut into pieces and pounded and then grinded to form tablet and consumed daily 2 to 3 times; non-vegetarian food is not allowed and leafy vegetable-*purai* is also tabooed during this period. |
| 32. Sardi-khasi (Cold and cough) | Leaves of sajina (*Moringa oleifera)*, garlic (*Allium sativum)* and salt. | Leaves of *sajina* are boiled for a long time and then its water is mixed with salt and garlic and again boiled; after that the hot drink is consumed to get relief. |

Mal Paharia as well as other local inhabitants in their vicinity depends on traditional medicinal plants for several reasons; of which the main ones are poverty, lack of availability of medical services in their rural area, which are secluded with poor communication. They are compelled to use traditional therapy through local medicinal practitioner or **baid** (*biropiyao*). The basic thrust of our study in this arena is furthering understanding, awareness and importance of existing traditional healthcare practices among the Mal Paharia.

## Discussion

The health care practices among the Mal Paharia-a forest-hilly terrain dweller is chiefly dependent on local resources for ailment where their belief system plays a key role. The currents of globalisation are yet to penetrate into their deep rooted value system on beliefs and practices. Therefore, wide spread real education with adult night schools are required. This area of Mal Paharia is the den of malaria and kalazar but in most cases they identify through their specialist as an effect of evil-eye of *jonkh* (malevolent spirit). Study also reveals that traditional medical practitioners among the Mal Paharia are more dependable and are a valuable resource for primary health care to communities. They stand in between communities and the divine beings. They are more respectable among the communities. Therefore, to implement modern health care practices one should not ignore their existing belief system and the dependable-respectable person of the community who is mediator between the celestial and terrestrial world of belief system.

It is however clear from the discussion above that these tribals, living under the penumbra of low literacy and having blind faith in the supernatural which can both harm and heal, cannot have any scientific knowledge of the causes of an illness. There are several causes of illness as per their emic view where sprit, psychology as well as their cultural value systems are responsible which in turn affect body and mind of the people; and to overcome all these they chiefly depend on their immediate natural resources, i.e. application of various herbs, tubers, roots, leaves, fruits and flower of their vicinity. The application of various local herbs for ailment clearly suggests their great heritage of possession of a traditional knowledge bank.

## Literature Consulted

Barua, I and R. Phukan, 1998, "Socio-religious Aspect of Health among Sonowal Kachari", Eastern Anthropology, 51(4), pp. 351-362.

Channa, S. M. (ed) 1998, Medical Anthropology, New Delhi: Cosmo Publications.

Dasgupta, Samira and Amitabha Sarkar, 2005, Reflection of Ethno-Science: A Study on the Abujh Maria, New Delhi: Mittal Publications.

Geertz, Clifford, 1963, Agricultural Involution: The Process of Ecological Change in Indonesia. Berkeley: University of California Press.

Kar, R. K. 2000, "Ecology of Health and Health Culture: A Case Study among the Tea Labourers in Assam, India, International Journal of Anthropology, 15(1-2), pp. 171-183.

Khatua, N. 1998, "Sickness and Healing among the Hill Korwa", Eastern Anthropologist, 54(1), pp. 51-61.

Munn, Nancy 1973, "Symbolism in a Ritual Context", in Handbook of Social and Cultural Anthropology, ed. J. J. Honigman, Chicago: Rand Mcnally and Company.

Rao, N. Sudhakar 2007, "Study of Tribal or rural Health in the Context of Globalisation: an anthropological Framework", in Anthropology, New Global Order and Other Essays, ed. K. K. Misra, New Delhi: Concept Publishing House.

Sarkar, Amitabha and Samira Dasgupta, 2011, Mal Paharia Culture at the Crossroad, New Delhi: Agam Kala Prakashan.

Singh, K. S., 1994. People of India, vol. III, The Scheduled Tribe, Delhi: Oxford University Press and Anthropological Survey of India.

Turner, Victor, 1967, The Forest of Symbols, Ithoca: Cornell University Press.

## (ii) USE OF HERBAL MEDICINE IN TRIBAL BASTAR

### Introduction

Each tribe of our country has its own unique cultural heritage which differs from the other. Increasingly, tribal communities all over the country are witness to the destruction of their habitat, though their life and culture is intimately linked with the forest they live in. (The Hindu, March, 30, 1999).

The abodes of most of the Indian tribes are in hilly terrain and in forest-clad environment. The impact of modern light in their habitat is marginal. The traditional knowledge which they have acquired from their ascending generation over a period of time is the key source of inspiration of maintaining their livelihood in such environment. Situation has compelled them to find out means through which they may recover or survive from any illness. As a result they often use their local environment resources for their ailment.

The study of traditional beliefs and practices regarding health and disease in different cultures is of great significance in understanding the human behaviour. An indepth study of folk medicine from an emic view will help in understanding the cultural symbols and meanings and their integration with the culture (Tribhuwan, 1998). Anthropological data on ethno-medicine is instrumental in understanding the native's or tribal's health related beliefs as well as it also preserves and conserves the surrounding bio-diversity of their habitat since they utilise the resources of a particular territory for their ailment over generation and also protect the resource base to sustain their future generations; this is ensured through certain cultural stigma which is religious value loaded like presence of sacred grove. Thus, ethno-medicine is belief and practices relating to health and disease, which are products of indigenous cultural developments and not explicitly derived from the conceptual framework of modern medicine. The Indian tribal people use their traditional knowledge in health care system where herbs, plants and roots locally available in their vicinity are used for their ailment.

The forest-clad district -Bastar of Madhya Pradesh (now Chhattishgarh) is the abode of the tribal population. The total area of the district (undivided) 15091 sq. miles, the density of population in the district is 6 persons per sq. km. It is the homeland of following tribal groups namely, Abujh Maria, Bison–Horn Maria (or Dandami Maria), Dorla, Dhurwa, Bhatra and Halba. Bastar can be treated as a single cultural zone.

**Details of the use of medicinal plants for Ailment.**

| *Sl No.* | *Common Name of the Plant* | *Local Name of the Plant* | *Name of the Disease* | *Process of application* | *Botanical Name* | *Family* |
|---|---|---|---|---|---|---|
| 1. | Gyapar | Hiran Khuri | i) Hyper acidity | i) Root extract consumed | Cissampelos pareira | Manispermacese |
| | | | ii) Snake bite | ii) Root extract is dropped in ear as well as root extract paste is rubbed in the affected parts | Cissampelos pareira | Manispermacese |
| 2. | Gilou | Gilou Guruch | Fever | Extract of the stem is consumed | Tinospora | Cordifolia |
| 3. | Safed Sarson | Safed Sarson | Head hair washing | Extract of the cereals are applied in hair | Brassica campestris | Brassicaceae (cruciferae) |
| 4. | Kakai | Kakai | Fever after delivery | The bark and leaf of the plant are boiled and consumed in the boiled water. | Placourtia indica | Placourtiaceae |
| 5. | Jhau | Jhau | Skin Disease | Root extract | Tamarix indica | Tamaricacese |
| 6. | Kharaiti | Zintijhari | Urinary Trouble | Root extract and juice of whole plant is consumed. | Abulilon indicum | Malvaceae |
| 7. | Pili kharaiti | Zintijhari | Urinary Trouble | Root extract and juice of whole plant is consumed | Sidacordifoliae | Malvaceae |
| 8. | Jangli Kapas | Jangli Kapas | Irregularity in mensturation | Root extract is consumed | Gosaypium hirsutum | Malvaceae |
| 9. | Senal | Kouhathodi | Leuchrrhoea (white discharge from vegina) | Root extract is consumed | Bomboxceiba | Bombacaceae |

*contd. . .*

*contd. . .*

| *Sl. No.* | *Common Name of the Plant* | *Local Name of the Plant* | *Name of the Disease* | *Process of application* | *Botanical Name* | *Family* |
|---|---|---|---|---|---|---|
| 10. | Marorphalli | Athimuri | Colic pain in abdoman | Fruit of the plant is consumed after grinding | Halicteresisora | Starculiaceae |
| 11. | Chota Gokhoru | Chota Gokhoru | Swelling of any parts of the body and impotancy among male (fragidity) | Fruits used | Tribulus terrestris | Bygophyliaceae |
| 12. | Khatti Buti | Chinchiniya vaji | Insomenia | Leaves are used as vegetables | Oxalis acetogella | Oxalidaceae |
| 13. | Bel | Bel | Constipation and bile problem | Cornel of the fruit is consumed | Aegle marmoleos | Rutaceae |
| 14. | Neem | Neem | Skin Disease | Oil is extracted from the fruit and applied in the affected parts | Azadirachta indica | Meliaceae |
| 15. | Malkangini | Peng / Pengu | Joints pain (Rheaumatoid Artharitees) | applicaion of oil of the seed in the affected parts of the body | Celestrus paniculatus | Maliaceae |
| 16. | Hadgod | Hadgod / Hadjor | Bone Fracture | Pulp is applied in the affected parts after grinding | Vitis quadrongulnris | Vitaceae |
| 17. | Achar | Charpak | Wound due to burning | Paste of the bark is applied | Buchinamia lansan | Anacardiaceae |
| 18. | Shahjana / Sajna | Munga | Headache, blood preasure | Leaves are boiled and water is consumed, fruit is also used as vegetables | Maringa aliefera | Moringaceae |

*contd. . .*

contd. . .

| Sl. No. | Common Name of the Plant | Local Name of the Plant | Name of the Disease | Process of application | Botanical Name | Family |
|---|---|---|---|---|---|---|
| 19. | Palas | Farsa | Hydroceal and urinary tract infection | i) Flowers are baked and fomented.<br>ii) Plant are burnt and then boiled in water to form a crystal and consumed. | Butea monosperma | Fabaceae (Papilionaceae) |
| 20. | Karanj | Karanj | Wound in mouth or gum | Oil is used, often twig is used as brush | Pongania pinnata | Fabaceae ( Papilionaceae) |
| 21. | Aparajita | Sankhapushpi | Throat infection | Root extract is consumed | Clistorla ternalea | Fabaceae (Papilionaceae) |
| 22. | Sarpunkha | Bajradanti | Inflamation in Gum | Root is used | Indigofera angulosa | Papilionaceae |
| 23. | Amaltash | Bandar danta or Sonarli | Removing constipalion | Endocarp of the fruit is used | Cassia fistula | Caesalpiniaceae |
| 24. | Lajwanti | Lajwanti | Impotency among male | Root extract is consumed | Minose pudica | Mimosaceae |
| 25. | Khair | Khair | Skin disease and abscess | Bark of the plant is boiled and consumed | Acacia catechu | Mimosaceae |
| 26. | Arjun | Kahu | Bone Fracture | Bark of the plant is boiled and added with milk and taken | Terminalia arjuna | Combretaceae |
| 27. | Baheda | Baheda | Skin tanning of cattle | Fruit is used | Terminalia bellirica | Combretaceae |
| 28. | Harra | Harra | Constipation | Fruit is socked in water and water is consumed | Terminalia chebula | Combretaceae |

contd. . .

*contd. . .*

| *Sl. No.* | *Common Name of the Plant* | *Local Name of the Plant* | *Name of the Disease* | *Process of application* | *Botanical Name* | *Family* |
|---|---|---|---|---|---|---|
| 29. | Dhawai | Dhawai | Food fermentation of alcholic drinks flower nectar is used | | Wood fordia fruticosa | Lythraceae |
| 30. | Indrayan | | Fruit is used for poisoning for fish catching | | Citrullus colocynthis | Cucurbitaceae |
| 31. | Mandook prani | | Epilepsy | Leave juice is taken | Cittells asiatics | Apisceae ( Umbelliferae) |
| 32. | Tejraj | Tejballi or Bhalukanda | Impotency among male | Root extract is consumed to cure impotency | Peucedanum nagpurense | Umbelliferae |
| 33. | Banleere | Jangli Ziri | Wound ind in the mouth or stomatities | Fruits are used | Carum pigram | Umbelliferae |
| 34. | Dekamali | Dekamali | Anti helminthis | Latex ( resin ) of the plant is consumed | Gandenia resinifera | Rubiaceae |
| 35. | Mundi | (unable to collect) | Skin Disease | Decoction of the whole plant | Mitragyna parvifoles | Rubiaceae |
| 36. | Sufed phetra | phetdra | Migrain and Sinocytis | Root extract drop at nose | Xeromphis spinose | Rubiaceae |
| 37. | Bringraj | Bhangra | Jaundice | Leaf extract is consumed | Felipta alba | Asteraceae (compositae) |

*contd. . .*

contd. . .

| Sl No. | Common Name of the Plant | Local Name of the Plant | Name of the Disease | Process of application | Botanical Name | Family |
|---|---|---|---|---|---|---|
| 38. | Akrkara | Akrkara | i) leucoderma | i) Leave pulp direct application | Spizanthes admilla | Compositae |
| | | | ii) toothache | ii) Buds | Do | Do |
| 39. | Rasana | Rasana | Rheaumatoid Artharities | Root extract | Rlephariapermum subscessile | Compositae |
| 40. | Kalisri | Banjira | Ulcer in the mouth (stometities) | Chewing the seeds of the plant | Verpomia anthelmintics | Compositae |
| 41. | Gojibha | Hathi bundhi | Proper milk lactation after delivery | Root are crushed and eaten | Elephantopus scaber | Compositae |
| 42. | Chitrak | Chitabarjari | Hydroceal | (i) Root is used, it is tied in the hand of opposite direction of affected parts | Plumbago zeylanics | Plumbaginace |
| | Chitrak | Chitabarjari | Ambebiosis | (ii) Root is used | Plumbago zeylanics | Plumbaginace |
| 43. | Bai birang | Bhaverang | Agti helminthis | Seeds are used | Embelia ribos | Myrsinaceae |
| 44. | Pila kaner | | Wound healing | Latex is used | Thevetia peruviana | Apocynaceae |
| 45. | Indra jota | Korai | Ambebiosis | Bark is used | Holarrhena antidysentarira | Apocynaceae |
| 46. | Saptparni | Chhatiban | Fever | Bark is used | Alstonia scholaris | Apocynaceae |
| 47. | Dudhi | Dudhi | Child diarohhoea | Old plant juice | Wrightia tinclores | Apocynaceae |
| 48. | Sarpagandha | Kukrachendi | For sleeping purpose | Root extract is consumed | Rauvolfia serpentina | Apocynaceae |
| 49. | Sarpagandha | Kukrachendi | Snakes avoid its smell | | Rauvolfia serpentina | Apocynaceae |

contd. . .

contd. . .

| Sl. No. | Common Name of the Plant | Local Name of the Plant | Name of the Disease | Process of application | Botanical Name | Family |
|---|---|---|---|---|---|---|
| 50. | Chhota madar | Arkjeladu | Joints pain (Rheaumatoid artharitees) | Tied up matured and ripe leaf in the affected parts | Calotropis procara | Asclepiadaceae |
| 51. | Nagbel | Nagbel | Snake bite | Root extract | Cryptolepis buchananil | Asclepiadaceae |
| 52. | Anantmul | Anantmul | Body strength | Root extract | Hemedesmus indicus | Asclepiadaceae |
| 53. | Gudmar | Chiti bhimari | Anti diabetic | Leave juice | Cymnena sylvestre | Asclepiadaceae |
| 54. | Nirmali | Khaza supari | Water purifier | Latex is used | Strychnos potatorum | Doganiaceae |
| 55. | Chiravata | Bhuilim | Stomach clear | Whole plant is soaked in water and consumed | Swertia corymbosa | Gentianaceae |
| 56. | Lasoda | Bohar | Cough | Leaf and fruit | Cordia myxa | Boraginaceae |
| 57. | Dhatura | Dhatura | Bronchial asthma | Used dry leaf as bidi (smoking) | Datura stramonium | Solanaceae |
| 58. | Bhathataiya | Vejribhata | i) cough | Fruit is used | Solamum indicum | Solansceae |
| | | | ii) alocacia | Application of root extract | Do | Do |
| 59. | Makop | Makoy | Jaundice and swelling of lever | Leaf juice | Solanum nigrum | Solansceae |
| 60. | Adhusa | Hagarlyata | Cough | Juice of leaf and flowers | Adhatoda vasica | Acanthaceae |
| 61. | Kalmegh | Kalabhuili | Fever | Whole plant extract | Andrographic paniculata | Acanthaceae |
| 62. | Bajradanti | Bajradanti | Dental infection | Juice of root | Barleris cristata | Acanthaceae |

contd. . .

*contd. . .*

| *Sl. No.* | *Common Name of the Plant* | *Local Name of the Plant* | *Name of the Disease* | *Process of application* | *Botanical Name* | *Family* |
|---|---|---|---|---|---|---|
| 63. | Pilikat saraiya | Kataban | Skin infection | Whole plant extract | Barleris prionites | Acanthaceae |
| 64. | Nili nirgundi (blue flower) | Nigur | Rheaunatoid artharitees | Leaves and root juice | Gendarussa vuigaris | Acanthaceae |
| 65. | Nrigundi (white flower) | Nigur | Rheaunatoid artuaritees | Leaves and root juice | Vitex negando | Verbenaceae |
| 66. | Dronpuspi | Gume | i) Nasal bleeding | Flowers and leaves extract use as nasal drop | Leueas aspera | Lamiaceae ( Labiatace) |
| | | | ii) Jaundice | Leaf extract | Do | Do |
| 67. | Tulsi | Tulsi | Cough and cold | Whole plant extract | Ocimum sanctum | Lamiaceae (Labiatace) |
| 68. | Tulsi dauna | Membrija | Ulcer | Seed extract | Artimesia indica | Lamiaceae (Labiatace) |
| 69. | Afamarg | Larjera | Safe delivery | Root extract | Achyranthes aspera | Amarantheceae |
| 70. | Lalchoulai | Jungli choulai | Painful mensturation or dysmenorrhoea | Root extract | Amaranthus spinosus | Amarantheceae |
| 71. | Pipra jadi | Pipra jadi | i) fever after delivery. ii) rheauumatoid artharitees | Root , noodle extract | Piper chaba | Piperaceae |
| 72. | Maida | Maidehal | Use during sprain | Bark is used as paste and apply in the affected parts | Litsea sebifera | Louraceae |

*contd. . .*

*contd. . .*

| *Sl. No.* | *Common Name of the Plant* | *Local Name of the Plant* | *Name of the Disease* | *Process of application* | *Botanical Name* | *Family* |
|---|---|---|---|---|---|---|
| 73. | Chandan | Balchandan | Swelling of any part of the body | Stem is pasted and missed with horn of antelope and applied in the affected part. | Santalum album | Santalaceae |
| 74. | Putrangiva | Jiyapota | Incase of still birth | Root and fruit are used | Potrangiva roxburghil | Euphorbiaceae |
| 75. | Arandi | Jara / rani jara | i) Jaundice.<br>ii) pain in the body and luxative | i) leaf extract.<br>(ii) seeds oil | Ricinus commnis | Euphorbiaceae |
| 76. | Awala | Awala | i) clear bowl<br>ii) bounty growth of head hair | i) fruit<br>ii) seeds oil | Phyllanthis emblica | Euphorbiaceae |
| 77. | Dudhi | Chota dudhi | Infantile diarrohoea | Whole plant extract | Euphorhia hirta | Euphorbiaceae |
| 78. | Ratanjot | Raijara | Apply on head hair for black | Seeds oil is applied. It is like a veseline | Jatropha gossypifolia | Do |
| 79. | Gular | Dumar | i) burn<br>ii) leucorrohoea or white discharge from vagina | i) paste of the bark<br>ii) fruit is dried up then powdered the same and consumed | P. glomerata | Moraceae |
| 80. | Kevkanda | Kevkanda | i) gastraritis | Root extract | Contus speciosus | Zingi beraceae |
| | | | ii) luxative | | | |
| | | | iii) rheaumatoid artharitees | | | |

*contd. . .*

*contd. . .*

| *Sl. No.* | *Common Name of the Plant* | *Local Name of the Plant* | *Name of the Disease* | *Process of application* | *Botanical Name* | *Family* |
|---|---|---|---|---|---|---|
| 81. | Jangli haldi | Jangli haldi | Joints pain | Only root parts is used | Cureouma longa | Zingi beraceae |
| 82. | Kali musali | Kali musali | Improvement of vitality power among male | Root is used | Curculigo orchioudes | Hyperdaceae |
| 83. | Satawar | Satawar | Lactation of new born's mother | Root extract or direct consumtion of root | Asparagus recemosus | Liliaceae |
| 84. | Kalihari | Kalihari | Abortion | Root extract is used and it is very poisonous | Gloriosa superha | Liliaceae |
| 85. | Safed musali | Musli | Afrodecia | Root extract | Culorophytum arundigaceum | Liliaceae |
| 86. | Jangli pyaj | Gondli | Alocacia in head | Root extract is applied | Urginea indica | Liliaceae |
| 87. | Ram datoon | Mutrijari | i) toothache | i) stem is used as datan | Smilax zeyianica. | Smilacaceae |
| | | | ii) urinary tract | ii) root extract | Do | Do |
| 88. | Nagarmotha | Unable to collect | i) skin disease | i) ash of the whole plant is mixed with *tora* oil and then apply in the affected parts of thg body (tora extract from mohua seed) | Cyperus | Cyperaceae |
| | | | ii) fever | ii) root extract decoction is taken | | |

The life of these tribal people are nourished and nurtured in the cradle of nature. So one may observe that impact of their immediate 'niche' (or environment) on their life is profound. The forest type of this district in tropical moist. The forestis characterised by humid monsoon climate.

Due to close association with the environment they have gathered an intimate knowledge of local resources of various floras having medicinal value and most surprisingly they always try to scrupulously guard this knowledge from outsiders. The exposure of these tribal people towards modernity is not remarkable and as a result they still depend on their indigenous way of treatment and have also developed its own method for the treatment and consumption of herbal medicines. They have a strong faith on this system and survive on such medicines. During winter they are even found without sufficient woolen garments, naked-footed but without any trouble. Data were collected from the medicine men of Abujh Maria, Dorla, Bison Horn Maria (or Dandami Maria) Muria, Dhurwa, Halba and Bhatra of the district.

## Discussion

The empirical observation reveals that indigenous system is closely woven into the social system of tribal Bastar. It needs further research and study. Infact, this indigenous system of use of herbal plants as medicine is confined to a region only. However, if the knowledge and scope of the system is widened a large number of population may be benefited. Before the advent of modern medicine like alloepathy, the use of herbal medicine was general in early social system. It is suggested to take proper study in this arena, which may open up a new horizon in the field of medicine.

## References

Cohen, Milton 1984, "The Ethnomedicine of the Garifuna of Rio Tinto" in Anthropology Quarterly, Vol. 57, No. 1, pp. 16-27.

Gindi Suresh Kumar 1994, "Ethnomedicineamong the Yanadi: A Hunter Gatherer Tribe in South India", Girijan Sanskriti, Vol. 2, No. 2.

Kurian, J. C. and B. V. Bhanu 1980, "Ethnomedicine: A Study of Nomadic Vaidus of Maharastra", in Eastern Anthropologist, Vol. 33, No. 1, pp. 71-78.

Tribhuwan, Robin D. 1998, Medical World of the Tribals, New Delhi: Discovery Publishing House.

### (iii) Use of Herbal Medicines Among the Toto

In connection with the ethno medicinal investigation of any community, a study of their geographical environment is urgently needed. This is true about the Totos too. . The Toto live in such a geographical situation that each and every moment they believe that there are evil spirits roaming in their vicinity, specially those like to stay in the water sources and are responsible to create sickness, disease and various types of misfortunes in their life. To get protection from their anguish they have several ways, and along with these, when they suffer from any type of disease, the remedial measures are also procured from that particular ecological niche. They collect their medicinal plants from the jungle of Dooars and live happily there with the help of those herbal medicines supplemented by with rituals and magical performances.

In Toto Para there is a person named Dhaniram Toto, who works as V. L. W. of his own village and the surrounding ones. He has a vivid knowledge of their medicinal plants and their application. He told that in their world there are medicinal plants that can cure all the diseases even cancer but unfortunately he does not know all about them. However what he knows is enough for the treatment of his people. . In Totopara the people generally suffer from *jwar* or fever, loose motion, dysentery, skin disease, headache, stomachche, bone injury, body pain and *bis bat* (arthritis). He diagnoses the actual cause of the disease and gives the medicine as per the need. He told that the villagers do not like to go to the doctor immediately. On the other hand, they prefer to consult their own *ojha* or *jhankri*. According to Dhani they not only give medicine but also at the same time give mental strength to a sick person, which is very much necessary for recovery from ailment. To study ethno medicine, one should consider these points too.

These are as follows—

#### Conception of ill health

**Illness etiology:** When a person feels weak/feverish /having cough and cold/body ache/head ache/stomach ache/loose motion/any type of skin disease/high fever etc. and in case of a child continuous crying, they feel that there must be some malevolent spirit causing the sickness/disease for the person.

**Role of medicinal practitioner:** The sorcerer or *jhankri* and the medicinal practitioner or *pau* are called immediately to identify the disease and the cause of the disease. The *jhankri* through his magical performances and counting suggests the exact cause of the disease. Sometimes the spirit who is responsible for the disease possesses him. According to it's prescription in his possession, he suggests the remedial measures to be taken for healing. Generally in his suggestions the primary item is to perform a ritual as per the prescription of the spirit who gave direction during his possessed state.

In case of *pau,* he first tries to identify the disease by feeling the person's pulse. It is known as *kui kanowa.* When the pulse runs fast, then he is sure that the person is attacked by some evil spirit and because of that he/she became ill. How much the malevolent spirit is powerful, or how much the intensity of its evil work depends on the rate of the person's pulse. Again, if the pulse runs very slow with some interruptions then he becomes very disturbed. He thinks that there must be a very dangerous spirit who attacked the person to take his or her life. Feeling the pulse rate, the *pau* also gets assured whether he will be able to cure the patient or not. Another method of identification of disease is ritual reading in *marua.* He keeps some *marua* on the floor . This time the person gets possessed by *Senjha/ Saiyenja,* and he begins to shiver. He requests the deity to tell him which spirit attacked the person and through fingers these maruas are stirred with chanting of some mantras and ultimately in this way he can easily identify the exact cause of the disease and the particular spirit responsible for the suffering. He gives medicines but along with that he also advises to arrange for a ritual offering to appease the displeased spirit. It is already mentioned that the evil spirits are also worshipped time to time to keep them quiet. Their *cheising* and all the benevolent spirits are also to be worshipped. Otherwise, they also will be angry and will become harmful. In any disease or distress the *pau* and *jhankri* suggest the patients what to do along with the proper medicine (in case of a disease).

**Body symbolism:** When a person suffers from high fever and tremendous shivering, then the *pau* suggests that it may be malaria. Similarly, when a person suffers from fever and his/her eyes become yellow then the *pau* suspects that there may be *pilia* or jaundice and he applies the herbal medicines along with sacrifice of chicken for the displeased spirit who is suspected responsible for the disease. When a person is suffering from severe cough and cold, his voice is choked, he feels pain in his chest and there is breathing trouble, then the *pau* becomes sure that the person is suffering from pneumonia. In this way the *pau* detects the disease through body symbolism.

## Cultural Values

**Ritual Healing:** Ritual healing is major component under cultural cognition of a disease which has already been discussed.

Omens and restrictions to be mentioned–When the medicine man goes to collect medicinal herbs he has to observe certain strict rules. He will not sleep with his wife, not take food cooked by her. He will not take any food and tea with salt before entering jungle. He has to collect the plant before sunrise. Otherwise, the plant will lose its medicinal value and ingradients. He will go very silently without knowledge of anybody except the patient's family who can accompany him. The *pau* has to worship *Mahakal* before entering the jungle. He will enter with uttering the mantra of *Maniprem* which he got from his Bhutia guru–Chundu Lama who has got it in his dream. In due course he will give the mantra to his youngest son (as he can give it to only one person). After he returns from jungle, at first he prepares the medicine and then takes some food cooked by himself.

## Role of ethno-medical specialist and application

### Application of Traditional Knowledge in Ailment through Herbs and available Natural Resources

| *Sl.No.* | *Name of the disease* | *Symptom* | *Plants with scientific name or any other item used* | *Method of preparation and application* | *Deity/spirit responsible* | *Restriction if any* |
|---|---|---|---|---|---|---|
| 1(a) | Haiwa (Fever) | Rise of body heat, bodyache, giddy feeling, weakness | Korola (a variety of bitter gourd) | It's leaves are ground and the juice is taken; sometimes whole leaf is taken. In that case the leaves are kept fold in thick leaf of *Muihira* leaf and the whole thing is kept inside the hot ash for sometimes till it gets soft. After taking it out of the ash, it is ground with salt and chilly and taken. It is continued for 3 days and 2 times daily. If not cured then they try for 1(b). | | Sour food items are strictly avoided. |
| 1(b) | -do- | -do- | Kasabu or vasak (Adhatoda Vasica) flower. | The flowers are packed in *Muihira* leaves and kept in hot ash till it gets soft or boiled in water and chatni is prepared with that. It is taken 2/3 times daily for 2 days. If not cured, then they try for 1(c). | | -do- |

| Sl. No. | Name of the disease | Symptom | Plants with scientific name or any other item used | Method of preparation and application | Deity/spirit responsible | Restriction if any |
|---|---|---|---|---|---|---|
| 1(c) | -do- | -do- | Kasai (? ) flower. It is red in colour and very juicy. It grows in the hilly forest. It is a herb. | Bioled for 20/25 minutes in water and the whole water is extracted and taken for 2 times at least every day, for 3 days. The water is very bitter in taste. If not cured then they try for 1(d). | | -do- |
| 1(d) | -do- | -do | Ambarshi or Bhat patta( ? ). | The tender leaves are taken and ground. The juice is extracted. It is very bitter in taste. The juice is taken for 2/3 times for 3 days. If not cured then consult Ojha or *Jhankri*. | | -do- |
| 2 (a) | -do- | -do- | Kising (Phlogocanthus thyrsiflorus) (Flower blossoms during Chaitra) | The juice of flower is extracted and stored in bottle, used during rainy season when fever is very common. It is taken 2-3 times daily for 2-3 days. If not cured, then they try for 2 (b). | | -do- |
| 2(b) | -do- | -do- | Kasai (?) a type of herb | Total herb or a portion of it is washed and ground / smashed and the juice is taken for 3 days; if not cured, then try for 2 ( c). | | -do- |
| 2 (c) | -do- | -do- | Ambarashi (a big tree) or Bhat patta | The bargo (bark) is extracted and burnt. The bark is bluish in colour and to is the ash. The ash is taken with water for 2-3 times daily for 3 days. If is very bitter in taste. | | -do- |
| 3 | Haiwa | -do- | Kulein (?) tree | Kulein roots are ground and mixed with water and taken 2-3 times daily for 3 days. | | -do- |

| Sl.No. | Name of the disease | Symptom | Plants with scientific name or any other item used | Method of preparation and application | Deity/spirit responsible | Restriction if any |
|---|---|---|---|---|---|---|
| 4 (a) | Dodoinya (Malaria) | Shivering and fever, bodyaches, vomiting tendency | Kulein tree (?) | Kulein roots are dried and powdered, then mixed with water and pasted. It is taken with water for 3 days at least. | | -do- |
| 4 (b) | -do- | -do- | Tyei sing plant (?.) | The *bargo* (bark) is ground, juice is extracted and taken with hot water. | | -do- |
| 5. | Mewong-po (Burn) | Irritation, skin becomes red, blisters develop and even ulcers develop. | Sinthi (?.) tender and unripe + *euimba* (turmeric) or alu (potato) saithi (juice) | These two are mixed together and ground. The juice is extracted. The mixture is applied on the burnt surface. Ghee is sometimes added to it. | | |
| 6. | Eyn gchu (abscess or boil) | A portion on the surface of skin swells and it becomes bigger and very painful when it is matured, pus is formed. | Tenga / Tengi / Tengke(? ) | The juice of the leaves is extracted, applied on the affected area leaving the central portion of the boil. It helps in quick maturity of the boil and relieves the pain. | | Sour food items are strictly avoided. |
| 7. | -do- | -do- | Parucha ( ? ) | Leaves and roots are ground together. A sticky milky juice comes out. The juice is used as poultice on abscess. | | -do- |
| 8. | -do- | -do- | Ghee and amenyeme leaves ( ? ) | Traditionally they used to operate it with a sharp bamboo strip when it is fully matured. The pus with the hard substance known as bij (seed) is extracted. Then they used to clean the place with a piece of clean cloth. After that ghee (old) is heated and applied on the sore for 3 days. If the bleeding is not stopped, naturally, they apply the juice of *amenyeme* leaves. The bleeding will definitely stop. | | -do- |

| *Sl.No.* | *Name of the disease* | *Symptom* | *Plants with scientific name or any other item used* | *Method of preparation and application* | *Deity/spirit respons-ible* | *Restriction if any* |
|---|---|---|---|---|---|---|
| 9. | Toothache | Pain sometimes bleeding, swelling of gum | Tamprasi or Guava (Psidium guajava) | Leaves are chewed and the juice helps to reduce pain. Gargle lukewarm water added with salt. | | |
| 10. | Loose or unstable tooth | Pains and uneasy feeling | Odla (?) | Thread is extracted from the bargo (bark) of the plant. The affected tooth is tied by the thread and is pulled out . | | |
| 11. | Kandukhe (earache) | Pain | Mustard oil | They put mustard oil in the earhole. | | |
| 12. | Insect intrusion in the ear | Pain and rusting noise in the ear | Gurja (?.) creeper | The creeper is torn vertically into two halves but not totally detached. A person whiffs in it putting the other end just on the earhole. A juice with bitter taste goes inside the ear and the creature comes out. | | |
| 13. | Naisang (Intestinal worms) | Itching in anal region | Mat Kila (?) | The leaves are taken, backed and then they formant the naval portion with it. | | |
| 14. | -do- | -do- | Manuma (or Kattali kala in Bengali) (Musa parade siaca) | 4/5 are taken and smashed and then the naval portion is coated with it. | | |
| 15. | -do- | -do- | Ash | Ash is mixed with water and taken during evening or night for a few days. | | |
| 16. | -do- | -do- | Mun gai straw (?) | Roots of mungai straw is ground with water and taken twice daily for 7 days. | | |

| Sl.No. | Name of the disease | Symptom | Plants with scientific name or any other item used | Method of preparation and application | Deity/ spirit respon-sible | Restriction if any |
|---|---|---|---|---|---|---|
| 17. | Naisang (Intestinal worms) | Itching and when it comes out from mouth. | Tamprasi or Guava (Psidium guajava) | The juice of tender leaves is extracted and taken for 2-3 days. It gives relief. The worms come out from anus. | | |
| 18. | Bat (Joints pain) (rheumatis m) | Pains in the joints of the body | Simbuli (Nishinda) (vitex negun do – verbena ceae) + Methi (fenu greek plant and its grain) + Kalijira (black cumin) + 1 full garlic (Allium sativum) + 250 gms of mustard oil. | At first the oil is heated upto its boiling point. Then left to reduce its heat. When it is less warm they pour all the items in the oil and it is stirred. These are fried but not burnt. Then all these are crushed in that oil. After it is totally cold, the oil mixed with all the items is poured in a glass bottle and kept and used to massage the affected portion. Prior to that the oil is heated. | | Sour food meat and cold en are prohibited. |
| 19. | Gathia / Gath darad (rheumatis m) | Swelling, joints with red colour, pains, the area is hot | Hariuhara or Tikraj in Bengali (?) | Oil of the seed is extracted and massaged on the affected portion to get relief from pain. | | -do- |
| 20. | -do- | -do- | Dungchu (Artemisia nilagririca), Titapani in Nepali | Roots are crushed and coarse powder is applied to the affected areas as poultice to relieve the pain. The plant is also used as an antiseptic medicine. | | -do- |
| 21. | -do- | -do- | Chulkani ( ? ) | Leaves are heated and put on the affected area to warm slowly to relieve the pain. | | -do- |
| 22. | Eye disease | Red eye, hazy vision, Itching and irritaton, wet eyes | Mimaising | Juice of the plant extracted and applied to the affected eye. | | |

| Sl. No. | Name of the disease | Symptom | Plants with scientific name or any other item used | Method of preparation and application | Deity/ spirit respon-sible | Restriction if any |
|---|---|---|---|---|---|---|
| 23. | Midoi / Anjani (Sty or Stye on the eye lid) | Pains, rheum exuding from eyes. | Mango (Mangifera Indica) | A mango leaf is torn from the tree. The portion of the leaf which was attached with a branch of the tree starts to secret white milk fluid. That portion of the leaf is touched on the sty. The eye immediately will get relief and become fresh. | | |
| 24. | Pushya (Dandruff) | White scale like substance on the scalp, itching and hair fall. | Bichi/Budhi (Acacia pennata (Linn) willd) (a type of creeper) | The vein of the leaves are extracted. Those are ground and pasted. It is applied on the scalp with water and massaged lightly. Soap like foam comes out of it. Then the scalp is thoroughly washed with water. It is repeated for a few weaks and the scalp will be *pushya* free. | | |
| 25. | Snake bite | Sleepy or drowsy feeling A mark of teeth of snake bite, burning sensation. | Bichi / Budhi creeper (Acacio pennata (Linn) willd) antidote for snake bite | It is crushed with water. Soap like foam comes out Applied to the affected area after cutting the wound in certain depth, and squizing the bad blood with poison. Some bindings are given. Some ropes are tied at the upper and lower portions of the wound leaving 4" gap between them.. | | |
| 26. | Bichhu Kata (scorpion bite) | Sign of bite burning sensation | Ahmicha ( ? ) | Juice of the leaves is extracted and applied on the affected portion. | | |

| Sl.No. | Name of the disease | Symptom | Plants with scientific name or any other item used | Method of preparation and application | Deity/ spirit respo-nsible | Restriction if any |
|---|---|---|---|---|---|---|
| 27. | Peme-chi-cho-wa (Stomach trouble) and Yoyo (Jaundice). | Stomach-che, loose motion. In Jaundice yellow colour of skin, eyes, nails and urin and stool. | Lanchkicha ( ? ) | Juice of root is extracted and taken 2-3 times daily atleast for 3 days. (Lashe Toto of Panchayat gaon of the village is expert in curing Yoyo disease) | | Avoid sour items, and non-vegetarian food. Pumpkin is strictly prohibited. In case of Jaundice oil, ghee are also harmful items. |
| 28. | Stomach trouble | -do- | Hariuhara (Tikraj in Bengali) | Bark is soaked in water, ground, juice is extracted. The juice is taken. | | -do- |
| 29. | Wind | Indigestion, farting. | Juing or Joy sing (sing means tree) | Flower and juice of fresh, tender bark is extracted and those are given to the patient to take 2 times daily after meal for a few days. | | -do- |
| 30. | Gastric trouble | -do- | a. Ticha, b. Pendra sing (Murraya Koenigil | a. Juice of the leaves extracted and taken with warm water thrice daily. b. Juice of the leaves is used in acidity and gas problem. | | -do- |
| 31. | Peme-chi-chno-wa (Diarrhoea) | No solid stool only water. Rumbling of belly. | Tamprasi or Guava. (Psidium guajava) | Tender leaves are chewed and swallowed. | | |
| 32. | Masi (Dysentery) | Falling of thick slippery substance with excreta frequent | -do- | -do- | | |

| *Sl.No.* | *Name of the disease* | *Symptom* | *Plants with scientific name or any other item used* | *Method of preparation and application* | *Deity/spirit responsible* | *Restriction if any* |
|---|---|---|---|---|---|---|
| 33. | -do- | Loose motion frequently with semi-solid substance, pains in abdomen. | Duta / Dhuta (Gyno cardia odorata) | The bargo (bark) of the plant is washed and thoroughly cleaned. Then it is ground in mortar and pastle and juice is extracted and kept in a bottle. It is given to the patient after mixing with water for 2-3 times a day for 2-3 days. Oil of the seeds is used as a medicine to cure skin disease. | | |
| 34. | -do- | -do- | Nyiui Sing (?) | Leaf of Nyiui plant is ground and consumed. | | |
| 35. | Mashi / Masi ( Dysentry) | Falling of thick, slippery substance with excreta, stomachache | Main root of Dhotisal tree(?) | It is ground and mixed with water. Taken once and cured. | | No spicy food is allowed. Minimum oil is allowed. Boiled food is preferred. |
| 36. | Edam bemi (Acidity) | Vomit, wind, flatulence | Juing (?) leaves | Juice is extracted and taken without or with a little water. | | |
| 37. | Jaundice | Three types – white, yellow and black. The skin colour, eyes, nails become yellow or black or white. | Sonapatta ( ? ) | It is boiled in 1 cup of water which becomes ½ cup and taken 2-3 times daily for 3-4 days. | | -do- |

| Sl.No. | Name of the disease | Symptom | Plants with scientific name or any other item used | Method of preparation and application | Deity/ spirit respon-sible | Restriction if any |
|---|---|---|---|---|---|---|
| 38. | Maka/Ghav, Sleeplessn ess, Mental tension. | Wound, bleeding, sleepless nights, mental tension. | a. Ahemnangmi / Makaibi or Nagbeli (Cryptolepis buchananil ).<br>b. Ameneme / Yamenyame (Hal Kamli) | i. Juice of the plant is extracted and applied on the wound. It stops continuous bleeding.<br>ii. Juice of the plant used as laxative and also taken in disorder of digestive system.<br>iii. Often leaves are roasted and inhaled for recovery from cold.<br>iv. Juice is taken in sleeplessness.<br>v. Juice of the root is massaged on scalp for recovery from mental tension and sleeplessness. | | |
| 39. | Maka (Sores and wound) | Wound, bleeding, irritation. | Egdi (Cissampelos pareira) | Juices of the leaves are applied on the sores and wound and also in inflammation.<br>Fibers from bark are strong and used for tying purpose. | | -do- |
| 40. | -do- | -do | Loyai (?) | Bark is used. It is ground and the juice is extracted, applied on the wound 2 times daily during morning and evening for a week. | | |
| 41. | -do- (Chronic wound or sore) | -do- | -do- | Bark is ground and the juice is extracted. The place is washed with a piece of clean cloth soaked in water. Then they apply the juice, 2 times daily till the maka is not totally cured. | | |

| *Sl.No.* | *Name of the disease* | *Symptom* | *Plants with scientific name or any other item used* | *Method of preparation and application* | *Deity/ spirit respon-sible* | *Restriction if any* |
|---|---|---|---|---|---|---|
| 42. | Dying person | Breeding trouble, Death pain | Root joint of Bikma | It is ground with water and given to the patient. It works like coramine. | | |
| 43. | Nyachpuna (wound due to cut) | Bleeding and sore. | Yamenyame or Halkamli in Bengali | It is a creeper. Juice of the leaves is extracted. The juice is deep green in colour and smells like Iodine. It is applied on the wound. If immediately the juice is applied after the skin is cut, then bleeding is stopped at that moment and there is no chance of septic as it acts as an antiseptic drug. | | |
| 44. | Maka+ scabies and itches | Irritation, itching | Aru or Akanda (?) Lapa (leaf) | The lapa (leaf) is torn and white sticky milky juice comes out which is at that moment applied at the affected portion and is cured within 2-3 days. | | |
| 45. | Skin disease | | Luto dabai (?) | Paste of leaves, applied in that affected portion 2-3 times for at least 3-4 days. | | |
| 46. | Scabies, Itches | Itching, scabs and or bubble on the skin. | Patash (?) or Bara Kasai (?) | The bark is burnt and the ash is collected. The ash is smeared on the affected portion. | | |
| 47. | Bata (a kind of old sore). It is also called as Toto sore. | It is found on feet and this infection occurs during winter. Irritation, Itching and burning sensation. | Goat's wool. | The wool is burnt and the ash is applied on the affected area for 2-3 days. | | |

| *Sl. No.* | *Name of the disease* | *Symptom* | *Plants with scientific name or any other item used* | *Method of preparation and application* | *Deity/ spirit respon-sible* | *Restriction if any* |
|---|---|---|---|---|---|---|
| 48. | Ghomra (Prickly Heat) | | Tamarind leaf (Tamarindus indica) | The leaves are boiled in water and with the water they take bath. Within 4-5 days it will vanish. | | |
| 49. | Dadra (Chicken Pox) | | Hill crab called as keya. It's colour is red. | It is killed and the juice is extracted. It is taken by the patient. All the germs come out. | | Has to take protection from cold and wind. In food-minimum salt, ghee allowed, chilli is restricted, non-veg items are avoided. The patient is covered with cloth. Incense burning essential. |
| 50. | Tipuing wa Maka (Small Pox) | | a. Bahera seeds and roots (Terminalia belerica)<br>b. Kurthi pulses<br>c. Harsoo (Pothos scandens) | a. Behera seeds and roots are ground together and taken with water once for 3 days. All the germs will come out.<br>b. Boiled kurthi is taken for less itching. | | -do- |
| 51. | High Blood pressure | Headache, dizzy or giddy feeling, tired feeling and restless-ness. | a. curry leaves (Murraya koenigl)<br>b. Sajne (drumstick) leaves<br>c. Myacho/ Mhyecho (?)<br>d. Pagra (Laportea erenulata) | a. Taken as sabjji or the leaves are boiled and taken with that water 2 times daily.<br>b. Boiled and taken with that water. Within 2 days the patient will feel comfortable.<br>c. Leaves are boiled, then salt, chilli, garlic, turmeric are added and taken.<br>d. Young leaves are fried with ghee and taken. Juice of roots is used for prolonged fever. Nos. b and c medicines, | | |

| *Sl.No.* | *Name of the disease* | *Symptom* | *Plants with scientific name or any other item used* | *Method of preparation and application* | *Deity/ spirit respon-sible* | *Restriction if any* |
|---|---|---|---|---|---|---|
| | | | | especially no. c reduces blood pressure very quickly. So no. c is taken once after 7 days. | | |
| 52. | Tumor | Swelling, pain or without pain | Lime + Lemon | After extraction of all the seeds some lemon are boiled with lime in a copper container in 5 litre of water. When it becomes 1 litre, it is kept for cooling. After it gets cool, it is kept in a glass container. Prior to application of the medicine, the place is first anointed by lime. Then they take a paper and anoint the paper with the medicine prepared. Then that paper is put on the affected place by touching the tumor. It is kept for 3 days. Then the dressing is repeated for 7 times. Prior to dressing they wash the place by clean cloth, soaked in hot water. Within 7th dressing the tumor is ruptured. If not cured then they advise to go to hospital. | | |
| 53. | Gathia (Rheum-atism) | Pains in joints, knees. | The bulb of archid (Vendra Roxbur Ghil) | It is dried and ground with garlic. The paste is massaged on the affected area. | | Cold and sour food are avoided. |
| 54. | Tyara (Ring worm) | | -do- | Archid bulb is dried and pasted with garlic. The anal – portion is anointed with the paste. | | |

| Sl.No. | Name of the disease | Symptom | Plants with scientific name or any other item used | Method of preparation and application | Deity/ spirit respon-sible | Restriction if any |
|---|---|---|---|---|---|---|
| 55. | Tonsil | Throat sore, difficult in swallowing, bad breath, coughing. | Sahara herb ( ? ). Chinijhar (?) | Ground together and the juice is extracted. The juice is taken 1-2 times for relieves of throat pain, sore, breathing problem, Pneumonia and bad breath | | |
| 56. | Dama (Asthama) | Breathing trouble | Chiprai (?) | Flower of the plant is taken with water. | | |
| 57. | Pneumonia | Fever, cold and cough, breathing problem, voice chocked, speedy heart beat, and put-up belly. | a. Gising (Callicarpa arborea roxb) b. Chinijhar( ? ) c. New betel nut tree or sapling | a. Juice of the bark is extracted and taken 3 times for 3 days. b. Chinijhar flower and leaves are ground and taken with water for 3 times and 3 days. c. Root of the sapling is ground and taken with water. | | |
| 58. | Chhati Darad (Acute chest pain) | | Silaji (It is the sedimentation on rock due to weathering. | It is ground, mixed with honey and taken 3 times daily and relief comes within 2 days. | | |
| 59. | Dog bite (chances of hydro phobia) | | The dog is first identified, Tender Datura (Datura Stra monium) seeds are collected. | The dog is first identified. Tender Datura seeds are taken. 2-3 seeds are then mixed with rice and offered to the dog to eat. If the dog eats the rice with Datura and gets mad, then there will be no chance of hydro phobia for the person. | | |
| 60. | a. Pneum-onia b. Throat pain c. Tongue sore d. Cough | Fever, cold and cough, pain, uneasy felling, burning sensation, irritation, severe coughing | Chinijhar ( ? ) | It's fruits, seeds and tender leaves are ground, mixed with honey and taken 2 times daily for 3 days. | | |

| Sl.No. | Name of the disease | Symptom | Plants with scientific name or any other item used | Method of preparation and application | Deity/ spirit respon-sible | Restriction if any |
|---|---|---|---|---|---|---|
| 61. | For breast milk | No milk or insufficient milk to feed a new bom / lactating child | Myrunsha or Mathari sak.** (Deeringia amaranthoides) (Lam.) | The leaves are boiled. The boiled sag (leafy vegetables) are taken with the water in which it is boiled. It is taken 2-3 times daily. | | |
| 62. | Saimowa (cough and cold) | | Pipul / Piplee (Piper mullesna) | They take a piece of bark whenever they feel irritation in throat. Cured within 2-3 days. Immature fruits and roots are taken in cough and cold. | | |
| 63. | -do- | | Juing or Joy sing. | Flower and juice of fresh bark is extracted and mixed with honey and taken at least for 3 days. | | |
| 64. | -do- | | Hill crabs called as Keya | It is burnt and then taken. | | |
| 65. | -do- | | Kamui / Ka myul (?) | Juice of the leaf is extracted and taken with hot water 2-3 times daily for 3 days. | | |
| 66. | Bleeding due to cut. | | Lime | Applied on the cut and a finger is kept on the lime (Put on the cut) pressing the lime for a few seconds, immediatedly bleeding will stop. | | |
| 67. | Any type of cut / pricked by thorn / any type of pain (26 types of pain (26 types of disease they believe are cured) | | Onh Kako Keya (It is oil extracted from scorpion) | Oil is extracted after killing the scorpion and then boiled in water. Apply the oil in affected area and immediately get relief and the thorn will come out.. | | |

**With the help of Dr Tapas K Paul of Botanical Survey of India. this plant was identified.

| Sl.No. | Name of the disease | Symptom | Plants with scientific name or any other item used | Method of preparation and application | Deity/ spirit respon-sible | Restriction if any |
|---|---|---|---|---|---|---|
| 68. | Bone fracture | Swelling and acute pain in that portion | Root of harjur tree (Cissus quandrangularis) + Lashing debe (Simul root) (?), Naya paraibo(?) grown on betel nut tree looks like fish+Lampa (Duba grass)+ Silaji/ Siraji. | All these except Silaji are ground. The bone is set perfectly. They are very much expert. They can understand which portion of bone is broken by touching the place. After setting the bone the mixture is applied to the injured place and it is tied tightly by a piece of cloth and kept for three days. On the fourth day the bandage is changed and new bandage is done with some mixture. It is repeated for seven times. Silaji is ground and taken with water for pain relief. | | Sour food is not allowed. |
| 69. | Pain due to bone fracture | -do- | Silaji / Siraji. It is sedimentation on rocks. The sedimentation is of dust, soil, water which becomes hard. It is of yellow or black or white in colour. | It is mixed with water. It is dissolved within 5 minutes then taken twice a week. It quickly relieves the pain. | | Do |
| 70. | Bone fracture. | -do- | Simric. It looks like stone. | It is ground, mixed with honey and egg. The mixture is taken 2 times day for atleast 7 days. | | -do- |
| 71. | Markapana (sprain) | -do- | The roots / tubers of Bhui Chapa (?) | It is dried and powdered, then applied at the affected portion. Then covered with plantain leaf and bandaged with cloth. It is repeated for 2-3 days and cured. | | -do- |

| *Sl.No.* | *Name of the disease* | *Symptom* | *Plants with scientific name or any other item used* | *Method of preparation and application* | *Deity/ spirit respon-sible* | *Restriction if any* |
|---|---|---|---|---|---|---|
| 72. | Bone fracture | -do- | Harchur (?) leaves | The leaves are ground and mixed with hot water and kept in bottle after it gets cool. Taken atleast 3 times daily atleast for 7 days with hot water. | | -do- |
| 73. | Bone facture | -do- | Podam Chal (?) | The root is ground, mixed with hot water. After it gets cool, kept in a bottle. It is taken 3 times daily for 7-10 days with hot water. | | |
| 74. | -do- | -do- | Harjora (?.) + Munipatta (?) + Sona patta (?) + Bark of Madar tree | These are ground together till these become a sticky substance which is applied on the area. Then a leaf is kept over it and plastered with a cloth. Prior to that the portion is set accurately. If not set, then again they try to set it acureately (which they feel through their naked hand). After accurate setting the plaster is done. Then the Harchur and Sing rep fruits are ground finely and taken with water, preferably with milk and taken for 2 weeks. After 15 days they untie the plaster and massage with hot mustard oil with garlic. | | |
| 75. | Bleeding due to cut. | | Matka plant / Assam jhar( ? ) | Leaves are ground and juice is extracted and applied on the wound. Immediately beleeding is stopped. | | |

| *Sl.No.* | *Name of the disease* | *Symptom* | *Plants with scientific name or any other item used* | *Method of preparation and application* | *Deity/ spirit respon-sible* | *Restriction if any* |
|---|---|---|---|---|---|---|
| 76. | Bone fracture | Swelling, pain. | Harjor (Vitis quadrangularis) root + Leaves of Munipatta (?) + roots of sajne tree (drumstick) + roots of Simul / Simbuli (Vitex negundo, Verbana ceae), It looks like potato + bark of Totela tree (?) + Ginger + black piper 3-4 globules + leaves of Gurjal creeper (?) + Ashur (?) leaves are dried. | All these are mixed together. An egg is mixed with that. This mixture is applied on the affected portion, after setting the bone. Two bamboo strips are taken and kept on two sides of the broken bone as a support so that the bone can not move. Then the medicine is applied. A leaf is kept on it and it is tightly bandaged by cloth daily for 21 days at same tiem. The Simbuli and Ashur leaves which are ground, from next day is taken. After 10/15 minutes sugar mixed with honey is stirred. It becomes hot when it is cold then taken by the patient. After 21 days massage starts. Oil massage (Mustard oil + onion + garlic are boiled together in 5 lit. oil till it is 1 lit) is done. Sometimes ghee is added during massage. But ghee is not used regularly as in it muscles will get soft. | | Green vegetables, pulses except mung dal. Fish, meat, egg are not to be taken. |

## Discussion

The empirical data suggests that young generation of Toto are literate but understand the value of education. They are chiefly terrace cultivators. They cultivate cash crop like Ginger, Arecanut and turmeric and recently some among them have started pineapple cultivation as cash crop. As per Primary Health Centre report they mainly suffer from malaria (Plasmodium vibex), acute respiratory tract infection, cold and cough, fungal infection and T. B. There are five individuals who suffer from cleft plate but now operation has been done. Recently delivery patients are coming at PHC. But before coming to PHC they (Toto) used to practice initial medical attention through their traditional healer in which they have a strong faith.

From the aforesaid discussion on empirical findings it can also be said that biological explanation of a disease among this tribal population, who are secluded, live in hilly-forest terrain, light of literacy is poor and burden with beliefs in celestial world, cannot delineate all about illness. There are several causes of illness as per their emic view where sprit, psychology as well as their cultural value systems are responsible which in turn affect body and mind of the people; and to overcome all these they chiefly depend on their immediate natural resources, i.e. application of various herbs, tubers, roots, leaves, fruits and flower of their vicinity. The application of various local herbs for ailment clearly suggests their great heritage of possession of traditional knowledge bank which are becoming eroded in the light of modernity.

.

### References

Bhattacharya, R. K. and B. N. Sarkar, 1995, "The Totos in Present Perspective". in *Sociology in theRubric of Social Science*, ed. R. K. Bhattacharya and Asok K. Ghosh, Calcutta, Anthropological Survey of India.

Bhowmick P. K., 1994, *Primitive Tribal Groups in Eastern India: Welfare and Evaluation*. New Delhi: Gyan Publishing House.

Chakraborty P. and K. Chattopadhyay, 1964, "Some Aspects of Toto Ethnography". *Bulletin of Cultural Research Institute.* Vol. III. No. 2.

Cultural Research Institute,1980, Underdeveloped Tribes: Project Report on the Totos of Jalpaiguri, West Bengal, SC and ST Welfare Department, West Bengal.

Das, Amal Kumar 1969, The Totos, Calcutta, SC and Tribes Welfare Dept, Govt. of West Bengal.

Dhali, Debendranath 1987, Toto (in Bengali), Calcutta: Cultural Research Institute, Govt. of W. B. (Sp. Issue No: 31) Ganashakti (Newspaper in Bengali Dated 02.11.2002).

Lowie, R. H., 1929, "Relationship Terms", in the Encyclopaedia Britanica, 14th edition. 19. London, pp. 84-89.

Lowie, R. H., 1950, Social Organisation. London. Routledge and Kegan Paul.

Majumdar Bimalendu, 1997, "Toto Janojatir Gram Sangathan O Samajik Niyantran bidhir Rupantar". *Lokoshruti,* No. 13 (in Bengali).

Milligan, J. 1919, Final Report on Survey Settlement Operation in Jalpaiguri District.

Misra, Baidyanath, 2002, "Hazards of a Billion Plus Population", in *Population Stabilisation and Development,* editor in chief, Baidyanath Misra, Cuttack, Council of Cultural Growth and Cultural Relations, The Universe.

Murdock, G. P., 1949, Social Structure, New York: Collier Macmillan.

Rao, Sudhakar Rao 2007, "Study of Tribal or Rural Health in the Context of Globalisation-An anthropological framework",in Anthropology, New Global Order and Other Essays, ed. By Kamal K Misra, New Delhi: Concept Publishing Company

Roy Burman, B. K., 1966, "Structure of Bridge and Buffer Communities in the Border Areas" *Man in India,* Vol. 46, No. 2.

Sanyal, Charu Chandra, 1973, The Meches and the Totos of North Bengal, Darjeeling, The University of North Bengal.

Sarkar, Amitabha, 1993, *Toto Society and Change: A Sub-Himalayan Tribe of West Bengal.* Calcutta: Firma KLM Pvt. Ltd.

Sarkar, Amitabha, A.V. Arakeri, Suresh Patil, 2012. *Traditional Knowledge in Indian Society,* Kolkata : Anthropological Survey of India.

Sinha, Debasish and Bikash Chandra Pal, 1984, "A Study of Eco-Sociological Changes among an underdeveloped Tribe: The Totos of North Bengal". *Bulletin of the Cultural Research Institute,* Vol. XVI. No. 1-4.

Sunder, D., 1895, Survey and Settlement of Western Duars, The Times of India (Kolkata edition, Dated 10.9.04, p. 12).

# 12

# Anthropology of Signals, Signs and Symbols in Indian Context— A Study on Culture and Communication

## Prologue

"The main aim and objective of Socio-cultural anthropologist is the analysis and interpretation of ethnographic fact, and of customary behaviour as directly observed. The most fundamental way in which the procedures of modern anthropologists differ from those of their predecessors a hundred years ago is that the modern treatment of ethnographic evidence is always functionalist. To-day, every detail of custom is seen as part of a .complex; it is recognised that details, considered in isolation, are as meaningless as isolated letters of the alphabet. So ethnography has ceased to be an inventory of custom, it has become the art of vivid description; the intricate interweaving of plot and counterplot as in the work of a major novelist (Geeretz,1973)".

"All social anthropologists take as their subject matter the variety of human culture and society, and they all assume that their task is not only to describe what the varieties are but to explain why they exist (Leach, 1976)".

The modes and channels through which we communicate with one another are not only diverse but complex. Human communication is achieved by means of expressive actions like *signals, signs* and *symbols*. These three terms are closely linked with one another. Culture is learned and acquired behaviour which is transmitted through generations. During the process of enculturation the various *signs, symbols* and *signals* of a particular culture is also transmitted for posterity and value gets attached with the particular *signs, symbols and signals*etc. are only understood by the particular cultural group. These are a kind of cultural communication before its ethnic group.

The modes and channels through which we communicate with one another are very diverse and complex ; human communication is achieved by means of signals, signs and symbols (Leach, 1976). In fact, these are some aspects of a culture which are normative in nature.

According to Leach (1976) human communication is achieved by means of expressive actions which operate as signals (which is mundane), signs (which is mundane as well as abstract), and symbols (which is totally abstract). These cultural traits of a community, that is, signals, signs, and symbols of a community which are significantly their own cultural ethos and are again intrinsic and value loaded cultural behaviours, considered as vehicle of communication which are transmitted over generation.

In the following lines we shall try to apply this theoretical concept among the Toto and the Mal Paharia social-system.

### A. Role of Bakung–the auspicious Drums and Social Division Among the Toto

Culture is learned and acquired behaviour which is transmitted through generation. During the process of enculturation the various *signs, symbols and signals* of a particular culture is also transmitted for posterity and value attached with the particular *signs, symbols and signals* etc. are only understand by the particular cultural group. These are a kind of cultural communication before its ethnic group.

According to Geertz (1973), "the modern treatment of ethnographic evidence is always functionalist. Every detail of custom is seen as part of a complex".

The modes and channels through which we communicate with the another are very diverse and complex; human communication is achieved by means of signals, signs and symbols (Leach, 1976). In fact, these are some aspects of a culture which are normative in nature. The present paper highlights the Toto–a small secluded vulnerable tribal group living in only one village–Toto para–their auspicious musical drum, *bakung*, one of which represent as male and other is female, centering it their all religious activities are not only performed but there exists a complex network of clan wise social division which was based on their nature of traditionally assigned work with Bhutan and Coochbehar from early days and often known as bridging one community with another (Roy Burman, 1966).

## II

The Totos are a little known particularly vulnerable tribe, numerically small and a mongoloid tribal group of Jalpaiguri district of West Bengal. Their life and culture are nourished in Sub-Himalayan Doars area of W. B. in only one village of the country. They are a primitive tribe living in Totopaṛa--a small village (J. L. No. 33/Old No. 13) situated in 89° 20´ latitude and 26°50´ longitude of the Madarihat police station of Alipurduar Sub-division of Jalpaiguri District. At present they have extended the boundary of their locale and the Puoar gaon is included in Toto Para. They have also purchased some cultivable land in Halla Para and Lanka Para of Ballalguri village, which is very close to their village. They, besides their permanent settlement in Totopara, have established their temporary huts and *nion kosha* to guard their harvest from destruction. (It is told that there are elephants in the jungle that come out to eat the cultivated products. To protect them they stay in the temporary huts especially when the crop starts ripening). In Aryampa hamlet of the village near Howri river, there are some Toto houses. According to Sanyal (1973), Totos live on a cluster of three small hillocks (750´ to 1250´ above sea level) at the foothill of the Himalayas to south of the border between Bhutan and West Bengal. The height of the village varies from 750 to 1500 feet. The hilly range, looking just like a wall, binds the northwestern side of the village. On the east of the village river Torsa is flowing with a tremendous current and river Haori is flowing on its southwest. On the western side of river Haori–there is everlasting bed of greenery, known as Titi forest–the tropical rain forest, popularly known as Dooars.

It is told that the Totos live in this village for at least seven generations (Dhali, 1987, Das, 1969, Roy Burman, Unpublished report), but earlier they were not confined in Totopara but there are evidences of their habitations in other neighbouring places in the Dooars region. Sanyal (1973) referred Sunder to a *taluk* named Totgaon in Chengmari *pargana* within the *tahsil* Maynaguri at present. It is situated on the eastern bank of the river Teesta, near the confluence with a tributary, the river Leesh, just opposite to Champasuri Teesta ferry. Sundar believes that the *taluk* was named after the name of Toto who once used to reside there. It is told that once there was a devastating flood of Teesta. Due to this natural calamity three fourth portion of Totgaon was washed away. Then, it is believed that a group of Toto had migrated to Nepal (Dhali, 1987). Sanyal (1973) mentioned that during his field work, he met a person named Hastonarayan Pradhan. He came from Nepal and settled at Totgaon. When Sanyal met him he was very old and Sanyal met him at Ellen berry Tea Estate. Hastonarayan Prasad informed that after the flood, one batch of Toto migrated to Nepal and the other people went to Cooch Bihar. Two persons were found there who were absorbed in Mech tribal community but used to claim themselves as Toto. The rest of the portion of Totgaon is presently renamed as Sundari Basti. Nepali, Oraon and Mech people live there.

Interestingly, it is told by them that at the time of migration, those persons had taken two big percussion musical instruments–*bakung* with them (one is male drum small in size and locally known as *chighaimu* or *Saiyenja* while the other drum–a little bigger in size is considered as female and known as *mogaimu* or *Sainjani*, she stays at the right side of her husband Saiyenja and both are considered as pious to Toto and are kept in *demsha* (sacred place) at Puja gaon of the village), which are still there in their village of present habitat at Totopara. They play the drums during their rituals and festivals and are kept in their sacred place of worship at Puja gaon.

The chief deity among the Toto is Ispha. To outsider it is known as *Mahakal–Mahakali. Ishpha* is the deity in whom both male and female deities jointly exist. Separately they are called as *Saiyenja* and *Sainjani. Sainjani* is the female expression, thought to be present inside *Saiyenja. Saiyenja* is the joint expression of *Mahakal* and *Mahakali*. According to Mahanirvan Tantra (Saptahik Bartaman, 6th Nov. 2010), the deity who swallows all the living creatures of universe is called *Mahakal.* In fact Lord Siva of great tradition is known as *Mahakal* at Toto Para. On the day of Sivaratri Toto appeases *Mahakal* with pomp and éclat. The puja is performed with rice, meat, and eu, once in a year at the last week of *Bhadra* (Aug.-Sept), officiated by *kaiji*–thechief priest assisted by some others known as *pau. Mahakal* is the most powerful deity among the Toto.

Apart from the worship of *Ispha* they also observe two important rituals communally. One of those is *ongchu*–on the 14th day of the darker half of the month Sraban (July–Aug). This is also the worship of *Kaleshwar/Ishpa* on different occasions. It is performed for three days in the month of *Sraban* (July-Aug. ) after they harvest *kaon* (a kind of millet) in their field. The *eu* (home brew liquor) is prepared from *kaon* and is offered to the deity in *ongchu* where they also sacrifice chicken. They appease the deity to get bumper crop, proper rain and to protect the village from evil eye. Twenty-two days after the performance of *ongchu* ritual the other ritual named as *mayu* is held in the month of *Bhadra* (Aug-Sept) or *asomase* (Sept-Oct) where they worship *Kaleshwar/ Ishpa*. It is also known as worship of orange. It continues for five days instead of nine days as they used to perform earlier and each day they sacrifice a cow to appease the deity. In all the rituals and worship there is no an anthropomorphic image or idol. During this ritual, contributions are collected from each and every household. Traditionally each family compulsorily had to contribute 15 kg. of rice of maize and eleven cock. In the past, the Toto, irrespective of male, female, old and children used to assemble in their temple called *demsha* and stay there during the occasion. They used to take their food and sleep, dance, sing, and enjoy throughout the festival. At present, they form a *puja* committee, which is responsible to take all the responsibilities to arrange a *puja*. In that committee total 22 representatives (one or two members from each clan) are there as executive members. They are given the charge to collect contribution from the members of their own clan. Now-a-days, compulsorily they do not stay there throughout the festival but they generally do so during evening when there is incense burning and the *pau* sings and dances with the rhythm of the *bakung* to appease *Mahakal* and *Mahakali* or *Kaleshwar/Ishpa*. It is told that "The puja of *Mahakali* among the Toto seems to be derived from the Tibetan Ponist Tantric worship. " (Das 1969). In this way, they celebrate the festival. In all the rituals, they make offerings to the deity facing north towards Badu hills.

The Toto of Totopara is a model of bridge community (Roy Burman, 1966). In 1868 Totopara came under the British, prior to that several times it changed hands between Bhutan and the Cooch kingdom under the Bhutia rule, the Toto were engaged in carrying rice, salt from the market of the plains to Bhutan (?), during their return journey they used to bring orange and various jungle products from Bhutan which they used to sell to the people of the plains. Thus, they performed a very important role in maintaining the trade line in the area.

For this purpose they were divided into two groups–one group used to go to the south for carrying the commodities from Cooch market to Totopara and another group to carry the commodities form Totopara to places inside Bhutan. On return they used to bring orange from Bhutan to Totopara and from Totopara the other group which used to collect rice, salt, oil etc. from Cooch markets (of Coochbehar), would take oranges brought from Bhutan by the other group and sell in the Cooch markets. These two groups were formed sharply on the basis of clan division and by this device of segmental identification; it was possible for each section to establish rapport with the dominant political community, with which it was in contact, without separate identity. The Toto engaged in transportation of goods from one place to another was known as *huiwa* or *corvee* service.

Wareng bei were responsible for linking as well as exchange of goods with Bhutan with mainland and it was managed by *gappu karangpui (organiser)*. While, Waiyingting bei were responsible for linking Coochbehar through exchange of goods from Bhutan through Totopara and it was managed by *kaiji karangpui.*

**Whole Toto Community is territorially divided into two halves**

| **Wareng bei** (*Kaiji/Deishi* group) | **Waiying ting bei** (*Gappu/Mondal* group) |
|---|---|
| Clan groups like | Clan groups like |
| (Dantrobei, | (Dankobei |
| Bongobei, | Nurunchangobei, |
| Baudhbei, | Mankobei |
| Badubei, | Renkajibei/Linkajibei, |
| Dhirenchangobei (Kaiji) | Mantrobei |
| Manchingbei | Pisenchangobei |
| | Nubebei |

III

## Social Organisation

The Toto are an endogamous group with thirteen exogamous clans (*sarkhae*). It is also reported that in early days only 13 families migrated and settled here and in course of time the increasing members of the said families were divided into 13 separate exogamous *sarkhae.* These 13 clan members (with sub-clan) are settled in six hamlets of Totopara and these are as follows–*Baudhdei, Badubei, Linkajibei, Nurunchangobei, Dhirenchangobei, Nubebei, Bangobei, Dantrobei, Mantrobei, Dankobei, Mankobei, Manchingbei* and *Pisenchangobei*. According to Das (1969), those different clans have different ancestral deities (*cheising*). They are propitiated in different forms. The members of *Budubei, Baudhbei, Linkajibei, Nurunchangobei, Dhuirenchangobei, Nubebei,* clans cannot touch monkey and squirrel and cannot eat food cooked by women of any community except the women of Bhutan. Bangobei, *Dantrobei, Pisochangobei,* clan members cannot touch monkey and squirrel but are not to observe any restriction in taking food cooked by any community. It is also reported that each clan has a separate demarcated area for cultivation in the village and these areas have separate identity like *arum-pha, amring, eia, tamding, chanduba, gaitring* etc. Market economy has already appeared there with all its tenets, the rigidity of clan oriented cultivable land identity among them has also lost its importance. Chakraborty and Chattopadhyay (1964) observed one more clan namely, *Dikbei* or *Digbei*. During the intensive fieldwork it is found that *Baudhube* has two sub-clans named as *Badampa* and *Digbei* or *Dikbei*. They have separate *cheising* or kul deity. The name of the *kul* deity of *Digbei* is *Turu* and of *Badampa* is *Babu.* Again, *Digbei* means land in high slopes where porcupine was available. The

*Baudhbei* clan members, who occupy the area in the high slopes, due to their settlement position, often identify themselves as *Digbei*. The other group who live in comparatively low altitude are called as *Badampa*. Though both *Badampa* and *Digbei* have originated from the same clan; that is; *Baudhbei* even then they are allowed to marry with each other with the approval of *lachi-janguwa*. As areas on for such division they argued that the settlement pattern is responsible for that. Traditionally the total Toto habitation was divided according to the clans mentioned later. Dhumschi gaon was the place meant for the *Baudhbei* group of people where a portion of them lives. The other portion lives in lower altitude of the same. They hardly used to have interaction with each other. They used to perform separately the rituals including the worship of *cheising* or *kul* deity. In this way gradually they became two separate groups having two separate *kul* deities which ultimately allowed them to marry each other. Again, another clan *Dantrobei* takes the above mentioned sub-clans; that is; *Digbei* and *Badampa* separately. Dantrobei are allowed to marry from the subclan *Digbei* but they establish *sanga bhai* relation with *Badampa*. As Badampa is regarded as their cousins–descending from mother's sister, they are tabooed to have any marital alliance with them. It is observed that intra-clan marriage is noticed in *Dankobei* clan which has got two exogamous territorial divisions namely, *Deyeche* (in the west) and *Nayeche* (in the east) though their *kuldev* or *cheising* or ancestral deity is same, that is, *derlasche mechenda*.

Interestingly, it is found during the present fieldwork that there are some clans clubbed together into two to three groups among whom marital alliance is prohibited now-a-days as they are regarded as consanguinal kins. As for example, *Dhirenchangobei* and *Nurinchangobei* were two different clans. Marital alliance was permissible among them. Another example is *Dantrobei* and *Mantrobei* were two different clans, among whom also marriage was not prohibited earlier. Now the situation is different. Now *Dhirenchangobei* and *Nurinchangobei* are clubbed together and are regarded as consanguinal kins, Similarly, *Dantrobei* and *Mantrobei* also became consanguinal kins. Among whom marriage is not allowed as it was done earlier. The reason for this type of clubbing together to form a *sange bhai* or consanguinal relation is not clear. However, after several discussions, it is concluded that once the number of persons of these clans were very less. To increase the number of persons and to strengthen the close knit kinship bondage of consanguinity, *Dhirenchangobei* and *Nurinchangobei* are clubbed together as were *Dantrobei* and *Mantrobei*.

## Name of the Clan and their deity with their House Facing towards

| *Sl. No.* | *Name of the clan (Kul/Serka)* | *Sub clan if any* | *Clan deity (Cheising)* | *Hamlet of people under a cheising* | *Facing of the house* |
|---|---|---|---|---|---|
| 1. | Budhubei | -- | Nidupa/Nirupa/ laze | Puja gaon | South |
| 2. | Baudhbei | 2 Sub-clans :<br>a. Badampa b. Digbei | a. Babu, b. Turu/ Gepdoji/Gepchi/Gema | Dhumschigaon<br>a. Lower<br>b. upper<br>chunder | East |
| 3. | Bangobei/Bangope | -- | Goja-go-Ampa/Lame | Mitranggaon | East |
| 4. | Dantrobei | -- | Basrang-kola/ Duba/ Purushi | Panchayatgaon Subbagaon Mondalgaon | East |
| 5. | Damkobei | 6 Sub-clans<br>a. Japa, b. Myapa<br>c.Yapa, d. syapa<br>e. Tyapa, f. Nipa | a. Gapu-gardoi/ Gupu-sitai/Gepchen<br>b. Dora, c. Karchan<br>d. Gushru, e. Gadau<br>f. Tamsepura | Mondalgaon<br>Panchayatgaon | East |
| 6. | Dhiring – Chang-kobei | -- | Nabyang-pa/ Lyabang-pa | Subbagaon | East |
| 7. | Machingbei | -- | Labam-pa/Nabam-pa/ Gepcheng | Subbagaon Mondalgaon | East |
| 8. | Mangobei/ Monkobei | -- | Aji-kola/ Aji-Ko-la/ Putinji | Subbagaon | East |
| 9. | Manrobei | -- | Dharang-kola | Subbagaon | East |
| 10. | Nube-bei/ Nubhi-bei | -- | Peisi-tya-ku-ya/ peisi-thiouo/gudru | Subbagaon Mondalgaon Panchayat para | South |
| 11. | Nuri-chang-ko-bei | -- | Keyeinpu/ Du-shanti | Subbagaon | East |
| 12. | Pischi-chango-ko-bei | -- | Yeje-ko-la/ yeje-go-la / yejela | Maidalgaon Subbagaon | East |
| 13. | Renka-ji-bei/ Lenka-ji-bei | -- | Oda | Subbagaon | East |

**Population Distribution of Toto Clan (hamlet-wise) (till 20. 12. 2010)**
**Village: Totopara**

| *Name of the para/hamlet* | *Family* | *Male* | *Female* | *Total* | |
|---|---|---|---|---|---|
| a. Dhumschi gaon | 32 | 73 | 67 | 140 | Budhubei :<br>a. Dikbei, (b) Badampa |
| b. Puja gaon | 23 | 69 | 58 | 127 | Badubei/Baudhubei |
| c. Mitrang gaon | 34 | 77 | 72 | 149 | Bongobei |
| d. subba gaon (almost middle of the village, market place) | 66 | 172 | 137 | 309 | Dhirunchangobei, Nubebei, Nurunchangobei, Mantrobei and Manchingbei |
| e. Mondal gaon | 28 | 58 | 57 | 115 | Dantrobei :<br>1. Tapa, 2. Mapa : Nubebei, Pisenchongobei |
| f. Panchyat gaon (Middle of village with market place, and hospital. | 114 | 277 | 256 | 533 | Dankobei, Nubebei, Dantrobei (Majority) |
| | **297** | **726** | **647** | **1373** | |

*1. Traditionally the hamlets were demarcated according to the Cheising's mythical place of abode. In one hamlet more than one Cheising used to stay and following them the members of the Cheising used to live. Now this practice is relaxed (which is shown in the table).

*2. Facing of house indicates the Cheising's favourable path of roaming. When it is from east then it is told that the Cheising has originated from sun or river Torsa or hill and when the hut is south facing, it is thought that the Cheising has connection with Hauri river.

The data are collected from Budhbare Toto (69 years, of Digbei clan, lives in the Dhumchigaon and also has land in Puar gaon. . He is the Pau (religious head) of the Toto community of Totopara.

Again, the Toto customarily practise clan exogamy. Most of the families are monogamous in nature. Empirical data reveals that two families have adopted sons (adoption is practiced through a ritual–*puiayawaha* during the day of communal worship of **Ispha** or **Mahakal** and Ongchu) due to absence of any issue. It is observed that Ekle Toto of *Budhbei* clan of Puja Gaon had two wives who were cousin sisters and living together. It is also reported during investigation that marriage within same clan is strictly forbidden; they practice cross-cousin-marriages–55 marriages were reported as MBD while 52 marriages were reported as FSZ, apart from these there were 19 such marriages reported which were also cross cousin but in distant relation. It is also observed that when a person is polygynous, that is, has two or more wives at a time and if the person dies then his young widow usually deserts her husband's house. She is allowed to marry a Toto again. Three families are polygynous and two families practice sororrate.

Though they practise clan exogamy, the marital alliance between *Nubebei* and *Dantrobei* is not usually allowed as they have legendic relation as cousin brother (mother's sister son). But if it happens they have to arrange for a community feast (*sangailama*) as punishment where 6 pitchers of *-eu* is served with beef.

## IV

Interestingly, it is told by them that at the time of migration, those persons had taken two big percussion musical instruments-*bakung* with them (one is male drum small in size and locally known as *chighaimu* or **Saiyenja** while the other drum–a little bigger in size is considered as female and known as *mogaimu* or **Sainjani**, she stays at the right side of her husband **Saiyenja** and both are considered as

**Marital Alliance among various clan groups of Toto at Totopara**

| emaN naC | apaJ | apa M | apA | iebhduaB | iebudaB | iebjiakni L | gnahcnu uN i ebo | gnhene hD i ebo | iebebuN | iebognoB | iebot naD | iebot na M | iebokna D | iebokno M | g- ainxna M i eb | nahcnes P i ebog | ebg D i ebK D | ap nadaB |
|---|---|---|---|---|---|---|---|---|---|---|---|---|---|---|---|---|---|---|
| Japa | × | √ | √ | √ | √ | [illegible] | √ | √ | √ | [illegible] | [illegible] | × | [illegible] | √ | - | - | √ | √ |
| Mapa | √ | × | √ | √ | √ | √ | √ | √ | √ | × | √ | × | √ | ? | x | √ | √ | √ |
| Apa | √ | √ | × | √ | √ | √ | √ | √ | √ | × | √ | √ | √ | √ | √ | √ | √ | √ |
| Baudhbei | √ | √ | √ | × | √ | √ | √ | √ | × | √ | √ | √ | √ | ? | x | √ | √ | √ |
| Badubei | √ | √ | √ | √ | × | √ | √ | √ | √ | √ | √ | √ | √ | √ | √ | √ | √ | √ |
| Linkajibei | x | x | x | √ | √ | × | √ | √ | √ | × (avoided) | × | √ | √ | × | x | √ | √ | × |
| Nuruncha gobei | √ | √ | √ | √ | √ | √ | × | × | √ | √ | √ | √ | √ | √ | √ | √ | √ | √ |
| Dhirunchang obei | × | × | × | √ | × | √ | × | × | √ | √ | √ | × | × | √ | √ | √ | √ | √ |
| Nubebei | √ | √ | √ | × | × *1 | √ | √ | √ | × | √ | × | √ | √ | √ | √ | √ | × | × |
| Bongobei | × | × | × | √ | √ | × | × | √ | √ | × | √ | √ | × | × | x | √ | √ | √ |
| Dantrobei | √ | √ | √ | √ | × | √ | √ | √ | × | √ | √ | √ | √ | ? | x | √ | √ | √ |

| Clan Name | Japa | Mapa | Apa | Baudhbei | Badubei | Likarbei | Nunchangbei | Dhunchangbei | Nubebei | Bongobei | Dantobei | Mantobei | Dankobei | Monkobei | Manchingbei | Pisenchangobei | Digbei | Badampa |
|---|---|---|---|---|---|---|---|---|---|---|---|---|---|---|---|---|---|---|
| Mantrobei | √ | √ | √ | [illegible] | √ | [illegible] | [illegible] | [illegible] | √ | × | [illegible] | × | × | × | [illegible] | [illegible] | √ | √ |
| Dankobei | √ | √ | √ | √ | √ | √ | √ | √ | √ | × | √ | × | × | × | √ | √ *1 | √ | √ |
| Mankobei | × | × | × | √ | √ | × | √ | √ | × | √ | √ | √ | × | × | √ | √ | √ | √ |
| Manchimgbei | √ | √ | √ | √ | √ | × | √ | √ | √ | × | √ | × | √ | ? | × | √ | √ | √ |
| Pisenchango bei | √ | √ | √ | √ | √ | √ | × | √ | √ | √ | √ | √ | √ | √ | ? | × | √ | √ |
| Digbei | √ | √ | √ | √ | √ | √ | √ | √ | × | √ | √ | √ | √ | ? | × | √ | × | × |
| Badampa | √ | √ | √ | √ | √ | √ | √ | √ | × | √ | × | √ | √ | √ | √ | √ | × | × |

*1 = Earlier not allowed because they live in same gaon and consider them as Sange bhai but now it is allowed but not practiced.

Informant –1. *Kalicharan Toto, 43 yrs,* S/o Late Sadra Toto, Mitrang Gaon, Bongobei clan, having 3 acres of land, owner of 200 trees of oranges. He is also medicine Man among Toto. (Data Collected on 18th Nov, 2010).

2. *Lora Toto,*70 yrs, Panchayat Gaon, Nubebei clan, having 20 bighas of land at Hallapara, Average earning Rs 1 Lac per year by selling of areca nut.

3. *Budhbare Toto*, S/o Late, Chandia Toto, 69 yrs, Poar Gaon, Digbey clan, having 20 bighas of land; he is *pau* of the village.

INDEX

✓ = Allowed

× = Not allowed due to Sange bhai or mother's sister's clan.

pious to Toto and kept in *demsha* (sacred place) at Puja gaon of the village), which are still there in their village of present habitat at Totopara. They play the drums during their rituals and festivals and kept in their sacred place of worship at Puja gaon. During any rituals at *demsha* the active role are played by *Wareng bei* or Kaiji group (the present *kaiji* is Sachin Toto s/o Wangchun who was adopted son of Late Shirang Toto, clan–Dhirinchankobei; it is hereditary post; the present *kaiji* is employed in Gramin Bank); while active role in arrangement of feasts are done by *Waiyingting bei* or *gapu/mondal* group (the present *gapu* is Sugrib Toto, Dankobei, s/o late Dhanapati Toto, Bank employee ; it is also hereditary post).

The chief deity among the Toto is *Ispha*. To outsider it is known as *Mahakal–Mahakali. Ishpha* is the deity where both male and female deities jointly exist. Separately they are called as *Saiyenja* and *Sainjani*. *Sainjani* is the female expression, thought to be present inside *Saiyenja*. *Saiyenja* is the joint expression of *Mahakal* and *Mahakali*. According to Mahanirvan Tantra (Saptahik Bartaman, 6th Nov. 2010), the deity who swallows all the living creatures of universe is called as *Mahakal* in fact Lord Siva of great tradition is known as *Mahakal* at Toto Para. On the day of Sivaratri Toto appeases *Mahakal* with pomp and éclat. The puja is performed with rice, meat, and eu, once in a year at the last week of Bhadra (Aug.-Sept), officiated by *kaiji*–the chief priest assisted by some priests known as *pau*. *Mahakal* is the most powerful deity among the Toto.

Apart from the worship of Ispha they also observe two important rituals communally. One of those is *ongchu*–on the 14th day of the darker half of the month Sraban (July–Aug). This is also the worship of *Kaleshwar/Ishpa* in different occasions. It is performed for three days in the month of Sraban (July-Aug.) after they harvest *kaon* (a kind of millet) in their field. The *eu* (home brew liquor) is prepared from *kaon* and is offered to the deity in *ongchu* where they also sacrifice chicken. They appease the deity to get bumper crop, proper rain and to protect the village from evil eye. Twenty-two days after the performance of *ongchu* ritual the other ritual named as *mayu* is held in the month of Bhadra (Aug-Sept) or asomase (Sept-Oct) where they worship *Kaleshwar/ Ishpa*. It is also known as worship of orange. It is continued for five days instead of nine days as they used to perform earlier and each day they sacrifice a cow to appease the deity. In all the rituals and worship there is no anthropomorphic images or idol among them. During this ritual, contributions are collected from each and every household. Traditionally each family compulsorily had to contribute 15 kg. of rice of maize and eleven cock. In the past, the Toto, irrespective of male, female, old and children used to assemble in their temple called as *demsha* and stay there during the occasion. They used to take their food, sleep, dance, sing, and enjoy throughout the festival. At present, they form a *puja* committee, which is responsible to take all the responsibilities to arrange for a *puja*. In that committee total 22 members (one or two members from each clans) are there as executive member. They are given the charge to collect contribution from the members of their own clan. Now-a-days, compulsorily they do not stay there throughout the festival but they should compulsorily stay there during evening when there is incense burning and the *pau* sings and dances with the rhythm of the *bakung* to appease *Mahakal* and *Mahakali* or *Kaleshwar/Ishpa*. It is told that "The puja of *Mahakali* among the Toto seems to be derived from the Tibetan Ponist Tantric worship." (Das 1969). In this way, they celebrate the festival. In all the rituals, they offer the offerings to the deity facing north towards Badu hills.

V

## Conclusion

From the above discussion it is evident that the *bakung*–a religious metaphorical symbol among the Toto played a *centripetal force* of solidarity through which all the community members are tied and also maintain a boundary with others.

### References

Dhali, Debendranath, 1987, Toto (in Bengali), Calcutta: Cultural Research Institute, Govt. of W. B. (Sp. Issue No. 31)

Geertz, Clifford, 1973, "Thick Description: Toward an Interpretive Theory of Culture", in Clifford Geertz, The Interpretation of Cultures: Selected Essays by C. Geertz, pp. 3-30, New York: Basic books Inc.

Leach, Edmund, 1976, Culture and Communication: The logic by which Symbols are connected, Cambridge: Cambridge University Press.

Roy Burman, B. K., 1966, "Structure of Bridge and Buffer Communities in the Border Areas" *Man in India*, Vol. 46, No. 2.

Sanyal, Charu Chandra, 1973, The Meches and the Totos of North Bengal, Darjeeling, The University of North Bengal.

Sarkar, Amitabha, 1993, *Toto Society and Change: A Sub-Himalayan Tribe of West Bengal*. Calcutta: Firma KLM Pvt. Ltd.

Sarkar, Amitabha and Samira Dasgupta, 2012, "Toto Society and Culture with special emphasis on Ethno-medical Practices", in *Traditional Knowledge in Indian Society*, ed. Amitabha Sarkar, A.V. Arakeri, Suresh Patil, Kolkata: Anthropological Survey of India.

Sacred Drum of Toto at Puja Gaon, Totopara

### B. Ritual symbolism: Cultural ethos among the Malpaharia

According to the Anthropologist Clifford Geertz (1976), "symbolic world is used as a vehicle for our concepts; they represent how we conceive of our world. The conception of the symbol is its meaning".

All symbolic representation has it's genesis in the social, ideological, and political concepts which define our cultural, ideological, and political concepts as a whole and define our culture. Symbols do not always remain same, but can transform through the ages and through various process of cultural adaptation.

Another interpretive anthropologist, Victor Turner, believed that symbols are not just vehicles for meaning, but by their very use, create meaning, understanding the solidarity in relationships. This is why he saw ritualistic symbolism as harboring core symbols which carried extra weight. The symbols function not only to represent a value or belief, but their use also affects the individual more profoundly. (©2011 by Kristine Millar, " The Power of Cultural Symbolism", from internet).

In this light the authors tried to highlight the symbolic expression of Mal Paharia (particularly a vulnerable tribal group) culture with special reference to their religious life.

The Mal Paharia people are mainly concentrated in Dumka district and local administrators identify them as Paharia who are one of the partiulcularly vulnerable tribal groups (PVTG) of Jharkhand. Mal Paharia live in a geographically difficult area where they always have a feeling of insecurity and uncertainty or of less predictability. In fact Mal Paharia is a separate group of the tribe Paharia. Paharia is a blanket term for three separate tribes namely, Sauria Paharia, Kumbharbhag Paharia and Mal Paharia. All of the three are endogamous groups and are confined in their habitat in *Damin–i–koh* (a Persian word means skirt of the hills) area of erstwhile Santhal Pargana district, which is now divided into Dumka, Pakur, Deoghar, Sahebgunj, Godda, and Jamtara districts.

In the *Damin-i-koh* area all the three groups of Paharia are distributed in the Rajmahal hills, which cover the entire *Damin* area. It consists of the upland, undulating, long ridges and depressions along with some fertile lands, which is intensively cultivated. There are three lofty peaks among which Massanjore is situated in Dumka sub-division.

The present study is carried out among Mal Paharia of Madhuvan village of Gopikandar block of Dumka district. The village Madhuvan is a multi ethnic village, which is situated in the northern side of the block Gopikandar. The village is secluded on the hill slopes and in the midst of forest. This village is dominated by Santal (66 families), followed by Mal Paharia (55 families), Ghatwar (12 families) and Maria or Lohar (12 families).

Madhuvan is a village situated in the forest and again the Mal Paharia hamlets are situated in the denser portion of the forest at the higher altitude of the village. As they live in such a geographical atmosphere where they have an uncanny feeling of unseen spirits that is in an adverse situation, to get strength in mind, to combat with the mysterious events, they get hold of the supernatural power, which are solely responsible to shape their culture and give them protections from all evils. Hence, their life is very much oriented by the belief of supernatural power and propitiation of spirits holds an important position in their religious life which are sometimes symbolically expressed.

On the issue of symbols let us start with symbolic expression of their sacred places locally known as *Than*. They have several *Thans* in their village for different deities which are symbolically their seats/ abode and their rituals and festivals are performed there. Some of those are *Goriya Than, Sing Bahani Than, Jahar Than, Kali/Chordanu Than, Chitipila Than, Kumhar Deo Than,* and *Ormu Than* etc. Each of these *Thans* is signalled by a clean and open place with bigger and smaller trees, some of which are valuable. *Thans* are in general situated at a corner of the village. Each of the *Thans* has its own identifying symbol of the deity whose abode is that particular *Than*. Seeing which one can easily understand which *Than* it is and who is the deity of that particular *Than*. Generally a *Than* is a place where, they believe, a particular deity resides and the trees in it's surroundings are believed to be of the deity's own choice. Now the deities are symbolised by stones of different shapes, sizes and colours. etc. As for an example, in *Goriya Than, Pahar Thakur* is established. According to them he is Lord Mahadeo, represented by a stone, and is established under a sal tree. There is a *trishul* or trident at the right side of the stone, symbolising Lord Mahadeo, regarded as *Pahar Thakur*.

Similarly, *Sing Bahini* is equivalent to Durga and represented by an oval shaped stone. This deity is established in *Sing Bahani Than* under a mango tree. Along with her in this *Than Mahadanu*, another form of *Lord Mahadeo* is established. It is a round stone installed by the right side of *Sing Bahini*. These two together are the symbol of fertility cult.

In any *Than* women are not allowed to sit or stand as they are believed to be impure. They have to stand at a distance. Again due to the impurity concept women are not allowed to attend many ritual/ festival in the *Thans*. Even they are tabooed to eat the consecrated food of the ritual of many of the deities. All these symbolise that women enjoy an inferior status to their men in their society.

In agricultural operation during the days of menstruation of his wife, a man is not liable to do *ropni* or seed sowing as his wife is regarded as polluted and hence he is tabooed to do the above mentioned works in the field as they believe it is an inauspicious act and the deity will be displeased and the land will be barren. Here woman is compared with land represented as *Dharti Ma* and both are same as productive unit. During her menstrual cycle fertilisation is not possible, and symbolising this in field the woman's husband is also not allowed to do those works related to fertilisation in the field.

In marriage when the girl that is the prospecting bride is chosen by the boy or the prospecting bridegroom's family, as a signal/sign of it, the bridegroom's side sends a thread anointed/coloured with turmeric paste which becomes a yellow thread. To finalise the date of marriage they tie several knots. Each knot indicates a day and the total count of knots signals the days left for the proposed date of marriage. It is tied with an arrow with a small pack of paddy grain at the arrow's head. Here arrow symbolises a weapon to keep all evils far from them and the paddy grains are symbol of prosperity. The bride's party can easily understand the date which is proposed by the bridegroom's party. If they have objection, they can change it by similar process. Now look at the whole thing. Marriage is a very sacred phenomenon. To fix up a date for marriage, *girha* (a sign) is done in a thread and they take turmeric and paddy grain. All these are very auspicious and symbols of prosperity. Girha is also done to invite other persons to attend the marriage ceremony. A person called as *girha denia* is send to the persons' house whom they wish to invite. He takes a long thread anointed with turmeric. The thread has several knots which indicate how many days are left for marriage. Suppose he visits a village to invite persons when ten days left then the thread has ten knots and if nine days are left then nine knots are there. The sign of invitation with turmeric symbolises of a fortunate and auspicious event as turmeric is very auspicious.

The bridegroom on the day of marriage on his journey towards the bride's house, as a customary rule, he has to marry a mango tree. It is known as *am biha*. Similarly, the bride is married with a *mahua* tree and it is known as *mahul biha*. Symbolically this ritual is performed to overcome any danger including death. In such a case, the *am* and or the *mahua* tree will face the danger or unhappy event and in this way give protection and the couple will have a safe married life. Interestingly it is seen that in *Goriya Than, Singh bahani* or *Durga* is seen seated under a mango tree and it is believed that she is fond of mango tree under whose shadow she takes rest. So mango tree enjoys a superior position. Here in marriage mango tree is taken symbolically as a bride. In case of a bride, she is married to a mahua tree instead of sal tree. Sal tree is a chosen tree of Mahadanu and under that tree Mahadanu - a form of Lord Siva sits. Why they have taken mahua tree instead of sal tree? They told that mahua tree is also a tree of *Mahadanu's* choice as he is fond of liquor extracted from it's flower. The liquor is a very important item of their life especially of ritual life. Its tree has a high position in their society. So they have taken *mahua* tree which symbolises a bridegroom.

Hunting became nearly an obsolete phenomenon. They generally go for hunting at the end of some ritual and it is a merry making event. Whenever they go for hunting, they go collectively from some villages. During the month of *fagun* and *jaith/ashad* they go for communal hunting. Several villages join the hunting party. When a village settle a date for hunting expedition, a person of a village during the market day broadcast the news holding a branch of Sal (sakhoa) tree as a sign for communal hunting. The willing village males of that particular village along with the willing males of other neighbouring villages join the party and it becomes a large group and they in smaller groups start their hunting expedition. The day before the hunting expedition the man has to observe some restrictions. The man should cook his own food and should not sleep with his wife in the same bed. Otherwise they feel that the hunter will be polluted and when he will proceed to forest for hunting he will face difficulties even including death. Again it symbolises a lower status for women in their society.

During the hunting expedition, the wife of a man has to spend those days with restrictions. She should not put vermilion, should not comb her hair and go for fasting during day time. She should cook and take food once daily after sunset. Otherwise they believe that it may bring danger for the man during hunting expedition. After the hunting party returns to their village, the wife of a hunter at first washes his feet with water. All these symbolises women are given an inferior status in their society.

To avoid natural calamities they have several ritual performances. Symbolically they drive out evil spirits such as in *Ormu Than* they worship *Dharti Ma* and during the ritual performances they speak the filthy language and abuses. They believe that when there was a great natural calamity known as *parlay, Dharti Ma* was disturbed by the evil spirits and shaken heavily and to get rid of that turmoil, filthy and vulgar words were used to drive out the ghosts-spirits. Ultimately, she was out of that crisis and became quiet.

They perform *Ashari Puja* collectively just prior to the start of monsoon cropping and also at family level, with a prayer to their deities and ancestors for plenty of crop for each and every household. They sacrifice a he-goat (as stated earlier) and Mal Paharia males consume it in the village border. The blood of sacrificed goat is sprinkled at the border by which they symbolically bind the village so that no evil spirit could be able to enter the village crossing the boundary. Along with this they set free two black pigeons symbolising that they are driving out all the evils in the form of those two pigeons. These are done to protect the village from all types of evils and malevolent spirits who may attack from outside the village.

There are several other examples of symbolic expressionwhich comes from the life and culture of the Mal Paharia community.

## Discussion

It appears from above discussion that cultural communication through various signals→signs→and symbols are obviously cognitive and very much confined to a culture of a ethnic community. According to Leach (1976) human communication is achieved by means of expressive actions which operate as signals (which is mundane), signs (which is mundane as well as abstract), and symbols (which is totally abstract). These cultural traits of a community, that is, signals, signs and symbols are significantly their own cultural ethos that are again intrinsic and value loaded cultural behaviours; that are considered as vehicle of communication which are transmitted through generations. Whether or not the symbols are sacred in abstract level or mundane among the Mal Paharia, make up a significant part of the cultural fabric of the community. These symbols speak without any words and emotional responses receive in return from the community members because it is not only value loaded but possesses an insight meaning which can only be realised through empathy.

## References

Firth, Raymond, 1973, Symbols Public and Private, London: George Allen and Unwin Ltd.

Leach, Edmund, 1976, Culture and Communication: the logic by which symbols are connected, Cambridge, Cambridge University Press.

Sarkar, Amitabha and Samira Dasgupta, 2011, Mal Paharia Culture at the Crossroad, New Delhi: Agam Kala Prakashan.

# 13

# Study of Ethnicity and Identity

## Prologue

One can identify himself or herself in various ways such as by name, affiliation, position through geographical territory or some interest groups as well as by ethnic terms and so on. In fact, ethnicity emerges from ethnic groups while, it creates identity consciousness and it is a kind of psychological feeling or group sentiment. Ethnicity is a term which arouses some emotional and psychological feelings in human mind. It "creates identity consciousness" (Goswami 1991). it gives the feelings or sentiments of "we" and "they" or in the group and out of the group.

"Ethnic identities and categorisation are based on the relationship between the ethnic groups at a particular point of time. The conditions which modulate the boundary of ethnic groups are a specific situational and historical condition"(Goswami, 1991). Ethnicity generates cognitive categories, that is, the notion of one ethnic group for others. According to Glazer (1975 ) ethnicity is a social group which consciously shares some aspects of a common culture and is defined primarily by descent or inheritance.

## A. Ethnicity: Identity and Conflict among Tribal Women Labours

The word ethnicity "stands for the ethnic quality or affiliation of a group bearing different meanings in varied situational contexts.

Members of an ethnic group may however distinguish themselves on the basis of certain common psycho-cultural characteristics" (Danda 1991: 92)

The ethnic groups are identified in two ways, namely, the **symbolic expressive group** and the **instrumental group** (Sengupta 1991: 14). the symbolic expressive groups are affective and are identified in connection with the place of birth, language, kinship relationship, social practices and religion. The instrumental groups are formed for certain common purpose and specially the common material interests. Ethnic groups are often in conflict with other one another and sometimes even within the same ethnic group. There are several views or theories on these conflicts such as modernisation theory, theory of internal colonialism and cultural plurality. The modernisation theory was postulated by Karl W. Deutsch (1961) who says that social mobilisation brings the ethnic conflict. In the changing situation from traditional to modern agriculture to non–agriculture, new patterns of behaviour arise which are not easily accepted by a section of people belonging to the same or other ethnic groups. Thus, a gap is formed between the two groups which often cause the conflicts.

It is obvious that economic development creates differences between people of any ethnic group or with the people of other ethnic groups. It differentiates the people as 'advanced' (those who get the opportunity of economic development) and ' retarded' (those with less scope of economic development). This conflict can easily arise between the two groups and it is theoretically framed as internal colonialism.

In the context above, in the present paper the author has taken an attempt to put on some of her observation at a micro level on the ethnic identity, grouping and conflict of the tribal women labourers attached with construction work as daily wage earners. The study was conducted in some construction sites situated at Girwa tehsil of Udaipur district of Rajasthan during 1979 to 1980.

In all these construction sites the study is concentrated upon the Bhil women labourers. The women construction labourers are locally called 'collie'. If one takes a look on the work structure of the construction site, he or she can observe that the women construction labourers are only associated with the unskilled type of works as helpers to the masons and earth diggers etc. They generally supply the concrete mixture to their masons, help them to erect temporary platform upon which the masons stand and do the construction work when they have to work at a height. These women labourers water the newly constructed walls, prepare concrete mixture, sweep the floor, assist the diggers in digging and throw the dug out rubbish (boulders and mud) to other places. They are also seen to carry heavy and big stone slabs from one place to another. Besides these, they always have to carry out various types of orders of the masons, supervisors, and mates etc. (e.g. bringing tea or snacks from the local canteen or tea stall etc.). These women labourers work on no-work no-pay basis at daily wage of Rs 5 per day. Their working hour starts from 8 am. to 8.30 am. and it continues for eight hours with a break of half an hour for lunch. In a construction site, 90 per cent (approximately) of the total women workers are Bhil and the rest 10 per cent belong to the other ethnic groups such as Banjara, Kalal and Meghwal.

Among the Bhil women construction labourers some women come daily from the neighbouring villages and some of them come from outside and are called migrant labourers (here they are referred as migrant labourers even when their migration is completely temporary. They return to their own villages whenever they finish the work or during the period of agricultural work at the rainy season). Those who come to work as migrant labourers, are always accompanied by one of their family members. The local women workers generally come daily early in the morning from their villages either on foot or by the transport arranged by the Contractor, and after finishing the day's work they return to their own villages. The migrant labourers usually stay in or around the construction site in temporary accommodation arranged by the contractors. Except the Bhil women, women of other ethnic groups are never seen to work as migrant labourers.

The contractors, supervisors and other workers attached with construction work have opined that the Bhil women are as a whole the most efficient and suitable helpers in construction work. They are labourious, simple, obedient, honest and dependable and very much ignorant of their right. They usually do not trouble the employers as is very frequently done by the Non-tribal women. So the contractors prefer to appoint the women labourers, from the ethnic group–Bhil for their own benefit. In this way Bhil as an ethnic group gets preference in the construction site.

In a construction site all the women helpers irrespective of their ethnic identities are called Coolie; an identifying marker, which gives all the women construction workers an in-group feeling "we" but it is very feeble. This "we" feeling is however very strong within the women of their own ethnic group; or within the Bhil coolies. They interact much among themselves than with the women 'coolie' of other ethnic groups for whom they have a feeling of "they". These two feelings are really psychological which separate them from others and for this their ethnic identity as Bhil is solely responsible.

The Bhil women labourers generally come to work in the construction site in groups–from a village or from some neighbouring villages. At the time of group formation they get the identity a 'coolie'. This grouping is completely an instrumental grouping for some material achievement (here to get some source of earning).

This new ethnic identity'coolie' for them is a secondary identity. To themselves primarily they are Bhil and then they are 'coolie'. Their ethnic identity as coolie never can supersede the ethnic identity–Bhil which is primordial and a symbolic expressive grouping.

These Bhil women generally have a very formal relation with the women of other ethnic groups with whom they do not like to mix. They have some sort of inquisitiveness for those women of other ethnic groups. It is already mentioned that they have a feeling "we" for all the Bhil women and "they" for all the non–Bhil women. This feeling gives them some psychological strength to keep their ethnic identity intact. Simultaneously, the non-Bhil women also separate themselves from the Bhilwomen whom they generally refers to as 'adivasi' coolie. They have a feeling of superiority over these 'adivasi collies'. It creates a distance between the two groups in spite of having another identity 'coolie' which is the same for all of them.

In a construction site they (the Bhil and the non Bhil) generally do not work as a mixed group and if they have to work together, such as, a Bhil women never accepts water from the hand of a Kalal or a Banjara or a Meghwal woman, even when they feel thirsty during the period of hard, and continuous work.

A construction site accommodates lots of skilled and unskilled labours. There are people of various ethnic groups with different cultural backgroundsand with different religious beliefs. They have to work together and interact daily in the work site. The Bhil women are not exceptional. They have to work as helpers to the masons who belong to various ethnic groups. In such a situation these women workerschit chat with the workers of other ethnic groups after the day's work. They exchange their ideas or views with others which increases their world view. Even the Bhil women indulge in some sort of immoral activities which again are against their own customary law. Due to exposure to other cultures these women knowingly or unknowingly borrow some cultural traits from the others or get acculturated. Many of their culture-traits have changed but minute observation says that changes only are found at the material level. They have started to wear cloths and ornaments of various designs and styles. They use powder, cream, colorful ribbons and clips etc. They prefer to use soap in the place of local mud used traditionally by the villagers. The have got interest in cinema or circus show, they have got the habit of taking tea and snacks. Their material aspiration has increased. They are allured by the colorful side of their local environment (that is; the material aspiration) at the construction site which is limited only at that level. It could not touch the core of their culture. In spite of all the attractions at the construction site they never like to forget their own identity as Bhil and feel proud of it.

These construction workers in general come to work form the villages to the urban and industrial sectors. They traditionally belong to the agriculturist families. Their shift from village to urban and industrial area and shift from the traditional occupation of agriculture to non-agricultural jobs brings changes in their thoughts and life style, which is different from women not working in construction site. The new pattern of behaviour and life style is not welcomed. So automatically a gap is formed between the two groups and it is expressed through disliking, avoidance, quarrels and even maladjustment between the two groups. In the present situation nobody likes to send his wife or daughter to earn through the construction labour, but their economic condition compels them to do so and in their society gradually a group with an identity as 'coolie' is established. This identity creates several social problems from those women. Their parents face difficulties to arrange their marriage, as they have got an impression that these women are of a doubtful and controversial character. The married women construction labourers often face troubles in their families, especially with their husbands who always suspect them. It is true that there are some women with such immoral character but everybody is not like that. Even sometimes an innocent women is also suspected.

The women labourers sometimes have to do overtime for which they get an extra pay. It is noted that in spite of having the opportunity to earn more these women always try to escape from this type of works. They say that in case of overtime work they have to stay in the construction site for one and a half an hour to two hours more. So automatically they reach late in their villages. It is not taken simply as a truth by the villagers and their family. They are scolded, suspected and have to face very unhealthy atmosphere. To avoid those they always deny to do overtime. It is found that due to the exposure of modernity and change of occupation these women face difficult situation within their own ethnic group. These women come into conflict within own society, own ethnic group.

The wage in the construction site was very lucrative (Rs 5 per day during 1979–1980). Their payment was made on either monthly or quarterly or weekly basis. Except this they have an opportunity to earn extra amount through overtime assignment. They have the facility to get money as interest free advance from their employers whenever they need it in their economic crisis. All these opportunities help these women to have a better economic condition and which automatically grows some superiority complex among these women. It generates disruptions and creates dissension between the two groups, the construction workers and the non-construction workers. There these women construction labourers receive threats of ex-communication as they are suspected to lead immoral life though acceptance of food and drink from the hands of persons of any other ethnic group, and to have pre or extra marital relationship (which are beyond their own social customs). Deutsch (1961) opined that social mobilisation is related to ethnic conflict which may be comparable in the present study that is, in the same ethnic group–Bhil, conflict is found due to change of occupation at industrial set-up and impact of urbanisation which breaks down the fealty to the traditional ways of living.

Agricultural labour is preferred the most among all the unskilled works but the scope to get a work in agricultural sector is very limited. Beside agricultural labour, there are other unskilled labours such as construction work, mud filling, work in brick kiln etc. Among all thes, construction work has its own charm. It is an easy source of cash earning. Wage earned from construction site is more than that of other sources. It separates them from the others and as a result two distinct groups are formed.

Therefore, from the above discussion it can be concluded that sections of people of an ethnic group can easily form an instrumental group for some material achievement but never can ignore or forget their own symbolic expressive group which is affective and primordial. The Bhil construction workers have got an identification as 'coolie' in the construction site which never go beyond their ethnic identity as Bhil. They primarily identify themselves as Bhil and then 'coolie'. They have "we"— a psychological in group feeling for all the Bhil 'coolies' and "they" for the non-Bhil 'coolies' by which they differentiate themselves from others. In the construction site the Bhil coolies are preferred most by the employers as they are sincere, honest and hardworking people. Here to the constructors and the supervisor, Bhil as an ethnic group gets importance. As an ethnic group their "we" feeling gives them some sort of mental strength to maintain their own ethnic identity in such a situation of cultural plurality. They work there as a separate ethnic group with its own boundary in spite of having been acculturated in several domains of their cultural life.

Due to the exposure of industrial and urban setting and due to better economic condition they come into conflict in their village and within their own ethnic group.

## References

Danda, A.K. 1991, Ethnic plurality and integration, In *Ethnonationalism: Indian Experience,* edited by Arun Ghosh and Radharaman Chakravarty, Chatterjee Publishers, Calcutta.

Deutsch, Karl W. 1961, Social mobilisation and political development, *American Political Science Review,* Volume 55, September.

Goswami, B.B. 1991, *Ethnic cognition in North-east India. In Ethnonationalism: Indian Experience,* edited by Arun Ghosh and Radharaman Chakravarty. Chatterjee Publishers, Calcutta.

Sengupta, P. 1991, *Ethnic group and ethnic conflict: A liberal perspective, in Ethnonationalism: Indian Experience* edited by Arun Ghosh and Radharaman Chakravarty. Chatterjee Publishers, Calcutta.

## B. Cultrual Mechanism of Ethnic Boundary Maintenance among the Dhodia

### Introduction

Ethnicity has been a key concept in anthropology and sociology for many years, yet many people still find uncertain as to its meaning, relevance and its relationship with concepts of race and nationalism. The term 'ethnicity' has been used to describe human social interaction, particularly in relation to groups that would previously have been designated as tribe and to minority migrant groups and their host societies.

In short, ethnicity can be defined as certain quality or affiliation based on hereditary as well as cultural considerations. According to Roy Burman ('72), 'Dissociation' is one concept which is a process of identification of a community with two different communities in two different contexts.

Barth ('69) emphasised that "ethnic groups are socially constructed (subject to environmental constraints) and that the content of the group–interns of both culture and personnel, has no a priori existence or stability" (Banks, '96). "Barth's main contribution is to urge a shift away from discussions of the content of ethnic identity through considerations of ethnic markers such as dress, food, language and so on, towards a consideration of the boundaries that mark the limits of such contents. First, that boundary persists despite a flow of personnel and information across them; secondly, as a corollary to the first that such groups cannot exist in isolation but only in contrast to other such groups. That is, the boundary does not bound something off from nothingness, but rather it distinguishes between two somethings" (Banks, '96).

Barth ('69) does not ignore the cultural content of the group, though he considers this to be of two types–diacritical markers such as dress and language and 'value orientation' such as morality and other social norms. In short, according to Barth, ethnicity is a super ordinate identity one which transcends or is at least equivalent to all other identities and as such his position is closer to that usually known as primordialism–ethnicity as a permanent and essential condition.

It can be said that an individual or a group can possess several identities in various situations, often this may be identified as "Interest Group" as told by Glazer and Moynihan ('75). Which particular identity the person will project would depend on his strategy adopted for the specific situation. Ethnicity, therefore, can be understood in terms of self–ascription or other's ascription but the stability of equilibrium of identity will depend largely on the degree of agreement between the two at any particular point of time. A citizen of India could be a Rajasthani, a Marwari, a Mewari, a Gujrati, a Kathiwad, a Meghwal, a Bhil or a Damor etc. depending on the context, this may be called as ethnic cultural plurality, under such circumstances the concept of ethnicity becomes extremely fluid.

The perception of identity of individuals and or groups varies not only over time but also in space. A series of criteria are involved which independently or in various combinations determine the ethnic identity of individuals or groups. Broadly the ethnicity may be classified as: (i) primordial where an individual derives attachment from place of birth, language, kinship relationship, religion and social practices; while and (ii) instrumentalist perspective emphasises the uses to which cultural symbols are put by elite's seeking instrumental advantage for themselves or the groups they claim to represent (e.g., Jharkhand movements, Bodo movement, Gorkhaland movement, etc. ). For them, ethnicity is a communal type of organisation which is motivated by interest group.

## The Dhodia

The present paper highlights on the Dhodia, a scheduled tribe of south Gujarat. The Dhodia are settled on the plains in Valsad and Surat districts. The distinct strip of valleys between the Arabian Sea and the Sahayadri range in the southern part of the Gujarat State is the region of Dhodias. They are mainly an agricultural community. Incomparison to other neighbouring tribal groups the Dhodias are well off agriculturists in the region but most of them are not able to produce enough to maintain their families round the year. Therefore, they seek other ways of getting extra income. Incidentally, due to rapid industrialisation and urbanisation of the area where they live, they find work in the industrial organisations. Their literacy rate is 31.2 per cent. In fact, in Valsad, Pardi and Vapi regions, through which National Highway No. 8 passes, the industrial labour in that region is becoming the principal means of livelihood for many Dhodias.

A good amount of changes has been observed in their socio-economic life. Due to their exposure and high literacy rate, they have always remained in constant contact with their non-tribal neighbours of the region. The growth of communication in this region has developed very fast and as a result the changing economic scenario in their region had forced the Dhodias to new patterns of life in which an urban and industrial economy is gaining importance over their traditional economy, i.e. agricultural economy.

## Field Area and Data

The author's observation and findings are based on synchronic comparison of three Dhodia villages in the district of Valsad, Gujarat. The village Kharedi, is situated in Dharampur taluka in an interior tract of hilly area which is not so well communicated and about 55 km away from the industrial centre. The next village Chanvai, is situated at the fringe of an industrial plant, hardly 3 km away, and is more exposed to communication. The third village is actually within the Atul industrial township, where Dhodia live along with other industrial workers in the factory township quarter.

The Dhodias of Kharedi village are mainly settled cultivator, their literacy rate is 43.3 per cent and about 68 per cent are engaged in agricultural pursuits. The economic organisation of this village still revolves round agriculture. Agriculture in the village is family enterprise and those who share the hearth shall share in the work of agricultural field and the harvest. The symbiotic relationship with forest is found among Dhodia (Sarkar, '93). The immediate environment, forests, also play a key role in their subsistence by providing wild edible tubers, roots, fruits, leaves, firewood, *mahuwa* seeds and flowers for consumption and *timru* leaves for bidi preparation, etc.

In the Chanvai village the literacy rate among Dhodia is about 59 per cent. Dhodias of this village have become involved in two economic systems which are sharply in contrast, one being subsistence peasant economy while the other is full blown industrial as well as commercial economy (Sarkar, '93). Of the total population, it shows that 5.53 per cent are engaged in agriculture as the main occupation while 45.42 per cent are engaged in agricultural pursuits as subsidiary occupation and about 25.42 per cent Dhodia in the Chanvai village are directly cash earners, either from service or wage earners which is their primary occupation These people who are directly cash earners from non-agricultural pursuits, were agriculturists in their past as evidenced from the genealogy. The wage earners of this village are mainly employed in Atul Industrial complex. It is found that majority of Dhodia earners in the industrial complex have agriculture as their subsidiary occupation. The wages earned at the factory are increasingly being utilised for development of agriculture and so gradually the subsistence sector is transformed into commercial sector which is reflected in many ways.

In contrast to earlier two villages the industrial township Atul is much urbanised in nature. The township has provided them all modern amenities. The literacy rate at the township is 79.08 per cent. The regular service holder among them is 29.71 per cent of which 9.42 per cent practice agriculture in part times as secondary occupation. There are 23.18 per cent who are employed in Atul industrial complex.

## Discussion

The Dhodia of Atul industrial complex and neighbouring areas are still in a limited phase of transformation. It is observed that the economic changes and development is very recent and tradition of urban life, wage earning occupation are generally lacking, the extent of technical, economic and social transformation that has taken place especially after independence has been locally identified as 'great'. Due to this the local tribal people have been thrown into a situation for which there is no set of prescribed behaviour in their traditions. This situation may be comparable to 'heterogenetic cultural transformation' of Redfield and Singer ('56). The urban mode of life is gaining its importance among the Dhodia of this region (Valsad, Pardi, Vapi region) and is increasing day-by-day due to more exposure to communication and industrialisation.

The other section of the Dhodia people who are still living in the traditional set up at forested hilly tract of Dharampur, are much behind their brethren of industrial zone economically. The Dhodias of Dharampur area are not good wage earner in comparison to Atul industrial area, and they are also not exposed to modern urban amenities and communication which has been observed through their mode of interaction with others. In short, the behaviour pattern among Dhodias of Dharampur are in contrast to their brethren of Atul region The Dhodia of Atul call the people of Dharampur as *raniparaj* (forest dweller).

With the introduction and wide spread money economy among the Dhodia socio-cultural area, drastic change in the outlook and behaviour pattern have developed among the Dhodias which has resulted in a sharp division of cultural boundary among the Dhodia ethnic groups. The data show that traditionally Dhodia is an endogamous ethnic group, but now due to the above mentioned economic differentiation with *rani-paraj* Dhodia in the level of socio-economic status, the Dhodias of industrial area are now avoiding to establish any marital alliance with the forest dwellers. It has been also observed that Dhodias are pushed towards industrial area in search of their subsistence. In fact, the brideprice and various other social customs which are prevalent among *rani-paraj* Dhodia, are found to be absent among the Dhodia who are living in the industrial area; their food habits, material possession, dress and personal adornments are also not alike.

It is revealed from above discussion that money plays a key role in the formation of two strata in an endogamous tribal group like Dhodia. Ultimately one distinct group is gaining an importance to form a single ethnic group which is guided by its socio-cultural behaviour. It is true that in the traditional set up of Dhodia, the role of money is essential but very limited as very little amount of money circulates among them. The Dhodias of the industrial sector are well aware about the significance of money which they earn regularly. The whole situation has created two sharp classes viz. *rani-paraj* Dhodia and plain land Dhodia, whose distinctive markers are obviously material wealth, possession of money and social-behaviour. This phenomena may be comparable with 'desociation' (Roy Burman, 1972, 1987), (which means, sometimes a process of separation of communities; which were earlier considered to be segments of the same community, takes place and transformation is brought in the society).

"Ethnic identities and categorisation are based on the relationship between the ethnic groups at a particular point of time. The conditions which modulate the boundary of ethnic groups are based on specific situational and historical conditions" (Goswami, '91). Since the ethnicity generates cognitive categories, the above mentioned discussion of the situation in Dhodias may be categorised as 'secondary-dispersion' (Riggs, '91), which is indicated when a population is scattered from its homeland in quest of new opportunities. Thus, it can be concluded that with the help of some socio-economic and cultural traits an ethnic boundary is maintained among the Dhodias of forest, hill tract, commonly called as *rani-paraj*, and the Dhodias of plain land especially who are more exposed to communication and industrialisation.

## References

Banks, Marcus 1996. *Anthropological Constructions.* Routledge: London.

Barth, Frederik (ed.) 1969. *Ethnic Groups and Boundaries: The Social Organisation of Culture Difference.* George Allen and Unwin: London.

Danda, A. K. 1988. Ethnicity and Nationality in India: Some theoretical issues. *Human Science,* 37: 103-119.

Danda, A. K. 1991. "Ethnicity, plurality and integration", in Arun Ghosh and Radha Raman Chakraborty (ed.), *Ethnonationalism: Indian Experience,* pp. 34-41. Chatterjee Publishers: Calcutta.

Glazer, Nathan 1975. The Universalisation of ethnicity. *Encounter,* 44(2): pp. 8-17.

Glazer, Nathan and Daniel P. Moynihan (ed.) 1975. *Ethnicity.* Harvard University Press: Cambridge.

Goswami, B. B. 1991. "Ethnicity, cognition in North-East India", in: Arun Ghosh and Radha Raman Chakraborty (ed.), *Ethnona-tionalism: Indian Experience,* pp. 62-71. Chatterjee Publishers: Calcutta.

Kumaran, K. P. 1992. Ethnicity, minority association and their socio-cultural function. *Man in India,* 72: pp. 141-152.

Redfield, R and Milton B. Singer 1956. The cultural role of cities. *Man in India,* 36: pp. 161-194.

Riggs, F. W. 1991. "Ethnicity, nationalism, race, minority: A semantic/onomantic exercise" (Part One). *International Sociology,* 6: pp. 281-305.

Roy Burman, B. K. 1972. Dynamics of persistence of tribal community in India. in B. C. Agrawal (ed.),: *Anthropological Approaches to the Study of Complex Society.* Indian Academy of Social Science: New Delhi.

Roy Burman, B. K. 1987. Ethnicity, ethno-history and stratification among the tribes of Manipur. *Journal of Social Research,* 30: pp. 23-48.

Sarkar, Amitabha 1993. *Dhodia: Industrialisation and Change in a Primitive Community.* Gyan Publishing House: New Delhi.

Weinner, Myron 1988. *Sons of the Soil.* Oxford University Press: Delhi.

# 14

# Anthropology of Religion

## Prologue

Religion is universal and pervasive in situation in human society. Religion may be broadly defined as a system of beliefs, emotional attitudes and practices by means of which a group of people attempt to cope with the ultimate problems of human life. Religions vary so widely in doctrine, practice and organisation and religious feelings are so personal and difficult to describe objectively that any definition of religion will necessarily seem inadequate. Each religion contains five basic elements:

1. Belief in supernatural power,
2. Belief in the holy,
3. Ritual,
4. Acts defined as sinful,
5. Some method of salvation or nirvana.

The tribal people under the present study mostly live in the hills, forest and in the islands, generally in isolated, less fertile and less accessible habitat. Since the tribal people live in isolation for centuries together in the lap of nature, they have developed a culture of their own adjusting with their local environment. In social and religious parts of their culture the sun, wind, moon, star, tree, animal, water sources, hills, birds and the earth etc. each and every natural object plays vital role. Their interaction with such natural objects became part of their great cultural heritage. In the primitive tribal groups, whatever happens in the world, any happening beyond human control or any oddity in their social environment is generally attributed to the influence or mechanism of supernatural powers which ultimately resulted in the beliefs in various malevolent and benevolent spirit. To overcome all the anxieties and feelings of uncertainty believed to be created by those spirits and to get strength in mind, they perform several rituals to appease all those spirits. Ritual is nothing but the functioning or active or the performing part of religion. "Religion is one of the most important aspects of culture" (Singh, 1982) and "Religion corresponds to the ecological setting to a great deal" (Chandra, 1981). Again religion has come out as per the necessity of human society. In fact, religion is the center or core of culture of a society. It guides the society in each and every sphere of life. A person is to abide by the norms of a society and definitely plays an important role to shape the culture of the society and to dictate the basic values.

To the authors' mind,*"religion is a phenomenon of social articulation followed by ritual and practices and by practising it, one feels secured as well as gets a feeling of an in group social bondage, which differs from other. The intricate dependence on various benevolent and malevolent spirits, become the part and parcel of their survival strategy in a particular ecological niche". (Sarkar and Dasgupta, 2011).*

The geographical or natural environment has an overall impact on the belief system of tribal people in a particular niche. Titiev (1955) has shown the inter relationship of the Universally accepted patterns of culture through the model of Bio-cultural triangle where the environmental relationship of man form the base whereas the other two arms of the triangle comprise Man-Man and Man-Supernatural (or Man-Social) interaction. Titiev opines that the three sides of the Bio-cultural triangle are always integrated but the emphasis is not equal in all the societies (Dasgupta, 1994).

"For many anthropologists, ecology has been an explicit and prominent component of their work. Others have approached it through the studies of cultural tradition. If one accepts the anthropological cliché that culture is the mechanism through which human beings interact with their environment, then the whole field of cultural anthropology can be characterised as human ecology. Studies of people's religious beliefs and practices implicitly, if not explicitly address their understanding of natural process and their responses to the environmental hazards" (Milton, 1993). It is obvious that different tribal groups possess different belief systems of their own which vary according to their local geographical environments. Their beliefs, rituals etc. are very much associated with their life and it is difficult even to isolate or separate those from the people. Infact these tribal people hold on to belief in various supernatural powers who wield a profound influence on their day-to-day life and livelihood. The whole religious belief system among the tribal people of India may broadly be classified as: (a) Sacred geography or territory, (b) Sacred being, (c) Sacred specialist and (d) Sacred performances.

### A. Mal Paharia: Impact of Belief System on Life and Culture

Religion is regarded as one of the most important aspects of human society. It cannot be touched but felt in mind, that is, empathy. It is a psychic and complex phenomenon of human kind expressed through some acts and performances. Religion as a whole has a very broad spectrum. Its structure consists of several rituals both benevolent and malevolent and each of which has functions expressed in the form of performances. Thus, religion has its structure as well as function, which are well knit with each other.

Again it is well-established that religion has evolved as per the necessity of human society. Infact, religion is the centre or core of the culture of a society. It guides the society in each and every sphere of life. A person is abiding by the norms of a society for all his life till death where religion shapes the culture of the society.

With the advancement of technology and flow of money the society is being changed and as a result even in the grass root level, that is village level the traditional interpersonal relation also gets affected. A vast section of Indian tribal people who are mostly marginalised due to their forest infested habitat are having three broad aspects of their expression in culture, namely, *nature*, that stands for geographical environment, while *Man* represents the society and the *spirit* which signifies the supernatural world as well as ideational aspects of culture like, ethos, value system, world-view, ideals, belief system and the like. With the advent of time, various agents of culture change are borrowed from alien culture elements, which make a traditional marginalised group to adapt to the new situation and as a result a culture synthesis or culture change occur among the group.

The authors, keeping in mind the above, have taken Mal Paharia for their present study. The authors tried to examine how far the Mal Paharia cultural life is dependent on their beliefs on supernatural power and whether they are able to go beyond their age-old tradition and belief system by the influence of the outside world.

Mal Paharia live in a geographically difficult area where they always have a feeling of insecurity and uncertainty or less predictability. In fact Mal Paharia is a separate group of the tribe Paharia. Paharia is a blanket term for three separate tribes namely, Sauria Paharia, Kumbharbhag Paharia and Mal Paharia. All of them are endogamous groups and remain confined to their habitat in Damin–i–koh (a Persian word means skirt of the hills) area of erstwhile Santhal Pargana district, now divided into Dumka, Pakur, Deoghar, Sahebgunj, Godda, and Jamtara districts.

In the Damin-i-koh area all the three groups of Paharia are distributed in the Rajmahal hills, which cover the entire Damin area. It consists of the upland, the undulating, long ridges and depressions, along with some fertile lands, which is intensively cultivated. There are three lofty peaks among which Massanjore is situated in Dumka sub-division.

The present study is carried out among Mal Paharia of Madhuvan village of Gopikandar block of Dumka district. For substantiate the qualitative data were also collected from Gando, Upar Murgathali and Asansol villages of Dumka block of Dumka district. The village Madhuvan is a multi-ethnic village, situated in the northern side of the block Gopikandar. The village is secluded on the hill slopes and lies in the midst of forest. This village is dominated by santal (66 families), followed by Mal Paharia (55 families), Ghatwar (12 families) and Maria or Lohar (12 families).

Madhuvan is situated in the forest and again the Mal Paharia hamlets are situated in the denser portion of the forest at the higher altitude. As they live in such a geographical atmosphere where they have an uncanny feeling of unseen spirits that is in an adverse situation, to get strength in mind, to combat with the mysterious events, they cling to the supernatural power, which are solely responsible to shape their culture and give them protections from all evils. Hence their life is very much oriented by the belief of supernatural power and propitiation of spirits holds an important position in their religious life.

To begin with the religious life of the *Mal Paharia*, it is necessary to mention that the *Mal Paharia* have their own priest or religious practitioner who is known as *Deohar* or *Pujar/Pujahar*. The post is hereditary. He has an assistant called *Fuljharia*. Along with them there is a messenger called *Gorait* who informs and invites all Mal Paharias to attend and participate in the rituals and festivals. He also collects contributions from the villagers in case of any ritual and festival organised by the community or by the whole village.

Besides them they have an *Ojha/Ojha guru*-sorcerer of their own community who is consulted in the crisis such as disease and death etc. To be an *Ojha* it is thought that one should have knowledge to detect and tackle the malevolent spirits and to neutralise their acts with suggesting the remedies. In addition to these in most cases the *Ojhas* also act as medicine man. If one *Ojha* fails to cure a person then they consult Jan guru–the sorcerer of the Santhal community who is believed to be more powerful than their own *Ojha.*

Among the Mal Paharias there are several sacred places meant for the performance of rituals. These places are called *Than* by the Mal Paharias. There are several *Thans* for the performance of different types of rituals. Some of these *Thans* in the studied village-Madhuvan of Gopi Kandar block are *Goriya Than, Jahar Than, Singh Bahani Than, Kali Than*/or *Chordanu Than Chitipila Than, Kumhar Deo Than* and *Ormu Than* are also important. In those *Thans* the worship of *Pahar thakur, Dharti, Bhui dev* etc. is done. In the village the Mal Paharias have their own *Thans* attached with their homestead where family deities are established.

Except all these *Thans,* each and every family has *Mara Morpa or Marha Morpa*–the place of their deceased ancestors. They establish those after the performance of *sradh* ceremony. In fact, in Madhuvan village they establish *Mara Morpa* in most of the cases beside the hearth. The *chulha* or hearth is regarded very pure and auspicious to them. So they prefer to establish it there. In some cases it is established at a corner of the courtyard but the place should be very clean. Three vertical lines are drawn there with vermilion, which signify the place as symbol of *Mara Morpa.* They believe that their deceased ancestors are their guardian deities who are worshipped every day and on every occasion, rituals and festivals. They offer new crops to those ancestors prior to their own consumption. In case of any unnatural death, they do not establish the ancestor in the place, such souls are regarded as malevolent spirit and they are driven out across the boundary of the village. Again within the boundary of the household, sometimes they establish their household deities also in the courtyard.

**Benevolent deities/Spirits**

They have divided their worldly deities and spirits into two divisions–the benevolent and the malevolent. Among their benevolent deities the *Surja Devata* is the supreme authority. Every day in early morning they salute the deity. The families who have taken Sun God as a lineage God perform *Surjaho*–the elabourate festival of the Sun God after the interval of three to five years. It is performed between the months of Fagun (February–March) to Asad (June–July).

Among other benevolent deities, *Pahar Thakur* (also enlisted among the malevolent spirits), *Dharti* or *Basumati Ma, Lit Mai, Lit Baba* (their originator), etc. along with their ancestors established at *Mara Morpa* are very important to them. They propitiate them through various rituals, which are mainly connected with their economic life, such as *Maghi Parab* and *Akhan puja.* These rituals are performed to get protection from the snake, scorpion and other ferocious animals of the jungle, and when they go for collection (a very important and compulsory occupation) in the deeper forest and also for a good harvest and protection of their cattle. *Maghi Parab* is performed within the last day of Pus (December-January) to Fagun (February-March). On the day of *Pus Sankranti* they prepare sweetmeat with new rice. Then on the first day of the Magh, customarily Maghi *Parab* starts. But they generally postpone the date due to their inability to accumulate money for Maghi parab, which is a very gorgeous festival for them. On the third day of the celebration, they perform *Akhan puja.* In this puja they worship their cattle. They also worship *Mahadano, Chordanu* etc. spirits (those will be discussed later) for protection of their crop. In each and every third year, just after *Maghi* puja, they perform *Bhui Dev* (mother deity) puja for the welfare of their village. They bring two *sakhoa* twigs and fit those in the courtyard of the *Pujahar*'s house. Upper portion of the twig is bifurcated and an earthen pot full with *pochai* is kept upon the twigs and then they dance encircling the vessel and worship all the *Bhuts* (evil spirits) to keep them quiet and harmless and Deos (the benevolent spirits) by telling their names and showing them regards with salute. During *Maghi Parab,* they also worship *Ghat Deo*–the deity stays at the *ghat* or boundary of the village, acts as the guard deity. In Madhuvan his place is situated between Madhuvan and Ormu village.

Another ritual associated with cultivationis *Rohini Puja,* performed in the month of *Jaith* (May-June). The villagers perform it collectively. Without the performance of this ritual they are not allowed to take out seed for sowing otherwise the *Bhui Dev* will be displeased.

They perform *Ashari Puja* collectively in the month of Ashad (June-July) just before the start of monsoon cropping and also at family level, with a prayer to their deities and ancestors for plenty of crop for each and every household. They sacrifice a he-goat as stated earlier and the Mal Paharia males consume it in the village border. The blood of sacrificed goat is sprinkled at the border with a belief that they are driving out all the evils from the village and in this belief they set free two black pigeons symbolising that they are driving out all the evils in the form of those two pigeons. These are done to protect the village from all types of evils and malevolent spirits who may attack from outside the village. In this ritual they offer all the new items of the season such as *chhati* (mushroom), new leafy vegetables, *phutka* or *kondki*–a potato like tuber etc.

In the month of Vaisakh (April-May), after the mango seeds are matured, they perform *Charak Puja.* In *Charak Puja* they worship *Sing Bahani,* whom they accord equal status with *Devi Durga,* and offer her the newly ripened fruit. After that they are allowed to eat it. Otherwise tiger will come to their village and attack them. Again they perform it to protect their houses from thunder.

*Makai Puja* - another similar ritual is performed at family level in the month of Bhado (August-September) to Aswin (September-October) when the maize or ghangra grains get ripened and are ready for harvest in the cultivable land. In this ritual, they worship *Kali, Mahadeo, Lit Mai, Lit Baba* (their originator), and their ancestors at *Mara Morpa.* They offer a pair of pigeon to *Kali Ma,* one red chicken to *Mahadeo,* black chicken to *Lit Baba, Lit Mai* and also to the ancestors at family level. Along with these items they offer five bunches of maize grain gratefully each to all of them with a prayer that they are offering the new crops to the deities and ancestors, as with the blessings of those they have been able to produce the crop. Then they go to the *Singh Bahani Than* where the Malpaharias of the village collectively perform the ritual. This is also a thanks giving ceremony when they offer five bunches of maize grain each to all of the deities at the *Than* with a prayer to get their blessings for a good harvest and also to get protection from any kind of stomach problem, headache and other disease after taking new crop, and also to get protection from snakebite and from other poisonous insects and ferocious animals. After that they go to the *bari* land, offer puja there and then they cut the maize and bring those at home. Then at first they have some rituals for purification of the harvested crop in a belief that if there is any evil eye on it, that will be driven out through the performance of those rituals.

Sing Bahani is worshipped also in the month of Aswin (September-October), when they offer her a sacrifice of kohora (pumpkin). It is known as Chhed Puja.

In *Manasa Puja*, performed in the month of Saon (July–August) they worship snake deity *Manasa Devi* to get protection from snakebite and other poisonous creatures in their vicinity. They perform *Banashakti* (a malevolent spirit that will be discussed later. ) *Puja* prior to the work of digging, locally known as *khobi* or *khonta*, for cultivation of *barbatti* or *ghangra* (a variety of beans) in their *vitto* land, with a prayer to protect them from scorpion, snake and other poisonous animals during the time of cultivation.

*Patjhari puja* is performed during the month *chaitra* the season of *pat jhora* that is, the falling of old leaves and coming of new leaves. In the heap of the falling leaves, poisonous snakes and other insects may hide themselves and may bite during cultivation in the hills.

When the new leaves come out in some fruit bearing trees including mango, jackfruit, *mahua*, they perform *Bisho/Bisho Puja*. It is also performed at family level. After the ritual they take the new fruits Otherwise there is a chance of any type of mishap in the village, Tiger and other ferocious animals may come out to kill them and their cattle.

*Bahal Puja* is another ritual performed prior to the harvesting of paddy in the *Bahal Than* to drive out all the evil spirits such as Kichling, Dakin etc. reside in and under the trees of the *Than* at a safe distance from their area and the surrounding area. Prior to the performance of the ritual if anybody cuts paddy, it is believed that he or his family members definitely will then be attacked or killed by the tiger.

They have several other rituals associated with hunting. The months April to June are regarded as their hunting season. They worship *Banashkti* (Durga) and *Pahar Thakur* (Lord Siva) prior to any hunting expedition.

*Baski Nath Puja* is performed during the time of *Makar Sankranti* and *Siva Ratri*. It is performed with a prayer for plenty of milk of the cattle. They pour water and milk at the root of a *bel (wood* apple*)* tree. They also perform rituals at their respective homes. In this way their economic life is very much oriented by their beliefs and rituals. It is observed that all these rituals and ceremonies are performed for their overall protection from all dangers and hazards during their economic operations, to get success in life, for a good harvest, for welfare of family and community seeking blessings from them.

To avoid natural calamities they have several ritual performances. In *Ormu Than* they worship *Dharti Ma* and during the ritual performance they speak the filthy language and abuses. They believe that when there was a great natural calamity known as *parlay, Dharti Ma* was disturbed by the evil spirits and was shaken heavily. To get rid of that turmoil several filthy and vulgar words were used to drive out the ghosts-spirits. Ultimately she was out of that crisis and became quiet.

It is found that they believe in Malevolent Spirits who also have influences in their life cycle. They perform several rituals to appease their deities with a hope to get blessings from them. Again there are some other ritual performances and taboos to get protection from all evil spirits. When a woman conceives, she is restricted to go to the forest and to any water source alone specially during noon and evening, as they believe that there are several types of *Jonkhs* (evil spirits) in their vicinity who through their mischievous/malevolent acts may do harm to the woman. Childbirth takes in a temporary shelter constructed outside the house but within the boundary of the house. If the child birth takes place inside the main room, it is regarded as a serious offence to the ancestors established in the *Marha Morpa*. They are excommunicated and a heavy fine is imposed on them. The mother and the child are not allowed to enter the house till the performance of the purificatory rites is over as it is a dishonour to their ancestors at Marha Morpa.

On the day of purification after taking bath, the woman goes to the ponds and other water sources of their hamlet with *sindur* (vermilion) and *kajal* (eyeliner). She draws three lines of *sindur* and two lines of *kajal* on the side/bank of all the water sources to protect the water sources from all evils and impurity. Then she goes to each and every Mal Paharia household and draws similar lines on the pitchers and all other water pots, husking pedal, on the *okkhal /khonta/akhal* (digging stick) to safeguard the water sources, containers and other utensils and implements. On the occasion of *handipoda,* and *muhjhutti* they offer cooked food to *Dharti Ma* and then *muhjhutti* for the child is performed. With the performance of these rituals, the family is allowed to take part in all rituals and festivals.

The time suitable for marriage starts from the month of *Fagun* (February-March) after the performance of *Siva Ratri* - one of their very important ritual. According to them *Siva Ratri* is the celebration of marriage ceremony of *Lord Siva* and *Parvati* in the celestial world. So it is a very auspicious time to arrange their marriage in the terrestrial world.

Prior to the marriage, the bridegroom is married with a mango tree and the bride with a *mahua* tree. This custom is known as am *biha* and *mahul biha*. It is believed that if there is any danger including death for the couple after marriage, it will happen to the tree with whom the first marriage is done and in this way they neutralise the probable crises, if there is any.

Just before the entry in the village, at the entrance, the bridegroom's *deheri* is given a red chicken, which he sacrifices at the boundary and the blood is sprinkled there. This is known as *Gaon Puja*. Through this ritual he drives out all the evil spirits and purifies the village. He in this way binds the village and obstructs all the evil spirits to enter and interfere on that auspicious occasion. Then the bridegroom's party crosses the boundary and enters in the village. After marriage when the newly married couple enters the main room at the bridegroom's house, they salute the ancestors established in the *Marha Morpa* and all other deities established in and outside the room. Then in the cooking of food for the ancesters, lineage members, and other invitees the bride takes part. After the cooking is completed, the bride has to offer it to the ancestors at *Marha Morpa*. Then they serve it to all present there.

It is noted that the Mal Pahariya always avoid talking on death. Death as usual like other communities of the world (with a little exceptions) is a very sorrowful event. The Mal Paharia are always very suspicious in any case of death happening in their village. As a reason for death, at first they suspect that there may be some evil act of mischievous spirits or caused by some malevolent act of some person. The soul of a person who due to some accident or suicide or some epidemic disease, is not established in the *Marha Morpa*. The other souls are established there and regarded as their guardian deities,

*Saraswati Puja*–It is not their traditional ritual but a new inclusion probably as an impact of spread of formal education in their village. Saraswati is the deity of learning. So they have started to worship her as other tribal and Hindu communities to appease her for better knowledge and education. They perform this ritual in their own vicinity, preferably at the school building. The school teacher (non-Brahman) officiates the ritual with the assistance of some Mal Paharia boys and girls. This is performed in the fifth day of the lighter half of the month of *Magh* (January-February).

They perform *Karma* and *Jitia*. Karma is performed in the month of *Bhado* (August-September) and after fifteen days they perform Jitia at family level for their children's welfare.

*Lakshmi Puja* -During *Diwali*, they perform *Lakshmi puja* when they worship cattle at their cattle shed. They anoint turmeric paste to the cattle and bathe their cattle; wash feet and mouth of those, burn incense, mark with turmeric and vermilion and offer food. That day they do not engage the cattle in any type of work.

**Table 14.1: Annual Ritual Calendar**

| *Sl. No.* | *Type of deity/ Spirit* | *Purpose* | *Month/ Date/ Time* | *Name of the deity/ Spirit/Ritual* |
|---|---|---|---|---|
| 1 | Benevolent | Performed by the members of Surja lineage for the welfare of the members | Between Fagun (Feb- – Mar) to Ashad (June – July) | Surjaho worship of Sungod |
| 2. | Benevolent and Malevolent | To protect them from any type of poisonous creatures hidden in the heap of fallen leaves specially in the jungle where they go for collection | Chaitra (March – April) – the season of Patjhora, that is, the falling of old leaves | Patjhari Puja – Deities/ Spirits – Banashakti, Kalgeriya, Pahar Thakur, Bhui Deo (Earth Goddess) |
| 3. | Benevolent | Offerings of newly ripened mango, jackfruit etc. After that they can consume it. Otherwise tiger will come from jungle and kill them. Again they perform it to protect their houses from thunder | In the month of Vaisakh (April-May) | Charak Puja Deity/ Spirit – Singh Bahani |
| 4. | Benevolent | When new leaves come out in some fruit bearing trees and seasons products such as mango, jackfruit etc. even if not ripened. After that they are allowed to take those. If this strict customary rule is broken, then there are chances of mishap in the village. Tiger and other ferocious animals may come out from the jungle and kill them and also their cattle. | Any Saturday or Tuesday of Vaisakh (April – May) | Bisho/Bisho Puja Deities/ Spirits – Ancestors, Bhui Deo, Banashakti |
| 5. | Malevolent | To appease her and to keep her quiet. They worship her with a prayer to get protection from scorpion, snake bite etc. during cultivation. | Vaishakh (April- May) Prior to the work of digging, locally known as *khobi* or *khonta* for cultivation of barbati (a variety of bean) | Banashakti Puja |

*contd. . .*

contd. . .

| Sl. No. | Type of deity/ Spirit | Purpose | Month/ Date/ Time | Name of the deity/ Spirit/Ritual |
|---|---|---|---|---|
| 6. | Benevolent | After performance of the ritual, they are allowed to take out seed from their respective houses for sowing, otherwise Bhui Deo will be displeased | Jaith (May - June) | Rohini Puja<br>Deity/ Spirit – Bhui Deo |
| 7. | Benevolent | Prior to the start of monsoon cropping the ritual is done with a prayer to the deities and ancestors for plenty of crops. In this ritual they offer new items, specially collected items of the season | Ashad (June – July) | Ashari Puja<br>Deities / Spirits – Ancestors, Bhui Deo |
| 8. | Benevolent | They worship snake deity Manasa seeking her protection from snake bite and other poisonous creatures in their vicinity | Saon (July – August) | Manasa Puja |
| 9. | Benevolent | To show respect to Sing Bahani Devi who is equalized with Durga for the welfare of family and village and to get protection from snake bite, other animals and for welfare of the family and village | Aswin (September – October) | Chhed Puja<br>Deity / Spirit – Singh Bahani (Ritual of sacrifice of *kohora* or Pumpkin |
| 10. | Benevolent | To get blessings for a good harvest and to get protection from any kind of stomach problems after consuming new crop. The ritual is performed to get protection from snakebite and other animals and creatures during harvesting. | Aswin (September – October) to Katick (October – November) | Ghangra/ Makai Puja.<br>Deity / Spirit- Sing Bahani, Kali, Mahadeo, Lit Baba, Lit ma, Ancestors |
| 11. | Benevolent | The ritual is performed prior to the harvesting of Paddy in the *bahal than* situated in the forest. Evil spirits such as *kichling*, *dakin* etc. reside in and under the trees at the *than* (alter). They perform the ritual to drive out all those evil spirits at a safe distance from their village and surrounding areas. It is believed that prior to the performance of the ritual if anybody cuts even a bunch of paddy plant, he and his family will definitely be attacked and killed by those evil spirits who will either come in a form of tiger or send a tiger from the jungle | Katick (October – November) to Aghan (November – December) | Bahal Puja |

contd. . .

*contd. . .*

| *Sl. No.* | *Type of deity/ Spirit* | *Purpose* | *Month/ Date/ Time* | *Name of the deity/ Spirit/Ritual* |
|---|---|---|---|---|
| 12. | Benevolent and Malevolent | Welfare of the village and protection of their crops. To drive out all the evil spirits and at the same time to appease some of the malevolent deities. Ghat Deo is regarded as the protector of the village from all evils and stays at the ghat or boundary of the village to resist the evils from outside the village | Between the last day of Pus (December – January) to Fagun (February – March). On the day of Pus Sankranti they prepare sweet meat with new rice. Then on the first day of Magh customarily Maghi Parab starts. But it depends on the villager's ability and decision but it should be within the above-mentioned time span. On the third day of Maghi Parab they perform Akhan Puja | Maghi Parab, Akhan Puja, Ghat Deo Puja. Deity / Spirit – Pahar Thakur, Dharti or Basumati Ma, Lit Mai, Lit Baba, Ancestors, Ghat Deo, Bhui Deo. Their cattles Goriya Devi, Chor danu, Mahadanu |
| 13. | Benevolent | With a prayer for family welfare, plenty of milk of their cattle and prosperity. | Maker Sankranti and Sivaratri | Baski Nath Puja Deities – Baski Nath (Lord Siva) and Dharti Ma (Durga) |
| 14. | Benevolent | To avoid natural calamities, they perform rituals of Dharti Ma | Several times in a year | Dharti Puja Deity / Spirit – Dharti Ma |

## Malevolent Spirits

It is worthy to mention that beside these benevolent deities, the Mal Paharia have a large number of malevolent spirits called *Jonkh* who have the mischievous power to do harm. Those roam in their vicinity always with a tendency to do harm to the people. They always have a suspicious mind and are scared of those. In case of all types of disease and death, they blame evil spirits. Even if wind blows heavily or if there is non-stop rain for a long, they blame the evil spirits. They lead their life with several self-imposed restrictions taken as protection from the evil act of those malevolent spirits. Some of the *jonkhs* are Rangadhari, Bisachandi, Kolkaowar, Kal Chaora, Kal Singh, Banashakti, Jalhari, Fulhari, Am Deo, Cham Deo, Goria Kali, Khunti Deo, Pat Bihar, Jonkh, Jokh Danu, Bhui Deo, Chordanu, Maha Danu, Singh Bahani, Patal Kali, Kiching, Smasan Kali, Maha Kali, Aghoriya Kali, Baghwas, Jora Jonkh, Karodanu, Mahul Baniya, Mal Jonkh, Kichling, Bel Kupia, Saonar, Bhowar, Pahar Thakur, Ichra Kudra Jonkh, Banashakti, Dalhar Jonkh, Swarga puriyatri Jonkh, Kalkumari Jonkh etc.

These *Jonkhs* always have a tendency to do harm to the Mal Paharias. But when they are established at the Thans at their own individual house they become the protecting deity for the family and lineage. They are worshipped time-to-time in each and every occasions and ritual performed by the family and lineage. Each and every family has one or two or even more Jonkhs of them. It is told that the villagers also worship the Jonkhs collectively in the ritual performances to appease those for their protection. Among the offerings, sacrifice of animal, bird, egg and *ganja* are compulsory.

They believe that when a person dies in unnatural death, he becomes a *bhut*. The *Jonkhs* are more dangerous that the *bhuts*. All the malevolent spirits together are referred as *masan*. Along with the worship of their deities known as *Gosain*, they also worship these evils with a hope that those will not do harm to them.

The women who become *bhut* are known as *dakin, kichling* etc. Dakin roams through the cultivable land, by the side of river, hills etc. Those prefer to stay near water. Those always have a target to attack men. Those do not attack women; rather are afraid of women. *Kichling* is more dangerous than *dakin*. Generally it does not go inside a person, but from outside it irritates a person who even sometimes becomes mad. As for example, *kichling* attacked once Buddha a Mal Paharia male of Gando village. He became mad. He saw a buffalo and began to tell that it is his *devar* (husband's younger brother). *Kichling* also prefers to stay at waterside such as in pond etc. places. It wears white dress and plays musical instruments. They do not worship this evil spirit. To drive out *Kichling* in most of the cases, their *ojha* fails. So, they consult *janguru* or *maulvi* of their locality.

Here a list of some of their Jonkhs with their activities is given below:

**Table 14.2**

| *Name of the Jonkh* | *Activities* |
|---|---|
| **Pahar Thakur** (a form of Lord Mahadeo) | According to the villagers Pahar Thakur is originally *Lord Mahadeo*. They worship him to safeguard themselves from ferocious animals and poisonous creatures during their hunting expedition. In each and every village, there is a Than of *Pahar Thakur*, represented by a stone placed under a *sal* tree. There is a *trisul* (trident) at right side of the deity. He is also worshipped in each and every occasion by family and at village level. At the rituals associated with cultivation, especially at the hills he is worshipped for bumper crop. During *Ashari* and *Maghi Parab*, they worship *Pahar Thakur* at village level. In this puja he is offered sundried rice, milk, sugar, liquor preferably of *mahua*, *batasa* and ganja. Ganja is one of the very important items among the offerings. Not only in *Pahar Puja*, in most of their pujas, especially of the evil spirits, they offer ganja and in its absence tobacco leaves as one of the compulsory items of offerings. |

*contd. . .*

*contd. . .*

| *Name of the Jonkh* | *Activities* |
|---|---|
| **Banashakti** | – Among their *Jonkhs*, *Banashakti*-the wife of *Pahar Thakur* is worshipped prior to a visit to jungle for hunting. Each and every hill has its own *Banashakti*. She is worshipped along with Pahar *Thakur*, whenever a person visits the jungle for hunting. She also protects the crops in the field. She is also worshipped during seed sowing both in hills and in their *bari* land. They dare not neglect her. If she becomes displeased, they will face various types troubles in cultivation and when they pass through jungle, it is sure that ferocious animals in the jungle will attack them. |
| **Chordanu** | Chordanu's primary duty is to protect the crops in the field, in the granary and other properties from stealing. *Chordanu* is worshipped both at family level and collectively by the Mal Paharias of the village. If any star falls from sky they are sure that there will be a theft very soon in the village at the direction where the star fell. Then *Chordanu* is immediately worshipped with a prayer asking for his protection from the theft. *Chordanu* is worshipped during any work attached with cultivation and in festivals of *Ashari* and *Maghi Parab*. *Chordanu's puja* is never performed inside the house but outside in the courtyard, in the *Chordanu Than* at the village and also in the hills. Women are also allowed to take the consecrated food except the pigeon offered to the spirit, which is cooked and consumed by the male there where the ritual is performed. If they do not perform the puja, then there will be less cereal produced in the field and the spirit will do harm and as a result cereals and crops will be stolen. |
| **Mahadanu** | Another malevolent spirit or a form of *Lord Mahadeo*. His worship is done along with *Chordanu* to get bumper crop. His *Than* is present in the *Goriya Than*. A round stone represents it where they pour milk. The family can install it at the courtyard or *bari* land under a tree. During seed sowing and cutting he is worshipped. It also protects their cattle. If at night a jackal howls or an owl cries then they are sure that *Mahadanu* is displeased with them giving them warning of any type of mishap, accident and even death in the village. Then they immediately arrange for its worship with the sacrifices to keep him quiet by satisfying him. |
| **Jonkh Dev** | Another spirit, important for its evil acts. It stays at the hills, in the jungle, river, trees etc. During her menstrual cycle a woman is not allowed to go to jungle and riverside and also to climb a tree. This spirit has a tendency to marry a Mal Paharia girl during her cycle and to lead a conjugal life. As a result the particular girl suffers from acute pain and obstruction in her monthly cycle and various types of health hazards. To get safety from his attack, they perform certain rituals. He is also worshipped in the hills at the time of plucking of *barbatti* in the month of *Aghan* (November-December). |

*contd. . .*

*contd. . .*

| *Name of the Jonkh* | *Activities* |
|---|---|
| **Mal Jonkh** | This *jonkh* stays at the *ghat* of Kurho Pahari hills. This spirit tempts the villagers who pass through the pathway of the hills, by keeping bell metal utensils, garland, silver coin etc. valuable items in the path. If by chance any villagers feel greedy and take the items at home, the *Mal Jonkh* follows him and enters his home and begins to stay there. As an impact of his entry in the home, family starts to face several types of disturbances and sickness within two or three days. Then they go to *ojha* to detect the cause and for remedies. They go to the *ojha* with a *sakhoa* leaf on which they keep mustard oil. The *ojha* rubs the oil on the leaf and tells the cause of the disturbances. He also tells how the spirit entered the house. The family then confesses what wrong they have done. Then the *ojha* worships the spirit with oil, vermilion, sundried rice, and a pot full with water, at the courtyard. He sprinkles water on the family head and other members of the family from the pot as significance that he is purifying the family. Then he worships **Mal Jonkh** at a corner of the room and establishes the spirit there. From then it is compulsory to worship the spirit once in a year as one of the deity of the family. The spirit is offered a white he-goat, rice, vermilion, puffed rice. The puja is officiated by the male head of the family. The family will consume the sacrificed meat. The family is liable to worship the spirit throughout the life. |
| | This spirit is also known as *Dhani Mal Jonkh*. He originally stays under a *simul* tree or a stream beside his original abode at the hills. He is also worshipped during harvesting time. |
| **Tumba Jonkh** | It roams in *Nandi Pahar* with a violin. He plays the violin at night roaming on the hills. He does no harm if he is worshipped during the cultivation of *barbatti*. |
| **Dalhar Jonkh** | This Jonkh stays in water sources such as in river, rivulet or stream, In the *khet* (cultivable land) prior to the harvesting, along with other deities and spirits he is worshiped during the month of *Aghan* (November-December). They worship it at a corner of the field. It is performed by the family head and women are tabooed to participate in the ritual. |
| **Swargapur Yatri Jonkh** – | It comes on the males to kill them. The person attacked by this *Jonkh* gets seriously ill. Then the Ojha detects the cause of disease through his *tel patta* (mustard oil on *sakhoa* leaves) magic. The *Jonkh* is then worshipped with an offering of pigeon, red chicken and a he-goat. |
| | They worship the spirit to keep it quiet. Sometimes a stick is taken and beaten in the open air as if they are cutting the spirit into pieces. Sometimes the stick is touched on the body of the patient. |

*contd. . .*

*contd. . .*

| *Name of the Jonkh* | *Activities* |
|---|---|
| **Baghowas** | It resides in hills. Prior to the harvesting of *barbatti*, they worship the spirit with sacrifices of pigeon, chicken or he-goat. They believe that if they do not worship him, then he will bring tigers from jungle to their village. |
| **Bhaman Jonkh** | It lives in Karaleta hills and also roams in Konda and Tanter Pani hills. It scares people by taking different shapes and sizes in the shadow. |
| **Yam Raja** | It stays in Murga Pahari hills and is worshipped by them for safety in the hills when they work there. If it is displeased, death comes in the village. |
| **Karodanu Jonkh –** | This spirit is established beside *Kali Mata*. They worship him to keep him quiet otherwise there would be illness in the village. |
| **Rangadhari Baba** | It is a very dangerous type of Jonkh. Generally they avoid it and keep safe distance but when it enters a house, they are forced to establish it as a family deity and perform its puja. Then it becomes a deity of family welfare. He is established inside or at the backside of the house, worshipped at family level with the offerings of a red chicken. He is worshipped specially for the welfare of their children and family. |
| **Ichra Kudra Jonkh** | This spirit is also worshipped at family level for the welfare of family during the month *Aghan* (November-December) at the side of a river or rivulet or under *peepal* or a baniyan tree. |
| **Bel Kupia** | He is another *Jonkh* worshipped at family level for the welfare of the family. He is worshipped after 14th January, that is, after the performance of *Makar Sankranti*. The consecrated food is taken by males and unmarried girls. |
| **Saonr Bhonwar** | This Jonkh takes shape of a Bhonwar (wasp) and flies here and there. If they worship it, their property will be increased. Otherwise it will bite. |
| **Bandro** | When there is whirlwind, they think that Bandrois passing through the place. If anybody especially the children fall in that whirlwind, he or she becomes ill. The Ojha is called to drive out the *bhut* or the spirit. |

**Pat Bihari Jonkh**–He stays in the paddy field, worshipped prior to the performance of works associated with cultivation such as seed sowing, transplantation and harvesting. Otherwise the spirit will create trouble. Women are not allowed to participate in this spirit's puja and are restricted to take the consecrated food. It is a puja at family level performed in the field. Among the offerings sacrifice of a pigeon or a red chicken or a he-goat is compulsory. In this puja they also worship *Chordanu, Mahadanu* etc. spirits.

Besides their traditional beliefs and ritual practices, there are influence of several other religious beliefs and practices. It is obvious that side by side their own traditional rituals, they have already taken several Hindu deities and rituals as their own transforming those as per their own beliefs and convenience. Such as the *Jonkh Mahadanu*. He is a transformation of *Mahadeo* (Mahadeo is originally not a Hindu deity). In Hindu religion *Mahadeo* is never offered any animal sacrifice but they sacrifice pigeon, chicken, he-goat in his honour.

They worship several Hindu deities like *Brahma, Vishnu, Shiva, Parvati, Lakshmi, Saraswati, Ganga, Tulsi, Hanumanji along with Dharti Ma, Pahar Thakur, Banashakti* etc. It is found that in some villages such as Gando and Upar Murgathali, the Hindu dominated villages, they worship Siva, Durga, Kali, Bajrangbali etc. collectively with the Hindu neighbours in the temple where Hindu play the dominant role. No service is taken from them (Mal Paharia) for being associated with the ritual. In those Hindu dominated villages the Mal Paharias are also found to worship *Tulsi*. In many of their houses there is a *Tulsi Than* where they worship *Tulsi* daily in the morning and also in the evening. They pour water on the plant, light the lamp and offer flower and betel leaves to the deity. In this village there are persons who are confused whether *Tulsi* is God or Goddess. They pour water to get the blessings of the deity. A very few of them told that *Tulsi* was a very pious woman. Once her husband gone out without telling her. Tulsi was very unhappy and started to meditate with a hope for her husband's return and ultimately her husband returned to her. This is a very important aspect, which gave *Tulsi* a very important status of Goddess. In her ritual *batasa, mihidana* etc. are offered during the morning time. After taking meat they are not allowed to do her puja. Those who believe that Tulsi is goddess do not pour water on Tulsi on Sunday as it told that on that day she gets menstruation.

Incidentally it is observed that when they worship Siva-Durga, Manasa, Saraswati, Bajrangbali and also Lakshmi etc, they worship them as per their own rules. No Brahman priest officiates the ritual. Lakshmi puja is performed on the day of Diwali when they worship cattle at their cattle shed. They annoint turmeric paste to the cattle and bathe them; wash their feet and mouth, burn incense, mark with turmeric and vermilion and offer food. That day they do not engage the cattle in any type of work. Their rituals are never officiated by the Brahman but the village barber has some duties in their certain purificatory ceremonies. They perform *Karma* and *Jitia*. Karma is performed in the month of *Bhado* (August-September) and after fifteen days they perform Jitia at family level for their children's welfare.

But above all their religious beliefs and practices are enriched with the beliefs in spirits and most of which are malevolent.

They have belief in *Dayen* (witch). In case of any mishap or sickness they suspect that either any malevolent spirit or a *Dayen* is responsible for that. They cannot touch the spirit but can catch hold a woman suspected as *Dayen* and torture her brutally even sometimes kill her only out of their suspicion.

There are some Mal Paharias who got higher education. They have daily contact with the block headquarters and even with Dumka proper. They have got opportunities to come in contact with different types of people with different religious beliefs, people with better technical knowledge and logical expression of various ideas and beliefs. In this situation these people have got a chance to exchange their ideas with them, got new ideas and they began to make an effort to give logical interpretation of their beliefs specially on the spirits and in most of the cases they failed to give satisfying interpretation. Again the Dayen or belief on witch and the horrifying torture on a suspected witch created a negative feeling on their society. Side by side they are influenced by the other religious beliefs and practices. Some have taken the membership of *Satsangh* of Sat Palji Maharaja of Hardwar. This Sangha has an ashram in Naihat of Dumka, 60 kms far from Dumka town from where some Mal Paharia families have taken *diksha*. They are the disciples of Sattananda Swami. He had taught the Mal Paharia disciples to have a disciplined life with vegetarianism and abstinence from taking liquor. They are told not to tell lie though for a good work telling lie is not a sin. Each and every day they worship Sat Palji and Hanji Maharaja. They are told to wear white dress and to stop the traditional beliefs and practices, which are thought by the sect as superstitious. These traditional beliefs and practices sometimes brings unpleasant atmosphere in the village. Rajindar Deheri, a 26 years old Mal Paharia of Madhuvan village, a disciple of Satsangh, told that though they do not take any non-vegetarian food but they do not follow the dress code. They try to eradicate the beliefs, thought by the sect as superstitions but till date, have not succeeded. At family level they have stopped to keep *Mara Morpa* and *Thans* for different spirits and deities but they cannot deny contributing in rituals performed collectively by the Mal Paharia of the village. Otherwise they will be excommunicated. They contribute half amount, as they do not take the consecrated food.

A few persons have come across during our field investigation who belongs to the Pentecostal group of the Christian religion. Some of them have informed that they are converted because of being tired with the superstitions beliefs, which sometimes act as disease of a society.

**Case:** Kalicharan Dehri (Age-63), a Mal Paharia, Bandajori, Dumka, Retd. Govt. Servant informed that in Jharkhand there are atleast 2000 Christians Mal Paharia of the Lutheran group of the protestant division. There are also some persons of the Pentecostal group. Kalicharan Dehri told that his parents and the family became Christian after they used to face several problems from their own people basing on their religious beliefs and practices. He informed once his elder sister became ill. They called Ojha who after reading *telpatta* oil (putting on a *sakhoa*leaf) detected the evil spirit responsible for the disease. As per his advice they arranged for the puja of the spirit to appease it. They spent at least rupees five thousand in it. It was a very hard task to spend such an amount on those days. Even then after a few days his elder sister died. Then they stopped to attend and participate and perform their own rituals and festivals. For this the other Mal Paharia relatives and friends were displeased. The Ojha was his father's elder brother. He through his magical performances detected Kalicharan's mother as a dain/dayen. He tried to kill her by throwing arrow. He convinced the other Mal Paharia of the village that she is a dain/dayen and it is necessary to kill her. The villagers attacked them and beaten them brutally. Then his mother decided to leave her own religion and to take to *Christianity*. They followed her and they all were converted as *Christians*. The other Mal Paharias became very angry with them. After the death of his father's elder brother his father attend the *sradh* ceremony where he was insulted. When he sat with others to take food he was told not to sit with others in the same line and was called later to take food but at that time the food was exhausted. In this way the other Mal Paharias insults them. Interestingly, it is also informed by them that previously they were the priests, and in spite of their conversion to another religion, even today they are consulted in rituals and festivals. They give them the instruction and process of ritual but they do not attend the ritual and neither takes the consecrated food. Kalicharan told that though they have taken Christian religion even then they follow many aspects of their religion specially their life cycle rituals along with the performances of the Christian rituals.

## Discussion

Thus, it appears from the above discussion that in the background of dependence of the ecological setting for pursuing their ritual activities, Mal Paharia culture may be viewed through the eye of Vidyarthi (1963). Their existence as Man as a social animal and the process of socialisation and enculturation are very much dependent on the forest niche and it has been observed that the manifestation of their culture especially the sacred pantheon which accommodates a number of deities and spirits, both malevolent and benevolent, have control over their socio-cultural life (Dasgupta, 1994). Before Vidyarthi, however, Titiev (1955) has elaborated the inter relationship of the universally accepted patterns of culture through the model of bio-cultural triangle where the environmental relationship of Man forms the base while the other two arms or sides of the triangle comprise of Man-Man and Man-Supernatural (or Man-Social) interaction. This observation of Titiev opens up a new dimension of study in anthropology, which has been, in later years, followed up by cultural ecologists. To understand Mal Paharia culture one has to look at it with functional perspective since they have adapted to the specific natural environment since hoary past. The Mal Paharia culture cannot be conceived without its present natural settings; at the same time it is not fair to conclude that Mal Paharia culture is a product of the specific forest environment. This is, of course, not a one-way process but the dependence is partly reciprocal (Dasgupta, 1994). The various cultural prescriptions adapted by the Mal Paharia for sustainable living clearly suggest for survival strategy in a particular ecological niche. More so, as a result of contact with Hindus they have adopted some of the Hindu deities and rituals in their own way again adjustment with the local niche.

The influence of *Satsangh* and *Christianity* only has come due to the negative impact of their beliefs and practices. They are trying to teach the people about the negative aspects of the Mal Paharia religion but till date it has very negligible impact on the Mal Paharia and their religion.

Thus it isrevealed from above discussion that the religious life of the Mal Paharia is full with beliefs on deities, spirits both malevolent and benevolent and all of those have sprouted in their ways of life to cope with immediate ecological niche in which they live.

## References

Biswas, Sushanta, 2005, *Mal Paharia* (in Bengali), Calcutta: Loko Sanskriti O Adibasi Sanskriti Kendra, Govt. of West Bengal.

Das, A. K., B. Roychowdhury and M. K. Raha, 1966, *The Mal Paharia of West Bengal*, Calcutta: Bulletin of the Cultural Research Institute, Tribal Welfare Dept. Govt. of West Bengal (Sp. Series No. 7).

Dasgupta, Samira, 1994, Birjia: Society and Culture (A Study in Cultural Ecological Perspective), Calcutta: Firma KLM Pvt. Ltd.

Elwin, V. 1941, *The Loss of Nerves*, Oxford Pamphlets of Indian Affairs, No. 14, Oxford: Oxford University Press.

O'malley, L. S. S. 1910, *Bengal District Gazetteers*: Santal Parganas, Calcutta: The Bengal Secretariat Book Depot.

Sarkar, Amitabha and Samira Dasgupta 2000, Ethno-Ecology of Indian Tribes: Diversity in Cultural Adaptation, Jaipur and New Delhi: Rawat Publications

Sarkar, Amitabha and Samira Dasgupta 2011, Mal Paharia Culture at the Crossroad, New Delhi: Agam Kala Prakashan.

Vidyarthi, L. P. 1963, The Maler: Nature-Man-Spirit Complex, Calcutta: Bookland.

Vidyarthi, L. P. 1968, "Cultural Change in the Tribes of Modern India", Presidential Address at 55th session of *Indian Science Congress Association*, held in Varanasi (Anthropology Section).

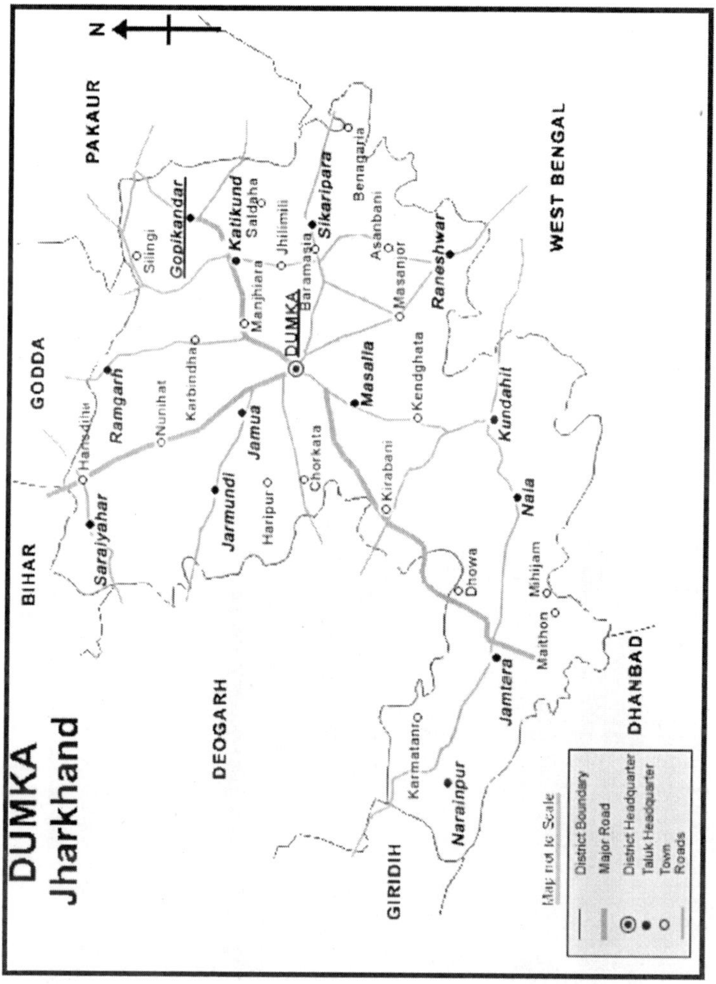


Map of Dumka of Jharkhand (Studied Area)

**Attacked by Bhaman Jonkh**

**House Type of Mal Paharia**

Animal Sacrifice in Maghi Parab

Jonkh Cluster

Distribution of Concecrated meat in Maghi Parab

## B. Religious Belief: Rituals and Festivals at Pargana or Village Level at Bastar

Life in India is a mosaic of colourful happenings. The festivals are not mere occasions but deep-rooted traditions and customs woven into the fabric of Indian life. One of the most important outward manifestations of religion is the performance of festivals and it has been an important feature of group life all over the world. Festivals are woven into our cultural fabric. All of them brighten the Indian landscape and add spice to the variety of our life. Each one of these festivals has its own distinguishing features but taken together they have an underlying rhythm and tenor, which signifies Indianness (Singh, 1982).

Religion cannot be seen but is only felt through empathy. Outward manifestation of religion comes through its active part that is through the performance of rituals and festivals. These are the ways to propitiate and show honour to the supreme authority to appease him for blessing. A person gets mental strength out of it. Ritual is the process of propitiation of deities (Sarkar and Dasgupta, 1996).

India is a country of multi-ethnic with heterogeneous culture having various religious faiths, which are respected as well as honoured by all the ethnic groups. In spite of possession of various religious stigmas by ethnic groups, there are some occasions where some rituals and deities are equally respected/honoured by all the ethnic groups perhaps, chiefly as their survival strategy.

Bastar being the study area is a region where people of various cultures lived together, often sharing each other's culture traits. Through their sharing and borrowing of such traits of neighbouring communities, the people of Bastar represents a clear picture of cultural admixture, especially, in religious pantheon.

It also appears that there are three main categories of deities prevalent among the tribal of Bastar:

(a) Earth goddess

(b) Lineage deity and

(c) Matagudi

### Earth Goddess

In each and every village in Bastar all the ethnic groups propitiate these three categories of deities where ethnic boundary is not taken into consideration. It is reported from Tamakoni, Machkot, Nagarnar, Pandripani and Tiriya villages that earth is referred to as *bhum*or *matideo* or *mutak* or *murtal* or *tallurmutte* or tallin. The earth includes the spirits of river, forest and appeased separately. In Tamakoni village these are appeased with the help of *Pujari* from Amnit Bhatra group while at Machkot it is officiated by Dhurwa priest or *perma.*

The tribal people of Bastar venerate the earth goddess in different names, which varies according to their territorial settlement pattern. Abujh Maria and Muria refer her as *tallurmutte*. *Tallin* by Dandami Maria, *mutak–murtal* by Dhurwa of Kanger ghati area and *bhum* or *mati deo* by Bhatra, Halba and neighbouring villages of Jagdalpur. They have also a belief that they are her offspring as she feeds them by providing various types of crops and cereals. The Hindus identify the earth deity as *matti deo/matideo*. It is worshipped in the lighter half of the month of Chait (March-April) and the ritual is officiated by a *gaita or sirha* of tribal origin or by a Mahara caste and referred to as *matipujari* and it is performed in day time. They have a belief that *matideo* also gives protection to their cattle. They worship the *matideo* to protect the village from all types of diseases and dangers. It is observed that each and every village of Bastar including our studied villages, has its own deity called *gaon devi* or *mata gudi*; in Tamakoni village *Maolimata* and *Jaliniburi mata* are presided in village *matagudi* while in Machkot village it is presided by *Maolimata, Pardeshinmata* and *Telangin mata*. They are worshipped for the welfare of the village. Besides all the deities, the village under study has its guard deity who in usually established at the outskirts of the village. The deity protects the village from all types of evils (Dasgupta and Sarkar, 2003). These deities are identified as *Dand deo* (male deity) in both the studied villages.

## Lineage Deity

Ancestor worship is one of the essential parts in the life and action of the tribes of Bastar. They believe that their deceased ancestors are among their own household deities who protect them from all sorts of problems and act for their welfare. The ancestral spirit holds a very important position in their culture and religious world. All tribes of Bastar practice ancestor worship. It is also reported that Abujh Maria, Dandami Maria, Muria and Dorla have their own *pen* (clan) deities (Dasgupta and Sarkar, 2002). This *pen* deity is a guardian deity of a particular clan to which a person belongs. These entire *pen* deities of the celestial world are mythically connected with each other through the network of social relations; more so, these deities have their own specified territory. *Anga* is the blanket term for all the clan deities. Some of the *pen* deities are male and represented by a frame of three parallel log of *saja* wood or log held together by cross-pieces of bamboo to which they are tied by cords of *siyari* creeper or twisted thongs to the outer ring of bamboos (Grigson, 1991). When the *pen* deity is a female then it is represented through *lat* (which is a long bamboo stick with a piece of coloured cloth which indicate the flag of a particular deity and tied at the top and above that at the extreme end there is a small conical or round bell metal piece in which the *lat* is inserted). This is known as *gura*. The log gods are commonly known as *anga deo or pat deo*. The *pat deo* deity is propitiated by the communities living in and around Jagdalpur, Dantewada and Chote Dongar areas while *anga deo* is the deity of Muria tribe of Narayanpur area. It is also reported that each and every clan has its own log god and among the log gods there are some sorts of hierarchy (Sarkar and Dasgupata). To detect the culprit they usually take help of their own clan god (log god). In case of any crisis, problem in a house then even Hindu of the village invite log god to visit their house and offer blessings. The clan god is carried on shoulder of four people from some other village. They carry it around the village, visiting each and every household. The clan priest also accompanies the party. It appears that the carriers of the log god are possessed and each and every act of them during such carrying procession is considered as the directives of their supreme authority of celestial world.

## Matagudi

The site of a *mata gudi* is found in each and every village of Bastar. In a village beside *mata gudi* there are places for other various *matas*, which are related with family welfare activities. Some of such deities are *Pardeshin mata, Bhandarin mata, Sitala mata, Telangin mata, Jalini mata, Maolimata, Kankalin mata, Kodai mata, Jamindarin mata, Danteshwari mata, Mahamai ma, Hingala devi* etc. of which *Danteshwari* (or *Yayal muttey*) being the supreme among them.

## Annual Ritual Calendar

The empirical data has been collected chiefly from Tamakoni, Machkot, Nagarnar and Pandripani villages. The ethnic composition of the studied villages is as follows :

**Table 14.3: Ethnic composition of studied village**

| *Name of the villages* | *Ethnic groups* |
|---|---|
| 1. Tamakoni | Bhatra (ST), Raja Muria (ST), Dhurwa (ST), Kurak/Dhimar. |
| 2. Machkot | Dhurwa (ST), Raut |
| 3. Nagarnar | Bhatra (ST), Kumhar, Sundi, Ghadwa, Panika, Mahara, Lohar |
| | Chandal |
| 4. Pandripani | Halba (ST), Gond (ST), Muria (ST), Dhurwa (ST), Sonar |
| | Dhakar, Sundi, Khatri |

In Bastar both tribal and non-tribal people observe several rituals and festivals. Some of these rituals are performed at the family level, some at community level while the rest at regional level. The empirical data also speaks that they have a celestial world where there are a large number of deities and which are genealogically related and are propitiated by them. Numerous *devis* (mother goddess) are in their belief system for various socio-economic welfare. Their celestial belief system is full of myth and legend which are directly influence their sustenance activity.

**Table 14:4: Annual Ritual Activities under Studied Villages**

**Category: (i) Earth Goddess (E); (ii) Lineage Deity (L), (iii) Matagudi (M)**

| *Month* | *Name of Village* | *Name of Deity / festival* | *Purpose* | *Place* | *Level of Worship* | *Officiated by* | *Category* |
|---|---|---|---|---|---|---|---|
| 1. Chait (March-April) | Tamakoni, Machkot, Nagarnar & Pandripani | Maoli mata (or matti deo or bhum deo) | For welfare and especially for good harvest. She is appeased first after that bijputni ritual is practiced in the next month. It is also a worship of earth | At village mata gudi | Village level | Tribal Priest / Pujari (Bhatra) | 'M' and 'E' |
| 2. Baisak (April- May) | | Bijputni | . It is associated with agricultural activities | Close to village Matagudi | Family level | Do | 'E' |
| | | Bhima deo | For good rain | Courtyard of village priest | Communal participation | Tribal priest | 'E' |
| 3. Landi (May – June) | | Deogudi Bazar (Soshon pahin mata) | To save them from disease and dange's | Outskirt of village | Village level. Both Tribals and Hindus jointly perform this. All the neighbouring deities are invited who attend the ritual with chata or lathi | Do | 'E' and 'M' |

| Month | Name of Village | Name of Deity / festival | Purpose | Place | Level of Worship | Officiated by | Category |
|---|---|---|---|---|---|---|---|
| 4. Goucha (June – July) | | (a) Goncha (Cart festival) | Welfare | Jagdalpur | Communal participation | Aryanak Brahma | 'E' |
| | | (b) Amush (or hariali) | Protect them from witches/ evil spirits roaming in the air as well as cattle worship | At village individual houses | Family level | Family head | 'E' |
| 5. Amos (July – August) | | | | | | | |
| 6. Bhado / Rassa (Aug. – Sept) | Tamakoni, Machkot, Nagarnar & Pandripani | Pola and Naya Khani / dhan noua | Harvested paddy is offered to their ancestors | At individual house | Family level | Family head and village pujari | 'E' and 'L' |
| 7. Kuar (Sept. – Oct.) | | Dushera | Welfare | Jagdalpur | Communal participation | Brahmans | 'M' |
| 8. Kartik (Oct – Nov) | | | | | | | |
| 9. Aghan (Nov. – Dec.) | | Lakhmi Jagar | For prosperity and fertility | Village mata gudi | By all tribal and Hindus | Tribal priest/ perma and sometimes along with Hindu priest | 'M', 'L' and 'E' |

| Month | Name of Village | Name of Deity / festival | Purpose | Place | Level of Worship | Officiated by | Category |
|---|---|---|---|---|---|---|---|
| 10. Pus (Dec. – Jan) | | Diari | Cattle worship | Individual houses | Family level | Family head | 'E' |
| 11. Magh (Jan – Feb) | | Marai | Thank giving ceremony to earth goddess | Collectively in one place of several neighbouring villages | Communal participation | Tribal priest (Perma / Gaita) | 'E' |
| 12. Fagun (Feb. – Mar) | | Amanua / amakhani (sometimes it is performed in chait depends on perma / pujari | To offer new mango to their ancestor, only after this ritual they are allowed to eat mango | Village mata gudi | Communal participation | Tribal priest | 'E' and 'C' |
| | | Anga Deo/ Pat deo (clan deity) He is worshipped in all rituals/ festivals | Tribals worship their clan deities to show reverence to them from whom they have originated. Again both tribals and non-tribals take help of those deities to get protection from all evils and also to detect the presence of any evil eye. | | Community level | Tribal of Bastar | 'L' |

Apart from these there are number of *Mata's* in the respective villages, which are also appeased time to time in order to get blessings and welfare for family. In the following lines we shall try to picture some of such *Mata* deity in the studied villages

### (A) Tamakoni Village

**(i) Jhanda Deo and Duarmundia:** It is situated in the village boundary to protect the village from any kind of calamity and both these are male deities, officiated by Bhatra *pujari*. He is appeased through *pujari* where all the members of village participate and contribute. Stone and stick represent him.

**(ii) Maolimata:** She is worshipped for the welfare of village and cattle. She is worshipped at *mata gudi* of village by Bhatra priest (of Amnit Bhatra group, wearing sacred thread) and is represented by a piece of stone. She is especially appeased during Holi and failing which people would face bad thing in the village, known as *dath parna*. She is also worshipped on every Saturday and Tuesday. She is regarded as the Sister of Mata Danteshwari–the tutelary deity of Bastar king.

**(iii) Jaliniburi mata:** She is represented at village *matagudi* with unhewn stones, ritual officiated by village priest (from Bhatra community), she is appeased for Cholera, Pox, dysentery and vomiting etc. During Fagun she is worshipped by all the villagers community especially on every Tuesday and Saturday of the week.

**(iv) Dongar deo:** He is also situated in the outskirt of the village. He is a male deity, appeased once in a year by buffalo sacrifice. The ritual is officiated by village Bhatra pujari for protection of village from any outside hazards.

**(v) Dand deo:** He is a male deity. He is appeased by village *sirha* (sorceror) who is from Raja Muria. He is a malevolent deity. He is appeased in order to have protected from malevolent spirit. All the villagers take part in this ritual.

### (B) Machkot Village

**(i) Pardeshin mata:** She is presided at village *matagudi*, represented by small terracotta icon. She is worshipped for welfare in family. Before eating of any new seasonal fruits/cereals firstly she is appeased like, during *amakhani* ritual (first eating of mango in a season). In each Wednesday and Saturday she is worshipped by Dhurwa pujari/ perma with incense and cocoanut. Apart from this she is worshipped with éclat during brighter half of the Chait month. She is also worshipped during *noakhani/nayakhani* in the month of *bhado* by village *sirha* (sorceror). All the villagers participate in it.

**(ii) Telangin mata:** She is a very ferocious and angry deity, represented by throny seat with iron nails in the village matagudi. Before harvesting of paddy she is appeased on behalf of village by Dhurwa *pujari/perma* by sacrificing egg at *matagudi,* which is known as *pit kutani,* only after paddy harvest is started by villagers. She protects from the evil eye during harvesting.

**(iii) Bhairam devi:** She is worshipped for the welfare of cattle and to save village from fever and appeased by *sirha* of tiger or nag clan. Stone represents her.

**(iv) Bhandarin mata:** She is represented by a khuta of wood equivalent to the horn of a wild buffalo, officiated by *pujari* and rituals performed for a cluster of neighbouring villages for welfare in family.

**(v) Maoli mata:** Represented by small terracotta icon, officiated by Dhurwa pujari, worshipped for welfare in family and for cattle and also considered as sister of Danteshwari ma or Hinglajin mata. In Gondi she is called as *yagal muttey.*

**(vi) Ganesh Puja:** It is a recent induction in the village, officiated by Brahmin priest of Jagadalpur in the month of Bhado. This puja continues for nine days where all the villagers subscribe for the ritual. During this puja Hindi songs are played through loudspeaker.

### (C) Nagarnar Village

The village shrine or *matagudi* is presided by *Jalini Mata, Pardeshin Mata* who is chiefly worshipped during Fagun (Feb-Mar) and Landi (May-June) communally by village Bhatra priest (Name–Aito Baghel). There is also a *bhima khuta* (rain deity) in the village, officiated also by a Bhatra priest for good rain. This ritual is performed sometimes from Chait (March-April) to Landi (May-June). *Bhandarin Mata* and *Telangin Mata* are worshipped by Bhatra pujari (Name–Nilo Baghel of this village) during Kuar (Sept-Oct.). Unhewn stone represents all these deities. Another *Mata,* living goddess, named *Kankalin Mata* is appeased by a different Bhatra *pujari* (Name–Somia Baghel) during Magh (Jan-Feb). The purpose of this ritual is thanks giving ritual for good harvest who is equally considered by them as *Danteshwari mata.* It is also a communal ritual in the village where all the villagers voluntarily contribute for such ritual. Apart from this, a few household in the village practised *Lakshmi Jagar* ritual during Pous (Dec-Jan). Though it is an individual family level worship, but all the villagers participate in it. The priest is Brahman in this ritual. Case history reveals that this ritual is performed at Bhatra family last during 2002 in this village.

### (D) Pandripani Village

Some tribal household of this village, namely, Bhatra and Halba, have *tulsitala* (Basil plant) in the courtyard. According to the Hindu mythology *tulsi* is equivalent to Narayan and these tribal people (only male) wears *Kanthi* garland in the neck. Pujari is from Dhakar and Muria tribe of the village.

There are following *matas* in the village who are appeased time to time by *pujari* and where all the villagers both Hindu caste group and tribal jointly participate and perform their respective role for happiness and welfare of their village, cattle, crops and family.

At Hazariguda Para of the village there is a seat for *mata* who is especially appeased during Holi (i.e., in the month of Fagun) and Goncha (cart) festival by Muria *pujari* in order to save themselves form pox. It is performed communally where all the villagers contribute. An anthropomorphic icon represents her.

At Maoliguda *para* of the village there is a place for *Maolimata* who is represented by unhewn stone, she is regularly appeased on Saturday and Tuesday by Dhakar priest. She is also considered as the sister of *Danteshwari mata*. During Holi in the month of Fagun she is specially appeased communally by collecting contribution from the villagers, otherwise her wrath will be harmful for them.

The *Banshbhundi Mata* is situated at the entrance of main road, near *damor* factory and on the western outskirt of the village. Unhewn stone represents her. All the villagers communally perform her ritual by collecting contributions twice in a year and her ritual is officiated by Dhakar (cultivating caste) priest. First she is appeased during Goncha/Ashar month in the lighter half for good rain and secondly, she is worshipped during the lighter half of the Pus month for the welfare of their cattle. On the same day they also perform *Diari* festival of the village. Along with this ritual on the same day at Karehkote para of the village Boriyadi Mata is appeased communally which is also officiated by Dhakar priest. She is also represented by an unhewn stone.

They also appease *Hinghlaji Mata* communally for peace and welfare of the village during Fagun (Feb-Mar). It is continued for three days and officiated by both Muria (ST) and Dhakar pujari of the village. Pig, cock and goat are offered in this ritual for sacrifice. Muria (ST) sacrifices pig while goat are sacrificed by Halba (ST). During this ritual all the neighbouring village deities are invited since all these *Matas* are genealogically related in their celestial world.

They also perform worship of *Bhima-Bhimul Khutha* for good rain by the Muria (ST) tribe communally in the village. She is appeased by *pujari* twice in a year that is during Holi in the month of Fagun and during *Goncha* (cart) festival in the month of Goncha (June-July). The seat of this benevolent deity is at Hazariguda para of the village.

Besides these, in each and every shrine of village *matagudi* there is an open space for *Dand deo*, whose wrath is harmful for village. He is also appeased with the help of *pujari* of the village.

The villagers also have faith and perform *Lakshmi Jagar* in the month of Aghan to Pus. This ritual is continued for a month and officiated by Muria (ST) and Dhakar priests. Though it is performed at family level yet all the villagers participate and take active part in it. Once this ritual is performed in the family, it is then obligatory for such family to continue it for two more years. This ritual is a symbol of prosperity among them and is widely accepted by both Hindu and tribal neighbours of the village.

The seat of *Pardeshin Mata* is also at Hazariguda para along with *Mata*. She is specially worshiped during harvesting, *amakhani* and *nayakhani* ritual by Muria (ST) *pujari*.

## Conglomeration of Mata Cult Network and Impact

There are mainly two kinds of religious organisations found in human societies. In primitive and archaic societies, religion is a different phenomenon; many forms of human association from the family to the work group, have in some important respects a religious character. In these societies, religion is one aspect of the life of all social groups. However, religious and magical specialists appear early in societal development and religious individualism may be found in contemporary non-literate societies (o'dea, 1969).

Religious institutions evolve as patterns of worship, that is, as cult; they evolve at the same time as patterns of ideas and definitions, that is, as beliefs; and they emerge as forms of association or organisation. The cult has a mysterious value, that we cannot fully rationalise (Mead, 1934, p. 296). The relationships acted out in the cult are first of all relationships with the sacred object.

In each and every villages of Bastar there are a number of *matas* (or a kind of Mother goddess cult) who are appeased from time to time for welfare and blessings, their wrath may usher in a troublesome life. The seats of these *matas* are in village shrine and some of those *matas* are already discussed in the preceding pages. Incidentally these *matas* are genealogically related to each other in their celestial belief system that again have some consanguineal or affinal relations with the supreme deity of Bastar–the *Danteshwari mata,* the tutelary deity of Bastar king/royal family.

The whole concept of various *matas* as found in different villages of Bastar centers around the principle mother cult, *Danteshwari,* acts as a centripetal force. During *Dussehra* festival we have observed the centripetal nature of the worship of the mother cult since all the individual village deities are brought in to Jagadalpur town for propitiation centering around *Danteshwari mata.* The forces of decentralisation of all these individual deities take place soon after the *Dushera* festival when these individual deities return to their respective villages after performing *bidai* or *gangamunda yatra* ritual at Gangamunda ward of Jagadalpur town.

The whole idea of centripetal nature of religious beliefs percolates in all strata of the society where the tribal and non-tribal ways of life form a bond of synthesis, at least in their religious world-view and socio-economic understanding of life. This impact is strongly evident in the life and culture of the people of Bastar at large even to this day though it might have crystallised during the reign of feudatory chiefs, who ruled Bastar till the recent past.

## References

Chandra, Ramesh, 1981. "Ecology and Religion of the Kinner", in the Nature-Man Spirit Complex in Tribal India, (ed) R. S. Mann, New Delhi: Concept Publishing Co.

Milton, Kay (Ed), 1993. Environmentalism: The View from Anthropology, London: Routledge.

O'dea, Thomas F., 1969. The Sociology of Religion, New Delhi: Prentice Hall of India Pvt. Ltd.

Sarkar, Amitabha and Samira Dasgupta, 1996. Spectrum of Tribal Bastar, Delhi; Agam Kala Prakashan.

Sunder, Nandini 2001. "Religion and Culture in Bastar: The Politics of Conversion", in the Eastern Anthropologist, Vol. 53, No. 3-4.

Titiev, Mischa, 1955. The Science of Man: An Introduction to Anthropology, New York; Henry Holt and Co.

# 15

# Cultural Synthesis

## Prologue

Dusshera in Bastar is devoted entirely to the goddess–*Devi Danteshwari*. The most important festival in Bastar is the Dusshera when local deities from all Parganas and villages are invited and they gather at the temple premises of Danteshwari in Jagdalpur–the district headquarter. The Dusshera in Bastar, unlike Dusshera in other parts of India, has nothing to do with the triumphant return of Rama to Ayodhya. The mother cult–*Danteshwari* acts like a centripetal force where both Hindu and tribals are roaming from apex to center. It has tremendous attractive force, which one can realise through *empathy;* they think that if *Danteshwari* is not appeased, people of the State will become restless, starved and ill. Because of the the subalterns of Bastar worshipped her. She is the supreme in the heavenly world of Bastar people. Her dictum is final and she controls her subalterns through the dreams of chief priest as the position of king is simply obligatory now.

## Mata Danteshwari being an element of Cultural Syncretism

The Bastar (undivided) district of Chhattishgarh is a tribal habitat with forest-clad environment. More than 75 per cent population are tribal and they are chiefly Muria, Abujh Marias, Bhatra, Halba, Dandami Maria (or Bison-Horn Marai), Dorla, Dhurwa and there are a few pockets of Gadaba along the bordering Orissa belt. These tribal people are distributed sporadically in the district of which Abujh Maria are confined in North-western part, Dandami Maria are in South-central that is in Dantewada region while Muria are in north and north-west, Dorla are in southern part, that is, Konta region and western Bijapur area, Dhurwa are in south-eastern part of Kanger valley, Bhatra are confined in Indrawati plain in northern Jagadalpur while Halba are sparsely distributed in north and south Bastar. All these tribal groups are endogamous in nature and possess theirown belief systems, which are different from eachother and in this way ethnic boundary is maintained. Apart from these there are sizeable populations of immigrants who are chiefly business community from Gujarat, Rajasthan, U. P., there are also Govt. employees and some pockets are dominated by Bengali refugee settlements rehabilitated by the government in various pockets of the district after the partition.

### Bastar Dussehra Festival–The Process of Assimilation and Integration

Bastar Dusshera is something unique. It is one of the chief festivals of Bastar, originally patronised by the Royal family. The Dusshera in Bastar, unlike Dusshera in other parts of India, has nothing to do with the triumphant return of Rama to Ayodhya. Dusshera in Bastar is devoted entirely to the goddess–*Devi Danteshwari*. Bastar Dusshera has several components each with a history of its own in which specific division of labour among the various ethnic groups of the district or subalterns of the state is highly marked. Dusshera in Bastar is an occasion to propitiate the supreme goddess–'*Danteshwari mata*' of the local pantheon. It is also reported from old inhabitants of Jagdalpur town that in early days during the regime of Late, Pravir Chandra Bhanjdeo, on the eve of this occasion the village/*pargana* headman and other office bearers and the feudal chiefs, the local diviners, shamans, priests (*pujari* or *gaita*), sorceror (*wadde)* etc. used to attend the function at Jagdalpur along with the respective village deities (i.e., either carrying the umbrella or *chhata* or *lathi* of the deities), carried in litters. Tribals from distant villages used to stay in the neighbouring forested area and within the open space of the town during these festival period, which continues for about 15 days.

It is also reported that Dusshera and circumambulation of *rath* or chariot was started during the regime of *Raja Purushottam Deo*–the one of the king of Bastar *during 1468–1534*. The Dusshera is intricately inter related with a number of villages and *parganas* with various ethnic groups. In Bastar Dusshera, this festival is usually started on

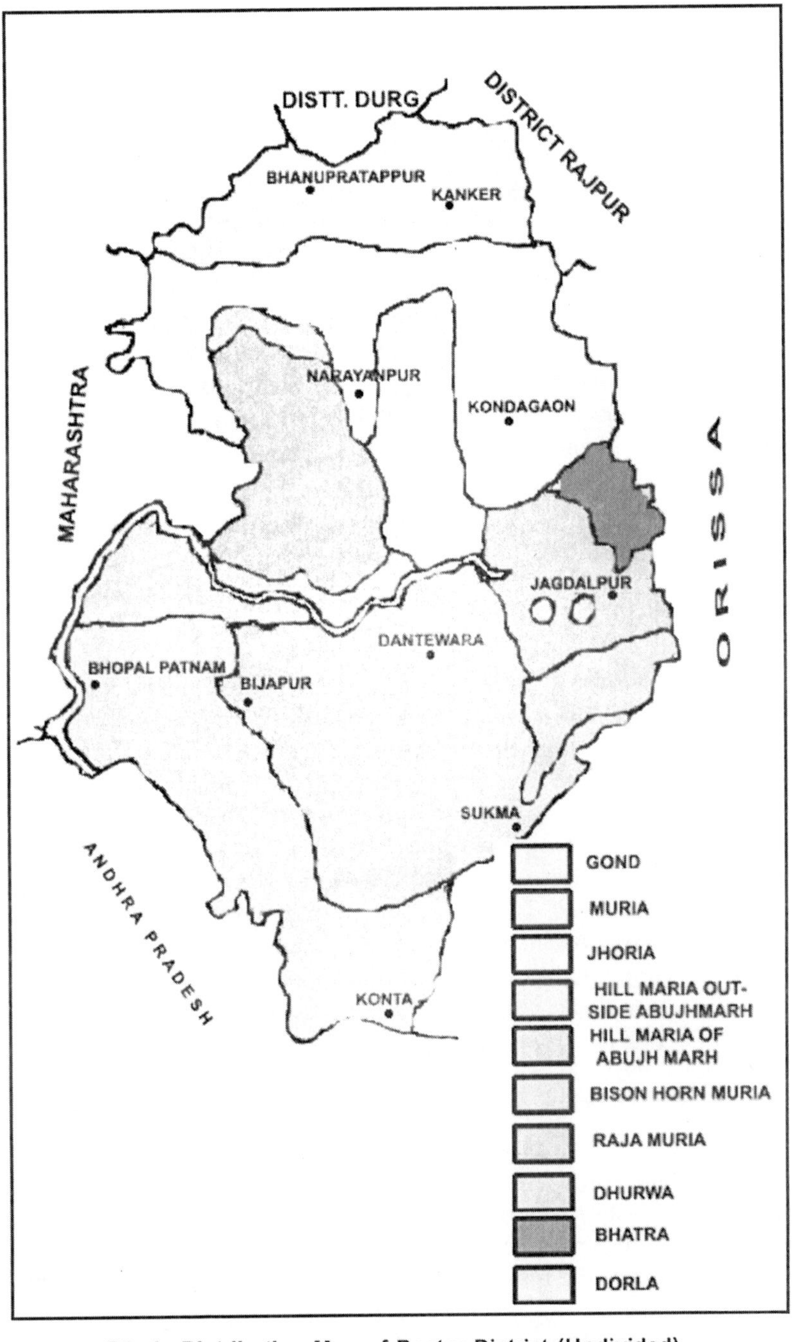


Ethnic Distribution Map of Bastar District (Undivided)

the day of *kumb* or new moon of the month Saon (July-Aug. ). On the same day the villagers also perform *Amush* or *Hariali.* From that day they start to bring wood for the construction of eight/four wheeled *rath.* On that day they worship the *pata* wood (the main support of chariot) before Danteshwari temple. The construction of base of chariot is initiated by ritual *magar muhi* when wooden support is provided to the base. Blacksmith of Pandripani and Tekamera villages and Agarias does the fixing of wooden joints with iron nails. Before construction of chariot they perform a ritual–*barsi utarni* when they worship the tools and equipments used for construction of the chariot. A goat is sacrificed and liquor, bangles, camphor, incense sticks, cocoanut are offered. After the construction of chariot wheels are over and before the holes are perforated *nar phodani* ritual is performed and offerings are similar to *barsi utarni.*

There is an intricate division of labour in making *rath. Raini rath* (or *vijay rath*) is eight wheeled while the *phool rath* is the smaller or four-wheeled chariot. The overall responsibility of the construction of chariot is traditionally vested in the "Savara Naiks" of the village 'Bera umargaon' and 'Jhar umargaon' of Bakawand block of Jagdalpur. The ethnic groups involved in this construction work are Bhatra (ST), Saora (ST) and Raut; and they are altogether 177 in number and Dalpati Naik is *mukhia* of this group who hails from Saora community. It is also reported that there are a few Agaria who are traditionally iron smelters and provides nails for these work and Bhatra and Dhurwa are engaged in making rope for pulling the *rath.* The wood for various parts of the *rath* are supplied from various villages of Bastar and it is estimated that in this work about 75-80 villages as well as villagers are directly involved. There are some important pieces of wood used in *rath* construction, namely *pata wood, magar muhi, acchanda diwas, golasarai, kaichi*wood–cross beam (for support), *khamba* wood (wood from base to top), *dhaman* wood (for *rath* top), *kami sarai, tarla patta* (for roof purpose), and *parla whokana.* It is also observed that the size of *raini-rath* is about 30 to 32 feet long, 18 feet wide and 18 feet tall while the size of *phool rath* is about 32 feet long, 17 feet wide and 17 feet tall.

It has been also observed that only one chariot is constructed yearly. In one year they construct the *raini rath* and the next year they construct the *phool rath.* After the chariot is constructed, the villagers of Mograpal decorate the chariot and it is known as *rath singarni.* At the beginning of the movement of chariot they perform a ritual–*rath-rengani.*

Next phase of the ritual is to take permission from *Kachan Devi* to celebrate Dusshera festival. It is a swing in the *'kachan gudi'*–the abode of the deity at Pathraguda of Jagdalpur town. The seat of the swing is made of thorns of *'bel'* tree. They perform the ritual on the new moon day of the month Aswin (Sept.-Oct) i.e. on the day of *pitrapaksha* or *mahalaya*. On this day both *Kachan devi* and *Raila Devi*–the most revered deities of both Panika (weaver caste) and Mahara (untouchable caste) communities are appeased. They believe that *Kachan devi* protects their wealth. As per their legend Kachan devi and Raila devi are two sisters and Raila is the younger one who married outside in a community of lower in hierarchic ladder and thus was disowned by her family as a daughter. Perhaps during that time Mahara and Mirgan accepted her as their deity when her elder sister is also worshipped. In fact with the blessing of Kachan devi Raja Vir Narayan Deo's(1639–54) wife gave birth to a daughter. The *Kachan gudi* ritual is officiated by Panika priest since time immemorial while the priest of "Raila Devi" belongs to Mirgan jati–Harijan community. On this occasion they select a virgin of Panika caste who becomes possessed by the deity–*Kachan*. During field investigation it is observed that the duty of virgin girl is performed by Kunti Baghel, Panika Caste, Age–8 and student of class-IV; for the last 4 days she is maintaining fasting. The priest -Sukul Das, Age-40, hails from Manikpuri Panika caste of Rajen ward, Jagdalpur. On this occasion *'gurumaya'*–the two women of Panika caste play on *dhankul*–a musical instrument (a bow with string) to invoke the deities. The virgin becomes possessed and moves round the swing for three times along with sorcerer and *Bhairam dev* and then she is seated on the swing and gives permission to celebrate Dusshera festival. Previosly Raja used to come to take such permission now the same tradition is also followed and present Raja accompanied by chief priest–Laloo Pujari and other dignitaries of *rajparibar* approach the swing and their journey route is cleared of all sorts of malevolent spirits by *Angadeo*, often it is also known as *Pat deo*, who is carried on the shoulder of four persons who are at that time possessed and they are also Panika and Dhakar by caste.

Next day after *Kachan gudi* that is, on the first day of the lighter half of the month Aswin (Sept-Oct) they perform the ritual *Kalash Sthapana* or place of brass tumbler in the interior of temple premises of *Danteshwari mata* filled with paddy grain. On the event 36 figurines of *Durga Devi* are made of silver, one nail like structure made of gold and the materials of offerings are given to the priest to start the ceremony. Twenty-eight Brahman priests are invited to perform the rituals associated with *kalash sthapana*. Fourteen of them recite the holy book Chandi and the other fourteen recite Saptapadi. It continues throughout the days and nights of *Navaratri*.

In the evening of the same day *Jogi bithai* ceremony is performed at Sirasar Chawk Bhawan–adjacent to Palace of Jagadalpur town. According to myth when the king–Annam Deo left Warangal for Bastar, the Jogi of Halba community followed him and behind them *Mata Danteshari* too. As per the dictum of the king one married man from Jogi of Halba caste keeps *sanjam* during Dusshera for remaining 7 days at a stretch. There is a pit in Sirasar Bhawan. The Jogi sits in the pit in the prescribed posture. All these days he keeps fast on behalf of Royal family and feeds on small quantity of milk. At the time of "*uthai*" or end of ritual, they are given cash along with goat, liquor etc. During present field investigation Jogi came from Bade Amabal village name–Bhagat Sinh, Nag bash, age-25. On that day from the temple premises of palace Jogi comes with procession of *manjhi* (red turban), *chalki* (red turban), *member manjhi* (blue turban), *mundabaja* (beating of small drums by Munda community) along with chief priest–Laloo pujari and before coming to Sirasar Bhawan, he visits *Maoli/Mavli mata* temple for blessings. A Kalash or brass tumbler and sword of the king are kept beside Jogi. The rituals are performed throughout the day and on the 9th day and on the day of Mavli Parghav the Jogi breaks his *sanjam* (Self-restraint) and leaves his seat from the pit.

On the next day after *Jogi bithai* ritual the *phool rath* is drawn and during this period *navaratri puja* is performed every day for nine days. After the holy recital by the priest in the *Danteshwari* temple at Jagdalpur and the emblem of the deity is placed on the *phool rath*. Then the chariot is drawn from Sirasar Chowk in a procession round the *Mavli Mandir* (considered as sister of *Danteshwari mata* and infact she is the tutelary deity of Royal family; it is reported that when Annam Deo fled from Warangal, he fled along with their tutelary deity whose position in Bastar is considered as sister of *Danteshwari mata*) and finally up to the *Singh Dyodhi* of *Danteshawri* temple. During circumambulation some persons continuously keep fanning the deity with *chavar/chamar* (whisk). The *rath* is drawn for five days and about 800-1000 people of about 30-35 neighbouring villages are assigned to pull the *rath* during these days (Sarkar and Dasgupta, 1996).

On the fourth day of the lighter half of the month Aswin (Sept-Oct) the *magarmuhi charani* ritual is performed. After the completion of construction of new *rath* (chariot) when new wooden wheels are inserted this ritual is performed with the sacrifice of a goat and two hens and labourers engaged in this work are from 'Bera Umargaon' and Jharumargaon of Bakawand block which has already been mentioned earlier. This ritual is important because in it the rope is tied for pulling the *rath* for circumambulation.

Next important ritual is *Nisha Yatra*. It is performed on the 8th midnight of *Navaratri'*. During the night at about 11.30 p.m. to 12.00 midnight they perform *Nisha Yatra* (*nisha* means night and *yatra* means sacrifice). On this event they prepare rice, pulses and milk porridge at the Mavli mandir and at midnight those are carried in earthen vessel by Dhakar, Halba (ST) and Bhatra (ST) in a procession to *Khemeshwar devi* temple followed by Bhatra men carrying the earthen lamps known as *mal diya* lighted by oil of the bark of *char* tree. The lamp bearers carry on their shoulders the lamps that are arranged in a series of wooden frame. At the *Khemeshwar devi* temple *bhog* ceremony is performed by present Raja, Raj Guru and Chief Priest and goats are sacrificed by *pharsa* (*tangi* or axe). Raja Muria (ST), known as *jalal* of Bhatpal village, does thesacrifice. It is also learnt that this ritual is performed to appease their ancestors and *Khemeshwar* temple is regarded as thevillage guard deity.

After the ritual at *Khemeshar* temple is over the procession returns to *Mavli* temple, goats are also sacrificed there. There after goats are also sacrificed at *Danteshwari* Mandir. In *Danteshwar*i temple a pumpkin is also offered now, which is a symbolic offering for a buffalo in early days.

On the 9th day they perform *Kumari puja* in the Danteshwari temple. On this occasion nine virgins and one bachelor all less than 10 years old are worshipped. They are given *saris* and *dhoti* respectively. The bachelor is regarded as *Bhairam deo*. He seats separately in front of the virgins (*Kumaris*). On the same day Jogi leaves his seat. This ritual is the forerunner of *Mavli Parghav* (i.e. reception of *Danteshwari* of Dantewada) in the evening on this day. On this auspicious day the invited deities from various places of Bastar reach at Jagadalpur and it is represented in the form of *doli* (palanquin), *lat* (stick) and *chatter* (umbrella) etc. of the deities which are brought from the villages. The main deities are *Danteshwari mata* of Chhote Dongar of Naryanpur and Bade Dongar of Naryanpur tehsil. These two are the special invitees on this occasion. Formal invitations are sent to them in the form of cash Rs 5.00 each and one goat each and cocoanut, camphor, incense, bangles, vermilion etc. The priest of the two deities along with their companions also come to Jagdalpur on the day of *Mavli Parghav* and participate in the ritual procession (Sarkar and Dasgupta, 1996). Besides this, others gods and deities of various villages and *parganas* also participate viz. *Chepra guddanMata* from Asana village, *Mavli Mata* from Madpal village, *Chorni Mata* from Morath Pal village, *Shitala Mata* from KankaPal, *Pardeshin Mata* from NengaRas, *Badi Mata* from Nalpawand, *Ganga dei* from Parwa, *Hingla Dei Mata* from Bakawand etc.

In the evening of 9th day of *Navaratri* or *nabami* the *Mavli Parghav* ritual is held. On the first day of *navaratri* the Rajguru sends invitation through a *majhi* to *Danteshwari* of Dantewada. Invitation are sent with Rs 101.00, a piece of towel, cloth, one cocoanut, incense, camphor, bangles, hair pins, bindi and red *tikli* (used in the forehead by a Hindu married girl) as a mark of homage to her. After that on the 9th day the 'palanquin' and *chhatra* of *Danteshwari mata* of Dantewada along with her some ornaments are brought to Jagdalpur with procession and are placed at *'Jiya Dera'*. The *chhatra* of Jagdalpur of *Danteshwari mata* is also brought to *jiya dera* and placed there in the company of *chhatra* of *Danteshwari* of Dantewada. In earlier days the Raja of Bastar used to go to receive the palanquin and *chhatra* of *Danteshwari* on this occasion. Now Rajguru, chief priest receives her along with District Administration. The people of Jagdalpur receive her in a big procession. They light lamps, burn cracker, dance, and play and sing song. The Bison-Horn Maria or Dandami Maria come in groups with traditional attire and dance with the rhythm of *mandal* and *nagera*. After receiving the *chhata/chhatra*, the chief priest (Laloo Pujari–Aryanak Brahman) brings it to the temple of *Danteshwari Māta* at Jagadalpur. At temple a goat is sacrificed then and *prasad* is distributed.

On the tenth day they perform *Bhitar Raini* when eight wheeled chariot–*Raini Rath* is drawn. Since this chariot is moved for the first time on the tenth day, the offerings are given before its movements and goats are sacrificed. During the afternoon the chief priest sits holding the *chhatra* (umbrella) of *Danteshwari* of Dantewada ceremonially placed on the *Raini Rath*. Previously the king played this role. Offering of *mogra* fish is made before the start of the movement of *rath*. The *Raini Rath* is drawn by Dandami Maria of Kilepal village area and this practice is continuing since time immemorial. In *Bhitar Raini* the chariot is drawn from Sirasar Bhawan taken round the *Mavli mandir* in circumambulation like *Phool Rath* and is taken to *'Singh Dyodi'* (main gate of palace). At this place the *chhatra* is taken down from the *rath* and kept at *Danteshwari* temple of Jagdalpur. Then some rituals are performed before the *rath* by some married women who sprinkle mustard seed and salt to protect it from evil eyes. On the same day at night the chariot–*Raini Rath* is ceremonially stolen by the Bhatras (ST) who brings it to Kumbharakot.

The main ritual of *Bahar Raini* is performed at Kumbharakot on the 11th day of Dussehra festival. All the invited deities of various villages and *parganas* along with the villagers are assembled at Kumbharakot from early morning. On this day Raja used to partake the food at Kumbharakot prepared from newly harvested crop. This ritual known as *Nayakhani.* Now a days, this ritual is attended by present Raja (symbolically because he has no authority, power, etc. ) with Rajguru and chief priest. Some sacrifices (goat and pumpkin) are also made there. A thatched hut on the bamboo pole is prepared; it is almost closed with single circular opening known as *Rani Mancha.* It is learnt that in early days *Rani* (queen) witnessed all the ritual activities at Kumbharakot sated on this *Rani Mancha* through the circular opening and villagers of Karanpur is entrusted traditionally with the construction of *Rani Mancha.* Now-a-days construction of such hut is simply a ritual behaviour among them. On that day Dhakar and Panika communities worship *Kachan devil,* made goat sacrifice in view of protection from infectitious diseases. In the evening of the same day the *rath* is drawn back by Dandami Maria with a large procession where present Raja stands on a jeep under the ceremonial umbrella of his kingdom.

On the 12th day of the ceremony of *Kachan Yatra* is performed at *Kachangadi*. On this event goat, pig and cocks are sacrificed and the same virgin girl who was seated on the swing made of thorns of 'bel' tree is brought and given cash and new clothes. Thus the ceremony ends with a belief that with this ritualistic performance the girl becomes free from her possessed state.

On the evening of the 12th day the next event of *Dussehra* festival is *Muria Darbar* which is an annual feature of Dussehra function since 1906 (Sundar, 1997) at Sirasar Bhawan. It is told that "it was started with the intention of training the king in administration and what we would today call 'communication skills'. It is an occasion when the adivasis of Bastar are told of noble intention of the state, exhorted to conserve forests and engage in improved agricultural practices. It is a moment for the profession and rewarding of loyalty and even for the voicing of those minor notes of dissent that are permissible within the structures of official patronage". (Sundar, 1997).

During *Manjhi Darbar* or *Muria Darbar* customarily the King sits on the dais with the *pargana manjhi* (headman of cluster of villages, hereditary post; wearing red turban with black coat), *Naik, Chalki* (he is assistant to *manjhi*, hereditary post *Chalki* wears blue turban while

*Naik* wears yellow turban and he is supposed to receive the *chata* or umbrella of Danteshwari of Dantewada ), *Munda baja* (hereditary post of a community and wearing pink turban) *Member/Memberin, Kotwar* and *Sarpanch, Patel, Mukhiya* (these posts are government posts and are selected through election) etc. to.discuss and solve their problem and their request were also taken care of. Now-a-days instead of King the dais is chaired by (during 2004 Dussehra) Chairman of Dussehra Committee, Minister and MLA of Chhattisgarh, Collector of Bastar district and Executive Officer of Panchayat (a woman). It is essentially an assembly of *Manjhi, Chalki* and *Member* where they are allowed freely to express their demand, problem of their area before this *Darbar* (assembly) where administrators and policy makers are also present and it becomes a direct interaction with state officials. Due to pressence of *Manjhi*, often this Darbar is known as *Manjhi Darbar.*

It has been observed during *Muria Darbar* on 25.10.2004 at 2.30 p.m. that *Manjhi*'s expresses their grievance and demand before the district and state authority:

*Case 1:* Tulsiram Pujari, Age-56, *Manjhi* Chotedongar Pargana, Muria (ST), he expresses his dissatisfaction about village roads, deforestation etc.

*Case 2:* Sadasiv Thakur, *Manjhi*, Hamirgarh Pargana, Age-55, Caste–Dhakar, he is demanding Rs 1000 per month being remuneration for carrying out the duty of *Manjhi.* Till date they have not received any such amount from administration. Chief Minister assured them through the officials of State on the dais that from now onwards State administration will incur Rs 500 and Rs 300 p.m. to *Manjhi* and *Chalki* respectively.

*Case 3:* Koram Kaunreya, Age-52, *Manjhi* Goalkunda Pargana of Bhopalpatnam, Dorla Gond (ST).

He resent about unemployment in the area and due to which young generation are inclined towards Naxalite activities.

*Case 4:* Lakhindar, Age-65, *Manjhi* Chitapur Pargana of Jagdalpur Tehsil, Bhatra (ST).

He expresses his satisfaction that due to good yield in this year with the blessing of *Danteshwari mata* the number of crowd is more and earlier it happened during 1965.

From the above discussion it is clearly revealed that right from the days of Maharajas, the system of political organisation in Bastar has been a very interesting one. The rulers, who were also the chief priest of the goddess *Danteshwari*, were regarded as the political heads. The hierarchical authority is as follows–Diwan, Pargana Manjhi, Panchayat, Manjhi-Mukhiya-Member and Memberin. At every level an official enjoys its authority and sustenance directly from the one above it (Das, 1974). Therefore, from the top of power structure–*Maharaja* to the village grass root level with the help of the institution of *Manjhi*, the political network and authority was well interconnected and firmly established. This helped Maharaja to unite its subalterns who are even of various ethnic groups.

On the 13th day they perform *Ganga Munda Yatra*. This is held in Ganga Munda tank of Jagdalpur. This ritual is also known as *Kutumba yatra*. All the invited gods and deities brought from various villages assemble at this place for collective farewell through community sacrifices of goat, pigeon, chicken, egg (fertilised) etc. With the performance of some ritual, they offer some money to the persons who have brought the invited deities and then the deities return to their respective villages.

On 15th day *Danteshwari* of Dantewada is given a farewell and it is the final ritual of Dussehra function. Her palanquin, *chhatra* and escorts return to Dantewada. In her farewell she is offered rice, wheat, flour, pulses, sugar, jaggery, ghee, mustard oil, lamp oil, chilies, three saris with silver embroidery, cocoanut, dhoti, goat, incense, camphor, cash, vermilion, bangles, mirror, comb, ribbon, hair pin and shawls etc.

Thus, Dussehra is the ritual, which brings the tribal and non-tribal Hindus, irrespective of their caste/ethnic boundary and status, close to each other, and it binds all of them by a single thread (Sarkar and Dasgupta, 1996).

### *Associated Ritual Component of Bastar Dussehra and Involvement of Ethnic Communities/Villages*

| *Ritual Components* | *Communities / villages involved* |
|---|---|
| (i) Barsi Utrani | Bhatra (ST), Saora (ST), Raut, Agaria |
| (ii) Nar Phodan | - do - |
| (iii) Rath Construction | - do - |

*contd. . .*

*contd. . .*

| *Ritual Components* | *Communities / villages involved* |
|---|---|
| (iv) For bringing of various pieces of wood for rath construction : | Name of the villages involved: |
| (a) Pata wood | Ulnar, Talnar, Chitaloor, Nangur, Billori, Madmoor, Nagarnar, Sadgud. |
| (b) Magar Muhi | Pandripani, Bade Marenga, Bade Morathpal, Lendra, Rajur |
| (c) Acchanda Diwas | Kurundi, Dhanaloor |
| (d) Gola Sarai | Khutapar, Baniagaon, Belgaon, Mejpadar, Dhanpunji, Chokawada, Maganpur, Bahmni, Amaguda, Jirgaon, Khumli, Markel, Kopaganda, Chote Kawali, Chilkuri, Bademurma, Jamawada, Keshapur, Phurapal, Magnar, Neganar, Badepara, Telegarapur, Alanar, Merawada, Parpa,Duganpal. |
| (e) Kaichi wood(cross beam) | Erikpal, Koyapana, Sendwa, Chingpal, Arshkot. |
| (f) Khamba wood (wood for base to top) | Bringpal, Dimrapal, Khumar Marenga, Kilepal, Mahakapal, Kaknar, Chindbahar, Koyanar. |
| (g) Dhaman wood (for top of chariot) | Tondapal, Badebadam, Chizaukutti |
| (h) Kami Sarai | Keshloor, Badearapur, Rajkot, Netmoor, Telimarenga. |
| (i) Tarla patta (for roof purpose) | Birasguda, Badebadam, Kolabada, Bade Kawali, Parati. |
| (j) Parla whokana | Mavli Padar village. |
| (vi) Rath Singarni | Aryanak Brahman of orissa, Panera (Mali). |
| (vii) Rath Rengani | Aryanak Brahman, Dhakar, Bhatra (ST), Jogi. |
| (viii) Kachan Gadi/gudi | Panika, Dhakar, Aryanak Brahman along with Royal family. [It is also observed in this ritual that two aged women known as *gurumaya* play *dhankul* (a musical instrument which looks like a bow with a string)]. Dhankul signifies for wealth; it is also playing during Lakshmi Jagar ritual. This instrument may be symbolises for end of bow and arrow era which is full of uncertainity and entry of stable |

*contd. . .*

*contd. . .*

| *Ritual Components* | *Communities / villages involved* |
|---|---|
| | economic condition in view of practise of settled cultivation where food is secured.) |
| (ix) Raila Devi | Mahara, Mirgan, Aryanak Brahman along with Royal family. |
| (x) Kalash Sthapana | At the temple premises by 28 Brahmans. |
| (xi) Jogi bithai | Jogi of Halba (ST) caste, Aryanak Brahman, Munda (ST), Manjhi-Chalki (Bhatra Dhakar, Murias Dandami Maria, Abujh Maria etc.), Member Manjhi (of Munda, Bhatra, Dhurwa etc.) |
| (xii) Navaratri Puja<br>(a) Circumambulation of rath within town - for rath pulling | Brahman<br>Chiefly Dandami Maria for pulling rath, mundebaja (Munda) and others. |
| (xiii) Magarmuhi Charani | Lohar, Agaria |
| (xiv) Nisha Yatra | Royal family, Brahman, Dhakar, Bhatra, Raja Muria, Halba and others |
| (xv) Kumari Puja and Mavli Parghav (reception of Danteshwari mata of Dantewada) | Brahmans, Royal family, Dandami Maria, Rajguru and District administration. |
| (xvi) Bhitar Raini | Brahman, Dandami Maria, Bhatra. |
| (xvii) Bahar Raini | Raja, Rajguru, Brahman, Dandami Maria, Dhakar, Panika and villagers of Karanpur. |
| (xviii) Kachan Yatra | Panika, Dhakar. |
| (xix) Muria Darbar | Manjhi, Chalki, Member, Patel, District and State Administrator. |
| (xx) Kutumba Yatra/Gange Munda Yatra | All the invited deities are given farewell with the help of Brahman, Sirha (Sorceror) and leske (tribal priest). |
| (xxi) 'Bidai' (of Danteshwari mata) | Brahman, Dhakar, Dandami Maria. |

Bastar, in fact, had been a stronghold of Saivaism from time immemorial. This aspect was fully exploited by the founders of the Bastar dynasty who fled from Warangal with an idol of their tutelary family deity–Danteshwari/Maoli–an incarnation of Durga and installed it at Dantewada and also declaring himself as a chief priest of Danteshwari. By declaring themselves as the prime worshipper of Danteshwari, "the kings of Bastar could integrate the tribal population of Bastar with the State. As stated above, the animistic religion of Bastar had already possessed the 'mata cult' complex in different names shades and hues such as *Maoli mata, Bhandarin mata, Pardeshin Mata, Jaliniburi mata, Telangin Mata* etc. The cult of deities is inseparably woven with the cultural fabric of the tribal Bastar. The tribal social

**Contents of Dusshera Ritual -2004 of Bastar**

| *Days* | *Date* | *Time* | *Ritual Activities* |
|---|---|---|---|
| 1. | 13.10.04 | Evening | Kachan Gadi ritual |
| 2. | 14.10.04 | Morning | Kalash Sthapana |
| | | Evening | Jogi Bithai |
| 3-9. | 15.10.04 | Morning | Navratri Puja |
| | | Evening | Circumambulation of Phool Rath |
| 10. | 21.10.04 | Morning | Durga Asthami |
| | | Evening | Nisha Yatra |
| 11. | 22.10.04 | Morning | Kumari Puja |
| | | Evening | Jogi Uthai |
| | | Night | Mavli Parghav |
| 12. | 23.10.04 | Morning | Bhitar Raini ritual |
| | | Evening | Circumambulation of Raini Rath |
| 13. | 24.10.04 | Morning | Bahar Raini ritual at Kumbharakot |
| | | Evening | After Nayakhani ritual at Kumbharakot, the |
| | | | Chariot is pulled back to Palace. |
| 14. | 25.10.04 | Morning | Kachan Yatra |
| | | Evening | Muria Darbar/Manjhi Darbar |
| 15. | 26.10.04 | Morning | Kutumba Yatra |
| | | Evening | Farewell to invited village deities |
| 16. | 30.10.04 | Morning | Farewell to Danteshwari of Dantewada |

organisation is linked closely with the kinship organisation found among the deities–smaller villages are the seats of secondary and tertiary relatives of a more prominent deity who is housed in another village and becomes a nucleus of a bunch of villages. It can be illustrated in the following manner.

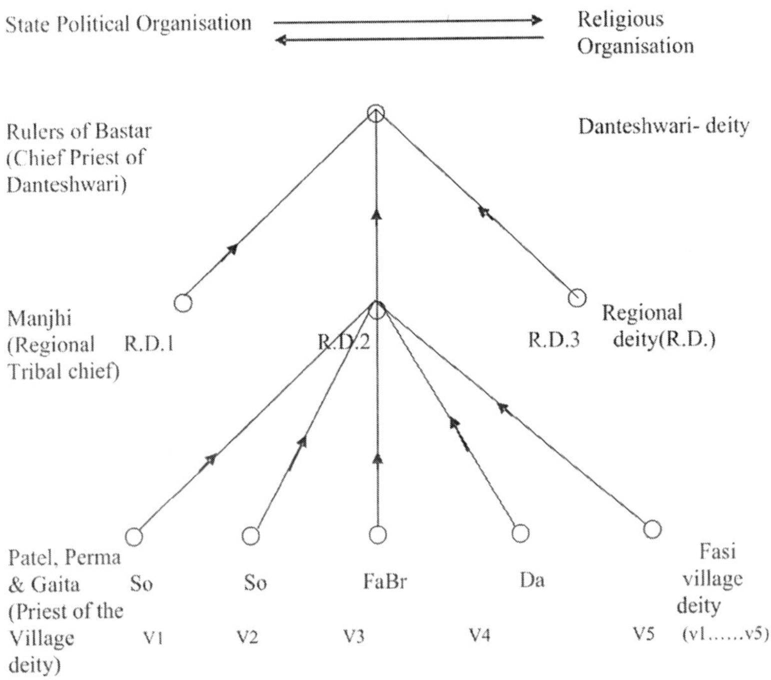


In the above illustration it has been shown that v1, v2, v3, v4,v5 are villages having their own deities who are related in turn with R. D. 2 which is regional deity and similarly R. D. 1 and R.D 3 are other regional deities forming separate cluster of villges. Each of the regional deities is the various manifestations of *Danteshwari mata.*

Looking at the process of State formation in Bastar it has been observed that by becoming the *purohit* or chief priest, the Rajput kings of Bastar carved out a religio-political niche for themselves to which they remained inseparably attached till the last king-cum-priest-Pravir Chandra Banjdeo was assassinated in 1965. The political control of the ex-rulers of Bastar ran more or less parallel with the religious organisation.

Dussehra festival on the other hand clearly signifies that it is an "integration rather than displacement of tribal elements in the development of 'nuclear areas' of sub-regional power. Ultimately, it was the fusion which helped legitimise rule in these areas. " (Sunder, 1997).

It can also be said from the empirical observation on Dussehra festival that within the agricultural mode of production, the Dussehra is an extension of the village *jatra* (sacrifice)–local festivals necessary to preserve fertility and avoid sickness. According to Dubey and Mohril (1961) *Kachan gudi* ritual is claimed to be a fertility ritual. To them, *Kachan* being an earth goddess associated with fertility and reproduction and song sung by the *gurumaya* women. According to Panika priest, a Panika sorceror helped a childless queen to conceive and in return she was asked to pray to *Kachan devi,* who is a symbol of prosperity.

The contextual, date also suggest that the king was seen as necessary to the performance of this Dussehra function for the interest of his kingdom. Induction of various role assigned to specific ethnic groups as participants and contributors to the Dussehra ceremonies, the Royal family simultaneously ensured their contribution in terms of revenue, administration and control even at grass root level for sustenance which makes them cohesive adaptation and adjustment and synthesis of cultural behaviour between two or more ethnic groups which ultimately lead towards harmonious environment in the region.

The annual ritual during Dussehra since 1906–the *'Muria Darbar'/ 'Manjhi Darbar'*–wherein the tribal or village chiefs (*Manjhi* or *Chalki*) are allowed freely to speak about their problems in the village regarding agricultural practices, land irrigation, forest and its resources, wages of labour, drinking water facility, induction of developmental activities in their area, and unemployment vis-à-vis rise of Naxalites etc. A kind of promise is assured from the ruler of Bastar who would do everything in his power to alleviate the sufferings of his subalterns.

This integrated system of political control remained intact till the death of the last ruler of Bastar in 1965 and after his death the system gradually collapsed, though present democratic set up government has not been able to maintain the same degree of cohesion between rulers and ruled as it existed earlier but Dussehra ritual being a kind of cohesive agent it functions as a *centripetal* force through which all the communities are integrated and as a result fusion of cultural behaviour as well as synthesis in religious arena has occurred. Dussehra of Bastar in other word may be termed as a meeting place for gods and goddess as well as of various ethnic groups on a larger scale. During the field investigation year (i.e. 2004) it is reported that altogether 79 *Parganas*/Villages gods and goddess who are in most cases genealogically related in their celestial world, were invited at Jagdalpur who were represented by a silver umbrella (*chatta*) or *lathi* etc. In this regard Sundar (2001) observed that the ritual division of labour between different groups for Dussehra parallels that of different lineages in the propitiation of village gods. The whole Dussehra ritual may be identified as a royal or political ritualistic activity, which acts as a cohesive agent of Bastar state. Here religious activities was shaped through the demands of state legitimacy or "in other words, how royal hegemony has been dependent on the appropriation of popular religion" (Sundar, 2001). It is also reported that the priest of all the temples of Jagdalpur were headed by non-Brahman or low caste and gradually within the past few years specially after independence these are replaced by Brahmans only.

## Conclusion

From the aforesaid discussion it is revealed that –

(i) the whole Dussehra ritual process is a kind of little tradition which became great tradition when in such ritual Brahman service is inducted and recitation of *Chandi* during *Navaratri* session and link the Danteshwari with *Devi Durga* of great tradition by also putting some arms and weapons in her hand which are typically vedic in nature.

(ii) Dussehra of Bastar is becoming sacred secular continuum.

(iii) The whole process of ritualistic behaviour is a kind of *cultural osmosis* where ethnic as well as religious boundary is not a decision making factor.

(iv) The mother cult–*Danteshwari* acts like a centripetal force where both Hindu and tribals are roaming from apex to center. It has tremendous attractive force, which one can realise through *empathy;* because in their mind if *Danteshwari* is not appeased, people of the State will become restless, starved, ill, so the subalterns of Bastar worship her. She is the supreme in the heavenly world of Bastar people. Her dictum is final and she controls her subalterns through the dreams of chief priest since now the position of king is simply obligatory.

(v) To our opinion the essence of Bastar Dussehra which is unique in the country and evolved as a way of consolidating political power (through *Manjhi, Chalki, Patel, Gaita* etc. ) using cultural and religious symbols through *Danteshwari Mata*. The various *matas* in different villages are directly or indirectly related with *Danteshwari* which clearly reflects the extent of political power of Raja (or King) to the grass root level.

(vi) The then king of Bastar intended to involve all the ethnic groups of his states and even villages in this festivities and thus a network of bondage was formed both at terrestrial and celestial level (i.e. through their deities in which they have a strong supernatural belief).

(vii) The political connotation of the festival is most evident towards the end. On the performance of *Muria Darbar* all tribal /parganas chiefs or *Manjhi* voice their grievances and problems at the *Darbar.* Earlier it was presided by the King but now-a-days it is done by District administration.

(viii) The influence of Chhattisgarhi language is very low among the studied groups of Bastar.

Thus, above picture clearly reflects that in the interest of political power various ethnic groups were assigned to perform certain specific and important role during Dussehra, which is still continuing and thereby assimilation as well as *synthesis of cultural traits* between two or more ethnic groups has occurred and which is certainly a product of acculturation.

Bastar Dussehra, is a clear signal towards *inclination of secularisation of culture.* Though people of Bastar are integrated through religious activities but due to apathetic attitude and negligence of government machinery for a practical developmental works in the remote forest areas, the young generation are becoming arrogant and hostile towards the administrative–political environment where they are not only marginalised but have no place for earning their bread.

**References**

Chapman, R. A. B., 1898. Political Agents Notes (unpublished manuscript in Jagdalpur, Record room, Bastar district, Chhattishgarh).

Cornford, Francis. 1957. From Religion to Philosophy, New York: Harper.

Dasgupta, Samira and Amitabha Sarkar, 2003. "A New Dimension on Social Organisation of Abujh Maria of Tribal Bastar: Communion between Celestial and Terrestrial Life", Journal of Indian Anthropological Society, Vol. 38, pp. 41-54.

Dasgupta, Samira and Amitabha Sarkar. 2005. Reflection of Ethno-science: Study on the Abujh Maria, New Delhi: Mittal Publication.

Glasfurd, C. L. R. 1862. Report on the Dependence Bastar, (Record room, Jagdalpur, Bastar district, Chhattishgarh).

Grigson, Sir Wilfred. 1991. The Maria Gonds of Bastar, Delhi: Oxford University Press and Nauya Prakashan (reprinted).

Jay, Edward J. 1968. A Tribal village of Middle India, Calcutta: Anthropological Survey of India, Memoir No. 21.

Jagdalpuri, Lala. 2000. Bastar Etihas ebong Sanskriti (in Hindi), Bhopal: Madhya Pradesh Hindi Grantha Academy.

Jagdalpuri, Lala. 2003. Bastar-Lok-Kala Sanskriti and Prasangha (in Hindi), Jagdalpur: Aakriti Sansthan.

O'dea, Thomas, F. 1969. The Sociology of Religion, New Delhi: Prentice -Hall of India, Private Limited.

Sarkar, Amitabha and Samira Dasgupta. 2010. Religion Belief and Practices: A portrayal of the integrative Process, New Delhi: Agam Kala Prakashan.

Sundar, Nandini. 2001. "Religion and Culture in Bastar: the Politics of Conversation," in Eastern Anthropologist, 53: 3-4.

Swami Ranganathanande. 2004. The Essence of Indian Culture, Kolkata: Advaita Ashrama.

Tylor, E. B. 1871. Primitive Culture, London, John Murry.

Watts, Neville, A. 1970. The Half-clad Tribals of Eastern India, New Delhi: Orient Longman.

# 16

# Anthropology of Art and Culture

Art is an emotional expression of tangible cultural attributes. The expression of feeling is the central function of art, dance, music etc. The artistic activities are chiefly cultural and it varies according to culture. In case of pyramidal type Kokna dance of Maharashtra and Gujarat or Worli (Gujarat and Maharashtra) painting or Saora (of Odisha) painting or body decoration and adornment by Jarwa (of A. and N. Islands) etc. all are very much value specific of particular cultures. The forms and styles of artistic expression vary from society to society. The artistic creation reflects the local environment—the materials and technologies that are available to a culture. "Creativity involves breaking out established pattern to look at things in a different way. . . . Creativity is the ability in man to bring something new into existence. It is closely linked with imagination which involves dreaming and seeing vision. " (Chauhan, 2006). Here in the following lines Dokra or Ghadwa art form of Chhattishgarh will be discussed.

## Dokra–a Dwindling Art Form of Chhattishgarh

Ghadwa or Ghasia – a folk artisan community as well as a marginal ethnic group of Chhattisgarh are the image-makers of brass metal by *cire-perdue*, that is, the lost wax process. They are distributed in Bastar of Chhattisgarh, in some pockets of Orissa, Jharkhand and West Bengal. A similar community is there with different name, that is; Malhar/Malhor/Malar who also follow the same occupation with similar technology-making brass images by the lost wax process. In Jharkhand the people with same occupation is called Jadupetia. Hazra of Anthropological survey of India opined that Ghadwa are actually Kaser. In fact, Kasers have several names, which vary from place to place and in Bastar they are named as Ghawda. Mukherjee (1976) also gave the same opinion and according to her they are also called as Gharua or Ghadwa. The Ghadwa informants told that they are a group of metal workers working with alloy of bronze, tin and copper. The groups are: (a) Bharewa-the artisans who work with bell metal and prepare items except any image, (b) Kaser - similarly works with bell metal but generally prepares utensils of household use, (c) Tamrakar who prepare household utensils of copper and (d) Ghadwa or Ghasia-the brass/bell metal workers who traditionally only prepare the images of gods and goddesses and some special items such as measuring pots, liquor pot etc. by lost wax process. It is told by them that they are not Kaser. On the other hand they told that they are an endogamous group and customarily their marriage with Kaser is not allowed.

The Ghadwas produce a large array of brass/bell metal image, locally known as dokra, of gods and goddesses either riding on a horse, or an elephant or a single image of a monkey–a representative of Mata Sitala, votive items, and various types of artefacts as well as decorative items. Their primary customers are local tribal groups of Bastar namely, Dandami Maria, Muria, Dhurwa, Halba, Bhatra, and Abujh Maria who used their items for veneration and worship in the shrines. According to Mahawar (2011) "the Ghasia craftsmen have introduced idolatry icons for the animistic abstract and unseen forces of nature. Some such images were already in existence in their tradition and in their ancient technique of metal casting. They have developed in association with the tribal priests some salient features in their iconography, and in due course this art has flourished around tribal religion and culture". The local buyers, as mentioned earlier, primarily buy the votive items for the ritual purpose. The buyers from outside use these objects as decorative pieces to enhance the aesthetic appeal of their drawing room in urban set up. The art form of the 'lost wax' process is very old and from historical point of view it's ancestry is traced from the time of Indus Valley Civilisation. Surprisingly this technique is still prevalent in several pockets of India. In Bastar, the community Ghadwa practice this technique for their survival. They are found in Jagdalpur, Kondagaon. Keshkal, Chilkutti, Ulnar, Besoli, Sirmur, Baniagaon, Orcha, Dilmili, Bastaner, Narayanpur, Chhota Dongar etc., places. Fagnu Sagar–a Ghadwa of Chilkutti village informed that in the social hierarchy Ghadwa hold a rank below

Brahman, Rout, Dhakad, Kalar, Sundi, Thakur, and higher to Dhobi, Nai, Mahar, Ghasia, etc, and also local tribal groups who are considered as beefeaters. They do not accept any *pucca* food from them. They claim that they are settled in Bastar since 13th century during the reign of Raja Annam Deo.

It is observed that there are sharply two *gharana* or school existing among the Ghadwa artists of Chhattishgarh, viz, Kondagaon-Keshkal gharana which is characterised by artistically elongated shape idols while Jagdalpur gharana is of small sized, decorative and minute design shaped; the designs are prepared out of wax thread. The present treatise highlights chiefly the artists of Jagdalpur gharana.

The Ghadwa society is endogamous, divided into a number of exogamous clans or *vansa* such as *nag, sagar, mahua, kachhua, sher, meen vansa* etc, with totemic affiliation. They practise clan exogamy. If a Ghadwa boy marries a girl from a community having lower social status he will be excommunicated but when the girl is brought from a community of higher social status, she is accepted after performance of *ratan kaniya*–a purificatory ritual in which the couple is purified before the *birandar* -the elders of the community by sprinkling the *pobanpani* (sacred water from Danteshwari temple) with a *tulsi* leaf (basil plant leaf) followed by feast. Marriage with MBD (mother's brother's daughter) and FSD (father's sister's daughter)–the marriage with cross cousin is allowed.

They live in multi ethnic villages forming a hamlets having cluster of at the most six to seven houses. In Kondagaon there is a bigger concentration with 300 families living in separate *paras* and hamlets. They try to set up their households near the market place to facilitate the sale of their products. The selection of place for establishment of their habitation also depends on the availability of the clay necessary for their work. They claim themselves as Hindus. Some of their important deities are their clan god, ancestors, Danteshwari mata, Karmaikola Tado and several other mother goddesses etc. Other deities are Sun, Moon, Dharti Ma, Bhairam Deo, Telengin Mata, Sat Bahan, Samria, while nag vans worship Jalni Mata, Gumdakarin etc. They observe Hindu rituals and festivals such as Holi, Diwali, Dussehra, and Vishwakarma puja.

## II

It has been observed that each and every image they prepare for the tribal groups has a unique feature. Some of those have a sign of crescent star (*chand tara*) somewhere upon the image. According to the informants of Chilkutti and Sirmur villages the meaning of such symbol is *'jab tak chand-tara rahega tab tak* Ghadwa *rahega.* 'It means that the Ghadwa will survive till the star and moon remain there (in the universe). While the elite groups of Jagdalpur say that the symbol is particularly used by the Chandravans kings, the ruling chiefs of Bastar.

Among the items produced by the Ghadwas some are:

1. Icons of purely local gods and goddesses, which are purely classical such as Chitla Dei (Sitla Mata), Ganga Dei, Linga Dei, other *mata*s such as Kal, Danteshwari mata, Jalni, mata Khoriya, Kankalin, Banjarin, Pardeshin, Mahamai mata, a horse with a rider, an elephant, and a *jhula* (swing), and also a pair named as Jhitku-Mitku, Bhima-Bhimi, Burha Deo, Chikat Raj, Harma Raj, Thakur Deyi, etc.
2. The horse rider is Siva called Bhairam. He has a sword, or a spear.
3. The elephant image is actually the representative of Danteswari Mata-the tutelary deity of Bastar State. The artisans who belong to a low caste are not allowed to see the image after it is put in place in the temple or in other ritual places. Their contact with the goddess occurs only during the annual procession when they are allowed to see and salute the elephant, horse, chariot, *jhula,* bull etc and also the umbrella–the symbol of Danteswari Mata.

   Utensils and other ornaments such as *payari* (anklets), *hansuli* (nacklace), pendent, earrings, and bells to wear, etc. and other items such as *turi* (sounding horn), *kalas* (pitcher), *duti* (coin container).
4. Decorative items such as hanger, pen stand, flower vase, ashtray, table lamp, lamp shed, hurricane, wine pot, teapot, bells, funnel, etc.

Now for preparation of *dokra* items the following raw materials are needed:

1. At first they collect three types of clay namely–
   (a) Mun *mitti*–the clay collected from agricultural field. It is in generally very fine. This variety of clay is sticky in nature.
   (b) Rui *mitti*–this variety of clay is reddish brown clay, taken from river bed where water flows very swiftly driving out all the darts but enough sand will be there. The clay is fine and necessary for *dokra* work. They avoid collecting mud from riverbed during rainy season.

(c) They use *dengur matti*–the mud of anthill.

2. Wax–wax from beehive is preferred for this work but now a day as it is very costly, they use paraffin wax.
3. Dhoop (resin) and *damor* (coal tar or pitch) at Kondagaon, the Ghadwas mix these two with wax to increase the density of wax.
4. A piece of fine cloth–used as strainer for wax after it is melted.
5. Semi leaves–used to rub it on the paraffin image. It gives a sticky texture at the surface of the image, which helps in designing. Due to the sticky texture the paraffin does not slip during designing.
6. Bhusa (paddy husk)–used to mix with *mun mitti* and *dengur mitti* to make it hard and it protects the clay image from breaking.
7. Chhedi *lendi* (goat–dung)–it is mixed with the *rui mitti*. It is very black in colour and glazy. They also mix coal after it is crushed. Coal is mixed as it keeps heat for a long duration.

Implements required for *dokra* work–

1. Hathora–a hammer, used to break clay.
2. Matni–it is a wooden strip of various sizes. It is used to the wax threads to get plain texture.
3. Chipna–it is prepared by bamboo strip, used to prepare eyes and mouth etc. (for minute works).
4. Chaku–it is an iron cutter, used to cut wax.
5. Sansi–it is an iron tongs/pincers. It also has various sizes, is used to hold the container filled with hot melted metal to pour that in the figure.
6. Jhara/*Jhari*–it is a thin brass disc. It is of various sizes, used to extract wax threads. Each of the *jharis* has some apertures of similar diameter through which wax threads come out.
7. Thesa/*dheta*–it is a solid wooden bar. It's diameter varies as per the diameter of pichkias it is inserted and fitted in *pichki* during work. It has a wooden handle straight, without any bending. Thesa/*dheta* works as piston and is used to make wax thread.
8. Pichki–it is a hollow, cylindrical brass container with outward projection throughout the circumference at the opening and inwardly projection at the bottom in which a *jhari* can be fitted. The wax is kept inside the *pichki* and then the *thesa/dheta* is

inserted into the *pichki*. The handle of the *dheta/thesa* is larger in height than the *pichki.*

9. Farni–a pair of wooden bars, which are, separate but kept together one upon another during work. These bars are of lozenge shape, broader at the middle and tapering at both of the ends. These two are hold together at both of their ends by the Ghadwa worker. Each of the wooden bars has a hole at the centre. The hole at the centre of the lower one of the two bars is broader in size through which the outer projecting part of the *pichki* as mentioned earlier comes out and is fitted with it. The hole of the upper bar, better to tell it a notch than a hole, is smaller in size keeping parity with the handle of the *thesa/dheta*. The upper portion of the handle coming out from the *pichki* is fitted there.

   Pidha–it is a wooden platform A Ghadwa worker rolls or flattens the wax as per his needs.

10. Bhatti (Furnace) –They prepare *bhatti* on the ground by bricks. It is not a permanent structure but it can be arranged as per the necessity of the workers. Bricks are arranged nearly in a half circle fashion, arranged in at least three to four rows, one upon another. They use fuel wood, small branches and twigs as fuel.

**Method:** At first they prepare *mun mitti* or the clay collected from agricultural field very carefully. They ground the clay in a stone. Bhusa is mixed with *mun mitti,* as this variety of clay is very sticky and if they prepare an image only by *mun mitti*, the image may break during drying. It increases the grasping capacity of the clay. They keep the image on a plane surface, generally on a plate for drying. When the figure is dry they scrub it with sand paper to make the surface plain and even.

After that, they coat the figure with *rui mitti* added with water and *chhedi lendi* and are ground together in the same stone. Then this paste is applied on the figure as a coating and again dried.

Then the figure is rubbed with semi leaves. A sticky substance comes out of the leaves and sticks on the figure and it gets a greenish tinge and a sticky appearance. Due to the sticky nature during coating the wax gets fixed and does not slip during the designing which, thus does not get disturbed.

Prior to that, the wax is prepared. Traditionally they used to work with bee wax but as the it is very costly now a days, they use paraffin wax along with bee wax for the work. At first, they mix both the types of wax and then melt it. After melting a strainer is used to extract all the unwanted particles from the melt. Then to increase it's thickness, especially the Ghadwa artists of Kondagaon, add resin and coal tar and again some bee wax with it. Then they let the wax solidify into cake and break it into smaller cakes. After that the cakes are put under the sun and near a lighted *chulha,* at a distance where the heat will be not so high, not to get it in a liquid form but only to soften it. When the wax cakes get too soft, they pour those into a *pichki.* The *dheta/thesa* is kept in the *pichki,* upon the softened cakes. The handle of the *dheta/theta* is fitted at the notch. The worker then holds those two bars together at their ends and applies his pressure. This pressure ultimately reaches to the softened wax through the *dheta/thesa* via it's handle fitted with the upper bar of *dheta/thesa.* As a result the wax comes outside through the holes of *jhari* fitted at the bottom of *pichki* in the form of several threads. The wax threads are collected and kept with care in a warm place to keep those soft but not melted. Now-a-days instead of total pressure (as it is a heavy task), the worker ties the two ends of *farni* of a side together with tree by strong thread and that of another side is fitted with a strong wooden pole then apply pressure at the side of the tree with which it is tied. Traditionally the work was completely done by men but presently as the work is easier, their women also can do this.

Then the wrapping of the clay figure by the wax threads is done. A slightly hot iron rod joins all the ends of the wax threads used during wrapping with each other. The wrapping is done spirally and the total figure is covered by it. After wrapping the figure is ornamented again by wax threads. This is done with the help of fingers and nails. Among the decorations popular are lines of threads–sometimes it is a straight line, or some parallel lines, or half circle, round etc. Others are dots, spiral binding just like the *beni*–girls' hairstyle etc. All these are done on the wrapped figure after the wax wrapping is completed. At the time of wax wrapping they keep opening or prepare a channel at a place generally at the base of the image or figure or at a suitable point where they fit *muchhi* connected with *ghaila.* Just after wax wrapping, the figure is again coated by clay. In case of smaller items they take at least six to seven items and all of those are coated together by clay of the *dengur mitti* (clay collected from anthill). It is mixed with paddy husk. It becomes very hard, not easily breakable. They coat all of those figures together along with a single *muchhi* and *ghaila* meant for all of those. Then the total item is kept in *bhatti* covered with firewood, small branches and twigs.

Now prior to further discussion, it is essential to give some ideas on *muchhi* and *ghaila.* These two are prepared with clay collected from ant hill–*dengur mitti* mixed with paddy husk. At first they prepare *muchhi.* It works as a lid attached with the figure. It is a funnel or glass like structure with openings at both the ends. One of the two openings is situated just at the centre of the *muchhi,* which is fitted with the figure at it's opening where the channels for running of melted metal on the figure is already prepared. In the *ghaila*, they keep smaller pieces of broken utensils and other metal scrap. Then it is fixed with the other open end of *muchhi*. Both are joined tightly with *dengur mitti* mixed with paddy husk.

After the covering of the total figure by *dengur mitti* including *muchhi* and *ghaila*, the total thing is kept for drying in the sun and after it is dried, it is kept in the *bhatti*. In a *bhatti* at a time six to seven small items are kept and in case of larger items at a time single or at the most two items can be kept. They use firewood, twigs and small branches of a plant in the *bhatti* and then they ignite the *bhatti*. One quintal of wood is needed. Then the worker waits for sometimes at least for two to three hours till the greenish or sulphur yellow flame comes out. When they want to get the result quickly, then they add some coal with it or only with coal. After the green coloured flame comes out, the worker understands that the metal is melted and has become liquid. The worker, for further confirmation, takes out the object by *sansi* and shakes it. If it sounds like a coconut full with water he gets assured that the metal has liquefied as per the need. Then he holds the object and turns it upside down. The liquefied metal then runs through the wax channels and spread out throughout the object burning the wax. The metal takes the position of the wax replacing it including its designs. Due to the heat of the metal the wax covering with its designs are melted leaving the impression and all are replaced by that metal which takes the place of the wax including the designs.

In Kondagaon, as they make bigger items, the workers heat the metal in a container and after it is melted like water it is poured directly in the item, which is covered by clay. They pour the liquid metal through the *muchhi* prepared at the base of the figure. The metal as usual melts the wax and takes it's place.

After taking out the article from the *bhatti*, they wait for at least an hour for it to cool off. They sprinkle water on it again and again and it to dissipate it's heat. By this time they become busy with breaking the clay covering. As it is so hard, sometimes they use hammer and with controlled hammering they break it.

After that the worker takes the item, washes it in water mixed with tamarind and polishes it by scrubbing with sand added with tamarind mixed water till the glaze with burnish gold colour comes. Presently, they polish the item with the help of machine, which is called by them as buff machine.

According to them, they have two different *gharanas* namely, Jagdalpuri *gharana* and other is Kondagaon–Keshkal *gharana* where a little difference in technique and in shape and size are noticed between the two *gharanas*.

In Kondagaon, they have slight difference in technique. They use the paraffin wax primarily and a small quantity of bee wax and these are mixed with *damor* and incense. They mix those to increase the density and the quantity of the wax. They in general prepare bigger items specially used as decorative items in the sitting rooms of the affluent people. In case of a bigger item, they do not put it directly in the *bhatti.* They prepare *muchhi* and attach that with the item preferably at it's base and keep it's another end open for pouring melted metal through it. They have a big *bhatti,* where they keep big clay made *ghaila* and in the *ghaila,* they keep broken metal pieces and ignite the *bhatti.* They use charcoal along with wood in the *bhatti* and wait for the melting of the metal pieces. After melting, they take out some metal in liquid form by a wooden ladleand pour it to the item through the *muchhi.* During the pouring of metal, if there is any crack found in the clay made item and the metal is oozing out from the crack, they immediately take a piece of wet cloth and compress it on the crack and stop the loss of metal. In Kondagaon they polish the item by a piece of iron along with rubbing with tamarind water. They sometimes polish the metal item by iron brush. In all the cases they apply tamarind mixed water. They smear *tora (mahua)* oil on the object and wrap it with straw then put that in fire. It gives a blackish colour with glaze to the image.

In case of *thos* item they prepare the item without clay but directly with wax. Then they cover it with *dengur mitt.* The clay made *muchhi and ghaila* filled with some broken pieces of metal is attached with it and then it is put in fire. The wax gets melted and the metal takes it's place. In this type, there is no support of clay; the image is made only by metal. So the metal quantity is more than the *mitti bhara kam.* Again the wax quantity required is also more and the item is costlier.

## Social organisation of production

The work is done jointly by both the sexes. Generally men select and collect the clay suitable for preparation of an image. They collect clay, break and mix it with paddy husk or goat dung and make the image. After the image gets dry, women rub semi leaves on it. Traditionally men only used to do the work of wax thread extraction but now both the sexes do it. Women preferably do wrapping of wax thread on the image and designing on it. The works of firing, melting of metal are done by men. The work of polishing is done by both the sexes.

The Ghawda worship several deities. Among their deities their clan deities, ancesters, and several other deities namely Danteshwari Mata, Bishwakarma, Karmaikola Tado Hinglagin Mata, and Dokri Mata etc are very important. In *bhatti* they worship Kheria Deo who is Danteshwari Mata's servant. Every day in the morning before starting work they worship him in the *bhatti* with the offerings of sun dried rice, incense, some flowers, and sal leaves. They (Mr Joidev Baghel– an artist of Kondagaon) believe that Karmaikola tado is their guardian deity. Incidentally Karmaikola Tado is again the guardian deity of a section of the Abujh Maria tribe and holding it Ghawdas of Kondagaon claim that originally they are Abujh Marias migrated in this area a long time ago and gradually they have forgotten most of the traits of their traditional culture and have taken a separate identity as Ghadwa. It is not supported by the Ghadwas of Jagdalpur. On the contrary, they strongly deny to it.

## Recent trend and discussion

It has been observed that due to economic constraints, to reduce the production cost, the *dokra* artisans presently mix paraffin wax with bee wax. Again sometimes they, specially the artists of Kondagaon mix *damor* (coal tar) and *dhoop* (resin) with the wax to increase the quantity. Some of them use buff machine for polishing. It saves their time and also gives an excellent result.

As a tradition, the prepared items are not so big in size. They used to prepare measuring pots, liquor container, and necklace, ear top, nose ornament, bangles, pairi or leg ornaments–all useful items of the local people. Day by day, the demand of the *dokra* items is not restricted among the tribals and only to fulfil the demand of the tribal people is not sufficient to fulfil their economic needs. Then to combat with such critical economic situation, they have broadened or expanded their artistic ideas and they have started to make some other items such as elephant, horse, bull, tortoise, bird, fish, flower vas, hanger, etc.

There is a sharp difference between two *gharanas* (schools) as mentioned earlier. The *jagdalpur gharana* artists generally prefer to make items of smaller size with a very little exception. The Kondagaon artists on the contrary prefer to make larger and big items. Again sometimes the items are not of their usual forms. As for an example, in the workshop of Jaidev Baghel of Kondagaon, there are tigers with disproportionate and unusual shape, with a longer size and smaller neck and face looking turning its head. There is a beautiful candle stand in the form of a bigger sized hawk. On its head there is a place to put a candle on it. All these items they make to get rid of boredom/

monotony and also to attract the outsiders and the tourists and the other elite groups who appreciate these items and the artists are able to sell their products at a higher rate to them. In this way they are trying to adjust with the present day economy of the country. Again it is necessary to mention that generally a Ghadwa worker gets lesser chances to expose before the markets of urban area.

Ghadwas being one of the marginalised artisan community is passing through a stage of technologically advanced wave of environment where the demand of their traditionally produced items /icons specially used by the tribals and local people are lessened day by day. On the other hand, those are appreciated by a section of people who are economically well–off and practically this art form is displayed in their drawing room and with their patronage only this art form is gaining importance and earned a reputable place in the folk art and craft industry. To get more attraction and to earn more the Ghadwa artists have come out from the tradition and turned or in other ward broaden/their artistic ideas and have started to make some other items such as elephant, horse, bulls, tortoise, birds, fishes, flower vas, hanger, etc. being the show-pieces of drawing rooms in urban set-up.

There is sharp difference between the two *gharans* (schools). The Jagdalpur *gharana* artists generally prefer to make items of smaller sizes with a very little exception. The Kondagaon *gharana* artists on the contrary prefer to make larger and big items. Again sometimes the items are not of their usual forms. As for an example in the work site of Jaidev Baghel of Kondagaon, there are tigers with a long size and smaller neck and face; looking turning it's head. All these items they make to get rid of the boredom/monotony and also to attract the outsiders and the tourists and the other elite groups who appreciate these items and purchase all these at a higher rate. In this way they are trying to adjust with the present day economy of the country.

Here, it is necessary to mention that in general they do not get the actual cost of the items due to the intervention of the middlemen and to give them protection, several Government and non–government organisations came forward. Presently there is an organisation named Tribal Cooperative Marketing Development Federation of India or in short TRIFED under the Ministry of Tribal Affairs who has extended their hands of cooperation for proper marketing of their products. This organisation takes the responsibilities of marketing of all the tribal products all over India. They have sister concerns such as TDCC, Girijan Cooperative Society (who now a days are promoting also the tribal handicrafts). They purchase products from the tribals and take the sole responsibilities of marketing of those. They also give loan or advance to the tribals, where payment of debt is done in several instalments. They are opening a raw material bank. There is another organisation named NABARD. They have a proposal of funding the artisans including the Ghadwas. The Ghadwas of Chilkutti village are interested in it, for which they should have to register their names. Later they will be given training and also advance money for their work. In this way they are trying to move towards the development not only of their craft but also for their development in all spheres and hopefully they are looking for a better future.

**Tentative Affinitiy of Gadwa/ Dokra Art**

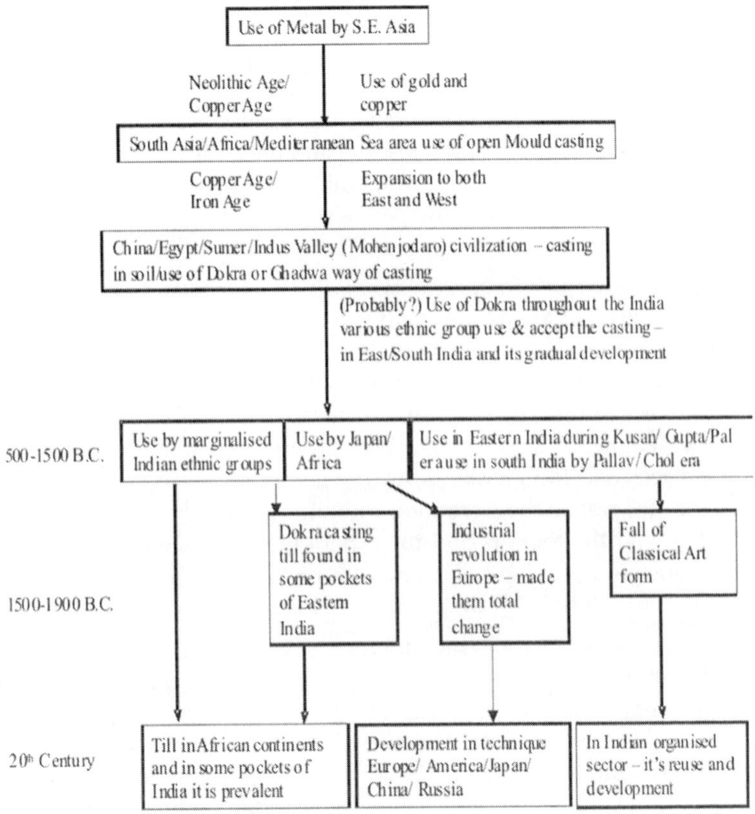


**(Ref. : Dutta, Prasanta, Loko Shruti, No. 14, Aug., 1998)**

Jhula Devi—Finished item

Country liquor container— Finished Product

Ghadwa artist in action

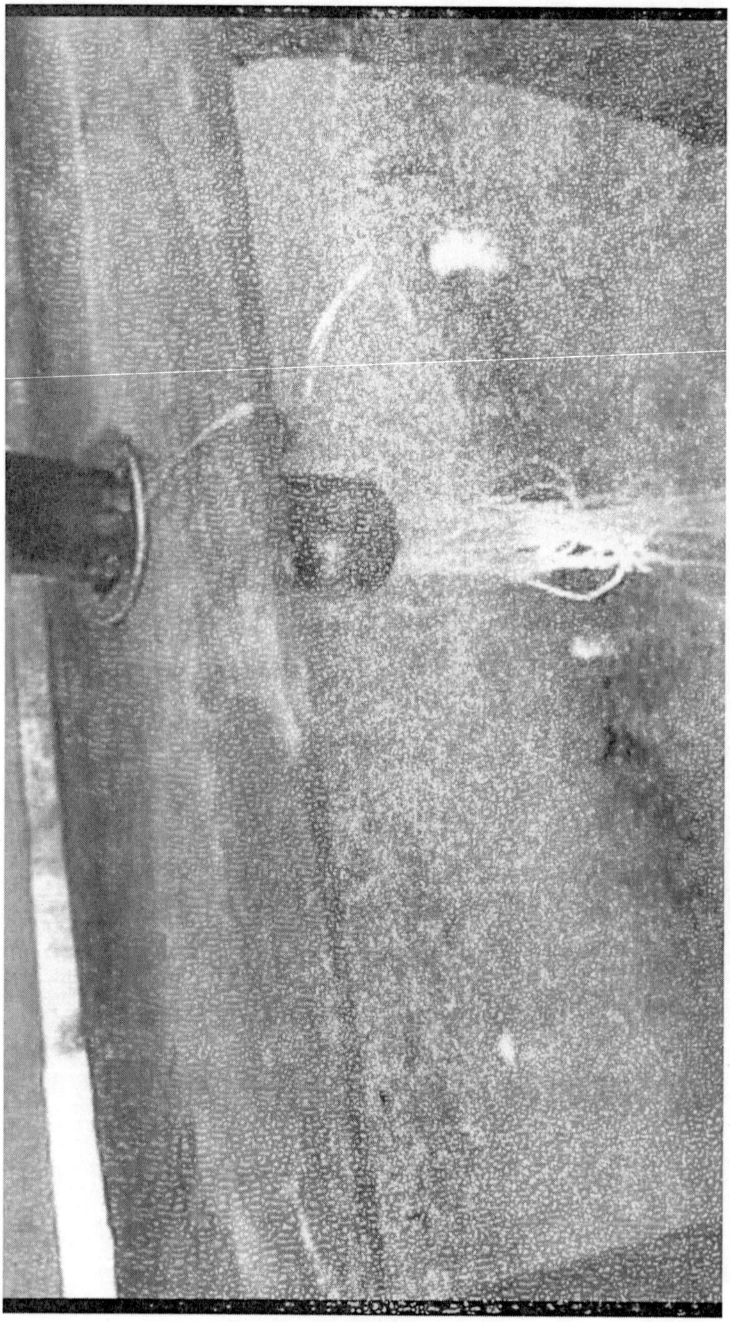

Preparing wax thread through pichki-pharni.

**Wrapping of wax thread**

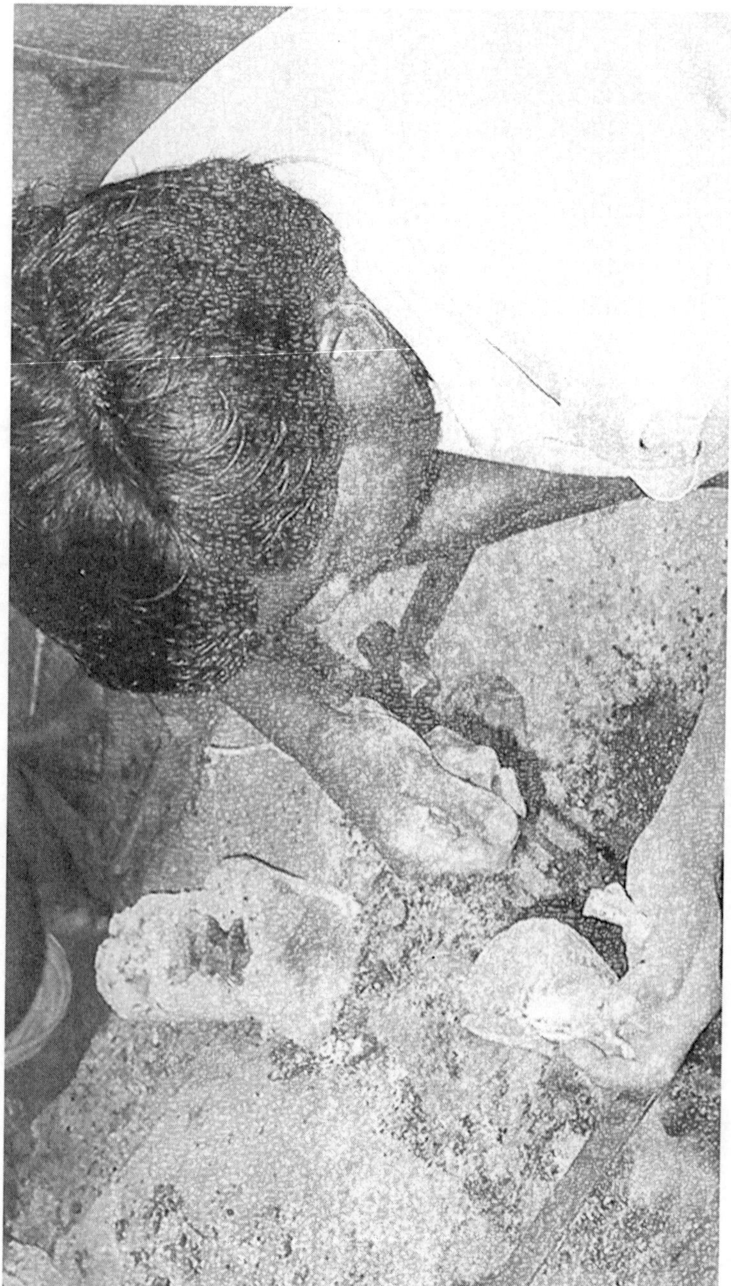

Breaking of clay to extract the metal item

**Brushing and Cleaning the finished item**

## References

Baghel, Jaidev 1982, Of 'Devis' and 'Devas' in *Shilapakar–The Craftsmen* ed. Carmen Kagal, Bombay: Indian Graphic Symbols.

Chauhan, Bijender Singh, 2006, "Creativity in Applied Art". *Employment News*, Vol XXXI, No. 19, Dt. 5–11 August.

Dutta, Prasanta, 1998, "Paschimbanger dokra silper adiparba," in *Lokshruti,* No. 14.

Kumari Pratibha, 2002, "The vanishing art in Metal: The Creativity of Malhar of Jharkhand" in *Jr. of Anth. Survey of India,* Vol. 51, pp. 5–34.

Mahawar, Niranjan, 2011, Bastar Bronzes: Tribal Religion and Art, New Delhi: Abhinav Publications.

Mukherjee, Meera, 1977, *Folk Artefacts of Eastern India,* New Delhi: All India Handicrafts Board.

Reeves, Ruth, 1962, *Cira Perdue Casting in India,* New Delhi: Crafts, Museum.

Sarkar, Amitabha and Samira Dasgupta, 1996, *Spectrum of Tribal Bastar,* Delhi: Agam Kala Prakashan.

# 17

# Concepts of Understanding Social/ Cultural Change

How one can conceive change? Change is simply variability in culture, and behaviour over time. 'Culture change' generally refers not to the short-term dynamics of particular culture but to large scale alterations in the organisation and operation of a society. The major changes are likely to be the accumulated product of much smaller changes occurring over a period of time. Culture is ever changing since it consists of learned patterns of behaviour and belief, culture traits can be unlearned and learned anew as human needs change. Thus, no specific cultural pattern remains impervious to change, just as no specific item of learning in necessarily immortal (Ember and Ember, 1977). Most of us are highly aware that 'times have changed' and along with this people's way of life and their behaviour pattern too. We being cultural anthropologists also try to understand how and why the changes have took place and its consequential effect on the society.

In the formative stage of Anthropology, the scholars were involved on speculation regarding the origin and development of culture. Cultural development was sought to be explained in terms of the origin of significant cultural elements and its ultimate diffusion to other areas.

The classical evolutionists believed in a unilinear course the evolution of culture. The elaboration of the stages of techno-economic development by the evolutionists was perhaps the most satisfactory. (Dube, 1993). One can also visualise the stages of such societal development viz :

A. Savagery -> Barbarism -> Civilisation.

B. In respect of marriage the following stages were recorded:
   1. Promiscuity -there was no incest taboo, beast like activities.
   2. Punaluan -Segregation of kin and lineage members.
   3. Group marriage
   4. Polynadry
   5. Polygyny
   6. Monogamy

C. It was apprehended family system evolved in the following way.
   1. Promiscuous intercourse -> Punaluan -> 'Consanguine' families based on group marriage ->Matrilineal -> Patilineal monogamous families.

D. Similarly, religion was believed to have originated from animism -> Polytheism -> Monotheism.

The evolutionist theory, for example, has been advanced in a refined and modified form by Gordon Childe, Julian Steward and Lessile White. To distinguish them from classical evolutionists, they are often identified as Neo-evolutionists. Childe traces the evolution of culture through four major strata like the Palaeolithic -> Neolithic -> Bronze Age -> and the Iron age. Each period represented by a technological revolution, which left its unmistakable mark on the economy, social institutions, religion and art of humankind. The transition from savagery through barbarism to civilisation is re-affirmed and is explained with infinitely more convincing data. Childe takes cognisance of contrasting environments and while he is convinced of essentiality of these "stages" on the road to civilisation, he recognises that the cultural consequences of each of the major neo-evolutions were different in different settings.

"Redfield and Singer (1954) have shown folk society, as an ideal type, represents a combination of societal elements that characterise a long established, homogenous and non-literate integral community. Such a society can be realised in a tribal band or a village, not in a city. The city, again as an ideal type, represents a community in which orthogenetic and heterogenetic transformation of the folk society have most fully occurred. "

"The orthogenetic transformations brings about the 'Great Tradition' and its special intellectual class, administrative officers and rules closely derived from the moral and religious life of the local culture and advanced economic institutions also obedient to these local cultural transformations. While, the heterogenetic transformation have accomplished the freeing of the intellectual, aesthetic, economic and political life from the local moral norms, and have developed on the one hand an individuated expediential motivation, and on the other a revolutionary, nativistic, humanistic viewpoint, now directed toward reform, progress and designed change" (Dube, 1993).

"Two hypothetical patterns of urbanisation are assumed: Primary and secondary (Redfield and Singer, 1954). Primary urbanisation takes place mostly within the framework of a core culture which develops and is transformed into an indigenous civilisation: the pre-civilised folk society, on the matrix of a shared culture, is transformed into a peasant society with correlated urban centres. In this process, first, a 'sacred culture' is produced, which is then gradually shaped by the urban literati into a Great Tradition. In secondary urbanisation a folk society pre-civilised "by contact with people of widely different cultures .... ", and in consequence a new form of urban life is produced. This form is, at least in part, in conflict with the traditional patterns. " (Dube, 1993)

## II

We the anthropologists are concerned with the study of group behaviour, that is, our unit of observation. Again, such group behaviour has two components one is overt or explicit behaviour which means the behaviour we can directly observe, that is otherwise known as 'norm', while the other component is covert or implicit behaviour which we cannot see in naked eye but we feel through empathy which is value of such behaviour when charges are occurred in the former level it is known as social change while changes are found both in norms and its value level, it is called as culture change.

There are various factors which are responsible for socio-cultural change in a society. Internal factors such as new invention may lead to an increased food supply, population growth or external factors like conquest, war or revolt, education, set up and as well as rise of industrial units, rise of communication facilities, migration, contact between two societies and even adaptation of a culture to its environment (Steward, 1955), etc.

According to E. Z. Vogt (1972, Reprint edition) culture change may be summarised in four basic questions:

(i) What are the internal or external factors that generate shifts in rates and types of culture change?

(ii) What are the process by which culture change takes places?

(iii) What models and methods are now available for the study of culture change?

(iv) How is the concept of culture change related to the closely associated phenomena of diffusion, innovation, evolution, acculturation and nativism?

Socio-cultural change in India indicates a profound impact on economic change. The effect of the new economic order upon the way of life of Indian society is clearly evidenced in industry. The reason behind such are induction of modern technology like radio, cable, TV, video cassettes, satellite network, pager, cellular telephone and various kinds of industrial set ups and overall globalisation of new open economic policy. Technology produces social inventions and also social change. Automobiles, e-network and electricity are now spreading industry almost everywhere. All these are responsible for changing scenario of socio-cultural life of human beings. Bottomore (1971) has noted that "two elements have played a decisive part in bringing about social change in India, first, western science and technology and secondly, social planning. The introduction of capitalist industry brought about changes in the property system and in the division of labour and gave rise to new social strata and classes which played an important part in the political development in India. "

Culture change can be studied as it occurs over long time spans and in the microscopic sense, as it occurs in short periods of time. In regard to microscopic models the works of White (1959) and Childe (1951) may be taken as examples for the study of cultural evolution. White's most significant proposition is that technological development expressed in terms of man's control over energy underlies social changes and cultural achievements. Childe is especially noted for his formulation of Neolithic revolution which means development of cultures from food gathering societies to settled agricultural food producing societies, in early human history. Another model which involves social and cultural changes over prolonged time spans is the contribution of Redfield (1941) when he studied folk and urban society and tried to show a continuum between the two as well as culture change. Among microscopic models the contribution of Murdock (1949) and Leach (1961) are focussed upon changing and cultural systems. Murdock is mainly concerned with changes in social organisation.

He proposes that change in social system regularly begins with a modification of rule of residence and other changes in kinship structure and terminology follow in predictable order, while Leach utilises "oscillation model" among Kachin society where a regular oscillation between two polar types with different political value systems takes place.

I

Changes can also be understood by following parameters or **Polar concepts** of cultural attributes where one can find a controlled group between two attributes. A few of such are discussed in the following lines—

**I. (a) Mechanical Solidarity:** As defined by Emile Durkheim, societal solidarity based upon a homogeneity of values and behaviour, strong social constraint and loyalty to tradition and kinship. The term applies to small, non-literate societies characterised by a simple division of labour, very little specialisation of function, only a few social roles and very little tolerance of individuality.

(Reference: Durkheim, E., 1947 the Division of Labour in Society, Translated by G. Simpson, Glencoe, Free Press).

**(b) Organic Solidarity:** As defined by Emile Durkheim, a type of societal solidarity typical to modern industrial society, in which unity is based on the interdependence of a very large number of highly specialised roles in a system involving a complex division of labour that requires the co-operation of almost all the groups and individuals of the society. In contrast to solidarity that is mechanical, that is, based on homogeneity of values, beliefs, and loyalties, this type of solidarity is called organic because it is similar to the unity of a biological organism in which highly specialised parts or organs must work in co-ordination, if the organism is to survive.

**II. (a) Folk-Urban:** A societal typology or conceptual model for differentiating types of societies formulated by Robert Redfield in 1947, that distinguishes between two contrasting ideal or generalised type of society: folk society and urban society. The typology provides a frame work for the comparative analysis of societies and also is useful in the study of social change in a society becoming urbanised.

**Folk–Urban Continuum:** This concept was developed by Redfield (1941) to explain differences between various communities on the Yucatan Peninsula of Mexico. He worked in Merida city, Dzitas town, Chankom peasant village and Tusik tribal village. Merida was placed near one end of continuum and Tusik on the other, while Dzitas and Chankom were regarded as intermediate types. Redfield found that as one moves along the continuum from folk communities to urban communities there is increasing group size, disorganisation, role segregation individualisation and secularisation.

**III. (a) Gemeinschaft:** A generalised or ideal type of society in which the social bonds are based on close personal ties of friendship and kinship. The term was used by Ferdinand Tonnies to distinguish between two basic types of society: Gemeinschaft and Gesellschaft. The term Gemeinschaft means "Community" in German and refers to a society characterised by the pre-dominance of intimate primary relationships and by emphasis upon tradition, consensus, informality and kinship. This pattern of society is most closely approximated by rural agricultural society.

**(b) Gesellschaft:** A type of society in which secondary relations predominate, that is, in which social relationships are formal, contractual, expedient, impersonal and specialised. The term Gesellschaft (means "society" in German) was introduced by F. Tonnies as an abstract or ideal type which is contrasted with Gemeinschaft. Although no actual society exactly matches an ideal type. Gesellschaft is most typically approximated in modern urban society, particularly as it exists in large metropolitan areas. It corresponds to the Gesellschaft type because of its weak family organisation, its emphasis on utilitarian goals, and the impersonal and competitive nature of its social relationships.

**(c) Great Tradition**:** According to Redfield the intellectuals influences that come from outside the village is great tradition. It refers to the formal, literate tradition of a civilisation, which is maintained by the elite society. The great tradition contrasts with the culture of rural people of the same civilisation, which is called little tradition.

**(d) Little Tradition**:** This is the culture of rural village living within a civilisation.

[** The two terms were criticised by Milton Singer]

**IV. (a) Universalisation:** The cultural trait which is widely prevalent or accepted. This was proposed by Mackin Marriott.

**(b) Parochialisation:** The cultural trait which is confined only a limited territory.

**V. Pushed–Pulled theory:** Pushed = Cultural osmosis, while Pulled = Cultural symbiosis.

When a group is unable to maintain its subsistence, livelihood and they are in search of new avenues, and when they work in new situation this is called 'pushed', but when in the new situation they are unable to adjust the alien culture, and they again go back to old situation, then is called 'pulled'.

**V. Sanskritisation–Westernisation:** The concepts sankritisation and westernisation, postulated by M. N. Srinivas, define these two types of sources of social change. According to Srinivas Sanskritisation represents actual or aspired for cultural mobility within the frame work of existing 'Great Tradition' and stratification system of caste. Westernisation on the other hand implies changes resulting from cultural contact with the west, particularly Great Britain.

According to Srinivas, Sanskritisation is "the process by which a low caste or tribe or other group takes over the customs, rituals, beliefs, ideology and style of life of a high and in particular, a twice-born caste". That is improving the position is the local caste hierarchy.

Westernisation refers to all cultural changes and institutional innovations in India as this country came into political and cultural contact with the western nations, primarily with U. K. However, Secularisation is a counterpart of the process of Westernisation.

**VI. Rank Concession Syndrome:** The term coined by M. Orans (1965) during his Santal study at Jamshedpur Steel city on Industrialisation. It means acceptance of social inferiority by the Santal in contrast with his neighbour Hindu.

Professor N. K. Bose through his article, "Hindu Method of Tribal Absorption (1941)" has shown how Hindu culture trait is borrowed by tribe due to their co-existence with the Hindus. Orans (1965) told quoting Bose reference that tribals used to concede their rank from economic determination and it is applicable to Santal.

**VII. Reference Group Theory (by Merton):** To evaluate one's position in relation to another section of population. During World War-II a group of unmarried solders and married soldiers raised their voice in view of their inconvenience, obligation and duties to respective families and Professor Merton addressed this as Reference group and here "unmarried soldiers" were treated as reference group.

**VIII. Bridge and Buffer:** This term coined by Professor B. K. Roy Burman during his study among the Toto of West Bengal, Meithei, Lushai, Naga, and Kachari at Manipur.

In case of a bridge community the segmentation is primarily ritual in character and the segments constitute parts of the same tribe.

They intermarry, inter dine and except some ritual matters, there is absolutely no difference among them, example Toto of West Bengal while, in case of buffer community, the segmentation is primarily political in character and frequently the segments are recognised as distinct tribes different from one another in language, material culture, social organisation and other matters. They do not also intermarry.

e. g., In Manipur and adjoining areas for instance the Kuki group of tribes appear to have played the buffer role between the —

(i) Meithei and Naga

(ii) Naga and Lushai

(iii) Naga and Kachari

(iv) Lushai and Kachari.

Among the Kuki constellation one tribe viz. Thado–is considered to constitute the core.

**IX. Cultural Oscillation:** This was proposed by Professor Binay Bhattacharya, Visva Bharati, Quarterly, Vol. 43, No. 3 and 4. Among the Patuas or Chitrakars in Bengal, he tried to find out the causes which counterbalance the process of assimilation and to explain the behaviour of a small community which is ordained to live in between two dominant socio-religious, in a word, cultural groups.

The Patua–semi-nomadic community left their original mooring somewhere in central India and migrated to various directions in search of food and one such branch came to Bengal in the remote past.

Gradually they came to contact with the Hindus and acculturised through process of induction and adopted some Hinduised occupation viz. scroll paintings, singing song of Hindu myths and idol making in addition to their original economic pursuit of snake charming. With the passage of time they were even not completely assimilated with the neighbouring Hindu community because of low status. The Patuas position therefore, became that of a rootless endogamous group.

The Patua swung toward Islam in order to escape repression and ostracisation by the high caste Hindus which reached its climax during the regime of Sen dynasty in Bengal in twelfth century A. D. The Muslim rulers showed favour to converts.

Scrolls were a good medium of mass communication and the Muslim rulers encouraged the Patuas to propagate Islam among the masses through scrolls. Coming in close contact with the Muslim, the Patuas acquired many traits of the Islamic way of life.

With the fall of Muslim rule after the battle of Palasi the Hindu gradually became powerful and dominant in economically and politically. Then Patuas found it possible to swing towards Hindus but could not give up certain Islamic traits such as burial of dead, circumcision etc.

This situation is obviously in search of economic and political security of the group.

**X. Phenomenon of Globalisation:** Globalisation refers to increasing interdependence of world community in many worldwide activities namely, trade, finance, communication, travel, culture, ideas etc. With the help of technology now one can connect himself or herself within a fraction time with the other part of world and exchange their ideas at his/her native place which can be explained as *'holding the world in the palm of one's hand'*. Arjun Appadurai (2000) explained the global connectivity in the following ways. Through which social change is possible where such tennets of globalisation reaches. Concept of global village is the result of global connectivity.

Global connectivities are ——

a. **Ethnoscape:** This is the movement of people, consisting of tourists, immigration, guests workers, refugees business class traveller etc.

b. **Mediascape:** The global connectivity is through. TV, computer, radio, newspaper, mobiles with whats apps, video messages through mobile apps etc.

c. **Technoscape:** Movement and and flow of technologies around the globe, e. g. satellite, radar etc.

d. **Financescape:** Global flow of money and capital often derived by interconnected currency markets, stock exchanges etc.

e. **Ideoscape:** Global flow of ideas and ideologies.

Apart from the popular polar concepts to understand the process of social change there are also other scholar's contribution to understand the process of change, namely,

a. Unity and Continuality of Indian Civilisation by Milton Singer (1958, 1972).

b. Vidyarthi's (1961) concept on "Sacred complex".

c. Marriott and B. S. Cohn (1971) developed the concepts of "Network and centres".

d. D. N. Majumbar (1957) concept on MARC (Man, Area, Resources and co-operation).

e. Nilakantha Syndrome by B. N. Saraswati (1975).

f. Concept of 'Maryada' and 'Parampara' by B. N. Saraswati (1975).

g. Morris Opler (1956) concept on 'Unity and Extensions'.

h. Oscar Lewis (1958) concept on Rural cosmopolitanism.

i. H. A. Gould's (1959) concept of 'Centripetal' and 'Centrifugal' social force to study the various facets of an Indian village.

In fact, to understand socio-culture change a controlled group must be identified for understanding change in synchronic level and when such changes are observed through prolonged time spans that are through diachronic level then the evidences of history and genealogy are essential.

In short, with the advent of agriculture, food supply becomes secure and firm in comparison to earlier feature of uncertainty in food through hunting. Thus, agriculture brought a change in the distribution of population in villages. Again with the introduction of industry in the subsistence sector, the monetary economy is gaining importance and as a result rapid changes are observed in socio-cultural way of life of the people. Thus, industrialisation has revolutionised the socio-economic and socio-cultural life of the people.

Anthropologists of nineteenth century and twentieth century first became interested in culture change as a result of contact with peoples who were altogether different from the western cultures with which they were accustomed. This explanation for the differences ultimately gave birth to the theory of evolution. More recently, interest has centred upon the process of modernisation in the third world countries where induction of industrial economy and its value system, migration of people and adaptation of western way of life have led a major cultural change.

Under the present scenario of globalisation of twenty-first century where electronic network of communication played a great role in social reforms, the polarisation of social relations and institutionalised behaviour are fast changing ; we the social scientists should take immediate attention towards the fast process of changing scenario which already affect our age-old social system and evolved some new institutions like Old Age Home, live together without any bondage of sacred institution like marriage, surrogate motherhood ship, in case of paternity only mother identity is essential which clearly signifies towards some kind of anomaly in family bondage, young generation are reluctant to age-old value system and very much inclined to mall culture and they are very much engulfed by hi-fi materialistic ways of life. Through these we are gradually alienated from traditional mooring of our heritage which ultimately brings 'boon or malison/curse' – which time will speak in future. In fact this modernisation process ultimately brings a change primarily at materialistic level which is more profound in City life than in village life. Anthropologists should focus their attention on these issues, supported with rich empirical data, and try to make a guideline for policy makers of the country for the actual developmental strategy of the nation where micro area interest should be given high priority.

## References

Bottomore, T. B., 1971. 'Sociology, Bambay: George Allen and Unwin (India) Pvt. Ltd.

Childe, V. G., 1951. Social Evolution, London and New York: copyright by H. Schuman.

Cohn, B.S., 1971. India: Social Anthropology of a Civilisation, USA: Prentice Hall.

Dasgupta, Samira, Amitabha Sarkar, 1996. Frontiers of Social Anthropology. New Delhi: Gyan Publishing House.

Dube, S. C. 1993. Understanding Change: Anthropological and Sociological Perspective, New Delhi: Vikas Pub. House Pvt. Ltd.

Ember, Carol R and Melvin Ember, 1977. Cultural Anthropology. New Jersey: Prentice–Hall Inc.

Gould, H. A. 1959. "The Peasant Life: Centripetal and Centrifugal", Eastern Anthropologists, Vol-13, No. 1.

Leach, E. R. 1961. Rethinking Anthropology. London: Athlone Press.

Lewis, Oscar. 1958. Village life in Northern India: Studies in a Delhi Village, Urbana: University of Illinois Press.

Majumdar, D. N. and T. N. Madan (1957). An Introduction to Social Anthropology Bombay: Asia Pub. House.

Mondal, Shekh Rahim. 2006, "Cultural Globalisation and Globalisation of Culture–Some Observation", The oriental Anthropologist, Vol. 6(2), pp. 297-306.

Murdock, G. P. 1949. Social Structure, New York: Collier Macmillan.

Opler, Morris. 1956. 'Extension of an Indian Village', Journal of Asian Studies, Vol. 16.

Redfield, Robert. 1941. The Folk Culture of Yucatan, Chicago: Chicago University Press.

Redfield, Robert. 1955. The Little Community, Chicago: Chicago University Press.

Saraswati, B. N. 1977. Brahmanic Ritual Tradition, Simla: Indian Institute of Advanced Studies.

Saraswati, B. N. 1975. Kashi: Myth and Reality of a Classical Cultural Tradition, Simla: Indian Institute of Advanced Studies.

Singer, Milton. 1958. Traditional India: Structure and Change, Philadelphia: American Folklore Society.

Singer, Milton. 1972. When a Great Tradition Modernises, New York: Praeger Publishers.

Steward, J. H. 1955. Theory of Culture Change, Urbana: University of Illinois Press.

Srinivas, M. N. 1962. Caste in Modern India and other Essays, Bombay: Asia Pub. House.

Srinivas, M. N. 1952. Religion and Society among the Coorg of South India, New Delhi: Oxford.

Vidyarthi, L. P. 1961. The Sacred Complex of Hindu Gaya, Bombay: Asia Publishing House.

Vogt, Evon. Z. 1972 (Reprinted) 'Culture Change', in International Encyclopaedia of the Social Sciences, (ed) David L. Sills, Vol. 3-4, New York: The Macmillan Company and the Free Press. (pp. 554-558).

Whites, A. L. 1959. The Evolution of Culture: The Development of Civilisation to the Fall of Rome. London: Mc-Graw Hill Company.

# Index

**N**